Brenton Hamline Badley

Indian Missionary Directory and Memorial Volume

Brenton Hamline Badley

Indian Missionary Directory and Memorial Volume

ISBN/EAN: 9783337060572

Printed in Europe, USA, Canada, Australia, Japan

Cover: Foto ©Suzi / pixelio.de

More available books at **www.hansebooks.com**

INDIAN
MISSIONARY DIRECTORY

AND

Memorial Volume,

BY

THE REV. B. H. BADLEY, M.A.

REVISED EDITION.

LUCKNOW.
METHODIST EPISCOPAL CHURCH PR.....
NEW YORK: PHILLIPS AND HUNT.

1881.

TO

THE PROTESTANT MISSIONARIES OF INDIA

OF WHATEVER NAME OR NATIONALITY,

WITH AN EARNEST PRAYER

FOR THEIR CONTINUED SUCCESS

IN WINNING TO CHRIST

THE BENIGHTED MILLIONS OF THE LAND,

This Unpretending Volume

IS RESPECTFULLY DEDICATED.

PREFACE.

The general favor accorded to the first edition of the Directory (issued five years since) has led to the preparation of the present revised edition. Great pains have been taken to make it as nearly perfect as possible, and it is hoped that the work may be found serviceable as a book of reference and interesting as a Memorial Volume.

Although not included by Mr. Sherring in his "History of Protestant Missions in India," Burmah is given a place in this volume. It is a part of the Indian empire and there is no reason why it should be excluded from a work of this kind. The names of Ceylon missionaries have also been inserted.

The enlargement of missionary operations in India during the past nine years as indicated in the following pages and the increase in the number of converts are causes of devout rejoicing and of thankfulness to God.

To the missionaries whose names are indicated by the bracketed initials under the historical sketches of various Missions, and to other friends in India and at home who have kindly given assistance, the compiler returns his warmest thanks. He will be glad to be informed of errors and omissions.

B. H. Badley.

Lucknow, April 27th, 1881.

WORKS CONSULTED IN PREPARING THE VOLUME.

I. A Cyclopedia of Missions. By Rev. Harvey Newcomb. New York; Charles Scribner. 1854.

II. Cyclopedia of Christian Missions. By the Rev. J. L. Aikman. London and Glasgow; Richard Griffin & Co. 1860.

III. The Missionary World; an Encyclopedia. New York: A. D. F. Randolph & Co. 1873.

IV. Report of the General Missionary Conference held at Allahabad, 1872-73; with Statistical Tables. Madras; C. Foster. 1873.

V. The History of Protestant Missions in India, from their Commencement in 1706 to 1871. By the Rev. M. A. Sherring, M. A., LL. B. London: Trubner & Co. 1875.

VI. Christianity in India. By the Rev J. Hough. 4 vols. 1839-45.

VII. History of the Tranquebar Mission. By J. F. Fenger. Tranquebar Evangelical Lutheran Mission Press. 1863.

VIII. The Life and Labors of Carey, Marshman and Ward. By John Clark Marshman. London: Alexander Strahan & Co. 1874.

IX. Christian Missions in the East and West (Baptist Missionary Society). 1792-1873. London: Yates & Alexander: 1873.

X. The Pioneers: a Narrative of the Planting of Christianity in Bengal. By Rev. George Gogerly. London: John Snow & Co. 1871.

XI. "The Land of Charity": a descriptive Account of Travancore and its People. With especial reference to missionary labour. By the Rev. Samuel Mateer, F. L. S. London: John Snow & Co. 1871.

XII. History of the Missions of the American Board of Commissioners for Foreign Missions in India. By R. Anderson, DD. LL. D. 1875.

XIII. Hand-book of Bengal Missions, in connexion with the Church of England. By the Rev. James Long. London: Shaw. 1848.

XIV. A History of Wesleyan Missions, from their Commencement. By the Rev. William Moister. London: Eliot Stock. 1878.

XV. India and Indian Missions. By the Rev. Alexander Duff, D.D. Edinburgh: John Johnstone. 1840.

XVI. History of the Missions of the Free Church of Scotland. By the Rev. Robert Hunter, M. A. London: T. Nelson and Sons. 1873.

XVII. A Manual of the Foreign Missions of the Presbyterian Church, U. S. A. By John C. Lowrie. New York: William Rankin, Jr. 1868.

XVIII. The Land of the Veda. By Rev. William Butler, D. D. New York: Carlton and Lanahan. 1871.

XIX. The Land of the Tamulians and its Missions. By the Rev. E. R. Baierlein. Higginbotham & Co. Madras. 1875.

XX. Mission Reports, General and Local, of various Societies.

CONTENTS.

ABBREVIATIONS.

A.—Arrived in India.
Ad.—Address.
B.—Born.
Col.—College.
E.—Educated at.
Eng.—England.
Engl.—English.
H.—Health-furlough.
I.—India.
Inst.—Institution.
L.—Literary efforts.
M.—Married.
O.—Ordained.
O. D.—Ordained Deacon.
O. E.—Ordained Elder.
O. P.—Ordained Priest.
R.—Returned.
Rt.—Returned to India.
Ret.—Retired.
S.—Station; field of labor.
Sem.—Seminary.
Theol.—Theological.
Ver.—Vernacular.
W.—Work.

INDIAN MISSIONARY DIRECTORY.

——ooo——

CHAPTER I.

THE EARLY DANISH MISSIONARY SOCIETY.

IN the year 1705, at the instigation of the Chaplain to the King of Denmark, Ziegenbalg and Plutschau, who had been students at the University of Halle, were sent forth as missionaries to Tranquebar, where they landed July, 1706. In beginning their work they met with little sympathy from those about them, and, notwithstanding the King of Denmark's injunctions, opposition was shown them, especially by the Governor of the Colony. Other difficulties were experienced, but the missionaries remained at their post, and continued to preach, teach, write and translate. Three years and-a-half after their arrival the Native Christian community numbered 160 persons. The need of funds being felt, attempts were made to raise money in Germany and also in England; as one of the results of which, the Society for the Propagation of the Gospel (established by royal charter in 1701) sent the missionaries a donation of £20, and a collection of books. From this time much interest continued to be taken in England in the welfare of the Tranquebar Mission. King George I. manifested his good-will by writing the following letter to the missionaries in 1717, which is worthy of being recorded as an example to be followed by other crowned heads :—

"George, by the Grace of God, King of Great Britain, France and Ireland, Defender of the Faith, &c., to the Reverend and Learned Bartholomew Ziegenbalg and John

Ernest Grundler, missionaries at Tranquebar in the East Indies, REVEREND AND BELOVED:

Your letters, dated 20th of January of the present year, were most welcome to us, not only because the work undertaken by you of converting the heathen to the Christian faith doth by the grace of God prosper, but also because that, in this our kingdom, such a laudable zeal for the promotion of the Gospel prevails. We pray you may be endowed with health and strength of body, that you may long continue to fulfil your ministry with good success, of which we shall be rejoiced to hear. So you will always find us ready to succour you in whatever may tend to promote your work, and to excite your zeal. We assure you of the continuance of our Royal favour.

We pray you may enjoy strength of body and mind for the long continuance of your labours in this good work, to the glory of God and the promotion of Christianity among the heathen, that its perpetuity may not fail in generations to come.

Given at our Palace of Hampton Court, the 23rd of August, 1717, in the 4th year of our Reign. GEORGE R."

It was not thought proper to extend the labors of the Propagation Society to the East Indies, and the Society for the Propagation of Christian Knowledge (established in 1699) became the Patron of the Mission. A fund with special reference to the Danish Mission in India was opened, and to this contributions came from all quarters.

Two years after reaching India, Ziegenbalg began the translation of the New Testament into Tamil and finished it on the 21st March, 1711. By 1719, the year of his death, he had translated as far as Ruth in the Old Testament. Schultz, who arrived in 1719, resumed the translation at this point, and finished it in 1725. This earnest and scholarly missionary proceeded to Madras in 1726, where he established a Mission, preached, translated the Bible into Hindustani, and gathered in a number of converts. Much interest was cherished both in the Tranquebar and Madras work by the Protestants of Denmark, Germany, and England, and especially by the Royal Families of these countries.

In and following 1732, the missionaries extended their labors to Negapatam, and thence to Sadras on the sea-coast; and to Fort St. David to the north of Cuddalore: the latter station was itself occupied in 1737. Meanwhile, several congregations of Christians had grown up in the adjoining kingdom of Tanjore, which were placed under the care of pastors. A Christian community was also formed at Pulicat. In 1736 the country congregations contained 1,140 members, and the Tranquebar congregations, 1,189. During the next ten years 3,812 persons were baptized, and the knowledge of Christianity was scattered through Tranquebar, portions of Tanjore, and cities, towns and villages on the Coromandel coast from Madras to Ramnad.

In 1756, half a century after the founding of the Mission, the missionaries, now increased to eight, on reviewing the Mission's history found that about 11,000 persons in this one Mission had abandoned idolatry and superstition and embraced the Gospel of Christ; a cheering and stimulating fact.

In 1758, after the capture of Cuddalore by the French, and the consequent interruption to missionary work, Kiernander, at the request of the Danish missionaries, proceeded to Calcutta, where he labored diligently for many years.

In 1760, Schwartz, who had arrived in India ten years before, and had been earnestly and successfully engaged in and about Tranquebar, paid a visit to Ceylon. In 1766, he established a Mission at Trichinopoly, under the auspices of the Christian Knowledge Society, where he labored with the enthusiasm which was characteristic of his entire missionary life. About 1773, supported by the Mission at Madras, and with the approval of Schwartz, a catechist was sent to Vellore, where he established a Mission, and where a Christian community was soon formed. In 1776, Schwartz took up his abode in Tanjore; and the Mission there may be regarded as commencing from this date. This "Apostle of India," as he has been called, continued incessant in labors at Tanjore and elsewhere until his death, in 1798.

The province of Tinnevelly, which for years had been considered as an outstation of Tranquebar, was occupied in 1785, a Mission having been formed at Palamcottah, the Capital. This proved a promising field, and when Gericke visited it, in 1802, he baptized no less than 1,300 persons. On account of the diminished number of missionaries of the Danish and Christian Knowledge-Societies, Tinnevelly was virtually left to itself and the Mission was correspondingly weakened. In 1817, mainly through the efforts of the Rev. J. Hough, Chaplain at Palamcottah, it was transferred to the Church Missionary Society.

With the death of Schwartz in 1798, the first period of Protestant Missions in India may properly be said to end. After this date, but five of the fifty-four missionaries of the Danish Society arrived in India, and although several continued to labor at Tranquebar and elsewhere during the early part of the present century, still the interest decreased, and the Missions were either abandoned or incorporated with those of the Church of England and the Propagation Societies. (*Vide* Sherring's "History of Protestant Missions in India," pp. 55; 341, 342; 385-387.)

The following list of the laborers connected with this pioneer Mission is taken from Fenger's "History of the Tranquebar Mission:"—

Henry Plutschau. B. at Wesenberg in Mecklenburg. E. at Halle, O. at Copenhagen, 1705, embarked from thence Nov. 29, 1705. A. at Tranquebar, July 9, 1706, left I. Sept. 15, 1711, D. in Holstein, about 1746.

Bartholomew Ziegenbalg. B. at Pulsnitz, Saxony, June 24, 1683, E. at Halle. O. and A. with the former, went home Oct 26, 1714, R. by way of England, landed at Madras Aug. 10, 1716, D. at Tranquebar, Feb. 23, 1719.

John Ernest Grundler. B. at Weissensee, April 7, 1677. E. at Halle, O. at Copenhagen, 1708, embarked there Nov. 17, 1708, A. at Tranquebar, July 20, 1709, D. March 19, 1720.

John George Bovingh. A Westphalian. E. at Kiel, O. and A. with the last mentioned, Ret. in 1711.

Polycarp Jordan. Sent out unordained with the two last mentioned, went home in 1714, where he remained.

Benjamin Schultze. B. at Sonnenburg, 1689. E at Halle, embarked at Deal, March 20, 1719. A at Madras, July 25, 1719, O. at Tranquebar, 1720, began the Madras Mission 1728, went home 1743, D. at Halle, Nov. 25, 1760.

Nicholas Dal. B. at Anslet, Denmark, April 2, 1690, E. at Jena and Halle, A with the last mentioned, O. at Tranquebar June 7, 1730, D. May 5, 1747.

J. HENRY KISTENMACHER. B. at Burg in Magdeburg, A. with the two last mentioned, D. Feb. 16, 1722. (Unordained).

M. BOSSE. B. at Nelben in Magdeburg, O. at Copenhagen, 1724, embarked at Deal, Feb. 15, 1725, was in 1749 discharged and recalled to Copenhagen. where he D. 1750.

CHRISTIAN FREDERICK PRESSIER. B. at Perleberg, July 26, 1697, E. at Jena and Halle, O. and A. with the last mentioned, D. Feb. 15, 1736.

CHRISTIAN TH. WALTHER. B. at Schildberg in Brandenburg, Dec. 20. 1699, E. at Halle, O. and A. with the two last mentioned, R. to Europe 1739, D. at Dresden, April 29, 1741.

ANDREW WORM. B. in Mecklenburg-Strelitz about 1704, E. at Jena and Halle, O. at Copenhagen 1729, A. July 1, 1730, D. May 30, 1735.

S. G. RICHSTEIG. B. at Landsberg, Brandenburg, 1701, E. at Halle, O. and A. with the last mentioned, D. May 12, 1735.

JOHN ANTON SARTORIUS. B. at Laufenselten, in Hesse-Rheinfels, Feb. 21, 1704, E. at Halle. O. in Lon. (by the Lutheran Court-Chaplain Ruperti), A. 1730. He began the Mission in Cuddalore, 1737, D. there, 1738.

JOHN ERNEST GIESTER. B. at Berlin, E. at Jena and Halle, O. 1731, A. 1732, went with Sartorius to Cuddalore 1737, R. to Madras, 1743, left the Mission, 1746, went to Batavia and there embarked for Europe, but D. on the voyage, 1746.

G. W. OBUCH. B. at Morungen, in East Prussia, May 20, 1707, E. at Halle, O. at Copenhagen, 1736, A. in Tranquebar Aug. 19, 1737, where he D. Sept. 3, 1745.

J. CHAR. WIEDERROCK. B. at Minden in Westphalia, Feb. 9, 1713, E. at Halle, O. and A. with the last mentioned, labored at Tranquebar until his death, April 7, 1767.

J. BALTHASAR KOHLHOFF. B. at Neuwarp in Western Pomerania, Nov. 15, 1711, E. at Rostock and Halle, O. and A. with the two last mentioned, labored at Tranquebar more than 53 years, D. there Dec. 17, 1790.

JOHANN ZACHARIAS KIERNANDER. B. at Linkoping in Sweden, Dec. 1, 1710, E. at Upsala and Halle, O. 1739, embarked at Gravesend April 1, 1740, landed at Cuddalore Aug. 28, 1740, labored there till 1758, when he went to Calcutta to commence a Mission, where he labored earnestly many years: D. at Chinsurah, in 1794.

JOHANN PHILIPP FABRICIUS. B. at Cleeberg, Jan. 22, E. at Giessen and Halle, O. at Copenhagen, 1739, A. with the last mentioned, labored at Tranquebar till 1742, when he became Schultz's successor at Madras, where he died Jan. 24, 1791, after more than 50 years' residence in I.

DANIEL ZEGLIN. B. at Stettin in Pomerania, Aug. 26, 1716, E. at Halle, O. with the last mentioned, and A. with him and Kiernander, labored nearly 40 years at Tranquebar, where he D. May 4, 1780.

OLUF MADERUP. B. at Maderup, Denmark, April 29, 1711, E. at Copenhagen, O. there, 1741, embarked Nov. 19, 1741, A. at Tranquebar July 1, 1742, labored at Tranquebar more than 34 years, D. there Nov. 20, 1776

JACOB KLEIN. B. at Elbing in Prussia, Jan. 20, 1721, E. at Halle. O. at Copenhagen, 1744, embarked at London, March 29, 1745. A. Aug. 3, 1746, labored nearly 44 years at Tranquebar, where he D. May 18, 1790.

J. CH. BREITHAUPT. B. at Dransfield in Hanover, O. at Wernigerode, 1745, A. with the last mentioned, learned Tamil at Tranquebar, went to Cuddalore, 1747, and to Madras, 1749, where he labored, and D. Nov. 17, 1782, after more than 36 years' residence in I.

CHRISTIAN FREDERICK SCHWARTZ. B. at Sonnenburg in Neumark, Oct. 26, 1726, E. at Halle, O. at Copenhagen, Sept. 17, 1749, landed at Cuddalore July 30, 1750, labored more than eleven years in Tranquebar, commenced (in 1762) the Mission in Trichinopoly, settled at Tanjore, 1778, D. there Feb. 13, 1798, after more than 47 years' residence in I.

DAVID POLTZENHAGEN. B. at Wollin in Pomerania, 1726, E. at Halle, O. and A. with the last mentioned, went to Cuddalore, R. to Tranquebar for two years (1758-60), D. at Cuddalore, 1781.

G. H. CONR. HUTTEMAN. B. at Minden in Westphalia, 1728, E. at Halle, O. and A. with the two last mentioned, went to Cuddalore, R. to Tranquebar 1758-60. D. at Cuddalore, 1781.

PETER DAME. B. at Flensburg, in Sleswick, May 22, 1731, E. at Halle. O. at Copenhagen, 1754, A. 1755, D. on a journey at Tanjore, May 5, 1766.

CHRISTIAN WILHELM GERICKE. B. at Colberg in Pomerania, April 5, 1742, E. at Halle, O. at Wernigerode, 1765. A. after a long and dangerous voyage at Point de Galle, Dec. 4, 1766, arrived after some stay in Ceylon, at Tranquebar, June 6, 1767, went to Cuddalore, labored at various places especially at Negapatam, until 1788, when he became Fabricius' successor, (and Chaplain of the Female Asylum) at Madras, D. at Vellore, Oct. 2, 1803, and was buried at Madras.

J. F. KONIG. B. at Konnern near Halle, Oct. 26, 1741, E in the Orphan-house at Halle, O. at Copenhagen, 1767, A. 1768, D. at Tranquebar Feb. 4, 1795.

F. W. LEIDEMANN. B. in Lippe-Schaumburg, Jan. 6, 1742, E. at Halle, O and A. with the last mentioned. D. Aug. 8, 1774.

W. JACOB MULLER. B. in Waldeck, May 24. 1734. E. at Halle, O. at Copenhagen, 1769 A. June 12, 1771, D. Dec. 30, 1771.

CHRISTOPHER SAMUEL JOHN. B. at Frobersgrun near Greiz, Aug 11, 1747, E at Halle. O. and A. with the last mentioned, D. after more than 42 years' labor at Tranquebar, Sept. 1, 1813.

J. CH. DIEMER. B. in Alsatia (Lower-Rhine, France), 1745, E. at Strasburg and Halle, O. at Wernigerode, 1773, A. at Bombay, 1774, and went to Calcutta, married, R. to Eng. 1785, R. to Calcutta, 1789, where he D. 1792.

J. W. GERLOCH. B. at Schlitz near Fulda, 1738, E. at Halle, O. at Copenhagen, 1775, A. Aug. 5, 1776, went to Calcutta, 1778, where he D. 1792.

J. P. Rottler. B. at Strasburg (Lower-Rhine, France), June, 1749, E. at Strasburg, O. and A. with the last mentioned. Labored at Tranquebar till 1803, when he was provisionally sent to Madras: was unconnected with any Home Mission, 1806-17, when he took charge of the Madras Mission under the "District Committee." D. after 60 years' residence in I. Jan. 24, 1836.

J. J. Schollkopf. B. at Kirchheim in Wurtemberg. 1748, E. at Tubingen, O. at Wernigerode, 1776, A. June 16, 1777, D. at Madras, July 11, 1777.

Ch. Pohle. B. in Lower Lusatia (Brandenburg) March 9, 1744, E. at Leipzig. O. at Copenhagen in 1776, A. 1777, D. at Trichinopoly, after more than 41 years' labor, Jan. 28, 1818.

Lor. Fred. Rulfsen. B. in Sleswick, April 7, 1753, E. at Copenhagen, was sent (with two unordained assistants for Calcutta) to Tranquebar, A. June 16, 1780. and died of fever soon after.

J. Dan Mentel. B. at Strasburg (Lower-Rhine, France), Feb. 13, 1755. E at Strasburg, O. at Copenhagen, 1780, A. 1781, R. to Europe in 1784.

Peter Rudek Hagelund. B. in Denmark, 1756, was sent out in 1785. D. at Tranquebar, Oct. 1, 1788.

J. Caspar Kohlhoff. (Son of J. Balthasar Kohlhoff) B. at Tranquebar, 1726, brought up by C. F. Schwartz, O. by him at Tranquebar, 1787, labored at Tanjore till his death March 27, 1844.

Jos. Dan. Janicke. B. at Berlin July 27, 1759, E. at Halle, O. at Wernigerode, 1787, A. 1788, labored at Tanjore and Palamcottah, and D. at the former place, May 10, 1800.

Aug. Fred Cammerer. B. in Brandenburg. June 22, 1767, E. at Halle, O at Copenhagen, 1789, suffered shipwreck at the Cape, A. 1791, was at Tranquebar for many years, D. Oct. 22, 1837.

C. W. Pazold. B. in Lusatia, 1764, E at Wittemberg, O. at Wernigerode, 1792, A. 1793, where he assisted Gericke, went to Calcutta as Professor of Tamil in the College of Fort William, 1802, R. in 1804 to Madras, where he labored till his death, Nov. 4, 1817.

E. Ph. H. Stegmann. B. at Cassel 1773, E at Marburg. O. at Copenhagen, 1795, A. 1796, R. to Europe in 1797, Rt. in 1799, R. to Europe. D. at Funen.

W. Tob. Ringeltaube. B. in Silesia 1770, E. at Halle. O. at Wernigerode 1796, A. 1799, R the same year to Eng. Joined the London Missionary Society, Is said to have been killed on a journey into the interior of Africa before 1820.

J. M Go. Holzberg. B. near Gorlitz, April 28. 1770, E. at Leipzig. O with the last mentioned, A. 1797, labored at Tanjore till 1803, and then at Cuddalore where he D. Dec. 19, 1824.

Lamb. Ch. Fruchtenicht. 1799-1802.

Christoph H. Horst. B. near Schwerin, 1761, studied medicine at Gottingen, joined the army and arrived with his regiment at Madras 1787, joined the Mission as a catechist at Cuddalore in 1792, removed to Tranquebar, 1803, then to Tanjore 1806, where he was ordained by Pohle, and D. July 18, 1810.

DAN. SCHREYVOGEL. B. at Lindau. Bavaria, Jan. 16, 1777, was sent out unordained as a catechist to Tranquebar 1803, A. 1804. O at Tranquebar 1813, resigned and joined the English Church by re-ordination, 1826, D. at Pondicherry, Jan 16, 1840.

CHRISTL. AUGUSTIN JACOBI. B. at Olbernhau in Saxony, May 26, 1791, E. at Leipzig and Halle, O. at Copenhagen 1812, embarked in Eng. 1813, A. at Tanjore, but died immediately after arriving, Feb. 21, 1814.

J. G. PH. SPERSCHNEIDER. B. in Schwarzburg-Rudolstadt, 1794, E at Leipzig and Jena. O. at Halle 1818, A. in Nov. 1819, went to Tanjore where he labored until 1826, when his connection with the Patron Society was dissolved.

LAUR. PET. HAUBROE. B. at Copenhagen, 1791, E. at Copenhagen, O. at Roeskilde, 1818, A. in Madras Feb. 1819, labored there till 1827, removed to Tanjore, where he D. 1830.

DAVID ROSEN. B at Ebeltoft, Denmark, 1791, E. at Copenhagen, O. and A. with the last mentioned, labored in Trichinopoly till 1824, at Cuddalore till 1829, then at Palamcottah till 1830, was at the head of the Danish colonization experiment on the Nicobar Islands, 1831-34, R. to Palamcottah, 1835, went home 1838, was appointed pastor of Lille Lyndby in Zealand, D. 1862.

K. E. MOHL. A. 1829, was pastor of Zion Church, Tranquebar, went home, 1835.

HANS KNUDSEN. B. at Copenhagen, Jan. 11, 1813, E. at the same place, came to I. in 1837, was pastor of Zion Church, Tranquebar till May 1843, when he fell sick and R. to Europe.

AARON. B. at Cuddalore about 1699, baptized at Tranquebar Aug. 5, 1718: O. Dec. 28, 1733: D. June 25, 1745.

DIOGO. B. of Roman Catholic parents about 1705: joined the Lutheran Church Nov. 17, 1713: O. Dec. 25, 1741: D. in Oct. 1781.

AMBROSE. B. of Roman Catholic parents in 1709: joined the Lutheran Church Aug. 8, 1717: O. at Poreiar April 9, 1749: D. Feb. 8, 1777.

PHILIP. B. of heathen parents in 1731: baptized at Tranquebar Sept. 3, 1841: O. Dec. 28, 1772: D. Feb. 4, 1788.

RAYAPPEN. B. at Poreiar in 1742 O. in 1778, D. March 25, 1797.

SATTIANADEN. O. Dec. 26, 1790, D. in 1815.

NAJANAPRAGASAM. O. March 17, 1811, D.—

ADEIKKALAM. O. March 17, 1811: D.—

VEDANAYAGAM. O. March 17, 1811: D. about 1813.

ABRAHAM. O. March 17, 1811: D.—

SCHAWRIRAYEN. B. in 1751 at Valipaleam. O. in 1813, D. Sept. 25, 1817.

NALLATHAMBI. O. in Aug. 1817, D. in 1857.

ABRAHAM. O. in Aug. 1817, D.—

PAKIANADEN. O. in Aug. 1817, D.—

CHAPTER II.

THE BAPTIST MISSIONARY SOCIETY.

THIS Society, the pioneer of the many Missionary Societies which have sprung up during the last century, was organized mainly through the tireless efforts of William Carey. In the year 1791, when preaching at Leicester, he pressed upon the attention of his ministerial brethren his favorite theme, the degraded state of heathen lands; and respectfully submitted for their consideration, "whether it was not practicable and their bounden duty to attempt somewhat towards spreading the Gospel in the heathen world." At the next meeting of the Nottingham Association, in May, 1792, Mr. Carey preached his memorable sermon from Isaiah 54, 1-3, and dwelt with great power on his two leading divisions—"Expect great things from God; and attempt great things for God." The impression produced by this discourse was so deep and general that the Association resolved upon instituting a mission to the heathen at their next meeting in Autumn. On the 22nd of October, 1792, the Society was formed, and although the collection on the occasion amounted to but £13 2s. 6d., ample funds speedily flowed in from various quarters.

After the formation of the Society, the next great question was in reference to its specific field of operation. Mr. Carey had thought long and anxiously about the South Sea Islands, and held himself in readiness to proceed thither if any Society would send him out with the means of support for one year. Just at that time he met with Mr. Thomas, who had been a surgeon in an East Indiaman, which situation he had given up in order that he might become a preacher to the heathen. He had learned the Bengali language, and, after some years of evangelistic work, had returned to England and was collecting funds for the establishment of a Christian Mission in Bengal. The Society's Committee, after consulting with Mr. Thomas, and being fully of the opinion that a door was opened in the East Indies for preaching the Gospel to the heathen, agreed to invite him to go out under the patronage of the Society, agreeing to furnish him with a companion if one could be obtained. Mr. Carey was willing to go at once: and, after encountering numerous and complicated difficulties, financial, domestic and political, they at length embarked for India in the *Princess Maria*, a Danish East Indiaman, on the 13th of June, 1793. They reached Calcutta in safety on the 11th of November. On arriving, they found the way closed by the restrictions of the East India Company against their openly pursuing their vocation as Christian missionaries, and being uncertain as to their future support from England, they went up country and took situations which were offered them in connection with indigo factories, in the neighbourhood of Malda.

On the 1st of November, 1795, the missionaries formed a church at Mudnabutty (where Mr. Carey had fixed his residence) consisting of themselves and two Englishmen. In 1796, the Rev. John Fountain was sent out to reinforce the Mission. In 1797, the missionaries made an excursion to Bootan, preaching Christ in many new places. During 1798, a school was established and a printing press set up at Mudnabutty for the printing of the Scriptures, the translation of which into Bengali was made a primary object of the Mission. In October, 1799, Messrs. Ward, Brunsdon, Grant and Marshman arrived in India, and, owing to the hostility of the British Government, proceeded to Serampore, a Danish settlement. After consulting with the other missionaries, it was determined to remove the Mission from Mudnabutty to Serampore, which was done early in 1800. On the 24th of April, 1800, the missionaries united together as a church. The printing of the New Testament in Bengali was begun May 26, 1800, and was finished February 7, 1801. The first Bengali convert, Krishna Pal, was baptized on the last Lord's Day in December, 1800.

The work gradually spread from Serampore. Dinagepore, Cutwa and Jessore were occupied as mission stations by 1804. In the early part of 1805, four additional missionaries from England arrived. In 1809, a new place of worship for Europeans and natives was opened in Calcutta, costing Rs. 30,000.

In 1806, and onward for several years, the Mission experienced severe trials from the opposition of Government, which seemed determined to conciliate the Hindoos by protecting their idolatrous forms of worship against all interference from the missionaries. Prejudice and bigotry joined hands in endeavoring to prevent missionaries entering India. Besides other forms of opposition, Government proceeded to prohibit the circulation of tracts and public preaching in Calcutta: and this opposition reached a climax when on the arrival of two new missionaries from England in August, 1806, they were peremptorily ordered to quit the country immediately. Like others who had preceded them, they at once placed themselves under the special protection of the Danish Governor of Serampore and even then barely escaped. At times the Government abstained from interference, but at other times it was violently opposed to missionary enterprises. In 1812 it ordered two missionaries to be expelled the country, and then all others brought to its notice, with the exception of those at Serampore. The last of those thus expelled was the Rev. Mr. Johns, who, in spite of all protestations, was sent home to England, at an expense to the (Baptist) Society of £500. In the same year, 1813, the new East India Company Charter came into force, removing all restrictions on missionaries entering the country.

The work at Serampore and in adjoining stations was energetically carried forward. "In no country in the world and in no period in the history of Christianity," says the author of *Protestant Missions in India*, "was there ever displayed such an amount of energy in the translation of the sacred Scriptures from their originals into other tongues, as was exhibited by a handful of earnest men in Calcutta and Serampore in the first ten years of the present century. By their own industry, and that of other persons in various parts of India, who had caught from them the inspiration for the work, during this short period, portions of the Bible, chiefly of the New Testament, had been translated and actually printed, in thirty-one Indian languages and dialects." The whole Bible was translated, through their agency, into a few, and the New Testament, into a larger number of languages.

In 1810 the missionaries arranged their labors under the

specific designation of "The United Missionaries in India," comprehending Bengal with five stations, Burmah, Orissa, Bootan, and North India with two stations, Patna and Agra. The missionaries Chamberlain and Peacock reached the latter place in May 1811, Lord Minto, strange to say, having given them a passport.

In 1811 the number of members in all the churches exceeded 300, one-third of whom had been added within a little more than a year. On the 11th of March, 1812, the mission printing-house at Serampore was entirely destroyed by fire, involving a loss of about £10,000, no part of which was insured. So great was the interest taken in England in the Mission that this whole loss was more than made good in the short space of fifty days: and a powerful impulse was given to the Mission by rendering it more generally known and producing a simultaneous feeling of interest in all denominations.

During the year 1813 work was progressing in ten stations in Bengal, the missionaries were preaching in ten languages and were preparing the Scriptures in many more. Allahabad was occupied in 1814. During 1815-17 upwards of 400 persons were added to the churches. Dacca and Monghyr were occupied in 1816: Howrah, Sewry, Benares and Delhi, in 1818. About this time the Serampore College was projected: in which knowledge was to be imparted in English, Hebrew, Greek, Sanskrit, Arabic, Chinese, and a multitude of Indian languages: and lectures were to be delivered by qualified professors in mathematics, medicines, jurisprudence, ethics, and theology. A charter was obtained for the College from the Danish Government in 1829.

During the interval 1817-27 a controversy arose between the Serampore missionaries and the Parent Society respecting the property at Serampore. This culminated in a breach which extended from 1827 to 1837, during which time the two bodies labored independently. The Serampore mission had nine outstations, including Delhi, where the Rev. Mr. Thompson was earnestly laboring. The Parent Society made its headquarters in Calcutta, where the missionaries prosecuted their labors with success. The printing press yielded a large revenue, chapels were built in various parts of the city, and schools were opened. Early in 1838 harmony was restored between the two bodies and the breach healed. The plan of union provided that the translations and all the movoable property at Serampore should be transferred to Calcutta, which thenceforth became the centre of interest in regard to translations, printing, etc.

The Society occupies the following stations: Calcutta, Serampore, Backergunge, Jessore, Dacca, Eastern Bengal, Dinagepore, Beerbhoom, Monghyr, Patna, Benares, Allahabad, Agra, Delhi, Simla, Poona, Madras, and Ootacamund; there are in all about 110 stations and sub-stations. It has 34 European and 11 Native missionaries or Assistant missionaries, and 104 Native evangelists. About 2,500 children are taught in the day schools and 400 in the Sunday-schools connected with the Society. The largest number of Christians connected with it is in Backergunge, where the Christian community exceeds 4,000. There are a considerable number of Christians also in the Twenty-Four Pergunnahs, in Jessore, and in Delhi and its neighbourhood. The native Church-members connected with the Society number over 3,000, representing a nominal Christian community of probably about 10,000. The Society has paid special attention to the work of Bible Translation, especially in the Bengali and Hindi languages, chiefly through the labor of Drs. Carey, Yates, and Wenger, and Mr. Parsons, all of whom have passed to their eternal reward. The Society engages mainly in preaching, as distinguished from educational work.

---o---

MISSIONARIES OF THE SOCIETY.

Allen, Isaac. B. Bristol, Eng. June, 1831. E. Oberlin Col., Ohio, U. S. A., 1860,-62, O. Aug. 1863, A. Nov. 1863. S. Beerbhoom and Dacca. H. to Eng., 1875-77. S. Dacca and Cachar. W. Engl. and Ver. L. Several Engl. Tracts. Ad. *Silchar, Cachar.*

Anderson, James Henry. B. in Lon., 1827, E. at Stepney Col., Lon. A. Nov. 2, 1854. S. Jessore, 1854-66, Acting Principal Serampore College, 1866-68; for a time in Calcutta. H. six months in 1862, and 1870-72, Rt. 1873. S. Allahabad. Work, Ver. at Jessore, Engl. and Ver. since. On account of wife's ill health went to Eng. in Feb. 1881.

BANERJEA, BROJONATH. Ad. *Dinajepore, Bengal.*

BANERJEA, TARA CHAND. B. Calcutta. Feb. 17, 1827. E. General Assembly's Inst., Calcutta, before the disruption of the Church of Scotland. For some years prosecuted medical studies. Became a Christian Feb. 17, 1844. Taught in Mission schools in the capacity of head-master about twenty-five years, for some years in the Cathedral Mission Col., Calcutta. O. by the Presbytery of the Church of Scotland in August, 1868. Was a missionary in connection with that Church till Feb. 1872, when he became a Baptist and afterwards joined the Baptist Missionary Society of Eng. at Calcutta. L. Translating the Koran and Institutes of Manu. Ad. *Lower Circular Road, Calcutta.*

BARNETT, T. A. 1880. Ad. *Dacca, Bengal.*

BATE, JOHN DREW. A. 1866 Ad. *Allahabad.*

BION, ROBERT. A. 1847. Ad. *Dacca, Bengal.*

BROADWAY, D. P. A. 1856. Ad. *Bankipore, Bengal.*

BUKSH, SAMUEL PEER. B. Calcutta, 1823. O Intally chapel, Sept. 1875. S. Pastor of the Native Baptist Church, South Colinga St. L. "Ainulkal," "Brazen Serpent," "Namaze" in prose and in Mohammadan Bengali, "Birth and Childhood of Jesus," and "Narration of Abraham" in verse and in Mohammadan Bengali, "Gulpa Ratno" and "Catholic Errors" in prose in Bengali; versification of the Proverbs and Ecclesiastes in Bengali—all these for Tract Society: Commentary on the Proverbs of Solomon in Bengali, to be had at the depository of Tract Society and in Baptist Mission Press. Ad. *Intally, Calcutta.*

CAREY, WILLIAM. (M.B. L.K.C.S, Edinburgh). B. July 12, 1849, at Serampore, Bengal. Set apart as a medical missionary in Oct. 1874. M. Oct. 26, 1874. A. Dec. 1, 1874. Ad. *Delhi.*

CHOWRRYAPPAH, SAMUEL JOSHUA. B. 1849, at Bellary. Spent nine years in Eng. two of which in Guinness' East Lon. Institute. O. in Southampton, Jan. 13, 1875. A. Feb. 26, 1875. Labored in Tamil and Telugu. Ad. *Vepery, High Road, Madras.*

DUFFADAR, ANUNDO C. Ad. *Jessore, Bengal.*

DUTT, GOGON CHUNDER. B. of heathen parents, in 1839, near Dacca. Converted in 1858. O. 1862. Since 1867, S. Khoolna. L. Three Tracts; two on "Romanism," and one on "Christian Baptism," Bapt. Miss. Press, Calcutta, Ad. *Khoolna, Bengal.*

EDWARDS, THOMAS RICHARD. B. Hanthewy, Abergavenny, Monmouthshire, Feb. 27, 1857. E. Pontypool Col., accepted by the Baptist Missionary Society for mission work in I. July 8, 1879. A. Nov. 27, 1879. Ad. *Barrisal, Backergunge, Bengal.*

EVANS, B. A. 1880. Ad. *Monghyr, Bengal.*

EVANS, THOMAS. B. Sept. 28, 1826 at Newport, South Wales. Entered the Baptist Theological Col. at Pontypool, Wales, in Jan. 1850. Set apart as pastor of "The Tabernacle" at Pontypool, in 1853. A. July 17, 1855. Appointed to Chitoura near Agra where he remained until Jan. 1856, when he removed to Muttra. In May, 1857 was driven into the Fort at Agra by the rebels, who destroyed all the mission property at Muttra. In Oct. 1858 lost all his property the second time by a fire in the Agra Fort. In Feb. 1859 returned to Muttra where he labored among the British soldiers and also among the Hindoos, until Jan. 1861 when he removed to Delhi : took an active part in the famine relief works. H. in April, 1863. While at home labored in the interests of the Missionary Society. R. Nov. 1865. Spent 1866 as paster *pro tem.* of the Baptist Church at Circular Road, Calcutta. Removed to Allahabad in Jan. 1867, where he labored as pastor and in general missionary work until March, 1873, when on account of ill health he was again compelled to leave I. After eighteen months in Eng. Rt. and was stationed at Monghyr, where he has since labored. W. both Eng. and Ver. Ad. *Monghyr, Bengal.*

EWEN, JOHN. B. Aberdeen, N. B. Oct. 1855, appointed by Free Church of Scotland Evangelist to Pachamba, Nov. 1874. A. April 1875. Resigned on account of change of views on the subject of Baptism and returned home Oct. 1876. Entered Bristol Baptist Col., Jan. 1877. Attended Medical School in that city. O. May 20, 1879. Appointed by B. M. S. to Delhi. Rt. Nov. 1879. At present in charge of Medical Mission. Ad. *Delhi.*

GUYTON, ROBERT FIRTH. B. April 5, 1845, at Norwich. O. at Chepstow, June, 1871. M. Oct. 1871. Labored three years as pastor of the Baptist Church, Chepstow, A. March 25, 1874. S. Delhi. Ad. *Delhi.*

HALLAM, EBENEZER CHARLES BETHLEHEM. B. at Worcester, Eng. Jan. 1. 1833. E. at King Edward's Grammar School, Birmingham, and Normal School, Toronto, Canada West. Converted at nearly 17 years of age, Baptized, December 16, 1849. Entered the ministry as a licentiate in 1852, in connection with the Free Baptist denomination. O. at Dereham. C. W., in 1855. Dec. 31, 1855. A. March 19, 1857. S. Jellasore, Orissa, from April 1857, until Feb. 1863. Was then removed to Balasore, and in June of the same year sailed for America (on account of Mrs. Hallam's ill-health, who died on the passage). Rt. Feb. 19, 1867. S. Balasore. Removed to Midnapore in April, 1870, and was appointed to the tutorship of the Theol. Class. Left the Free Baptist Mission in Dec. 1872. Resided in Calcutta for six months, acted for a short time, as Assistant Translator to the Bengal Government, and commenced the publication of an Oriya Grammar. In July, 1873, was appointed officiating pastor and missionary at Monghyr, under the auspices of the Baptist Missionary Society of Eng. In Jan. 1875 was transferred to Howrah, in Jan. 1877, transferred to Allahabad. From March, 1857 to April 1870 W. was wholly in Oriya : for the next three and a half years wholly in Bengali : following this, chiefly in Engl. In 1874 his Oriya Grammar was completed and made over to the Calcutta School Book Society : now to be had at their Depository. In July, 1874, the honorary degree of M. A. was conferred by Bowdoin College, U. S. A. H. in 1879, to Eng.

HEINIG, HENRY. B. Magdeburg, Germany, Jan. 30, 1810. E. Berlin, 1836-37. A. Dec. 1838. S. Patna, 1838-50, Benares, 1850-81. Ad. *Benares.*

JAMES, W. B. A. 1878. Ad. *Dinagepore, Bengal.*

JAMES, W. R. A. 1878. Ad. Bapt. Miss. Press, *Calcutta.*

JONES, DANIEL. B. in Nov. 1850 at Llantwit Major, Glamorganshire, S. Wales. Began to preach in Sept. 1869. E. Pontypool Col. Wales, 1872-74. O. Nov. 11, 1874. A. Dec. 7, 1874. S. Monghyr till 1876; Benares, 1878; Agra, 1878-81. Ad. *Agra.*

JORDAN, CHARLES. B. at Dulwich, Surrey, Oct. 1, 1841. E. Regents Park. Col., Lon. Afterwards had pastoral work. Designation, Aug. 1869. A. Nov. 8, 1869. S. Dec. 1869 to June, 1871, Barrisal: 1871-73, Engl. preaching, teaching and Ver. translation at Serampore and Calcutta: 1873-78, President of Serampore Col.: in 1878 transferred to Calcutta, in 1879 H. to Eng.

KERRY, GEORGE. A. 1856. Ad. South Road, Intally, *Calcutta.*

KOBIRAJ, R. K. Ad. *Calcutta.*

MARTIN, THOMAS. B. March 9, 1823, County Derry, Ireland. Converted at an early age. Entered the Baptist Col. Bristol, in 1849. Was accepted by the Baptist Missionary Society in 1853, and set apart for I. in May, 1854 M. June 28, 1854. A. Calcutta Nov. 2, 1854. S. 1854-64, Backergunge, engaged chiefly in itinerating and preaching; 1864-76, Serampore, engaged mostly in teaching in the Col.; in 1876 returned to Backergunge. H. 1866, one year: 1872, two and a half years. Ad. *Barrisal, Bengal.*

McCUMBY, ALEXANDER. B. Cawnpore, Dec. 1814. Enlisted in the 31st Regt., March, 1828. In 1838 left the army and joined Mr. Start's Mission, with which he was connected for about 39 years. His work has been Bazar and mela preaching. Has made extensive preaching tours in Bengal and North I. Went to Eng. in 1846 with Mr. Start. R. 1847. Joined the Baptist Missionary Society, 1878, Allahabad. Was previously located in Dinapore for 11 years. Ad. *Benares.*

McKENNA, ANGUS. B. Dec. 29, 1833. Entered the ministry in 1855. A. 1851. Joined the Society in 1856. M. in August, 1857. S. Serampore, 1857: Dinagepore, 1862: Chittagong, 1867: Dacca, 1870: Barrisal, 1874: Dacca, 1874: Soory, 1879. H. From Feb. 1870 to Jan. 1873. W. Engl. and Ver. Ad. *Soory, Bengal.*

MORGAN, THOMAS. A 1839. Ad. *Howrah, Bengal.*

PEARCE, GEORGE. B. at Canterbury, Kent. O. in June, 1826; M. the same month. A. Oct 22, 1826. S. Chitpore, Seebpore, Intally, Alipore, Seebpore, Serampore, and Ootacamund. Except about three years, W. has been entirely Ver. Translations: (1) "Doddridge's Rise and Progress of Religion in the Soul"; (2) Second Part of Bunyan's "Progress"; (3) "Pinnock's Bible and Gospel History"; (4) "Companion to the Bible" (London Tract Society). Original: *A Vernacular Hymn-book; A Compendium of Christian Duties; A Tract against Popery; The Voice of the Bible against Idolatry; A Scripture Tract-book;* Several smaller tracts. Several H. aggregating ten years. Ad. *Ootacamund, Madras P.*

PRICE, W. J. Ad. *Agra.*

ROUSE, GEORGE HENRY. B. at Melton. Suffolk, Nov. 18, 1838, Brought up in the Church of England: became a Baptist in youth: was baptized in 1854: studied for the ministry in Stepney and Regents Park Col. Was accepted for missionary service in I. in 1860: left Eng. for I. in 1861. M. Was sent to I. with the view of specially engaging in the work of Bible translation in Bengal. Remained in I. till May, 1863, when complete failure of health necessitated a return to Eng. Remained in Eng. nine years, most of the time as tutor in the Regents Park or the Haverfordwest Baptist Theol. Col. R. in 1872. and settled in Calcutta. For nearly four years had charge of the Baptist Mission Press. For over two years acted as pastor of the Circular Road and afterwards of the Lal Bazar Church. Has been to some extent associated with Dr. Wenger in the revision of Bengali Bible and has engaged in other Ver. works. H. to Eng. in 1880.

SHAH, GOOLZAR. B. near Calcutta about 1826. Appointed pastor of the Intally church in 1852. In 1853 the Baptist churches of Intally and Colinga were united and he became pastor of the united church, remaining at Colinga until 1865. In 1865 his secular employment called him to Simla where he founded the Baptist mission. Labors at Simla during the hot season and at Calcutta during the cold. 1871 visited Eng. where he spent four months Ad. *Simla.*

SMITH, JAMES B. at Morley, Yorkshire, March 4, 1817. M. Before coming to I. he was connected with the Leeds Young Men's Preaching Association. A. in 1841. O. in 1846. S. Cawnpore, then Muttra and Chitoura, and subsequently, immediately after the mutiny, Delhi, where he has since remained. W. has been Ver preaching in Delhi and surrounding villages, and establishing schools; and Eng. preaching in Delhi. H. 1861-62, to Australia: to Eng. 1867-68: again in 1870: and in 1876. Ad *Delhi.*

SPURGEON, ROBERT. B. Halstead, Essex, May, 17, 1850. O. at East Lon. Tabernacle, 1873. A. March 19, 1874. S. Soory, 1874-75, Jessore, 1876-78, Dacca, 1879.—Nov. 1880, Barrisal, Nov. 1880. Ad. *Barrisal, Bengal.*

SUMMERS, EDWARD SAMUEL. B. Lon. June 18, 1853. O. Oct. 1876. A. Dec. 1876. S. Calcutta, 1877, Serampore Col. 1878 to present Ad. *Serampore.*

THOMAS, JOSEPH WILSON. B. in Calcutta, Feb. 6. 1844. R. from Eng. Nov. 1867. S. Serampore Col. till 1878. H. Nov. 1878—Feb. 1880. Ad Bapt. Mission Press, *Calcutta.*

WILLIAMS, ALBERT. B in S. Wales, 1841. O. 1866. A. 1866. S. Circular Road Church, Calcutta, 1866-78, Principal Serampore Col. 1879. H. to Eng. March, 1875.—Oct. 1876. Ad. *Serampore, Bengal.*

DECEASED AND RETIRED MISSIONARIES.

JOHN THOMAS.—Mr. THOMAS had been educated for the medical profession, and, having obtained an appointment in the service of the East India Company, proceeded to Calcutta in 1783 as a Surgeon. Unable on his arrival to discover any one of a congenial Christian spirit, he advertised, as he said, for a Christian who would assist in promoting a knowledge of Jesus Christ in and around Bengal. Mr. Chambers responded to the notice, and offered to encourage the translation of the New Testament into the Persian and Moorish languages. This movement however led to no result, and Mr. T. returned to England. He embarked as a Surgeon the second time, and, on his arrival in Calcutta, was introduced to Mr. Grant, who was delighted with his piety and zeal, and raised a subscription to enable him to quit the Company's service, and devote his attention to the heathen. A missionary station was thus formed at Goamalty, near Malda, where he applied himself diligently to the Bengali language, into which he translated a portion of the New Testament. He was employed for three years in itinerating through the district, and made considerable impression on the minds of several natives. In 1792, for various reasons, he determined to visit England, and seek assistance for the establishment of a Mission in Bengal. On arriving he heard of the formation of a Missionary Society in his own denomination, and, after correspondence and consultation, he was accepted as a missionary to India. In company with Mr. Carey he proceeded to Calcutta, landing there in November, 1793. After remaining some months in Calcutta he removed to Malda where he took charge of an indigo factory. Was afterwards engaged in superintending some sugar factories in Beerbhoom. Amid all his secular engagements he never neglected the instruction of the heathen. In December, 1800, while at Serampore, he was so overjoyed at the accession of a hopeful convert that he began to exhibit symptoms of insanity and was placed in an Asylum. After a month's residence here he was restored to mental health, and proceeded to Dinagepore to take charge of an indigo factory. Here he died on the 13th of October, 1801. (Abridged from "Carey, Marshman and Ward.")

WILLIAM CAREY.—Born in Northamptonshire, August 17, 1761. His parents being in humble circumstances, he was brought up to the trade of a shoe-maker. A sermon by Mr. Scott, the commentator, is said to have been the means of his conversion, after which he first became a village school-master, and then the pastor of a small Baptist church. At an early period of his religious career he was imbued with a spirit of missionary enterprise far in advance of the times in which he lived. His heart was greatly drawn out to the heathen world, and he continued both with pen and voice to urge his views upon the attention of his brethren in the ministry. Nothing less than his sublime earnestness and unflagging zeal would have brought success: this at length rewarded him, when in October, 1792, the Baptist Missionary Society was organized. Mr. Carey at once with great gladness of heart offered his services to the Society, and, with Mr. Thomas, was appointed to India. After many vexatious delays and much self-denial in order to secure funds, (Mrs. Carey having consented to accompany him on condition that her sister should also go,) the party left England, June 13, 1793. Arriving in Calcutta the following November they took up their residence there; but before a month Mr. Carey was constrained to seek some cheaper residence. He removed to Bandel, about 25 miles up the river, but as this was in the neighborhood of European society, he proceeded with Mr. Thomas to Nuddea, but returned after a brief sojourn, to Calcutta. Here he was reduced to great distress, and with his family removed for a time to the Soonderbuns. He was rescued from this most unfavorable position through the efforts of Mr. Thomas, and the superintendence of an indigo factory was offered him. He accepted this at once and removed to Mudnabutty, distant thirty miles from Malda. In this secluded spot he passed more than five years of his life, preaching to the workmen of the factory, itinerating in the villages, etc. His principal attention was devoted to the translation of the New Testament into Bengali, for printing which a press was purchased in Calcutta. The press was set up at Mudnabutty, and is still preserved in the Serampore College. On the arrival of Mr. Ward and his companions in 1799, Mr. Carey, then at Kidderpore (a village which he had purchased), was not disposed to change his residence, but, influenced mostly by Government opposition, he yielded, and removed with his family to Serampore, where he arrived January 10, 1800. Soon after he became a teacher of the Bengali language in the College of Fort William, entering upon the duties of his office May 12, 1801. Shortly after he was likewise appointed teacher of the Sanskrit language; and compiled grammars of both languages. He was also diligently engaged in translations. In 1807, on the remodeling of the College, Mr. Carey was raised to a professorship, and his allowance increased to Rs. 1,000 per month. On the 8th of March, 1807, he received the diploma of Doctor of Divinity from Brown University, in the United States, a title of which he was well worthy. His wife having died Mr. Carey was married again in 1808. In July, 1809, he completed the publication of the Bengali Bible; and was at once seized with a fever which brought him rapidly to the brink of the grave: the fever was at length subdued, and he gradually recovered his strength. He continued to labor with unabated zeal. Amidst all his missionary, biblical and literary labors. he never lost sight of the material interests of the country. In April, 1820, he drew up the prospectus of the Agricultural Society of India which was organized soon after, chiefly through his efforts. On the 30th of May, 1821, he was visited with the loss of his second wife, who had been of "eminent service to him in the translation of the scriptures." During 1823 he was married the third time. In July, 1823, his labors were still further augmented by accepting the office of Government translator in the Bengali language: he also edited a Grammar and a Dictionary of the Bootan language, and completed his Bengali Dictionary. In the course of the year he was elected a fellow of the Linnæan Society, a member of the Geological Society, and a corresponding member of the Horticultural Society of London. On the

8th of October he was again brought near death, but was gradually restored to health. During the year 1833 he experienced several severe attacks of illness, and it was evident that his constitution was exhausted by his forty years of incessant labor in the climate of Bengal, without a visit to England, or even a voyage to sea to recruit his strength. After he had completed the last revision of the Bengal translation, he felt that his course was run, and his work accomplished. On Monday morning, the 9th of June 1834, he passed gently away to the better world. (*Vide* "Memoir of William Carey. By Eustace Carey": "Carey, Marshman, and Ward"; and other volumes.)

JOHN FOUNTAIN.—A resident of London. Appointed to the Mission in Bengal, he embarked on one of the Company's ships, rated as a servant, and entered India without attracting notice. He joined the Mission at Mudnabutty towards the close of 1796. He removed with Mr. Carey to Serampore in 1800, where, on the 20th of August of the same year, he died.

JOSHUA MARSHMAN.—Born at Westbury Leigh in Wiltshire, April 20, 1768. As he grew up, his reading became somewhat extensive, and when he was fifteen he spent several months in the shop of a London book-seller. Shortly after his return he united with the Baptist Church in his native village. In 1791 he was most happily married. In 1794 he removed to Bristol where he was baptized, and where he passed through a course of study in the Academy. The perusal of the Periodical Accounts, which recorded the labors of Mr Carey. gradually turned his mind to missionary labor in India, and when it was known that the Society was in need of laborers for that field, he offered his services and was accepted. In company with Messrs Ward, Brunsdon, and Grant he embarked May 29, 1799, and reached Serampore October 13th of the same year. On the 18th of May 1800, Mr and Mrs. Marshman opened two boarding schools which soon yielded a handsome income. On the 1st of October he delivered his first address to the natives in Bengali. In July, 1801, he visited Jessore, which soon after became a mission station. At the beginning of 1806, Mr Marshman commenced the study of Chinese, with the view of translating the Scriptures into that language. For fifteen years he devoted himself to this arduous task, and he has the merit of having carried the first Chinese translation of the Bible through the press. Mr. Marshman was eminently successful in collecting funds for the new Chapel in Bow Bazar, Calcutta: in less than ten days he secured £1.100 from those altogether unconnected with his own denomination. In 1808 he waited in person on every gentleman of eminence in Calcutta, and obtained no less than £2,300 to aid in the printing of the Scriptures. Two years later, in 1810, he published the first volume of his English translation of the works of Confucius, with a preliminary dissertation on the language of China; a monument of literary enterprise. Mr. Marshman's literary labors had attracted much attention in America, and in the month of June, 1811. he was honored with the diploma of Doctor of Divinity from Brown University. In the year 1814 he published his "Clavis Sinica, or Key to the Chinese Language," the result of eight years of study. About the year 1815 he published his memorable pamphlet entitled, "Hints relative to native Schools, together with an Outline of an Institution for their Extension and Management." The plan described in the pamphlet for the extension of vernacular schools succeeded beyond the most sanguine expectation. Within a year or two 45 schools were established within a circle of 20 miles around Serampore, in which 2,000 children were taught. On the 31st of May, 1818, the first number of the *Sumachar Durpan*, or *Mirror of News*, was issued from the Serampore press, conducted chiefly by Mr. Marshman. In the same year the missionaries also commenced the publication of a monthly magazine which was denominated the "*Friend of India*," a name which was associated with the periodical publications of Serampore for more than half a century. They also about this time issued the prospectus of the Serampore College which was drawn up by Mr. Marshman. In June, 1820, Mr. Marshman commenced the publication of a *Quarterly Friend*. These journals from the beginning took an active part in the discussion of all subjects of public interest. During the years 1820-21, Mr. Marshman was engaged in his celebrated discussion with Ram Mohun Roy, on the doctrine of the Atonement. The controversy attracted much attention and was beneficial to the interests of Christian truth. The chief object to which his attention was directed at this time was the completion of the Chinese version of the Bible, on which he had been engaged fourteen years and the last sheet of which left the press in December, 1822. A copy of it was presented to the British and Foreign Bible Society at their annual meeting in May, 1823. In January, 1826, in the interests of the Serampore College, Mr Marshman proceeded to England. where he landed June 17th. He visited prominent cities in Great Britain, addressing large audiences and awakening a deep interest in the work at Serampore. He also visited Denmark, and in a personal interview with the King obtained the royal sanction to the charter of the College. From Copenhagen he proceeded to Paris and thence to England. After several months of labor and travel he embarked for India, February 19, 1829, landing at Serampore on the 19th of May. For several years he was earnestly engaged in teaching and literary work. At the beginning of 1834 his health began to fail. The death of his colleague, Mr. Carey, in 1834, inflicted a blow on his enfeebled constitution: and in 1835 he took a journey to the sanitarium of Chirra Poonjee. During 1836, his health was precarious: his spirits rose and sank with the prospects of the mission, and these prospects were then not of the brightest. In 1837 it became evident that his days of labor were nearly ended. About the middle of the year he was disabled from all public services. He grew weaker until early in December, when he was called to enter into rest. (Abridged from "Carey, Marshman and Ward.")

WILLIAM WARD.—Born at Derby, October 20, 1769, the son of a carpenter, who died while he was a child. At an early period while only an apprentice, he manifested considerable mental ability, and was afterwards employed in journalism for six years, first at Stafford, and afterwards at Hull. At the place last named he became decidedly religious, was publicly baptized, and commenced his theological studies with a view to the Christian ministry. Shortly after, the Society called for laborers for India, and Mr. Ward was one of the four to respond. Landing at Serampore he with his co-laborers was soon busily engaged in missionary work: he set the first types of the Bengali Bible with his own hands and presented Mr Carey with the first sheet of the New Testament on the 18th of March, 1800. In October he went out to preach alone in Bengali. Neither of his colleagues, it is said, ever obtained that mastery of the colloquial language which he acquired. On the 10th of May, 1802, Mr. Ward was married to the widow of Mr. Fountain. Towards the close of 1810 he published the first edition of his work on the "History, Literature, and Mythology of the Hindoos, including a minute description of their manners and customs, and Translations from their principal works:" for which he had been collecting materials since his arrival in the country. Concerning this well known work it has been truly remarked, "The value of this rich store of information, which exhibits an unexampled acquaintance with the interior economy of native society, has not been diminished by fifty years of subsequent investigation. and the work continues to maintain its character as the most complete and accurate record yet published on these topics." It has passd through a number of editions. In 1818, impaired health necessitated a voyage to England, and he embarked on the 18th of December, landing in England the following May. During the voyage he partly composed a volume entitled, "Reflections on the Word of God for every day in the year, to be used in family Devotions." While at home he travelled, wrote and lectured in behalf of his brethren at Serampore and the perishing millions in India. Being the first missionary who had ever returned to England from the East he received in every circle a most enthusiastic welcome. He visited various parts of England, Scotland and Wales, and besides other labors succeeded in raising £3,000 for the Serampore College. He paid a visit to Holland; and also spent three months in America where he was heartily welcomed, and where he raised Rs. 20,000 for the College. Returning to England he embarked for India in May, 1821. During the voyage he employed his time in writing farewell letters to his friends in England and America, which he was subsequently prevailed on to publish; the work went through three editions. He reached Serampore, October 20, 1821: resumed charge of the secular department of the Mission, and of the printing office, and worked the nineteen presses with increased diligence in the printing of Scriptures and tracts; but the object to which he gave his chief attention was the training of the more advanced youths in the College for missionary duties. He revised and published his "Reflections:" and began another literary work. He was enabled for a few months to resume his labors with all the vigour of renewed health, when his career was suddenly terminated by an attack of cholera. On Wednesday evening the 5th of March, 1823, he preached the evening lecture, apparently in good health: the next day he attended to some work, but was seized with cramps in the afternoon, and expired on Friday, at the age of 53.

WILLIAM LEWIS GRANT.—A resident of Bristol. In company with Messrs. Marshman, Ward and Brunsdon he landed at Serampore on the 13th of October, 1799. The dampness of the house occupied by the missionary party caused Mr. Grant to be attacked with a severe cold which brought on a fever: from the effects of which he died on the 31st of October of the same year.

DANIEL BRUNSDON.—One of the four missionaries who came in 1799. He died in Calcutta on the 3rd of July, 1801, at the early age of 24.

FELIX CAREY.—Eldest son of Dr. Carey. He was born in England several years before Dr. C. came to India. Accepted by the Missionaries as a colleague in 1803. In 1807 he offered his services to assist in the establishment of a Mission in Burmah : and in company with Mr. Chater proceeded to Rangoon, at the close of the year. Hearing that he had introduced vaccination at Rangoon, the King of Ava ordered him to proceed to the capital and vaccinate the royal household He went to Bengal for supplies, and on returning to Rangoon received orders to bring with him the press which had been established there. The vessel in which he embarked was upset by a squall in the river, and his wife and two children were drowned. The press was lost. He resided some time at the Court and proceeded to Bengal as the representative of the King, but incurring his displeasure he was not able to return to Rangoon. After leaving Burmah he led a wandering life on the eastern frontier of Bengal for three years, when he returned to Serampore. From this time to the date of his death, in 1822, he continued to labor in connection with the Serampore missionaries.

JOHN CHAMBERLAIN.—Sailed for India with his wife, by way of America, in May, 1802, and reached Serampore, January 27, 1803. Hi progress in acquiring the language was very rapid. Early in 1804 he was stationed at Cutwa. Here he met with severe domestic afflictions but continued to labor for five years. On the 16th of November, 1810, Lord Minto granted a passport to Messrs. Chamberlain and Peacock, and with the approval of their brethren they proceeded to Agra to form a station. On account of disagreement with the Military authorities he was sent back to Serampore, after a lapse of eighteen months. Shortly after, he returned to the North-west, and took up his residence at Sirdhana : but in 1814, was again removed by the Government from the North-West Provinces. Mr. Chamberlain soon after made choice of Monghyr as his station, and there passed the remaining years of his life. Having declined in health, he sailed for England with the hope of recovery, but died on the passage, in 1821.

NAMES.	To India	FROM	STATIONED AT	REMARKS.
Joshua Rowe, ...	1805	Salisbury, ..	Dinapore, ...	Died 1823.
William Moor, ...	1805	Stogumber, ..	Ditto, ...	D. 1844.
Richard Mardon, ...	1805	Devonport, ..	Goamalty, ...	D. 1812.
John Biss, ...	1805	Plymouth, ..	Serampore, ...	D. 1807.
William Robinson,	1806	Olney, ..	Dacca, ...	D. 1852.
Ignatius Fernandez,	1806	Serampore, ..	Dinagepore, ...	D. 1830.
William Carey, ...	1807	Ditto, ..	Cutwa, ...	D. 1853.
Carpeit C. Aratoon,	1809	Calcutta, ..	Calcutta, ...	———
William Johns, ...	1810		Expelled, ...	by Govt. 1813.
John Lawson, ...	1810	Trowbridge, ..	Calcutta, ...	D. 1825.
Henry Peacock, ...	1810	Calcutta, ..	Agra, ...	D. 1820.
——Cornish, ...	1810	Ditto, ..	Dacca, ...	Ret. 1813.
——Petruse, ...	1810	Ditto, ..	Jessore, ...	Ret. 1813.
Owen Leonard, ...	1810	Ditto, ..	Dacca, ...	D. 1848.
J. T. Thomson, ...	1810	Ditto, ..	Delhi, &c., ...	D. 1849.
D. DeCruz, ..	1811		Goamalty, ...	———
William Thomas, ...	1811	Calcutta, ..	Jessore, ...	D. 1871
Jabez Carey. ...	1811	Serampore, ..	Amboyna, ...	D. 1862.
——DeBruyn, ...	1812		Chittagong, ...	D. 1816.
L. Mackintosh, ...	1812	Calcuttta, ..	Agra, &c., ...	D. 1848.
W. Smith, ...	1813	Cuttack, ..	Benares, ...	D. 1852.
Eustace Carey, ...	1814	Paulerspury,	Calcutta, ...	———
William Yates, D.D,	1813	Leicester, ..	Ditto, ...	———
John DeSilva, ...	1815	Calcutta, ..	Sylhet, ...	D. 1828.
James Penney, ...	1816	Shrewspury,	Calcutta, ...	D. 1845.
W. H. Pearce, ...	1817	Birmingham,	Ditto, ...	D. 1840.
——Hart, ...	1817	Calcutta, ...	Cutwa,	———
J. W. Ricketts, ...	1817	Amboyna, ..	Berhampore,	———
J. Phillips, ...	1818		Samarang, ...	D. 1829.
Nath. M. Ward, ...	1818		Sumatra, ...	D. 1850.
——Burton, ...	1819		Deegah, ...	D. 1828.
Charles Evans, ...	1819		Sumatra, ...	Ret. 1827.
John Statham, ...	1820		Calcutta, ...	Ret. 1827.
John Mack, ...	1821	Nailsworth, ..	Serampore, ...	D. 1845.
John Johannes, ...	1821	Calcutta, ..	Chittagong, ...	D. 1864.
R. Richards, ...	1821	Benares, ..	Furrukabad, ...	Ret. 1828.
James Williamson,	1823	Serampore, ..	Beerbhoom, ...	D. 1866.
Andrew Leslie, ...	1824	Edinburgh, ..	Monghyr, ...	D. 1870.
J. C. Fink, ...	1824	Calcutta, ..	Chittagong, ...	D. 1856.
——Hampton, ...	1823	Beerbhoom, ..	Beerbhoom, ...	Ret. 1824.
Thomas Swan, ...	1824	Edinburgh, ..	Serampore, ...	Ret. 1829.
——Albrecht, ...	1824	Dresden, ..	Ditto, ...	D. 1829.
——Fenwick, ...	1825		Chinsurah, ...	———
James Thomas, ...	1826	Bradford, ..	Calcutta, ...	D. 1858.
J. D. Ellis, ...	1831	Exeter, ..	Ditto, ...	Ret. 1841.

Names.	To India.	From	Stationed at	Remarks.
W. Greenway, ...	1830		Dinapore, ..	D. 1880.
A. B. Lish, ...	1831	Calcutta, ...	Agra, ...	D. 1852.
John Lawrence, ..	1831	Loughton, ...	Monghyr, ...	D. 1874.
H. Smylie, ...	1831	Dum Dum, ...	Dinagepore, ...	D. 1855.
John Leechman, D.D	1832		Serampore, ...	Ret. 1838
Henry Beddy, ...	1832		Patna, ...	D. 1854.
F. DeMonte, ...	1833	Calcutta, ...	Calcutta, ...	D. 1855.
G. T. Anderson, ...	1834	Stepney, ...	Ditto, ...	———
Richard Williams, ...	1838	Agra, ...	Agra, ...	Ret. 1859.
Louis Kalberer, ..	1838	Wurtemberg,	Patna, ...	D. 1866.
Robert Bayne, ...	1838	Cupar, ...	Calcutta, ...	Ret. 1840.
G. Parsons, ...	1839	Frome. ...	Monghyr, ...	D. 1840.
F. Tucker, ...	1839	Stepney, ...	Calcutta, ...	Ret. 1841.
T. Phillips, ..	1839	Ditto, ...	Agra, &c., ...	D. 1868.
W. W. Evans, ...	1840	Hackney, ...	Calcutta, ...	Ret. 1845.
G. Small, ...	1840	Bristol, ...	Calcutta, &c.,	Ret. 1852.
John Parsons, ...	1840	Frome, ...	Monghyr, ...	D. 1869.
Robert Gibson, ...	1841	Stepney, ...	Calcutta, ...	D. 1842.
J. Parry, ...	1841	Barrisal, ...	Jessore, ...	———
J. Makepeace, ...	1844		Agra, ...	Ret. 1855.
W. H. Denham, ...	1844	London, ...	Serampore, ...	D. 1858.
C. B. Lewis, ...	1845	England, ...	Calcutta, ...	Ret. 1878.
John Sale, ...	1849	Wokingham, ...	Calcutta, &c ,	D. 1875.
C. F. Supper, ...	1851	Wurtemberg,	Dacca, ...	D. 1871.
J. Trafford, ...	1852	Weymouth, ...	Serampore, ...	Ret. 1879.
J. Jackson, ...	1853		Allahabad, ...	D. 1866.
John Gregson. ...	1854	Beverley, ...	Agra, ...	Ret. 1872.
William Sampson, ...	1855	Bristol, ...	Serampore, ...	Ret. 1865.
J. Mackay, ..	1855	Scotland, ...	Delhi, ...	D. 1857.
R. Robinson, ...	1856	Agra, ...	Dacca, ...	Ret. 1869.
E. Dakin, ..	1857	Loughborough,	Serampore, ...	D. 1869.
J. G. Gregson, ...	1858	London, ...	Agra, ...	Ret. 1869.
J. Williams, ...	1859	Wales, ...	Muthra, ...	Ret. 1879.
F. T. Reed, ...	1860	Bristol, ...	Sewry, ...	Ret. 1879.
J. Parsons, ...	1860	Meerut, ...	Delhi, ...	Ditto, 1873.
R. J. Ellis, ...	1860	Scotland, ...	Jessore, &c , ...	D. 1877.
E. C. Johnson, ..	1861	London, ...	Jessore &c., ...	Ret. 1870.
E. Edwards, ...	1862	Pontypool, ...	Monghyr, &c ,	Ditto, 1872.
J. A. Campagnac, ...	1870	Calcutta, ...	Ditto, ...	D. 1873.
H. G. E. St. Dalmas,	1872	Wellington, ...	Ulwar, ...	Ret. 1878.
C. C. Brown, ...	1874	London, ...	Barrisal, ...	Ret. 1876.
J. Mintridge, ...	1874	Birmingham...	Jessore, ...	D. 1875.
E. B. Francis, ...	1874		Poona, ...	Ret.
W. S. Miller, ..	1874		Benares, ...	Ret.
H. J. Tucker, ...	1875		Sewry, ...	Ret.

John Chamberlain Page. B. at Monghyr, Nov. 28, 1822. O. at Calcutta in Dec. 1843, (having returned from Eng. in 1838 destined for the army). Labored at Calcutta, preaching in Hindustani and English : then in the 24-Pergunnahs : then stationed at Budge Budge preaching from Calcutta to Gunga Sagor : next at Calcutta, teaching, and preaching in Bengali, Hindustani and English in the city and suburbs. In 1848, transferred to Baekergunge. His health failing, in Dec. 1859 he went to Eng., returning to Barrisal in Feb. 1862. In 1865 went to the Australian colonies : was enabled to establish three Missionary Societies, and, returning in 1866, to put agents into two districts in Bengal. Health again failing, he went to Simla in 1867, and to Darjeeling in 1868. Traveled in Independent Sikkim. Re-visited England to recruit his health, and returned in Jan. 1875 : was stationed at Darjeeling, until 1876, when he retired.

John Wenger. B. August 31, 1811, in the canton of Berne, Switzerland. E. for the Swiss National Church. Resided in Greece as a private tutor for some years, until 1838 when he went to Eng. Was baptized in Feb. 1839. In June, 1839 A. and immediately joined the Rev. Dr. Yates in the work of translating the Holy Scriptures. The Old Testament was finished in Feb. 1840 : the entire Bible shortly before the close of 1845. An improved edition of the entire Bible was issued in 1852. A third and carefully revised edition was begun in 1855 and finally completed in 1861. While this was in press he visited Eng. for health. R. in 1862. He next prepared an annotated edition of the Bengali Scriptures, and following this, the revision of the text of 1861. He also translated the Bible into Sanskrit taking up the work at the death of Dr. Yates. The first volume was published in Nov. 1848. The second appeared in 1852 : the third, in 1858 : and the fourth, which completes the entire work, in 1872. After re-visiting Eng. Rt. early in 1876. Died at Calcutta, Aug. 20, 1880.

———o———

CHAPTER III.

THE LONDON MISSIONARY SOCIETY.

THIS Society was organized in September 1795, the Rev. David Bogue, D.D., of Gosport, taking the leading part in its founding. The constitution of the Society is thoroughly catholic, being intended to include in its management, support and practical working, Christians of all denominations. The chief support has always been drawn from the English Congregationalists, and of late years increasingly so, as other churches have been constrained to institute and support missions of their own.

The Society sent its first missionary to India in the year 1798. This was the Rev. N. Forsyth, who came in the first instance to Calcutta, but finally settled at Chinsurah, twenty miles to the north of that city. He labored at both places but chiefly at Chinsurah. He continued alone in the work until 1812, when he was joined by the Rev. Robert May, who succeeded him at Chinsurah, and was soon deeply engaged in educational efforts. He was so successful in this branch of labor that by the end of 1816 he had under his superintendence as many as thirty schools in which near three thousand children received instruction, and for which Government gave a monthly grant of Rs. 800. Mr. May was soon joined by the Rev. Mr. Pearson from England, and by Mr. Harle. The mission at Chinsurah passed in 1849 into the hands of the Free Church of Scotland: a printing press which was first set up there was afterwards removed to Calcutta and subsequently abandoned.

In the year 1804, the Rev. George Cran and the Rev. Augustus Des Granges were appointed to India by the Society, and arrived at Madras in March, 1805. They remained here a few months engaged in the study of the language, and then proceeded to Vizagapatam, the capital of the Northern Circars, where they founded a mission which has continued since. They opened schools and soon began translating the Scriptures into Telugu, in which they were greatly assisted by Anandarayer, a converted Brahman from Tranquebar. Their labors were cut short, however, as Mr. Cran died in 1809, and Mr. Des Granges in 1810. Other missionaries had arrived and the work was carried steadily forward. No converts were gained until about 1835. In 1837 a collegiate Institution was founded; and in 1840 a printing press was established. Chicacole was occupied as a branch mission station in 1844, and in 1852 Vizianagram was added. In 1871 the three missions had nearly 300 converts.

The London Society was the first to establish a mission in Madras next after that connected with the Christian Knowledge Society. In 1805 the Rev. W. C. Loveless and Dr. Taylor arrived from England on their way to Surat. The latter entered Government service, and Mr. Loveless was persuaded to remain in Madras. His labors were mostly among the English-speaking population. He became Master of the Male Asylum, which position he held until 1812. For years he did not find his way open to labor among the heathen. About 1815 he was joined by several missionaries from England, and more active operations were commenced. Schools were opened and a church formed. In 1852 an educational Institution was founded, which is affiliated with the Madras University, and is well attended. Out-stations have been formed at Pulicat and Tripassore.

Missionary work in Travancore was commenced by the Rev. Mr. Ringeltaube in 1806. He had previously been connected with the Christian Knowledge Society and appointed to Calcutta: but had suddenly resigned his position and returned to England. Subsequently, in 1804, he was sent out by the London Society in company with the Rev. Messrs. Cran and Des Granges. When the latter proceeded to Vizagapatam he travelled southwards to the extremity of India. He labored in Tinnevelly and along the coast from Tuticorin to Cape Comorin. Early in 1806 he sailed from Tranquebar to Tuticorin where he began preaching. He visited a number of places, among them Trichinopoly, and baptized many persons. Subsequently he took up his residence at Maladi, where he erected a church. By the year 1810 he had formed six out-stations: in this year he baptized 200, and in 1811, 400 persons. By the end of 1812 there were 677 communicants in all the stations of his mission. In the midst of his usefulness, in the year 1815, he suddenly and mysteriously disappeared and was never heard of again. He was succeeded in 1818 by the Rev. Charles Mead who has been called the "Father of the South Travancore Mission." The foundation stone of the Nagercoil Chapel, the largest in South India, was laid January 1st, 1819. In 1819 Mr. Mead and his co-laborers established a Theological School which has since been sustained mainly through the proceeds of a donation of Rs. 5,000 made at that time by the Ranee of Travancore. In a few years the converts had so far multiplied that the mission was separated into two divisions, with Nagercoil as the head-quarters of the one, and Neyoor of the other. At both these places printing presses were set up and sustained for many years: but they were eventually merged into one which has been active and useful. By 1840 the Christians in the two districts had increased to 15,000, while the schools in them had 7,540 pupils. In 1822 out-stations from Nagercoil were formed both at Trevandrum and Quilon. In the latter place a printing press was established, but was subsequently given up. In the year 1871 there were in connection with the London Society's missions in South Travancore 32,122 Native Christians.

In the year 1810 the Society began its operations at Bellary, the Rev. John Hands being the first missionary appointed there. Under his supervision schools were opened, a church was formed, and Tract and Bible Societies organized. In 1818 the Scriptures were published in Canarese, having been translated by Mr. Hands. In 1826 a much-needed press was established at Bellary. It was at this station that the celebrated Samuel Flavel, one of the brightest ornaments of the Native Church of India, labored for a score of years. He was ordained in 1822 at Bangalore, where he labored as pastor of the Native church until 1827, when he was transferred to Bellary. He was suddenly removed by cholera in 1847.

When the Society was organized in 1795, Surat was one of the places which it proposed to occupy: and in 1805 two missionaries were appointed to this place, but as has been seen, did not reach their destination. In 1815 two others, the Rev. J. Skinner and the Rev. W. Fyvie were appointed, and entered upon their work in Surat at the close of that year. The missions of the Society were transferred subsequently to the

Irish Presbyterian Mission, as it was thought that they were too greatly isolated from the other Indian missions of the London Society. Surat was thus transferred in 1846, the other stations, in 1859.

Calcutta was occupied by the Society in the year 1816, the first missionaries being the Rev. Henry Townley and the Rev. Mr. Keith. They established schools in Calcutta and preached both there and at Howrah. In May, 1820, the foundation stone of "Union Chapel" in Dhurrumtollah street was laid. The church was completed in April, 1821. Of the large sum expended on it nearly £4,000 were collected in India. By 1821 the Society occupied twenty-one stations in and about Calcutta: and the missionaries had charge of thirteen schools. Ramakalchoke and contiguous places were occupied in 1826 and have been held ever since. In 1837 the educational Institution at Bhowanipore was established. It has expanded from year to year and was early affiliated with the Calcutta University. The building was erected in 1853, at a cost of £6,800. The Society has given no little attention to the subject of female education here.

In August 1820, the Rev. M. T. Adam began the mission at Benares, which has continued to the present time. The missionaries, many of whom have spent long terms of service in this one station, have given themselves to teaching and preaching. The mission has here a large collegiate Institution besides other schools.

Belgaum in the Canarese country was occupied for the Society in the year 1820 by the Rev. Joseph Taylor, who labored there more than thirty years. The Rev. W. Beynon was stationed at Belgaum in 1828, and, after many years of labor, died there, in 1878. The mission at Bangalore was founded in 1820 by the Rev. Messrs. Laidler and Forbes. For many years but little progress was made and many reverses were experienced, but at present the mission is in a flourishing state. One fact which may help to account for this is, that the Society has kept from changing its agents there. The Rev. Messrs. C. Campbell, B. Rice and J. Sewell in their united terms of service have labored at Bangalore not less than one hundred years.

In the year 1822 the Rev. J. Hands established a mission in Cuddapah. Prior to 1848 but few converts were obtained but about this time a spirit of inquiry spread among the villages and the progress since has been rapid and encouraging. In 1855 a new station was formed at Nundial which has become an important centre of missionary operations.

Berhampore in the district of Moorshedabad was occupied in 1824. The Christian community is chiefly engaged in cultivating the soil.

The mission at Salem was founded in 1827 by the Rev. Henry Crisp. The Society has now fourteen congregations in the district, the chief of which are at Salem and Tripatore. Coimbatoor and Combaconum were occupied by the Society in 1830. Of late years a large number of converts has been added to the missions.

In 1838 a mission was established at Mirzapore by the Rev. Dr. Mather, who continued at the head of the mission thirty-five years. It possesses a flourishing educational Institution, a large Orphanage, two churches and an extensive press. An out-station was formed in 1863 among the Singrowlee hills to the south of Mirzapore.

The Society has two missions on the hills: one at Almorah, established in 1850 by the Rev. J. H. Budden: the other at Raneekhet, in 1868 by the Rev. J. Kennedy. Both are important stations. The statistics for 1880 are as follows :—

Stations occupied, ...	24
Foreign Ordained Agents, ...	45
Native do. do.	30
Native Christians, ...	50,098
Communicants, ...	4,632

MISSIONARIES OF THE SOCIETY.

Arumanayagam, Arulanandam. B. at Colachel, South Travancore. O. at Neyoor, Jan. 9, 1867. Labored as inspector of village schools in Neyoor district from 1852 to 1862: theological class at Nagercoil, 1861-62: evangelist in the Neyoor district, 1863-67 : since ordination, as assistant missionary at Attur. Ad. *Attur, Neyoor district, Travancore.*

Arumanayagam, Visuvasam. O. Jan. 3, 1867. L. a Handbill on

"Existence of the Soul." Ad. *Ananthanadangudy, near Nagercoil, Travancore.*

ASHTON, JOHN PERKINS. A. in 1859. Was stationed for six years at Madras and then transferred to the Bhowanipore Institution, Calcutta. Ad. *Calcutta.*

BACON, JOHN REDMOND. B. in London, Jan. 13, 1846. O. in Sept. 1875, A. in Nov. 1875, has since labored at (Ad.) *Cuddapah, Madras P.*

BUDDEN, JOHN HENRY. B. Nov. 19, 1813, in Lon. O. June 8, 1841. A. Dec. 3, 1843, S. Benares, Mirzapore, and, since 1850, Almorah, where he commenced the mission. Ad. *Almorah. N.-W.P.*

BULLOCH, GEORGE McCALLUM. B. Edinburgh, May 1, 1850. E. Western Col. Plymouth. O. at Edinburgh, July 13, 1874, A. Oct. 23. 1874. S. Benares, Nov. 1874 to July, 1876; Raneekhet, July, 1876 to Dec. 1876; Benares, Dec. 1876 to March 1880, Mirzapore, March to Aug. 1880; since, Benares. Ad. *Benares.*

CHATTERJEE, TARA PERSHAD. B. near Calcutta, in 1834. Embraced Christianity, (was a Kulin Brahmin) in April, 1851. O. March 20, 1861. Became a preacher of the Gospel in 1860. W. Superintending missionary and pastor of the village stations and churches, South of Calcutta and in the Soonderbuns Dist. Ad. *Kaurapookar, 24 Pergunnahs, Bengal.*

COLES, JOSEPH BENJAMIN. B. in Lon. Nov. 22, 1819. O. July 5, 1843. A. Dec. 25, 1843. S. Mysore, Bangalore, Bellary, Coimbatore, Madras, Bellary. H. from March, 1859 to Jan., 1862 and March, 1873 to May, 1875. Ad. Rockside, *Bellary, Madras P.*

COLEY, HENRY. B. at Stroud, Gloucestershire, Sept. 17, 1849. E. at Spring Hill Col. Birmingham. O. at Birmingham, Oct. 3, 1877. A. Jan. 1878. M. Has labored since A. at (Ad.) *Almorah, N.-W. P.*

DASS, NANDA LAL. B. (of Hindu parents) Sept. 30, 1840, at Barripore near Calcutta. E. at Bhowanipore. Baptized in Jan. 1857. M. July, 1864. O. in Feb. 1868. Labored as an evangelist at Bhowanipore, with pastoral work and teaching in the Engl. Inst. Since 1868 has labored at (Ad.) *Berhampore, Bengal.*

DAUD, C. O. 1865. Ad *Mirzapore, N.-W. P.*

DAVID, A. O. 1867. Ad. *Coimbatore, Madras P.*

DEVALAM, ANBUDIAN. Ad. *Trevandrum, Travancore.*

DUTHIE, JAMES. B. Stonehaven, Scotland, Nov. 2, 1833. O. Jan 31, 1856. A. March 15, 1856. S. L. M. S. Inst. Madras, three and-a-half years; Prin. Seminary, L. M. S., Travancore, from Nov. 1859 to present. L. Homiletics (Tamil) out of print; Editorial work in connection with Tamil Magazines, Tracts, &c. H. 1869-1871, and 1875 to 1876. Ad. *Nagercoil, Travancore.*

DUTT, KASHI NATH. O. in 1861, at Calcutta, where he labored until 1866, when he was transferred to (Ad.) *Benares.*

EMLYN, JAMES. A. in 1867. Ad. *Pareychaley, Travancore.*

FLETCHER, WILLIAM. A. 1865. Ad. *Pareychaley, Travancore.*

GOFFIN, H. J. A. in 1876. Ad. *Vizianagram, Madras P.*

HACKER, ISAAC HENRY. B. Birmingham, July, 1847. O. Carrs Lane

Birmingham, Oct. 3, 1877. A. Dec. 17, 1877. S. Neyoor. M. Ad. *Neyoor, Travancore.*

HAINES, THOMAS. A. 1870, Ad. *Bellary, Madras P.*

HAWKER, JOHN GILES. B. Boyn Hill, Berkshire, Aug. 21, 1839. O. Congregational church, Maidenhead, July 6, 1865. A. Dec. 18, 1865. S. Bellary, as itinerant missionary and pastor of the Native Church, 1871; since, Belgaum, principally in the Anglo.-Ver. School. H. from 1875-77. R. Nov. 24, 1877. Ad. *Belgaum, Bombay P.*

HAY, JOHN. B. April 23, 1812, at Stuartfield, near Aberdeen, Scotland. Entered Marischal Col. in Nov. 1829, and graduated with M. A. in 1833. Was engaged for a time in private teaching. Afterwards offered himself to the L. M. S. and was sent to Turrey, Bedfordshire, where he read theology for two years with the Rev. M. Cecil. O. in Aug. 1839, A. in Jan. 1840; was stationed at Vizagapatam, and took charge of the Engl. school. Private affairs called him to Eng. R. in 1844, after an absence of eighteen months. He continued his educational work and afterwards engaged in that of translating the Scriptures into Telugu. Proceeded to Eng. in 1860: while at home prepared a new translation of Genesis and Deuteronomy. On returning to India in 1863 revised and published (in connection with Dr. Wardlaw) the Pentateuch and other portions of the O. T., also the first part of "Pilgrim's Progress," besides a few tracts in Engl. and Telugu. In the beginning of 1869 was called home on account of his wife's illness. Was again engaged in the work of Scripture translation and R. in March, 1872. He again took charge of the Engl. school at Vizagapatam and of the Engl. congregation, continuing his literary labors. Has since labored here, with these and other duties. Has been the Convenor of the Telugu Scripture Revision Committee, and has had much to do with the Telugu translation of the Bible. Ad. *Vizagapatam, Madras P.*

HEWLETT, JOHN. B. June 11, 1836, at Keynsham. Somerset. O. in July, 1861, at Swansea A. Dec. 14, 1861. S Benares, Almorah, Benares, Mirzapore. Work both Engl. and Ver. H. 1869-70, and 1878-81. Has translated into Urdu Augustine's "Confessions": obtainable at the Mirzapore Press. Ad. *Benares.*

HILL, SAMUEL JOHN. A. in 1852. Labored at Calcutta until 1854: since. at Berhampore. Ad. *Berhampore, Bengal.*

HUTCHISON, HENRY ALEXANDER. B. in Glasgow, April 17, 1848. Studied medicine two years, and then prepared for the ministry. O. in 1874 by the Presbytery of Glasgow and joined the L. M. S.: A. Dec. 21 1874, and was appointed to Coimbatoor, as itinerating missionary. Ad. *Coimbatoor, Madras P.*

HUTTON, DAVID. A. 1865, Ad. *Mirzapore, N.-W. P.*

INSELL, THOMAS. B. Stratton, Eng. O. in Lon. June 23, 1873. A. Dec. 20, 1873. Ad. *Mirzapore, N.-W. P.*

JAGANADHAM, PULIPAKA. Entered the Engl. school at Vizagapatam about 1840. Renounced Hinduism. and was baptized April 28, 1847: O. at Vizagapatam in 1858. Shortly afterwards was transferred to Chicacole Has labored at Chicacole and (Ad.) *Vizagapatam, Madras P.*

JOHNSON, WILLIAM. A. in 1858. Has labored in connection with the Bhowanipore Inst. and Hastings church. Ad *Calcutta.*

JOSHUA, J. O. 1867. Ad. *Nagercoil, Travancore.*

JOSS, WALTER. A in 1869. S. Coimbatoor until 1876, when he was trans. to L M. S. Inst. at Madras, Ad. *Madras.*

KAMALAM, J. O. 1867, A. *Pareychaley, Madras P.*

LAMBERT, J. A. A. 1865, Ad. *Benares.*

LEE, WILLIAM. B. Piverton, Devonshire, Eng. May 29, 1841. O. Union Chapel Islington. Lon. July 6. 1864. A. Dec. 28, 1864. S. Nagercoil, 1865-68, Trevandrum, 1868: Neyoor, 1872. H. from 1875 to 1877. W. Supt. of Press, Editor of "South Travancore Christian Messenger (Tamil.) Ad. *Nagercoil, Travancore.*

LEMARE, EBENEZER. B. Manchester, Oct. 5, 1848 E. Owens and Lancashire Independent Colleges. O. at Manchester, Oct. 2, 1873. A. Dec. 4, 1873. M. Nov. 24, 1875. S. Bellary, 1873-77; Belgaum, 1877-80; since, at Salem W. Engl. and ver: mainly educational: L. a lecture for educated natives entitled "John Stuart Mill. His attitude towards Religion:" Addison and Co., Madras. Ad. *Salem, Madras P.*

LEWIS, EDWIN. A. 1865 Ad. *Bellary, Madras P.*

MASILLAMANI, CHRISTIAN. B. in Sept 1833. at Mylandy, Travancore. E. in Nagercoil Seminary. Labored from 1857 as an evangelist. O. Feb. 13, 1866 as pastor at Dennispuram, where he has since labored. L. a number of Tamil poems, handbills and lyrics; published at Nagercoil and Madras. Ad. *Dennispuram, Nagercoil, Travancore.*

MASON, G. O. 1864. Ad. *Cuddapah, Madras P.*

MATEER, SAMUEL. O. Aug. 10, 1858. A. Feb. 24, 1859. S. Pareychaley, 1859-63, Trevandrum 1863 to present H. from March 1868 to Jan. 1, 1872. L. "Land of Charity" a descriptive account of Travancore and its people (republished in America); Lessons in Botany and Sketches of Sermons, (Tamil); "Fifty-two Sketches of sermons;" "A tract for prisoners." "a tract for coolies on coffee Estates," "Medical Hints for the Poor," (Malayalam). Editor of Malayalam Christian Lyrics and Hymn-Book, Editor of "Balar Deepam" (magazine for children) and other school books and tracts. Ad. *Travandrum, Travancore.*

MOOTHOO, C. Converted about 1855, while a pupil in the L. M. S. Inst., Madras, where he was E. for the ministry. O. July 6, 1875. In charge of the Native Church at (Ad.) *Salem, Madras P.*

NEWPORT. GEORGE OLIVER. B. at Henley on Thames, Oxfordshire, March 2, 1840. E. at Cheshunt College. O. July 30. 1862. M.: A. Dec. 24, 1862. S. Pareychaley, 1863-67: Nagercoil, 1869-71, and 1873-76; Salem. 1876-79, since, Madras. Work, both Engl. and Ver. Has edited some Tamil periodicals and contributed to Tamil magazines. H. from July, 1871 to Dec. 1873. Ad. *Madras.*

NYANABRANAM, M. O. 1867. Ad. *Neyoor, Travancore.*

PAYNE, JAMES EDWARD. B. March 18, 1835, at the Lower Venn, Avenbury, Herefordshire. O. at Bedford, Eng., Aug. 22, 1860. A. Dec. 20, 1860. Appointed to Bhowanipore. H. from Jan. 1869, to Dec. 1870. M. June 2, 1870. Work mainly ver.; Bengali preaching, teaching, and editing Bengal Christian Literature for Tract and Bible Society. Ad. *Bhowanipore, Calcutta.*

PARTHASARADY, C. O. 1867. Ad. *Madras.*

PAUL, J. B. in 1840. E in the Bangalore Seminary. O. in 1871, as pastor of the Canarese Church at (Ad.) *Bangalore.*

PEERAJEE, PAUL. B at Belgaum, in 1830. E in Bangalore Seminary. O at Belgaum in 1862. Subsequently removed to Bangalore as pastor of the Tamil Church. Ad., *Bengal.*

PHILLIPS, E. A. A. 1878. Ad. *Ranee Khet, N.-W. P.*

PHILLIPS, MAURICE. B. April 11, 1838, in the parish of Llanboidy, South Wales. O. at Narbeth, South Wales, in Aug. 1861. A. in Madras, Jan. 4, 1862. M.: Commenced the mission station at Tripatoor and continued there until March, 1873. H. to Mar. 1875. Had also charge of the Salem station from 1869 to 1873. Rt. in March, 1875, and was appointed to Salem. W. Ver. Ad., *Salem, Madras P.*

PHILLIPS, WILLIAM BENJAMIN. B. Manchester, Sept. 8, 1848. O. Sept. 1875. A. Nov. 28, 1875. Ad. *Berhampore, Bengal.*

RICE, BENJAMIN. B. in Lon. May 28, 1814. E. at Homerton Col. O. in London, July 27, 1836. A.at Madras, Dec. 29, 1836. S. Bangalore, from that time to the present; H. but once, from Feb 1853 to Sept. 1856. M. Has been engaged in all branches of missionary work. Was one of the Revisors of the present Canarese version of the Bible; and is the author or translator of a number of Canarese and English Tracts, School books, and works for the benefic of Native Christ ians, published by the Bangalore Tract and Book Society: of which Society, and of the Bangalore Bible Society, he is Secretary. Is also Secretary of the South India District Committee of the L. M. S. Ad. No. 1 Mission Road, *Bangalore.*

RICE, EDWARD PETER. B. at Bangalore, April 26, 1849. Entered Cheshunt College, Sept. 1868. Graduated with B. A, Lon. Univ. 1873. O. in Lon. Nov. 4, 1873. Reached Madras, Dec. 13. 1873. Appointed to Bangalore: engaged in the itinerating and evangelistic department. During 1877-8 in charge of English Institution, in 1879 returned to itinerating work, L: A pamphlet in Engl. for educated Hindus, entitled: "*Jesus Christ, His Life, Character and Claims*": Ad. *Bangalore.*

ROBINSON, WILLIAM. B. Sheffield, Aug. 1, 1852. E. Rotherham, Col. O. Queen St. Chapel Sheffield, Sept. 10, 1877. S. Vizagapatam, one year; Coimbatore, 1879-80. Tripatore, July, 1880. M. March 25, 1880. W. Ver. Ad. *Tripatore, Madras P.*

ROTTI, JOHN MAHANTAPPA. B. Hubli. 1833. O. June 19, 1868. S. Belgaum. W. Pastoral, School and Preaching Ad. *Belgaum, Bombay P.*

RUNGANATHAM, C. O. 1874. Ad. *Madras.*

SHIDDALINGAPPA, PAUL. B. in 1835, at Byl Hongal. Called to the ministry in 1855: O. in 1868. Native pastor at (Ad.) *Belgaum, Bombay P.*

SLATER, THOMAS EBENEZER. Son of the late Rev. W. Slater: B. at Chesham, Bucks, April 10, 1840. Was ordained and married in Aug, 1866, and A. at Calcutta in Dec of the same year. Was connected with the Bhowanipore Institution till May, 1870, when he was obliged to leave I. on account of domestic affliction. R. at the end of 1871, and took charge of the Engl. Inst. at Madras. At the beginning of 1875 was relieved of his work in the Inst., and has since been laboring among the educated Natives of Madras, Is the author of an English tract, "God in Christ," and two lectures on "The Bible"—both written for educated Hindus—published by the Bangalore Tract and Book Society: an annotatated edition of Bushnell's "Character of Jesus," published by the C. V. E. S., Madras: and "Sunday afternoon Addresses to educated Hindus:" H. 1879.

SMITH, JAMES. B. at Bicestor, Oxfordshire. Dec. 6, 1839 Called to the ministry in 1861. O. in July, 1866, M. in 1866. A. Dec, 1866. Has. labored since at Belgaum. Work principally educational, in Engl: some ver. H. April, 1877-79. Ad. *Belgaum, Bombay P.*

STEPHENSON, W. W. B. Aug. 26, 1848. O. Nov. 7, 1876. A. 1876 Ad. *Nundial, Madras P.*

TAYLOR, JOSEPH FIELD. A. 1878. Ad. *Calcutta.*

THOMAS, MORRIS. A. 1878. Ad *Vizagapatam, Madras P.*

THOMSON, THOMAS SMITH. (L. R. C P. Ed.; L. M. L R. C. S. Ed.) B. Dec. 28, 1844, at Edinburgh M. Nov. 12, 1872, Was engaged as resident physician in the Medical Mission Inst. at Edinburgh before coming to I. A. Jan. 4, 1873. Has since been engaged as medical missionary at Neyoor. Work both Engl. and ver. Ad *Neyoor, Travancore.*

UNMEYUDIAN, V. O. 1867. Ad. *Coimbatoor, Madras P.*

WALTON, JOHN HEWENS. B. at Woolwich. Kent, June 17, 1841. Studied for the ministry, three years at Western Col., Plymouth and one year at the Missionary Inst, Highgate, Lon. O. Dec 12, 1866., A. at Madras, Jan. 24, 1867. Appointed to Bangalore to take charge of the Anglo-Ver. schools. M. Dec. 28, 1867. Ad. *Bangalore.*

WILKINS, WILLIAM JOSEPH. A. 1866. Ad. *Calcutta.*

WILKINSON, FREDERICK. B. Nov. 1, 1832, in the Island of Trinidad, West Indies. Studied for the ministry at the Theol. Sem., Bedford, where he was O. and appointed to India Sept. 16, 1859. A. January, 1860 and was appointed to James Town, Travancore. M. in July, 1861. Was transferred in 1862 to Santhapuram. In 1866 removed to Quilon. H. 1872, R. to Quilon in Dec 1873; Madras in Dec, 1876. H. to Eng. R. March, 1881. Ad. *Trevandrum, Travancore.*

WILLIAM, M. Ad. *Nundial, Madras P.*

YESUDIAN, C. Ad. *Tittuvilei, Travancore.*

ZECHARIAH, SAMUEL. B. June 21, 1823, near Colachel, South Travancore. E. at L M. Seminary, Nagercoil. O. Feb. 13, 1866 at Nagercoil: has since labored as pastor of Neyoor Church. L. a Pamphlet in Tamil, "The Pioneer Missionary work of the Rev. Charles Mead." Ad. *Neyoor, Travancore.*

DECEASED AND RETIRED MISSIONARIES.

Nathanael Forsyth B. 1769 Sailed May, 1798. A at Calcutta, Dec 1798 S. Chinsurah D. in Calcutta, in May, 1816.

William Tobias Ringeltaube. After joining the L. M. S., sailed from Copenhagen, Apr. 20, 1804. A. at Tranquebar, Dec. 5, 1804. S Palamcottah. 1804-9, Oodagherry, 1809-12, Mayilady, 1812-16. In 1816, on account of ill health left Travancore, when his connection with the Society ceased.

George Cran. A. Dec. 5, 1804. In July, 1805, in company with Mr. Des Granges proceeded to Vizagapatam where they founded a mission. D. at Chicacole, Jan. 6. 1809.

Augustus Des Granges. B. 1780. A. Dec. 5, 1804, and with preceeding went to Vizagapatam in 1805. D. at V. July 12. 1810.

William Charles Loveless. Arrived in India, June 24, 1805. Was appointed to Surat but landing at Madras. he proceeded no further. He became Master of the Male Asylum which position he held until 1812. In addition he preached to the English and other residents, and labored most earnestly in the face of strong opposition. Resigned, June 4. 1824.

John Taylor, M. D. O. Oct. 19, 1804. A. at Madras, June 24, 1805. Afterwards, accepting a Government post, his connection with the Society ceased. D. in Dec. 1821, at Shiraz, Persia.

John Gordon. Arrived in India Sept. 9, 1809. Labored at Vizagapatam; and at Madras, where he died January 16, 1828.

William Lee. Arrived in India, Dec. 11, 1809. Labored at Vizagapatam, and Ganjam. His health failing, he was obliged to return to England in 1817. Died.

John Hands. B. Dec 5, 1780. Arrived in India in 1810. Labored chiefly at Bellary: for some years also at Bangalore. Was one of the translators of the first version of the Canarese Bible. Ret. 1842. D. at Dublin, June 30, 1864.

Jonathan Couch Brain. O. Jan. 26, 1809. A. at Madras Feb. 5, 1810, at Rangoon, Mar. 23, 1810. D. at Rangoon, July 2, 1810.

Edward Prichett. B. 1772, at Birmingham. O. Jan. 26, 1809.. A. at Rangoon, Mar. 23, 1810. On account of war removed to Calcutta, Jan. 1811. S. Vizagapatam and Madras. D. at V. June 12, 1820.

John Thompson. A. at Madras Mar. 22, 1812. Ordered by Government to leave I., but before the order could be carried out, he D. at Madras, June 25, 1812.

Robert May. B. 1788. A. at Calcutta, Aug. 11, 1812. Succeeded Mr. Forsyth at Chinsurah in Feb. 1813. D. at Calcutta, Aug. 1818.

William Fyvie. B. Sept. 15, 1788, at Methla, Aberdeenshire. O. Dec. 28, 1814. A. at Bombay Aug. 9, 1815 and proceeded to Surat, where be labored many years. In Jan. 1847 on the relinquishment of the Surat mission, Ret. to St. Helier, Jersey, where he D. in Feb. 1863.

James Skinner. O. and A. with Mr. Fyvie. Labored at Surat and D. there Oct 30, 1821.

James Dawson. O. Dec 28, 1814. A. at Madras, Sept. 4, 1815. Labored at Vizagapatam, where he D. Aug. 14 1832.

Richard Knill. B. April 14. 1787, at Braunton, Devon. O. at Leeds, Oct. 6. 1815. A. Aug. 26, 1816. S. Madras and Nagercoil. H. to Eng. June 12, 1819. In 1820 was appointed to pastorate of an Engl. church at St. Petersburg, where he labored until Aug. 1833, when he R., to Lon. For eight years was engaged in deputation work; from 1842-47 was pastor at Wotton-under-Edge; in 1848 became pastor at Chester. D. at Chester, Jan. 2, 1857. (*Vide* "Life" by C. M. Birrell: Nisbet & Co. 1860.)

William Reeve. B. 1794. O. Feb. 7, 1816. A. at Madras Aug. 26, 1816, and at Bellary, Sept. 27. R. to Eng. Sept. 18, 1824. Rt. July 17, 1827. S. Bellary and Bangalore. Assisted in revision of Canarese Bible. Compiled two Canarese English Dictionaries. H. to Eng. Feb. 17, 1834. Connection with Society ceased, Nov. 23, 1835 Date of death unknown.

Samuel Render. B. 1787. O. Feb. 21, 1816. A. at Madras Aug. 26, 1816. Connection with Society ceased June 22, 1818.

Charles Mead. B. at Bristol Oct. 1, 1792. O. Mar. 6, 1816. A. Aug. 26, 1816. S. Madras, 1816-17. Nagercoil, Jan. 1818 to May, 1825, when he removed to Combaconum on account of his health and commenced a new station there. R. to Travancore in 1827, lived one year at Mandeycadoo, and removed to Neyoor in 1828. H. to Eng. Dec. 5, 1836 to April 5, 1838, when he R. to Neyoor. Connection with the Society dissolved in Dec. 1851, D. at Trevandrum, June 19, 1873. (*Vide* "The Pioneer Mission work of the Rev. Charles Mead" by the Rev. S. Zechariah, L. M. S. Press, Nagercoil.)

Henry Townley. O. Feb. 7, 1816. A. at Calcutta, Sept. 7, 1816, and with Mr. Keith commenced a station there. Removed to Chinsurah in Feb, 1821. On account of wife's ill health R. to Eng. Dec. 1, 1822. D. Aug. 9, 1861.

James Keith. O. A. and labored at Calcutta with Mr. Townley D. there, Oct. 6, 1822.

John David Pearson. B. in Lon. 1788. O. Aug. 29, 1816. A. Mar. 6, 1817. S. Chinsurah. H. to Eng. Apr. 8, 1824. Rt. June 20, 1826. D. at Calcutta. Nov. 8, 1831.

John Donaldson. B. 1793. O. Aug. 27, 1816. A. Aug. 1817. S. Surat, D. at Bombay, Mar. 25, 1818.

John Harle. A European, engaged, in 1817, as an assistant at Chinsurah. In 1820, removed to Tallygunge. Ret. 1821.

Cornelius Traveller. B. 1791. A. at Madras, in Jan. 1819. Ret. Sept. 29, 1823. R. to Europe and settled in Jersey.

John Hampson. B. 1793. A. Feb. 8, 1819. S. Calcutta, where he D. Aug. 29, 1819.

Samuel Trawin. B. 1794. A. at Calcutta, Feb. 8, 1819. Formed the station at Kidderpore, in 1822. D. at Berhampore, Aug. 3, 1827.

George H. Ashton. B. in India. Was engaged as an assistant in 1819 in Travancore. S. Quilon, Neyoor and Pareychaley. In 1860, Ret and went to reside at Quilon.

Charles Mault. B May 1, 1791. O. Oct. 24, 1818, A. at Bombay, May 18, 1819, at Nagercoil Dec. 11, 1819. In 1827 was appointed in charge of East Travancore Health failing, R. to Eng. in 1855, Ret. to Stoke, where he D. Oct. 17, 1858.

George Gogerley. B. in London, Nov. 10, 1794. A. Sept. 13, 1819. S. Calcutta O, June 2, 1828. H to Eng. 1835, Rt Jan. 19, 1839. Ret. Nov. 1841 D. in London, Feb 11, 1877. L. "The Pioneers of the Bengal Mission". London: Snow and Co. 1871.

Joseph Taylor. B in India, 1790. O., at Madras May. 1819. In Sept. 1820 commenced a new station at Belgaum where he labored many years. R. 1855, and removed to Bombay where he D. Nov. 19, 1859.

Thomas Nicholson. B. 1795. O. Mar. 31, 1819. A at Madras Sept. 16, 1819. D. there Aug. 2, 1822.

Matthew Thomson Adam E. at Gosport. O. Oct. 9, 1819. A. early in 1820. M. Aug. 1820 went to Benares and commenced the mission there. On account of ill health R. to Eng. in 1830. His connection with the Society subsequently ceased.

Andrew Forbes. B. 1792. O. Aug. 18, 1819. A. at Madras Feb. 16, 1820, and at Bangalore in April 1820, where, in connection with Mr. Laidler, he commenced the mission. Ret. 1821.

Stephen Laidler. B. Oct 12, 1789, at Wooler, Northumberland. O. Aug. 18, 1819. A. Feb. 16, 1820. S Bangalore. On account of wife's ill health R. tô Eng. in 1827. Ret. Sept. 24, 1827. D. Oct. 25, 1873.

George Mundy. A. at Chinsurah in March, 1820. O in Nov. 1825. H. to Eng. in 1829. Rt Nov. 7, 1832. S. Kidderpore, Chinsurah. H to Eng. in 1844. Rt. to Calcutta in 1849. D. there Aug. 23, 1853. L. "Christianity and Hinduism contrasted," 2 vols., Serampore, 1834.

John Smith. B. 1790. O. Aug. 18, 1819. A. Feb. 16, 1820 Commenced a station at Quilon, March 6, 1821. H to Eng. 1824, when he Ret. D. 1824.

Edward Ray. In 1820, was received in Calcutta as an Assistant. H. to England where he was O. March 15, 1825. A. Oct. 3. 1825, S. Berhampore, Calcutta, Kidderpore. On account of his wife's ill health R. to Eng. in 1831. His connection with the Society ceased in 1832. He afterwards setted at Twickenhem.

Hiram Chambers. B. 1792. O Aug. 2. 1820. A. March 20, 1821, S. Bellary 1823; Bangalore 1825. Being unable to bear the climate of India, he embarked for Eng. Jan 6, 1826. On the following day Jan. 7, D.

William Hugh Bankhead. B. 1799. E at Hackney College O. Dec. 14, 1820. A. Aug. 16, 1821, at Calcutta, where he D Nov. 7, 1822.

Micaiah Hill. B. at Walsall. O July 18, 1821. A. at Calcutta, March 5. 1822. Became editor of the "*Asiatic Observer.*" In 1824 removed to Berhampore, and commenced that station. H to Eng. Dec. 25, 1838. Rt. to Berhampore Oct. 1842. In Jan. 1847 removed to Calcutta. Early in 1849 set out for Benares for the benefit of his health, but D. Feb 3, in a boat on the Ganges, a few miles from Benares.

James Hill. B. May 17, 1795 at Stafford. O. July 18, 1821. A. at Calcutta, March 5 1822. R. to Eng. Dec. 9, 1833. Ret. Dec. 25, 1834. D. Jan. 12, 1870.

Joseph Bradley Warden. B. 1799. O July 18, 1821. A. at Calcutta, March 5, 1822, where he D. Jan. 8, 1826.

Samuel Flavel. An earnest Native preacher. Joined the mission at Bangalore in 1821. O in 1822. Was appointed to Bellary, in 1827, where he labored until his death, in 1847.

Alexander Fyvie. O. Sept 28, 1821. A. at Bombay, April 26, 1822, at Surat, May 13. R. to Eng. Oct. 15, 1832. Rt. to Surat Dec. 23, 1835, where he D. June 10, 1840

William Howell. B. in I. Nov. 1790. Engaged about 1821, as assistant at Bellary. Removed to Cuddapah, in 1822, and commenced that station O Sept. 29, 1824. at Madras Ret. in Sept. 1841.

Edmund Crisp. B. June 26, 1799, at Hertford. O. Oct. 3, 1821. A. March 26, 1822. S. Madras 1822-29, Combaconum, 1829-35. H. from Madras to Eng. Feb. 15, 1837. Rt Sept 1840. S. Bangalore. in charge of Training Institution. H to Eng. 1848, soon after Ret. D. London, Nov. 6, 1877.

Thomas Brown A. at Calcutta May 24, 1822. Was directed to proceed to Bellary. to carry on printing there. Died on his passage, between Calcutta and Madras.

William Crow. B. about 1797, O. July 11, 1822, A. July 12 1823. S. Quilon H. to Eng. March 29, 1826. His connection with the, Society eventually ceased and he entered the pastorate. D Nov. 27, 1872.

John Emanuel Nimmo. B in I. In 1823, engaged as assistant in Madras. In 1831, removed to Chittoor, in June, 1833 to Combaconun. O. at Madras, March 1, 1837, Removed to Tripassore in Jan. 1852, Ret. June 8, 1857.

James William Massie. B. Nov. 11, 1798, at Glasgow. O. July 11, 1822. A. at Madras, June 21, 1823. R. to Eng. in 1827, Ret. Sept. 24, 1827. Afterwards became pastor at Dunfermline.

William Campbell. B. 1799. O. Aug. 13, 1823. A. June 27, 1824. S. Bangalore. H. Dec. 1835. After being engaged for a time in deputation work Ret. D. at London in 1878 L. "British India," London: Snow. 1839.

William Taylor. O. Aug. 1823. A. at Madras, May 22, 1824. In 1827 took charge of Pursewakam. Ret. Nov. 14, 1834.

George Walton. B. in I. E at Bellary Engaged in 1824 as assistant missionary. Accepted as a missionary Oct 10, 1831. S. Bellary. and Salem. O. at Bangalore, Dec 23, 1832. D. at Salem, June 9, 1841.

John Edmonds. B at Poole, 1798. O. Poole, March 17 1824. A. Nov. 11, 1824. S. Chinsurah. His wife's health failing he R. to Eng. Sept. 23, 1826, after which he Ret. and took a Pastorate at Shelton, Staffordshire. D. March 21, 1858, at St. Helen's, Lancashire.

Thomas Salmon. B 1800 at Thetford. A. at Surat. Oct. 30, 1825. H. to Eng. in 1833, after which he Ret.

Charles Piffard. B. 1798 at Pentonville, Lon. O. May 2, 1825. A. at Calcutta, Oct. 3, 1825. S. Kidderpore. On account of wife's ill health R. to Eng. May 3, 1830. Rt. in March 1831. R. to Eng. May 18, 1833. Rt. Dec. 10, 1834. and labored at Calcutta, where he D. Dec. 11, 1840.

William Beynon. B. May 17, 1801, at Caermarthen. O. March, 31, 1825. A. Sept. 14, 1825. S. Bellary, 1825-28. Belgaum. 1828-70 when he Ret. to Eng. Rt. for residence, Nov. 1871. D. at Belgaum, Feb. 5, 1878.

Adam Lillie. B. Calton, Glasgow, June 18, 1803. O. at London, March 28, 1826. A. at Madras, Sept. 11, at Belgaum. Nov. 19, 1826. Soon afterwards serious illness compelled him to R. to Eng. Soon after his return his connection with the Society ceased.

Bennington Haill Paine B. 1805, at Ipswich. Appointed as a Printer to Bellary. A. Sept. 11, 1826. In 1831 began to assist in vernacular work. R. to Eng in 1839. Rt. Dec. 8, 1841. Labored at Bellary until his death, March 6, 1842.

Isaac David. Born at Tanjore about 1794. His parents were staunch Papists. O. at Bangalore in 1826. Labored at Salem, Trichinopoly, Bangalore, Madras and other places: was the means through God of numerous conversions. Of his twelve children, two of his sons were ministers, and all his daughters but one married clergymen of various Societies. He died at Madras, while actively engaged, April 15, 1862. Native Christians of all denominations, throughout Southern India, in token of their esteem and love for him, erected a monument over his grave.

James Robertson. B. in 1799. O. June 14, 1826. A. Nov. 1826. S. Benares, where he D June 15, 1833.

Alphonse F. Lacroix. B. May 10, 1799, at Lignieres, Switzerland. O. Aug. 11, 1820. Appointed to Chinsurah by the Netherlands Miss'y Soc'y; A. Mar. 21, 1821. Joined the L. M. S. Mar. 1. 1827. Labored at Chinsurah until April, 1829, when he removed to Calcutta. R to Eng. in Dec. 1841. Rt. Jan. 9, 1844. Devoted himself chiefly to Ver. preaching and itinerating. Was invited to R. to Eng. in 1856 by the Society but declined Health failing he visited North India and R. to Calcutta, where he D. July 8, 1859. (See "Memorials," by Joseph Mullens, D D Lon.: Nisbet and Co. 1862.)

James Charles Thompson. B Jan. 23, 1804. O. Feb. 27, 1827. A. Aug. 5, 1827. S. Quilon H. 1844-46. D. at Quilon. May 18. 1850.

William Miller. B. Dec. 1, 1804. O. Feb. 8, 1827. A Aug. 5, 1827. S. Nagercoil and Quilon. H. to the Cape, 1834-6. Ret. to Nagercoil in 1836 and D. there April 24, 1838.

William Bawn Addis. B. Sept. 17, 1800, near Bristol. A. Aug. 5, 1827. O Aug. 13, 1828 In 1830 commenced a station at Coimbatoor. Ret. in 1861 through failure of health to Coonoor, where he D. Feb. 18, 1871.

Henry Crisp. B. July 14, 1803, at Hertford. O. Mar. 20, 1827. A. at Madras July 17, 1827. Commenced the Mission at Salem, Oct. 25, 1827. D. Oct. 28, 1831.

Robert Jennings. B. Feb. 22, 1797. O. April 4, 1827. A. Madras, July 17, and at Chittoor (where he was the first resident missionary) Aug. 4, 1827, D. at Chittoor, June 1, 1831.

John Smith. B. 1801, at New Windsor. Designated April 3, 1828. A. at Madras Aug. 20, 1828. H. to Eng. Sept. 17, 1839. Rt. to

Madras Sept. 22, 1842. In March, 1843 went to Vizagapatam: embarked May 15 in the "*Favourite*," to return to Madras and is supposed to have been lost at sea with the vessel and all on board. L. "A Missionary's Appeal on behalf of Southern India," 1841.

John Adam. B. May 20, 1803 in Lon. O. Mar. 26, 1828. A. Sept. 4, 1828. S. Calcutta. D. at Kidderpore, April 21, 1831.

John Reid. B. June 17, 1806, at Soho, Lon. O. Aug. 18, 1829. A. at Madras Jan. 25, 1830, and at Bellary, March 1, D. at Bellary, Jan. 8, 1841. (*See* "Memoir" by R. Wardlaw, D. D., Glasgow: Maclehose, 1845).

George Christie B. New Mills. Bauffshire, July, 1802. O. Jan. 13, 1830. A. Oct. 24, 1830. S. Calcutta. Being unable to bear the climate, he proceeded to Cape Town in 1832. He afterwards laboured in South Africa, D. at Cape Town, Nov. 24, 1870.

Thomas Kilpin Higgs. B. Dorchester, Sept. 1803. O. Newport Pagnell, June 10, 1830. A. at Calcutta, Oct. 24; and at Chinsurah, Nov. 8, 1830. D. at Calcutta, Dec. 3, 1832.

William Harris. B. 1805 at Glasgow. O. Sept. 8, 1830. A. May 30, 1831. H. to Eng. Oct. 1832. D. Portsmouth, April 28, to 1833.

William Buyers. B Dundee, 1804, O. Woolwich, Feb. 16, 1831. A. Oct. 9, 1831. S Benares. H. March 13, 1841 to 1843. Again H. 1845. R. to Benares at his own expense. In Feb. 1859 he removed to Almorah and labored there till 1861. In 1863 resigned his connection with the Society. L. "Letters on India." "Recollections of Northern India." Lon. Snow.

John Bilderbeck. B. in 1809, in I. Was a Roman Catholic. Joined Black Town Con'l Church, Madras, Visited Eng. in 1831. O. Dec. 22, 1831. A. at Madras May 1, 1832. In 1833, removed to Chittoor. Resigned in 1841 and joined the C. M. Society.

James Paterson. B. July, 1807. O. Dec. 21, 1831. A. in Calcutta, June 8, 1832. Removed to Berhampore, July, 1832. H. to Eng. Dec. 21, 1847. Rt. Dec. 1850. Labored at Calcutta. D. Dec. 10, 1854, on the Ganges, while on a missionary journey to Dacca.

Orlando Thomas Dobbin. B. May 29, 1807, at Charlemont, Ireland. O. Jan. 6, 1832. A. at Calcutta June 8, 1832. On account of ill-health, Rt. to Eng. Dec. 1832. Ret. May 18, 1833. He subsequently became Pastor at Arundel, Sussex.

William Hoyles Drew. B. Dec. 21, 1805, at Plymouth. O. April 12, 1832. A. Sept. 16, 1832. S. Madras. H. to Eng. Aug. 19, 1840. Rt. Dec. 14, 1845. Labored at Madras, chiefly as a Ver. preacher (Tamil), D. of cholera, at Madras, May 9, 1856. (*See* "Memoir," by John S. Wardlaw, Vizagapatam; 1857).

John Campbell. B. in 1804, in I. E. at Homerton Col. O. Dec. 20, 1832. A. at Calcutta, July 6, 1833. S. Kidderpore. Ret. in April, 1846, R. to Eng.

Charles Miller. B. 1805, at Forfar. O. May 29, 1833. A. Oct. 5, 1833. S. Neyoor, 1833-37, Nagercoil, 1837-40, D. at Poonamallee, Sept. 9, 1841.

Robert Cotton Mather, LL. D. B. Nov. 8, 1808, at New Windsor, Manchester. E. at Edinburgh, Glasgow and Homerton Col. O. June 10, 1833. A. at Calcutta, Nov. 15, 1833, at Benares, Sept. 7, 1834. In May 1838, removed to Mirzapore, where he commenced a new station. H. to Eng. at the close of 1844. Rt. Nov, 26. 1846, and resumed his work at Mirzapore. H. to Eng. in 1857. While in Eng. revised and carried through the press the Urdu Bible ; also diglot New Test. (Engl. and Urdu). R. to Mirzapore, Feb. 7, 1861. In 1869 completed new edition of Roman-Urdu Bible, and commenced an edition in Urdu-Arabic with references. H. to Eng. in 1873. While in Eng. carried through the press a Hindustani version of N. T. portion of Annoted Paragraph Bible, and subseqently, O. T. portion of the same. Ret. in 1875. D. at Finchlay, near Lon, April 21, 1877.

John Adam Shurman. B. 1810, in Westphalia. O. June 10, 1833. A. Nov. 15, 1833. S. Benares. Devoted himself to the Educational and Scripture Translation department. Did much in preparing Urdu and Hindustani versions of the Scriptures. In April, 1842 went to Calcutta to superintend the printing of the Urdu version of O.T. R. to Benares in June, 1843. In Oct. 1843 R. to Eng Rt. *via* New York, Feb. 20, 1846, Labored at Benares until his death, Oct. 1, 1852.

George Welsh, B. 1803, at New Cunnock, appointed to Bangalore. O. A. at Madras, Sept. 1834. and D. there Oct. 21, 1834.

Thomas Boaz, LL. D. B. Aug. 10, 1806, at Scarborough. O. June 18, 1834. A. at Calcutta, Dec. 10, 1834. Was pastor of Union chapel. H. to Eng. in 1847. Rt. Jan. 7, 1850. On account of ill-health R. to Eng. in Dec. 1858, Ret. July 4, 1860, D. in Lon. Oct. 13,1861. (*See* "The Missionary Pastor ; Memorials of Rev. T. Boaz, LL. D." Lon. Snow, 1862).

James William Gordon. Son of the Rev. J. Gordon. B. at Vizagapatam, in 1811. O. Sept. 3, 1834, at Exeter. A. Feb. 4, 1835. S. Vizagapatam. H. to Eng, Dec. 12, 1839. Rt. to Vizagapatam, Dec. 28, 1842. In July, 1844 removed to Chicacole. R. to Vizagapatam in July, 1845. H. to Neilghery Hills, 1871-72. Ret. in 1875.

Edward Porter. B. July 12, 1810. O. May 19, 1835, A. Sept. 3, 1835. Labored at Vizagapatam until 1844, at Cuddapah till 1846, when he R. to Eng. for two years. Rt. and labored at Cuddapah from 1848 to 1867 when he Ret. ultimately to Eng.

Colin Campbell. B. Dec. 23, 1810, at Paisley. O. April 10, 1835. A. at Madras Sept. 3, 1835. S Bangalore, 1835-40, Mysore, 1840-50, Bangalore, 1850-61, Salem, 1861-62, R. to Eng. in 1862, Rt. June 4, 1864. Ret. to Eng. in 1875.

Gilbert Turnbull. B. in 1811, in the Isle of Wight. O. Aug. 4, 1836. A. Dec. 29, 1836. S. Bangalore. Health failing, he went to Australia in 1838. D. near Sydney, March 19, 1839.

William Thompson. B. May 23, 1811, at Leith, Lancashire. O. Aug. 15, 1836. A. Dec. 29, 1836. S. Bellary. H. to Eng. March, 1840—Jan. 1841. S. Bellary. In Aug 1844, proceeded to Madras, to superintend the preparation of new Canarese type. R. to Bellary in

Jan. 1845. R. to Eng. in 1849, on account of his wife's ill health. Having accepted the pastorate at Cape Town, his connection as a missionary with the Society ceased. Arrived at Cape Town June 24, 1850, served as Agent and General Treasurer for the South African Missions.

James Bradbury. B Sept. 22, 1805, at Mayfield, Staffordshire. O. Sept. 7, 1836. A at Calcutta, Feb 8, 1837. In 1842, removed to Chinsurah, in July 1849, to Berhampore. R. to Eng. in 1870 Ret. in 1872.

John Shrieves. B. 1802, in India. S. Bellary 1836-47 where he was O. Jan. 29, 1845. In 1847-49 Cuddapah, 1849-55, Bellary. D. Feb. 9, 1857.

J. A. Regel. B. in I Appointed assistant missionary at Pulicat near Madras, in July, 1836. In 1839, removed to Bangalore O. at Bangalore, April 10, 1840. Rt Dec. 11, 1843.

William Penman Lyon. B. Dec. 28, 1812, at Glasgow. O. July 7, 1837. A. Dec. 12, 1837. S. Benares. On account of wife's ill health R. to Eng. in 1840, when his connection with the Society ceased. Subsequently became pastor at Albany Chapel, Regents Park, London.

Thomas L. Lessel. B. Apr 23, 1807, at Aberdeen. O. Aug. 1, 1837. A. at Calcutta, Dec. 12, 1837. In Dec. 1838, removed to Berhampore. H. to Eng. May 20, 1852. R. to Calcutta, Dec. 14, 1861. Ret. 1868, and in 1870 R: to Eng.

Robert Caldwell. B. May 7, 1814, near Belfast. O July 7, 1837. A Jan. 7. 1838 S. Madras. On his joining the Gospel Propagation Society, he resigned his connection with the L. M. S. June 28, 1841. In 1842, he commenced a station under the Gospel Propagation Society at Edeyengoody, Tinnevelly.

James T. Pattison. B. 1811 in London. O. Oct. 4, 1837 A. Mar. 31, 1838. S. Quilon and Nagercoil. Connection dissolved June 1844.

John Abbs B. Dec, 20, 1810. O. Aug. 23, 1837. A. at Neyoor April 20, 1838. In 1845 removed to Pareychaley. In 1859 R to Eng. Ret. in 1861. L. "Twenty-two years' Missionary experience in Travancore." Lon: Snow and Co., 1870

John Cox. B. 1811 at Painswick, Gloucestershire O. July 27, 1837. A. Mar. 31, 1838. In April, 1838 commenced a station at Trevandrum. Ret. in Aug. 1861.

James Russell B. May 18, 1806, at Glasgow. Was Pastor at Rendall, Orkney. A. Mar. 31, 1838 S. Nagercoil, 1838-40. In 1840 formed a new station at James Town. H. to Australia, June. 1856 to May, 1857. Ret. in 1860 to England.

Archibald Ramsay. B. 1806, in London. A March 31,1838, and proceeded to Nagercoil, where he commenced a Medical Mission. Afterwards removed to Neyoor. Connection dissolved, June 30, 1842.

William Morton. Engaged in Calcutta about 1838. In 1840 R. to Eng. R. to Calcutta, in 1842. On account of ill-health Ret. to Eng. in 1845.

James Sewell. B. Nov. 7, 1809, at Thealby, Lincolnshire. O. Feb. 22, 1838. A. at Madras, July 28, 1838. S. Bangalore. R. to Eng. in 1845. R. to Bangalore, in 1849. Ret. to Eng. in Aug. 1864.

John Lumb. B. 1809, at Otley, Yorkshire. O. Aug. 2, 1838. A. Dec. 1838. S. Madras. After six months his health failed; R. to Eng. in 1839, when his connection with the Society ceased.

J. H. Edward Van Roer. B. 1806, at Brunswick. O. Sept. 6, 1838. A. at Calcutta Jan. 19, 1839. His connection with the Society was dissolved in June, 1841.

Ferdinand Van Sommer. B. 1803, at Covendon, Holland O. Sept. 6, 1838. A. at Calcutta, Jan. 19, 1839. Soon after left India. Connection dissolved in May, 1841.

James Kennedy. B. May 11, 1815, at Aberfeldy, Perthshire. O. Aug. 1, 1838. A. at Calcutta, Jan 19, 1839, and at Benares, March 31. H. to Eng. at the close of 1849. Rt. Feb. 24, 1854. Health failing R. to Eng. in 1862. Rt. Jan. 4, 1866, visited Almorah in 1867-68, and formed a new Station at Ranikhet, April 30, 1869. H. to Eng. in 1877, Ret. in 1877. L. "Essays on Fundamental Questions." Mirzapore, 1874: and other works. Has pastoral charge at Portobello, Scotland.

Henry Bower. B. in India. Was engaged, in 1838, as an Assistant Missionary in the Madras Mission. and appointed to Tripassore. In 1841, he joined Gospel Propagation Society.

William Dawson. B. Jan. 16, 1816, at Vizagapatam. Was engaged, in 1838, as Assistant Missionary at Cuddapah. In 1840, removed to Chicacole. O. in 1843. In June, 1852, removed to Vizianagram. To Eng in 1857. Rt. early in 1859. Labored at Vizianagram. In 1875 left I. for E but D. on the voyage, May 5.

Rudolphe DeRodt. B. in Switzerland. Went to I in 1835, and in Jan. 1838 joined L. M S. Labored at Calcutta, where he D. Aug. 29, 1843.

John Michael Lechler. B. in 1804. in Germany. Having resigned his connection with the C. M. S., joined the L. M. S., in 1839. S. Coimbatoor and Salem. H. to Eng. in 1854. R to Salem in July, 1855. D. at Salem, June 17, 1861.

William Flower B Aug. 16, 1811, at Botley, Hants. O. Feb. 6, 1839. A. at Bombay Aug 2, and at Surat, Sept. 1839. In 1844, joined Mr. Clarkson in commencing a new station at Baroda, Guzerat. On account of ill-health R. to Eng. 1846. D. at Titchfield, Feb. 3. 1847.

William Clarkson. B. 1817, at Salisbury. A. Jan 30, 1839. A. at Surat, Dec. 15, 1839. In Nov. 1844 removed to Baroda, afterwards, to Mahi Kantha. H. to Eng. in 1848. Rt in 1851. Ret. to Eng. in 1854 subsequently became pastor at Folkestone. L. "India and the Gospel;" "Missionary Encouragements in India;" "Christ and Missions." Lon. Snow and Co.

Ebenezer Lewis. B. Oct. 4, 1812, near Aberystwith. O. July 9, 1839. A. Jan 7, 1840. S. Coimbatoor, 1840-43, Madras, 1843-46, Nagercoil, 1846-55, (formed a new station at Santhapuram). H. to Eng, in Aug. 1855. Rt. in 1857. Labored in Travancore, chiefly occupied in revision of N. T. in Tamil. Health failing, R. to Eng. in 1862. Ret. in. 1867. D. at Buckhurst Hill, Essex, Nov. 30, 1873.

Alexander Litch. B. Feb. 27, 1816, at Edinburgh, O. June 12, 1839. A. at Madras, Jan. 7, and at Chittoor, Feb. 7, 1840. In 1842, removed to Madras. In 1847 health having failed, Ret. to Eng. and settled at Wigton, Cumberland.

Richard Daniel Johnston. B. Feb. 14, 1815 in I. Engaged, in 1839, as assistant at Vizagapatam. O. in 1843. In 1855 commenced a station at Nundial. In 1870 visited Eng. Rt. Nov. 11, 1871. Ret. 1878.

William Glen, M.R.C.S. B. Annan, Dumfriesshire, Oct. 2, 1811. O. Dec. 23, 1839 A. June, 1841. S. Mirzapore. His connection was dissolved by a Board Resolution of March 26, 1844. But Oct. 30, 1848, he was again appointed as an Assistant missionary at Mirzapore. He resigned his connection with the Society in Feb. 1854.

William Porter. B. Nov. 10, 1811, at Sherborne. O. May 28, 1840. A at Madras, Sept. 15, 1840. S. Madras. H. to Eng. in July, 1855. Ret. June 24, 1857. Undertook a boarding school at Hastings.

David Gilkinson Watt. B. in 1817, at Irvine, N. B. O. June 9, 1840. A. June 2, 1841. S. Benares. H. to Eng. in 1844. Rt. Dec. 1846. S. Benares. His health having failed, Rt. to Eng, in 1848, and Ret. soon afterwards, took a pastorate at Norwich, Cheshire.

John Smith Wardlaw, D. D B. July 25, 1813, at Glasgow. O. July 14, 1841. A. at Madras, Sept. 22. and at Bellary, Oct. 28, 1842, H. to Eng. in 1845. Rt. to Bellary in Oct. 1846. Had charge of the Wardlaw Inst. (opened Aug. 28, 1846) and assisted in Scripture translation. H. to the Cape, 1853-4. In 1856 removed to Vizagapatam to co-operate with Mr. Hay in revision of Telugu Scriptures. H. to Eng. in 1859. In 1861 was appointed President of the Highgate Inst , and conducted it until 1871, when it was closed. D Oct. 9, 1872. at St. John's Wood. L. "Memoir of Rev. W. H. Drew," Vizagapatam, 1857.

John Owen Whitehouse B. April 23, 1815, at Dorking. O. June 8, 1842. A. Sept. 22, 1842. S. Nagercoil, in charge of the Seminary, and in 1855 of the Printing Press and District. In 1856 the charge of the eastern half of the Santhapuram District rested on him and also the oversight of the James Town District. H. to Eng. Jan 22, 1857. As his wife's health did not permit her return to India, his connection with the Society ceased, June 30, 1861. From June, 1867 to April, 1875 assisted in revision of the system carried on in the Foreign Department of the Society, discharging at various times, in 1870, and in 1873-74, the duties of the Foreign Secretariat.

Matthew William Wollaston. B. Aug. 1802, at Calcutta. Had held a situation in the Government College at Agra, which he relinquished on conscientious grounds. Was engaged in the Mirzapore mission in 1843, and in Jan. 1844 was appointed Supt. of schools there. O. in Nov. 1844. Visited Eng. in 1847. Rt. in 1848 and labored at Mirzapore until his death, June 10, 1851. L " Grammar for the use of natives in India"; "Sanskrit Grammar."

Joseph Mullens, D.D. B. Sept. 2, 1820. O. Sept. 5, 1843. A. in Calcutta Jan. 9, 1844. Labored in the L M.S. Inst. and also in ver. preaching. H. to Eng. in April, 1858. Rt. Dec. 20, 1860. In May, 1865, was invited by the Directors to assist Dr. Tidman in the Foreign Secretaryship. R, to Eng. by way of South India and China, visiting the stations of the Society. A. in Eng. April 22, 1867. On the death of Dr. Tidman, March 8, 1868, he became sole Foreign Secretary. In 1870 visited Canada and in 1873-4 Madagascar (Deputation Work). While on a similar journey to Ujiji in Africa, he D. July 10, 1879, near Mpwapara, Africa. L. "Missions in South India," 1854. "Results of Missionary Labor," 1856. "Memorials of the Rev. A. F. Lacroix," 1862. "Ten years Missionary Labor in India" 1863. "London and Calcutta," 1868. "Twelve Months in Madagascar," 1875. "Statistical Tables of Missions in India;" and other works.

John Henry Parker. B. Nov. 14, 1816, at Hackney. O. Sept. 7, 1843 A. Jan. 9, 1844. S. Calcutta, laboring in L. M. S. Inst. and in ver. preaching. H. to Eng. in Dec. 1852. Rt. Aug. 2, 1856. Resumed work in L.M.S. Inst. and at Coolie Bazar Chapel. D. at Calcutta, Sept. 9, 1858.

Julius Ullmann. A German missionary who had labored some years in India. Educational work at Benares, from Aug. 1844 to 1847, when he resigned.

John Sugden B. 1821, at Woodsome Lees, near Huddersfield. O. March 20, 1845. A. Aug. 2, 1845. S. Bangalore Labored in the Tamil department of the Mission and Seminary. R. to Eng. in 1852. His connection with the Society soon afterwards ceased, and he took a pastorate at Lancaster.

Joseph Van Someren Taylor. B. July 3, 1820, at Bellary, I. O. July 15, 1845, at Bermondsay. A. at Bombay 28, 1845, and at Baroda, in Nov. 1846. In 1847 removed to Mahi Kantha. H. to Eng. in 1856. In 1859 joined the Irish Presbyterian Mission.

T. Artope. A German. Was engaged as an Assistant at Mirzapore in 1845. R. to Europe in 1854, when his connection with the Society ceased.

C. Droese. A German. Had labored in I under another Missionary Society. Was engaged in I. Sept 28, 1846, as Assistant missionary in the Benares mission. His connection with the S. ceased in 1847, when he R. to the scene of his former labours.

Edward Storrow. B. Nov. 1818, at Darlington. O. Dec 16, 1847. A. at Calcutta, March 6, 1848. Labored in L. M. S. Inst. and in ver. preaching. H. to Eng. Jan. 1858 to Sept. 1859. Served as pastor of Union chapel, 1859-66. Health failing R. to Eng. in Jan. 1866. Ret. in 1868. Subsequently labored at Rugby and at Brighton. L. "The Eastern Lily Gathered," Watson's "Apology for the Bible," "India and Christian Missions," 1859.

William Henry Hill. B. June 3, 1822, at Calcutta (Son of Rev. M. Hill). O. Jan. 6, 1848, at Plymouth. A. March 6, 1848. Labored in L. M. S. Inst. and ver. preaching and itinerating. In Jan. 1860 proceeded to the Cape for the benefit of his health, thence to Eng. in Jan. 1861. In 1863 his health not having sufficiently improved Ret. Settled at Faversham, Kent.

Carl Buch, Ph.D. B. Jan. 29, 1819, at Maaster, Westphalia. O. April 24, 1849. A. Madras, Sept. 23, and at Calcutta; Oct. 13, 1849.

Labored in L. M. S. Inst. In Oct. 1850, resigned his connection with the Society, and soon after was appointed Principal of the Government College, at Bareilly, where in the Mutiny, he was shot on June 1, 1857.

J. G. Stanger. Was previously connected with the Basel Miss. Soc. In June, 1850 was engaged as assistant missionary at Bellary. Work, preaching and itinerating. Ret. in 1855.

Charles James Addis. B. in Travancore. (Son of Rev. W. B. Addis). In Oct. 1850 was appointed assistant missionary at Coimbatoor. On account of ill health Ret. in 1861 to Coonoor.

Frederick Baylis. B. Nov. 18, 1825, at Rodborough, Gloucestershire. O. Aug 29, 1850, at Southampton, A. Dec 20, 1850. S. Madras, 1851-54, Neyoor, 1854-72. L. Numerous works in Tamil; for sevral years was joint, and afterwards, sole editor of the illustrated Tamil Magazine, "*Desopakari.*" H. to Eng. March, 1872 to Nov. 1874. D. at Moottam. near Neyoor, May, 1877.

Alfred Corbold. B. May 7, 1821, at Ipswich. O. Aug 7, 1850. A. at Bombay Jan. 9, 1851. S. Mahi Kantha and Borsad until 1860. H. to Eng. in June. 1860. Rt Jan. 31, 1862. S. Madras. Health failing R. to Eng. March 1. 1870. Rt Jan. 4, 1873. S. Madras. Health again failing Rt. to Eng. in 1875. D. at Bedford, Sept. 1877.

Charles Calder Leitch. (M. R. C. S. Ed) B Oct. 31, 1822, at Edinburgh. Appointed as Medical missionary at Neyoor. O. Sept 4, 1851. A. at Madras, Dec. 17, 1851, at Neyoor in Feb. 1853. Drowned at Moottam on seacoast, while bathing, Aug. 25, 1854. (*See* "Memoir," by the Rev D. Smith, D. D. Edinburgh, 1856).

Richard John Sargent. B. Nov. 19, 1822, at Plymouth. O Sept. 11, 1851. A. Dec 17, 1851. S. Bangalore. In 1857 removed to Madras and took charge of the Tamil church, etc. R. to Eng. on account of wife's ill health in 1861. His connection with the Society ceased in Sept. 1863, when he became pastor at Billericay, Essex.

Edward Josiah Evans. B June 30, 1826, in Lon. O. Aug. 28, 1851. A. at Belgaum, Dec. 22, 1851. In Apr. 1852, proceeded to Mirzapore, in Aug. 1856 to Madras. R. to Eng. in 1860. Rt. in 1863, settled at Poyle, Middlesex.

Philip Ludwig Mens Valett. Had been connected with the Dresden Missy Soc'y. In 1852, joined the L M S. and was appointed to Bellary. A. Feb. 10, 1853. In 1857 was transferred to Chicacole. Ret. to Eng. in 1859.

Matthew Atmore Sherring. B. Sept. 26, 1826, at Halstead, Essex. E. at Univ. Col. Lon. and Coward Col. O. Dec. 7, 1852. A. at Benares, Feb. 12, 1853. In Nov. 1856 removed to Mirzapore. R. to Benares, in 1861. In 1866 R. by way of America to Eng. Rt. Feb. 6, 1869. S. Benares. H. to Eng. in 1876. Rt. and labored at Benares, where he D. Aug. 10. 1880. L. "The Indian Church during the Rebellion." Lon. Nisbet, 1859. "The Sacred City of the Hindus." Lon. Trubner and Co. 1868. "The Tribes and Castes of India, as represented in Benares." Lon. Trubner and Co. 1872. "The History of Protestant Missions in India," Lon. Trubner and Co. 1875.

George Hall. B. Sept. 27, 1825, at Edinburgh O. April 7, 1851. Labored in Jamaica, 1851-53. R. to Eng. 1853. A. at Madras April 5, 1854, where he took charge of L.M. S. Inst. H. to Eng. July 6, 1863. Rt. in Oct. 1865. On account of wife's death R. to Eng. May 12,1871- Rt. to Madras in 1872. H. to Eng. in 1876. Ret. 1879.

C. E. Thompson. B. in I. Engaged in I. as assistant missionary at Chicacole. In 1853 removed to Vizianagram, in 1861, to Vizagapatam, in 1868, to Chicacole. Ret. in 1877.

Theodore Gottlieb Kubler. E. at Basle. O. March 4, 1855, in Lon. A. in 1855. S. Salem and Madras. In Oct. 1857, on account of ill health, R. to Eng. Ret. in 1858.

John Joll Dennis. B. Feb. 14, 1830, at Morice Town, near Plymouth. O. Oct. 4, 1855. A. Feb 12. 1856. S. Nagercoil. On account of his wife's ill health R. to Eng in 1862. Rt. Aug. 18, 1863, proceeded to Nagercoil, where he D. Nov. 15, 1864.

John Macarthey. B. May, 1828, at Castle Douglas, N. B. O. Jan. 7, 1857. A. July 1857, at Bellary where he took charge of the Wardlaw Institution. In Nov. 1863 resigned his connection with the Society.

William Jones. B. 1833 at Llanwrin, Montgomeryshire O. Sirhowy, Feb. 10, 1858. A. Calcutta April 9. 1858 In Feb. 1859 he was transferred to the Mirzapore mission. Labored at Benares and Mirzapore. In Dec. 1863 left Benares to establish a mission in the District of Singrowli, south of Mirzapore and settled at Duddhi: H 1867. R. Jan. 1869. D. at Duddhi, April 25, 1870.

William Moody Blake. B. Madras Aug. 1828. O. Jan. 1858. A. 1858. S. Calcutta, 1860; Benares 1861-68. R. to Eng. in 1870, and Ret. in Oct. 1871. Subsequently settled at St. Peter's Port, Guernsey.

Samuel Jones. B June 13, 1830, at Warrington. O. Nov. 3, 1858. A. 1859. S. Coimbatoor. H to Eng. in 1867. Rt. in March, 1871. S. Nagercoil. H. to Eng. in 1877. D. in Lon. May 29, 1877

John Crichton Dick. B. Edinburgh, April 27, 1834. O Feb. 16, 1859. Sailed March 7, 1859. Died on his passage out, June 27, 1859.

George Shrewsbury. B. May 6, 1833, at Hythe, Kent. O. Aug. 23, 1860. A. Dec. 20, 1860. S. Berhampore. His health not improving Ret to Eng. 1868. His connection with the Society ceased in 1870 when he become pastor at Ingress Vale, Greenhithe, Kent.

James Frank Gannaway, B. 1838 at Wartlington, Hants O. July 10. 1861. A. in Nov. 1861. S. James Town. His wife's health failing lef tIndia in Aug. 1864 for Eng. In 1865 Ret. and in 1866 became Pastor at Wotton-under-edge, Gloucestershire.

John Lowe, M. R. C. S. Ed. B. Mar. 2, 1835, at Banchory, Aberdeenshire. Appointed Medical missionary at Neyoor. O July 1, 1861. A. at Neyoor Nov. 21, 1861. In 1868 on account of wife's ill-health R. to Eng. Resigned Mar 13. 1871, and became Supt. of Training Inst, Edinburgh Medical Mission.

S. R. Asbury. B. Feb. 1833, at Hanley, Staffordshire. E. at Andover Theol. Sem. (U. S. A.) and Univ. Col. Lon. O. July 30, 1861. A. Jan. 3, 1862, at Mirzapore. Ret. to Eng. in 1864.

Frederick J. Bright. B. in Essex, Dec. 24, 1832. O. June 6, 1861. A. Jan. 3, 1862. S Mirzapore. In 1864 Ret. to Eng. when his connection with the Society ceased.

Goodeve Mabbs. B. 1835 at London. O. Aug. 13, 1861. A. Jan 1862. S. Salem, 1862-65. Nagercoil 1866. Res. Jan. 19, 1867 and Ret. Sept. 23. 1868. Subsequently became Pastor at Holy, Moorside.

William Edward Morris. B. Aug 3, 1855, at Llanfyllan, Montgomeryshire. O. Aug. 14, 1861. A at Coimbatoor. in Jan. 1862. Established a mission at Tirupoor, Apr. 9, 1863 Removed to Salem, in Nov. 1865. Health having failed R to Eng. April 9, 1869, Ret. Apr. 30, 1872. Settled at Market Harborough.

Alexander Thomson B. in 1834. O. July 1, 1861. A. at Cuddapah, in Jan. 1862. D at Bellary, Sept. 6, 1862.

Edward Allport Wareham. B. March, 1838, at Hampton Wick, Middlesex. O June 23, 1864. A. Nov. 1864. S. Belgaum. Suffering from sunstroke, H to Eng. in 1871. Ret. in 1872, and was appointed District Agent for Scotland and Ireland.

Thomas Haslam. B Oct. 17. 1839, at Egerton, near Bolton. O. Sept. 1, 1864. A. 1864. In April, 1865 opened a Mission at Pullachy in the Coimbatoor District At the close of 1866 removed to Coimbatoor, where he labored until his death, June 13. 1869

William G. Mawbey. B 1840, at Northampton. O. July 5, 1864. A. 1865. S. Cuddapah. H. to Eng. in 1876. Afterwards Ret.

David Meadowcroft. B. Feb. 1838, at Manchester. O. July 4, 1864. A. in Dec. 1864. S Madras. His wife's health having failed R. to Eng. Feb. 2, 1867, and Ret. Afterwards went to Australia.

William Whyte B. Oct 6, 1838, at Oban, Argyleshire O. June 5, 1866. A. at Madras, Oct. 21, 1866 and D. there Dec. 30, 1866.

Henry De Vere Gookey. B. Mar. 16. 1843, at Southampton. O. July 4, 1866. A. Jan. 12, 1867. S. Vizagapatam. H to Eng. in 1875, Ret. in 1878

John Naylor. B. Mar. 4, 1837, at Halifax O. July 26, 1866. A. at Calcutta, Oct. 29, 1866. H. to Eng. in April, 1875. Ret. Jan. 26, 1877

Henry Toller. B May 10, 1845, at Market Harborough. O. Sept. 2, 1869. A. Jan. 18, 1870: D at Salem. March 15. 1870.

Stephen Organe. B. 1839, at Bristol. O July 4, 1866. A. Jan. 12, 1867. S. Madras, Educational work On account of wife's ill-health R to Eng in 1867. R. Feb 7. 1868. S Madras. Jan 18, 1871 resigned connection with the Society. and accepted the pastorate of the Church at Davidson Street Chapel, Madras.

Edwin Midwinter. B. March, 1853, at Newbury. O Feb. 16, 1876. A. in 1876. S. Vizagapatam, where he D. May 27, 1877.

Alexander Strachan. B Nov. 26, 1853 at Fraserburgh, N. B. O. Oct. 5, 1877. A. in 1877. S. Calcutta, where he D. Sept. 20, 1878.

CHAPTER IV.

THE AMERICAN BOARD.

I. THE MARATHI MISSION.

THE American Marathi Mission was the first established by "The American Board,"* the oldest Missionary Society in America. This Society was organized in June, 1810, but the first missionaries did not sail till February, 1812. They landed in Calcutta the following June, and were peremptorily ordered out of the country by Government. Two of them escaped to Bombay, and endeavored to commence missionary work there. These were the Revs. Gordon Hall and Samuel Nott. They were at first forbidden to engage in missionary work at Bombay, but after suffering much annoyance, and once having their passage engaged to England by order of the Bombay Government, they at last received permission to remain. An earnest appeal by the missionaries themselves to the excellent Governor of Bombay, Sir Even Nepean, was mainly effectual in securing this result. The letter giving the permission was dated December 21, 1813. They were soon joined by the Rev Samuel Newell. When ordered away from Calcutta, Mr. Newell had taken passage in a ship to the Isle of France. But the hardships of the voyage proved too much for Mrs N. in her delicate health, and soon after landing at Port Louis, she rested from her labors. Having buried his young wife and infant child, Mr. Newell returned alone to India, to carry out his cherished purpose of preaching the Gospel to the Hindus.

Permission having been received to reside in the city, and preach to the Native population, the missionaries commenced their work in earnest. They experienced especially severe trials in the outset, but they were men of large faith, of untiring

---

* NOTE.—The full title of this Society is, "The American Board of Commissioners for Foreign Missions." But except in official documents, it is more commonly known as "The American Board."

energy, and they counted not their lives dear to themselves if they might win in the struggle. Others soon came to their support. In 1815, the Rev. H. Bardwell, who understood printing, joined the Mission. A press was soon at work, which with constantly improving types and other appliances, was one of the chief agencies employed by the American Mission till 1855. Other presses in the meantime having been established, at which all necessary printing could be done, this secular work was then dropped as no longer indispensable to the Mission.

Of the three founders of the Mission, Mr. Nott was compelled by failing health to return home in about three years, but lived in America till 1869. In May, 1821, Mr. Newell fell a victim to cholera, that fearful scourge of India which has so often thinned the ranks of missionaries as well as other classes of foreign residents.

Mr. Hall labored thirteen years at Bombay. His labors were various and arduous. Besides preaching to the heathen he spent much time in the translation of portions of Scripture, and the writing of suitable tracts in Marathi. He also made long tours into the Deccan, sowing the seed broad-cast. It was on one of these tours in March, 1826 that he finished his course. Visiting Nasik and Trimbakeshwar, he found the cholera raging, and the people in a panic, without any means of checking the disease. With characteristic self-forgetfulness, he began to give the sick medicines from his own little stock, till it was nearly exhausted. He then started on his return to Bombay. At the end of the second day he reached a place called Durli Dhapur about thirty miles from Nasik. Having no tent, he stopped in the verandah of an open temple for the night. The cold and other discomforts of the place, added to the fatigue of the journey, prepared his system for a fatal attack of the disease raging around him. This came on about four o'clock the next morning as he was preparing to start on his journey. Medicine administered by his attendants was rejected, and he then told them that he should not recover. Having given a few brief directions about the burial of his body and other matters, he prayed with them, and calmly awaited the end. He died about noon of the same day, one of the humble heroes whose record is on high.

His attendants wrapped the body in a blanket, and laid it in a grave in the Musalman burying-ground.*

In the few years following the death of Mr. Hall, several members of the Mission made long tours through the Marathi country, preaching and distributing tracts and vernacular portions of Scripture. In December, 1831, Ahmednagar was occupied by Messrs. Graves, Read, and Hervey, as an inland station. Since its occupation this city and the districts around it have engrossed a large part of the time and strength of the Mission. The greater part of the churches are organized here, and most of the Native Assistants are employed in these districts. Satara was occupied in 1849 by the Rev. W. Wood. Sholapur was occupied in 1861 by the Rev. C. Harding.

Schools for children of both sexes have formed an important agency in the operations of the Mission since its founding. At first, Hindu teachers were employed, as no others were available; the schools being carefully superintended by the missionaries or Native Christian catechists. But for the last twenty-five years, only Christian teachers have been employed. Miss Farrar, who was thirty-five years connected with the Mission, labored with untiring energy and zeal and with much success, in establishing and carrying on girls' schools. Many hundreds of girls were thus brought under Christain instruction. The school for Christian girls at Ahmednagar has numbered about 100 pupils for some years past. In the 60 schools of the Mission about 1,200 pupils are under the instruction of Christian teachers.

Other stations have been occupied by the missionaries in the districts around Ahmednagar, and one at Bhuinj in the Satara district. Sirur was occupied by the Rev. O. French in 1842; Khokar by the Rev W. P. Barker in 1855; Wadale by the Rev. S. B. Fairbank in 1857; Rahuri by the Rev. A. Abott in 1859.

There are now (January, 1881) five missionaries connected with the Ahmednagar district, two with Satara, one with Sholapur, two at Bombay, and one is in America on furlough. There is also a medical missionary lady in Bombay.

* NOTE.—One of the attendants of Mr. Hall at the time of his death, Mr. Thomas Graham, is still living (January, 1881) in Bombay. He was a most valuable Assistant in the "American Press" while this was carried on by the Mission, and is now employed in connection with the "Education Society's Press," Bombay.

There are 25 churches in connection with the Mission, of which fifteen have ordained pastors over them.

The following statistics show the growth of these churches. The first part of the statistics refers to the churches in Ahmednagar district only; the others to all the stations of the Mission.

Members received into the church on profession of faith:

1831 to 1840, inclusive,	...	...	16
1841 to 1850, ,,	...	...	138
1851 to 1860, ,,	...	...	441

In all the churches—received on profession:

1861 to 1870, inclusive,	...	...	463
1871 to 1880, ,,	...	...	1,190

Number of Communicants:

January 1, 1861,	... 473		
Do. do. 1871,	... 629	Increase	156
Do. do. 1881,	... 1,340	do.	711

The following literary labors of missionaries of this Mission may be mentioned. The books, if not out of print, can probably be obtained through the Treasurer of the American Board, L. S. Ward, Esq., Congregational House, U.S.A.

Memoirs of Rev. Gordon Hall. (1834). By Rev. Horatio Bardwell, D.D.; 260 p.

Memoirs of the converted Brahman, Babajee. (1836). Rev. Hollis Read. 2. Vols., pp. 264 and 275.

India and its People, Ancient and Modern. (1859). Rev. Hollis Read. Pp. 384.

India, Ancient and Modern, Geographical, Political, Social and Religious. (1856). Rev. D.A. Allen, D.D. 8vo, pp. 618.

Journal of a Missionary tour in India (1836). Rev W. Ramsay. pp. 367.

The Conquest of India by the Church. (1845). Rev. S. B. Munger.

A Grammar of the Marathi Language: Translation of the "Surya Siddhanta": "Antiquity and Unity of the Human Race." Rev. E. Burgess. [L. B.]

MISSIONARIES OF THE SOCIETY.

Ankaipagar, Mahipati Balaji. Professed Christianity Aug. 28, 1853. O. Dec. 26, 1867. In charge of the church in (Ad.) *Vedagar, Ahmednagar, Bombay P.*

Ballantine, William Osborne, M. D. B. at Ahmednagar, Feb 9, 1849. A. (from America) April 18, 1875. S. Ahmednagar. Rahuri. W. medical practice and ver. preaching. M. Ad. *Rahuri, Ahmednagar, Bombay P.*

Barase, Jayaram Damaji. Professed Christianity May 27, 1855. O. Dec. 6, 1867. In charge of the church in (Ad.) *Shingave, Ahmednagar, Bombay P.*

Bhambal, Vithoba Lakshaman. Professed Christianity Nov. 22, 1857. O. Nov. 27, 1867. In charge of the church at (Ad.) *Gahu, Ahmednagar, Bombay P.*

Bissell, Lemuel. B. at South Winsor, Ct. U., S. A., Dec. 12, 1822. O. at Milan, Ohio, April 9, 1851. A. Aug. 27, 1851. S. Sirur, Ahmednagar. W. preaching (ver.), itinerating, and instructing Theol. classes. H. Dec. 14, 1863, to Oct. 11, 1866: and from March, 1876 to Dec. 1877. M. Ad. *Ahmednagar, Bombay P.*

Bruce, Henry James. A. March 3, 1863. S. Ahmednagar, Khokar, Rahuri, Satara. W. preaching (ver.) and itinerating. H. from March 15, 1872, to Oct. 16, 1875. Prepared several works in Marathi, most important of which is "*Anatomy, Human and Comparative.*" Octavo, pp. 340. M. Ad. *Satara, Bombay P.*

Dhalawani, Kasam Mahamadji. B. at Ahmednagar, in 1837. Professed Christianity June 9, 1856. O. Nov. 19, 1863. S. Khokar 1863 to Dec., 1870, when he became pastor of the church at Sirur. Is now laboring as an evangelist at Satara. Ad. *Satara, Bombay P.*

Fairbank, Samuel Bacon. B. Dec. 14, 1822, at Stamford, Ct., U. S. A. E. Illinois College at Jacksonville, and received B. A., in 1842. After three years of theological study at Andover, was licensed in 1845: and received M. A. O. as an evangelist at Jacksonville, in 1845. Spent the following winter in the study of Marathi. Sailed from Boston, May 28, 1846: landed in Bombay, September 20, 1846. For more than four years beginning with 1850 resided in Bombay, and superintended the American Mission Press; which then did the work of the Mission and most of the Marathi work, as well as some Guzerati work of the Bible and Tract Societies. Afterward stationed at Ahmednagar and Wadale. Work almost exclusively in Marathi: preaching, itinerating, superintending village schools and native agents. Literary labors; revising Bible: editing the tracts of the Mission series and the school-books —compiling and revising rather than composing: H. May 2, 1855, to Jan. 12, 1857: and Aug. 18, 1869, to Aug. 26, 1871. Ad. *Ahmednagar, Bombay P.*

Gates, Lorin Samuel. B. at East Hardland, Ct., U. S. A. Ordained at Cambridge Vt., July 7, 1875. A. Dec. 28, 1875. W. preaching Eng. and ver. M. Ad. *Sholapur, Bombay P.*

GAYAKAWAD, HARIBA DAGADOBA. Professed Christianity Apr. 13, 1859. O. Dec. 24, 1868. In charge of the church at Sonai, Ad. *Manzari, Ahmednagar, Bombay P.*

HARDING, CHARLES. B. at Whately, Mass, U. S. A. Nov. 21, 1826. O. July 3, 1856. A. Jan. 12, 1857. S. Bombay, Sholapur. W., preaching (ver. and Engl.) and itinerating H. Mar 24, 1868, to Dec. 22, 1869. Second H. in Mar. 1880. M. (Ad.) Amherst, Mass. U. S. A

HUME, EDWARD SACKETT. B. at Bombay, June 4, 1848. O. at New Haven, Ct., U. S. A., June 2, 1875. Oct. 16, 1875. S. Ahmednagar, 1875, since, Bombay. L. Editor of *Dnyanodaya* one year. M. Ad. Byculla, *Bombay.*

HUME, ROBERT ALLEN. B. at Bombay, March 18, 1847. O. at New Haven, Ct., U. S. A, May 10, 1874. A. Oct. 29, 1874. S. Ahmednagar. W. Ver. preaching and teaching in Theol. Sem. Editor *Dnyanodaya.* M. Ad. *Ahmednagar, Bombay P.*

KARMARKAR, VISHNU BHASKAR Professed Christianity Oct. 2, 1853. O. June 27, 1860. Removed to Bombay in 1868, and soon after was installed as pastor of the Mission church in that city. Ad. *Tank St., Bombay.*

KSHIRASAGAR, ANAJI BHAGOBA. B. in 1842. Professed Christianity Dec 9, 1860 O in Dec. 1874. In 1879 became pastor of church in (Ad.) *Ahmednagar, Bombay P.*

MAKASARE, SONAJI CHANDRABHAU. Professed Christianity Nov. 22, 1857 O. Feb 25, 1874. In charge of the church at Ad *Parner, Ahmednagar, Bombay P.*

MAKASARE, VITHAL ABAJI. Professed Christianity Nov. 22, 1857. O. May 4, 1874. In charge of the chureb at (Ad) *Satara, Bombay P.*

MODAK, RAMKRISHNA VINAYAK Professed Christianity Sept. 25, 1842. O. Dec. 13, 1854. Remained here about five years: then accepted a call to become pastor of the church in Bombay, where he labored till 1866. On account of the health of his family he then R to the Deccan, and in 1870, when the two churches at Ahmednagar were united, he became pastor of the united church. Has written and translated several useful tracts and books. Resigned his place as pastor of the church in June 1879, and was appointed Instructor in the Theological Seminary at Ahmednagar. Ad. *Ahmednagar, Bombay P.*

OHOL, WANIRAM VESHAWANT. Professed Christianity Jan. 18, 1857. O Nov. 22, 1867. In charge of the church at (Ad.) *Rahuri, Ahmednagar, Bombay P.*

PARK, CHARLES WARE. B Sept. 8, 1845, at North Andover, Mass. U. S A. O. June 15, 1870. A Sept. 16, 1870 S. Ahmednagar, 1870-1 Sholapur, 1871-4. Bombay, 1874-80. L Founded the *Indian Evangelical Review,* 1873, and edited it until 1879: Editor of *Dnyanodaya,* 1873-80: Sec. Bombay Tract and Book Socy. 1874-76: Editor of Publications of Am Marathi Mission, 1878. H. to U. S. A., early in 1881. Ad *Bombay.*

PAWAR, RAWAJI DEWAJI. Professed Christianity in 1860. O. Dec. 28, 1860. In charge at (Ad.) *Parner, Ahmednagar, Bombay P.*

RATHAWAD, SAYAJI MUKINDA. Professed Christianity May 27, 1855. O. Dec. 13, 1867. In charge of the church at (Ad.) *Panchegar, Ahmednagar, Bombay P.*

SALAVE, LAKSHAMAN MANAJI. Professed Christianity Dec. 14 1851. O. Dec. 19, 1867. In charge of the church at (Ad.) *Chande', Bombay P.*

SMITH, JAMES. B. at Ontario, Canada, July 13, 1851. E. in Victoria College, and Knox Col Theol. Seminary, graduating from the former in 1876, and from the latter in 1879. M. April, 1879. Appointed to the Marathi Mission Sept. 19: O. at St. Mary's, Ontario, by the Presbytery of Stratford, Canada, Sept. 29. Sailed from Quebec Oct. 25, and landed in Bombay Dec. 13, 1879. Ad. *Ahmednagar, Bombay P.*

WAGCHAWARE, DHONDIBA TUKARAM. Professed Christianity Sept. 17, 1854. O. Dec. 5, 1872. In charge of the church at (Ad.) *Belapoor, Ahmednagar, Bombay P.*

WAGCHAWARE, GANGARAM LALABA. Professed Christianity Nov. 27, 1858. O. Dec. 12, 1867. In charge of the church at (Ad.) *Kolagav, Ahmednagar, Bombay P.*

WELLS, SPENCER REXFORD. B. at Albany, N. Y., U. S. A., Aug. 25, 1838. E. at Beloit College, Wis. In the war of 1860, was in the northern army, and lost an arm at Vicksburg. Attended the Chicago Theol. Sem., and graduated in 1867. O at Chicago in 1867. Preached two years in Dundee and London. Mich. M. April 6, 1869. A. Bombay Nov. 13, of the same year. Spent one year in Ahmednagar: has since labored at Bhuinj and Panchgani. W. mostly Ver. Proceeding to America on furlough in March, 1881. Ad. *Panchgani, Satara, Bombay P.*

WINSOR, RICHARD. A. Jan. 22, 1871. S. Sholapur, Satara, Sirur. W. preaching and itinerating. M. Ad. *Sirur*, Poona District, *Bombay P.*

ZADHAV, SADOBA MAKAJI. B. at Ahmednagar in 1842. Professed Christianity, July 2. 1854. O. Jan 25, 1853. In charge of the church at that place till 1876, then removed. Ad. *Mahad Konkan, Bombay P.*

RETIRED MISSIONARIES.

Hollis Read. B. at Newfane, Vt., U. S. A., Aug. 26, 1802. A. March 7, 1831. S. Bombay, Ahmednagar. W. preaching (ver.) and itinerating. Left I. March, 18, 1835. Ad. Congl. House, Boston, U. S. A.

Willam Ramsey. B. at Thompson, Pa., U. S. A, Feb. 11, 1803. A. March 7, 1831. S. Bombay. W. preaching (ver.) and itinerating. Left I. July 5, 1834. Ad. Congl. House, Boston, U. S. A.

Amos Abbott. B. at Wilton, N.H., U.S.A., in 1810. A. Oct. 15, 1834. H. 1847-57. S. Ahmednagar, Rahuri, Satara. Left I. in March, 1869. Ad. *Steel City, Neb., U. S. A.*

George W. Boggs. A. Sept. 14, 1838. S. Ahmednagar. W. ver. preaching. Left I. Dec. 22, 1838. Ad. Congl. House, Boston, U.S.A.

Allen Hazen. D. D. B Nov. 30. 1822. A. Feb. 27, 1847. S. Ahmednagar, Sirur, Bombay, Sholapur. W. preaching (Ver), itinerating, Bible revision, preparation of tracts, instructing Theol. classes. H. 1858-64. Left I. Feb. 24, 1872. Ad. *Agewam, Mass, U.S.A.*

William Wood. B. Dec. 2, 1818. A. Jan. 19, 1848. S. Satara, Ahmednagar, Satara. W. preaching (Ver.) itinerating, and preparing tracts. H. 1855-57, 1862 to 1865. Left I. March 15, 1872. Ad. *North Branford, Ct., U. S. A.*

Samuel Chase Dean. A. Jan. 12, 1857. S. Ahmednagar, Satara, Bhuinj. W. preaching (ver.) and itinerating. Left I. March 19, 1867. Ad. *Steele City, Nebraska, U. S. A.*

Henry Watkins Ballantine. A. March 3, 1863. S. Bombay, W. preaching. Left I. March 7, 1865. Ad. Congl. House, Boston, U.S.A.

William Henry Atkinson. B. at Bradford, Yorkshire, Eng. May 29, 1838. O. at Chicago, U.S.A., in April, 1867. A. Jan. 18, 1868. S. Ahmednagar, Wadale, Sholapur. W. preaching in ver. and Eng. and itinerating. Left I. in Jan. 1876. Ad. *Orchard, Iowa, U. S. A.*

DECEASED MISSIONARIES.

Gordon Hall. B. at Tolland, Mass., U. S. A. April 8, 1784. O. at Salem, Feb. 6, 1812. A. in June, 1812. Not being permitted to remain in Calcutta, where he and his companions landed, in company with Mr. Nott proceeded to Bombay where they opened the mission. He was engaged in preaching, itinerating and translating. D. while on a tour, near Nasik, March 10, 1826.

Samuel Nott. B. at Franklin, Ct, U. S. A. Sept. 11, 1788. O. at Salem, Feb. 6, 1812. Landed in Calcutta the following June, and with Mr. Hall escaped to Bombay. Was engaged in preaching. Left I. on account of failing health in Sept 1815. D. at Hartford, Ct., July 1, 1869.

Samuel Newell. B. at Durham, Me., U.S.A, July 24, 1784. O. at Salem, Feb. 6, 1812. Landed in Calcutta the following June. When ordered away he proceeded to the Isle of France. and thence to Bombay, where he joined the new mission. Was engaged in preaching, itinerating and translating. D. at Bombay May 31, 1821.

Horatio Bardwell, D.D. B. at Belchertown, Mass., U. S. A. Nov. 3, 1788. O. in 1815. A. Nov. 1, 1816, and joined the mission at Bombay. Was engaged in preaching and in superintending the Press. Left I. Jan. 22, 1821. D. in 1867.

John Nichols. B. at Antrim, N H., U. S. A., June 20, 1790. A. at Bombay, Feb. 23, 1818. D. Dec. 9, 1824.

Allen Graves. B. at Rupert, Vt., U. S. A. April 8, 1792. A Feb. 23, 1818. S. Mahim, Bombay, and Mahableshwar. Was in America from Aug. 1832, to Sept. 1834. D. Dec. 30, 1843.

James Garrett, Esq. B. at Utica, N. Y., U. S. A., July 16, 1797. A. Aug. 9, 1820. Labored in Ceylon and at Bombay in connection with the Press. D. July 16, 1831.

Edmund Frost. B. at Brattleboro, Vt., U. S. A., Nov. 16, 1791. O. in 1823. A. June 28, 1824. S. Bombay. D. Oct. 18, 1825.

Cyrus Stone. B. at Marlboro, N. H., U.S.A., June 9, 1793. A. Dec. 28, 1827. Labored at Bombay and Jalna in preaching and translating. Left I. in June, 1838. D.

David Oliver Allen, D.D. B. at Barre, Mass., U. S, A., in 1800. O.

in 1827. A. Nov. 27, 1827. S. Bombay, Ahmednagar, Jalna. W. preaching in Eng, and ver; itinerating, Bible translation and revision, and care of the Press. H. from Dec. 1832 to Jan. 1834. Left I. in 1852. D. at Lowell, Mass, July 19, 1863.

William Hervey. B. at Kingsbury, N. Y., U. S. A., Jan. 22, 1799. A. March 7, 1831. S. Bombay and Ahmednagar, and engaged in preaching. D. at the latter place May 13, 1832.

William C. Sampson, Esq. B. at Kingston, N. C., U.S.A., July 7, 1806. A. Nov. 22, 1833. Labored at Bombay in connection with the Press. D. at Allepie, Dec 22, 1835.

Sendol Barnes Munger. B. at Fairhaven, Vt., U.S.A., Oct. 5, 1803. O. Feb 12, 1834. A. Sept. 10. 1834. S. Bombay, Jalna, Bhingar, Satara. H. 1842 to 1846; May 18, 1853 to Nov. 1854; April 1860 to March, 1863. D. at Bombay, July 23, 1868.

George W. Hubbard. B. at Hanover, N. H, U. S. A., Dec. 25, 1809. A. Sept. 10, 1834. S. Bombay and Jalna in superintending schools. Left I. in June, 1837. D.

Henry Ballantine. B. at Schodack, N.Y., U. S. A., March 5, 1813. O. in 1834. A Oct. 11, 1835. S. Bombay and Ahmednagar. W. preaching (ver) itinerating, Bible translating, Christian books in the ver. instruction of Theol. classes H. from Dec. 1849, to Nov. 1852. Left I. Sept. 4, 1865. D at sea. Nov. 9, 1865.

Elijah A. Webster, Esq. B. at New Hartford, N. Y., U. S. A., Feb. 20, 1813. A. Oct. 11, 1835. S. Bombay as Supdt. of the Press Left I. in 1842. D.

Ebenezer Burgess. B. at Grafton. Vt, U.S A., June 26. 1805. A. Aug. 10, 1839. S Ahmednagar and Satara. H. Dec. 1844 to Feb. 1847. Left I. in Jan. 1854. D at Newton Centre, Mass., Jan. 1, 1870.

Ozro French. B. at Dummerston, Vt, U. S. A., June 8, 1807. A. Aug 10, 1839. S. Ahmednagar and Sirur. W. itinerating and ver. preaching. Left I. July 19, 1849. D Sept. 28, 1865.

Robert Wilson Hume. B. at Stamford, N. Y, U.S A, Nov. 8, 1809. O. in 1838. A. Aug. 10, 1839 S. Bombay. W. preaching, in Engl. and ver.; editing the ver newspaper "*Dnyanodaya.*" Was Sec. of the Bombay Tract Society. Left I. Sept. 20, 1854. D. at sea Nov. 26, 1854.

William Wilberforce Chapin. B. at Somers, Ct., U S.A., Dec. 2, 1836. O. Sept 24, 1863. A. May 19, 1864. S. Ahmednagar and Pimplas. D. March 22, 1865.

Hari Ramchandra Khishti. Professed Christianity April 14, 1839. O. Dec. 13, 1854. D. in Bombay, Jan. 11, 1864.

It is but proper here to add the name of Miss Cynthia Farrar, who was B. at Marlboro, N.H, U S.A., April 20, 1795, and A. Dec. 28, 1827. She labored at Bombay, Ahmednagar and Satara, superintending girls' schools. Visited America in 1837, Rt. in 1839. She D. at Ahmednagar, Jan. 25, 1862.

II. THE MADURA MISSION.

The District of Madura covers an area of about 8,000 square miles, and contains over two millions of inhabitants.

The Jesuits have had a mission in Madura for more than 250 years. In 1606, Robert De Nobilibus presented himself before the Brahmans of Madura claiming to be a Brahman of great purity from the west, strengthening his declaration by a solemn oath. He labored in the district for about forty years, making with his coadjutors, many converts. After the wars between the French and English, the number of Roman Catholics was greatly diminished, being estimated in 1776, at 18,000. In 1839, the Romish population of the district was 25,476, and they have probably not increased much since that period.

The American Mission was commenced in July, 1834, permission having previously been obtained from Sir Frederick Adam, then Governor of Madras. The first missionaries were the Rev. William Todd and the Rev. Henry R. Hoisington, who came from Jaffna, Ceylon, with three native assistants.

Early in 1835, the Rev. Daniel Poor, after visiting Madura, was so much impressed by the importance of the field that he removed permanently to this mission, and entered with enthusiasm upon his new work. A large number of vernacular schools were soon established, and also an English school in which many of the present native officials of the district were educated. At first the teachers of the schools were idolaters, as no others could be procured in the district, but the lessons were so arranged that no heathen books could be introduced. The schools were generally popular, as they were greatly superior to ordinary native schools, but they were occasionally interrupted by absurd rumors, which were circulated respecting the object of the missionaries in establishing the schools. At one time it was said the missionaries intended to carry off the boys and sell them for slaves: then they were training them for sepoys: again, that they gave the boys "spiritual milk"—some magical potation, to make them Christians; gradually, however, the people gained confidence in the missionaries.

As the first catechists of the Mission were brought from Jaffna, Tanjore, etc., and, being strangers in the district, were not always so contented, or satisfactory as could be desired, it early became a matter of much importance to raise up in the field the helpers that were needed. Accordingly, a number of boarding-schools were established in different parts of the district, as the first step towards the desired object. Some difficulties were met at the outset, in bringing boys upon the mission compound, from a caste feeling, but this obstacle was gradually overcome, and boys of various castes were brought to live together in harmony.

In 1842, the most advanced scholars in the boarding-school were brought together at Tirumangalam and formed the commencement of a Mission Seminary. The primary object of this institution was the raising up of suitable mission agents. The course of study was at first six years. The students were under no obligations to enter mission service, but were free to choose their future occupations as they pleased. The divine favor was vouchsafed to the institution in a remarkable manner, over 200 of the students having made a profession of religion while in the Seminary previous to 1867.

Subsequently, a class was received for a shorter course, to be prepared for schoolmasters, and a class of catechists was afterwards received to take a two years' course, after which they would return to the stations from which they came. Most of the present native pastors of the Mission, and many of the catechists and schoolmasters, received their education in the seminary. In 1870, the seminary was changed into an exclusively theological school, but experience seems to indicate that a varied course of study, including theology, is better adapted to the wants of the Mission than one exclusively theological.

Although at the commencement of the Mission, vernacular education was considered as of so much importance, it was not, as an end, but as a subsidiary means of accomplishing the great object of the Mission, the conversion of souls, and the building up of the kingdom of Christ. The schools gave the missionaries access to the people which they could secure in no other way, and each school was a preaching station, where the missionary was always sure of a good and attentive audience of parents as well as children. Preaching was carried on daily in the villages near the different stations, and frequent tours were made in more remote parts of the field. In 1843, a new feature of the Mission's history was the application from communities in villages, to be received and acknowledged as Christians. The motives which prompted these applications were sometimes of a worldly nature—the desire to escape from oppression or some indefinite hope of improving their temporal condition, and sometimes, in connection with this, was an evident longing for a purer faith. Whatever the motive was, they placed themselves under Christian instruction, and renounced all forms of heathenism. When persecution arose, some went back to their former idolatrous worship, but many others proved, by their firmness under trials, sometimes very severe, that they were sincere in their acceptance of Christianity. The system thus inaugurated, gained strength from year to year, and, under the regular instruction imparted, with the blessing of God, some of these nominal Christians gave evidence that they had truly become the children of God.

As the field of labor enlarged, without a corresponding increase of missionaries, the Mission became impressed with the importance of a more systematic visitation of the whole field, so far as possible; and in 1863, the missionaries and helpers were divided into companies, each of which was to spend a portion of time in itinerating. In 1865, over 1,200 villages were visited, and the gospel was preached to about 60,000 hearers, and a large number of Scriptures and tracts were distributed. Subsequent years have shown much the same result. The number of actual conversions in this form of labor has been small, yet a knowledge of truth has been spread far and wide, and in many cases men have been led to serious inquiry as to the truth of the strange doctrines brought to their hearing.

Churches were formed at the different stations, soon after the commencement of the Mission and were at first composed almost entirely of the native helpers. In 1843 the church members numbered 18: in 1875, there were 32 churches, with 1,880 members in good standing. The first native pastor was ordained on the 25th of March 1855; the number of ordained ministers in 1880 was 18, of whom 13 are in pastoral charge of native churches. A few of these pastors have had only a vernacular education, but they are well versed in the sacred Scriptures. The most efficient of the whole number, are those who, to earnest piety, have added a good education in English, as well as in their native tongue.

At first the native pastors received their entire support from the Mission, but at the present time they are supported in whole or in part by the churches over which they have been placed, and in part by the Native Evangelical Society. Most of the native churches are progressing towards entire self-support. A "Church Union" has been in existence for several years, in which the pastors and delegates from the churches meet for consultation and action on the interests of the churches. The subject of Christian benevolence is constantly kept before the people, and though most of them are very poor, they are increasing in their contributions from year to year. These amounted in 1880 to Rs. 4,868. Female education has not made much progress except among Christians, but at several stations schools for Hindu girls have been established and are fairly prosperous. In Madura, a desire for education has, to some extent, been awakened among Hindu women of good caste, and there is much encouragement to labor among them, though there are many difficulties to be overcome.

The question of caste, was one which was forced upon the attention of the Mission at a very early date. It was discouraged, as far as possible, and no distinction was recognized in the administration of the Lord's Supper but no other definite test of the renunciation of caste was at first proposed. In 1847, however, the subject became a matter of discussion throughout the Madras Presidency. The excitement was general in this district. There was no difference of opinion among the missionaries in Madura as to the nature and evils of caste, but there was some as to the best method of dealing with it. It was finally decided that a test should be proposed to all the helpers, and to the scholars and teachers of the Seminary. On the application of the test many of the helpers declined to take it and left the service of the Mission, as did also most of the teachers and scholars of the Seminary. Many of the scholars returned, however, when the first excitement passed off. For a time the tempest, which had passed over the Mission, seemed almost to have left only a wreck behind it, but the storm had cleared the atmosphere, and a more healthy state of things was the result. The position of the Mission was distinctly understood, and though it may not be said that all *feeling* of caste has been obliterated from the minds of Christians, its outward manifestation in an offensive shape is very rare indeed.

From a very early period the Mission has had the privilege of a missionary physician, who, in addition to the care of the mission families, has had considerable practice among the natives of the district. A dispensary was early opened in Madura, and subsequently in Dindigul. For seven years past Dr. Chester has had the care of both these dispensaries, besides the superintendence of several smaller dispensaries at other stations. The whole number of patients treated at the two principal dispensaries in 1880, was 39,000.

There are two societies supported by the native Christians in connection with the Mission. The Native Evangelical Society, to which reference has already been made, was established twenty-five years ago, and uses its funds in aid of native churches for the support of their pastors, requiring as a condition of its aid, that the church shall itself pay a certain portion of the pastor's salary.

The Widows' Aid Society was organized in September 1864, and has now nearly 160 members, with funds to the amount of about Rs. 10,500.

It is only necessary to add a brief summary of the state of the Mission at the end of 1880 :—

Stations 11 : missionaries 12 : single ladies 5 : churches 33 : native ministers ordained 18 : congregations 217, containing 11,372 men, women and children, of whom 3,138 are able to read : church members in good standing 2,591 : village schools 160 : scholars 3,772 : contributions Rs. 4,868.

———o———

MISSIONARIES OF THE SOCIETY.

BARNES, A. Professed Christianity in Oct. 1840. O. Nov. 30, 1871. Ad. *Pasumalai, Madras P.*

BUCKINGHAM, W. A. Professed Christianity July 2, 1854. O. March 13, 1872. Ad. *Pasumalai, Madras P.*

BURNELL, THOMAS SCOTT. B. at Chesterfield, Mass., U. S. A., Feb. 3, 1823. M. Feb. 4, 1847. A. at Madras, Feb. 20, 1849. Was engaged as printer of the Ceylon Mission at Jaffna, from March 6, 1849, to Dec. 1855. Joined the Madura Mission, and was O. at Pasumalai, Sept. 10, 1856. Labored at Tirumangalam till Aug. 1857, and since then at Melur. W. has been chiefly ver.: some editorial work. H. to America from April 19, 1869, to Dec. 19, 1871. Ad. *Melur, Madura, Madras P.*

CHANDLER, JOHN EDDY. B. in Woodstock, Conn, U. S. A, June 12, 1817. E. at Yale Col., and Lane Theol. Seminary, Ohio. O. Sept. 4, 1846. M. before coming to I. Reached Madura in April, 1847. S. Shevaga, Dindigul, Battalagundu, Tirumanagalam, and Madura. W. has been among the heathen, as well as the care of Christian congregations: for several years he was the treasurer of the Mission. H. to America in 1861, R. early in 1864, second H. in 1873. R. in 1876 and was stationed at (Ad.) *Palani, Madura, Madras P.*

CHANDLER, JOHN SCUDDER. B. in Madura, South India, April 12, 1849. Studied for the ministry in New Haven, Conn., U. S A, 1870-73. O, May 18, 1873, as an evangelist, in the same place. M. May 21, 1873. Was engaged in pastoral work before coming to I. A. at Madras, Dec 4, 1873. Appointed to the charge of the Battalagundu Station in Aug. 1874. Engaged in Ver. work. Received the degree of M. A., (Yale Col.,) in July, 1873. L. "The Everlasting Way," and "The Children's Gracious Lord" (Tamil lyrical Tracts, compiled); "The Pastor's Manual" in Tamil (original but in connection with Rev. G T. Washburn): essays and a hand-bill; Tamil Christian Almanac for 1881. Tracts and Almanac obtainable at Madras Religious Tract and Book Depot; "Manual" at Madura. Ad. *Battalagundu, Madura, Madras P.*

CHESTER, EDWARD, M. D. E. at Yale Col., and Union Theol. Sem., New York, where he graduated in 1858. O. by the Fourth Presbytery of New York. Studied medicine at the New York University Medical Col, from the Faculty of which he received his medical degree. Came to I. M.: reached Madura in May, 1859. He was stationed first at Tirupuvanam, but shortly afterwards removed to Dindigul, where he engaged in usual missionary and medical work. Besides the charge of the dispensaries at Dindigul and Madura, has under his care a large class of medical students. Ad., *Dindigul, Madras P.*

CHRISTIAN, D. O. Feb 2, 1860. Ad. *East Karisakulam via Mandapasalai, Madura, Madras P.*

CLARK, ALFRED. B. near Dindigul, Sept. 1, 1834. Attended the Sem. at Pasumalai from 1847-54. Labored as a catechist eighteen years. O March 10, 1872, over the church at Pukilapatti, where he has since labored. Ad. *Dindigul, Madura, Madras P.*

COLTON, JOHN. B. at Tanjore in 1830. Removed to Madura in 1842. Graduated from the seminary at Pasumalai October 2, 1848, and for twenty-seven years was engaged as one of the teachers in the same. O. pastor of the church at Dindigul June 24, 1875. Has been engaged in compiling a Church History for mission use: has translated several books for the C. V. E. S. His "Manual of the Madura District" has passed into the second edition. Has translated or prepared for the use of theological students a number of brief memoirs of eminent men. Ad. *Dindigul, Madras P.*

CORNELIUS, J. Professed Christianity Dec. 20, 1838. O. July 14, 1872. Ad. *Madura, Madras P.*

DEVASAYAGAM, M. O. Jan. 1877. Ad. *Pommanpatti, Madura, Madras P.*

EAMES, M. Professed Christianity in 1846. O Oct. 29, 1870. Ad. *West Karisakulam, via Mandapasalai, Madura, Madras P.*

GUTTERSON, GEORGE. H. B. in Andover, Essex Co., Mass. U. S. A. May 12, 1847. E. Andover Theol. Sem.; graduating in June, 1878, A. March 4, 1879. Ad. *Pasumalai, Madura, Madras P.*

HERRICK, JAMES. B. March 19, 1814. Graduated at Williams Col. Mass., in 1841, and after teaching for a year entered Andover, where he completed his studies in Sept. 1845. O. Oct. 8th of the same year, and M. Nov. 2nd following. Embarked for I. Nov. 12, 1845, and reached Madras in March, and Madura, in April, of the next year. S. at Tirumangalam. Was in charge of the seminary at Pasumalai, from Nov. 1850, to April, 1854. Resumed charge of the Tirumangalam station which he retained till Dec. 20, 1863. H to America in 1864, Rt. in 1867, and was again placed in charge of the seminary, remaining there until 1870, since which time he has been stationed at Tirumangalam. Had the superintendence of the Mandapasalai Station for four years, and of the seminary at Pasumalai for two years, in addition to the labors of his own station. Ad. *Tirumangulam, Madras P.*

HOWLAND, WILLIAM SOUTHWORTH. B. in Jaffna, Ceylon, July 8, 1846. (Parents, missionaries in Jaffna.) Graduated at Amherst Col. U. S. A, 1870: at Andover Theol. Sem., 1873. O. May 8, 1873. M. June 19, 1873. A. Jan. 1, 1874. Appointed to charge of Mandapasalai Station, Jan. 1875. W. itinerating and preaching. Ad. *Mandapasalai, Madura, Madras P.*

. ISAAC, SANTHAPPAN. B. in the Madura District in 1840, his parents embracing Christianity when he was ten years old. Graduated at the Pasumalai Sem. in 1860. Labored as a catechist until 1872, when he took charge of the church at Kambam over which he was O. Dec. 11, 1872. Ad. *Kambam, Madura, Madras P.*

JONES, JOHN P. B. in Denbighshore, Wales, Sept. 4, 1847. Removed to America in 1865. E. at Western Reserve Col. and at Andover Theol. Sem., graduating in 1878. A. Dec. 1878. S. Madura until Sept. 1879; since, in charge of (Ad.) *Manamadura, Madura, Madras P.*

MATHURANAIGAM, S. Professed Christianity April 15, 1864. O. Jan. 25, 1870. Ad. *Pasumalai, Madura, Madras P.*

Noyes, Joseph Thomas. B. in Newburyport, Mass., U. S. A., March 4, 1818. United with the Presbyterian Church in that city in 1834. Pursued his preparatory studies at Phillips Academy. Entering Amherst Col. he graduated in 1845, and after studying theology for three years at Andover, he was ordained by the Newburyport Presbytery. M. and was appointed to the Ceylon Mission of the American Board, where he A. March 10, 1849. Was transferred to the Madura Mission in 1853, and stationed for one year at Tirumangalam, after which he was placed in charge of the Periakulam Station, where, with the exception of a visit to America from 1871 to 1873, he has continued to labor until the present time, his work being in the ver. among the heathen, and in Christian congregations. Ad *Periakulam, Madras P.*

Pilaventhrum, D. Professed Christianity Oct. 29, 1854. O. March 10, 1872. Ad. *Battalagundu, Madras P.*

Rendall, John. B. near Halifax, Nova Scotia, Jan. 21, 1821, but removed at an early age with his father's family to Utica, New York. He remained there until fifteen years of age, when he went to Quincy, Ill., and entered the Mission Institute where he pursued his studies for nine years. M. Aug. 18, 1845: O. by a council at West Boylston, Mass., in Sept. 1845. He joined the Madura Mission April 29, 1846, and was stationed at Dindigul, where he continued for about three years, after which he was appointed secretary and treasurer of the mission, and placed in charge of the station at Madura. In 1867, he visited America. On the passage, Mrs. Rendall died suddenly from apoplexy. Mr. Rendall R. to Madura in 1870, accompanied by one of his daughters. He took charge of the station at Battalagundu until 1873, when he returned to his former station and duties at Madura. W. has been partly among the heathen, and partly the charge of Christian congregations, with the financial business of the Mission. Ad. *Madura, Madras P.*

Rowland, A. G. Professed Christianity Sept. 1, 1842. O. March 1, 1868. Ad. *Madura, Madras P.*

Savarimuttu, A. O. in June 1858: Ad. *Kodikanal, Madura, Madras P.*

Seymour, E. O. in June 1858: Ad. *Kombai, Madura, Madras P.*

Thomas, Muttian. B. 1841, at Paliamputti, Madura. M. Oct. 3, 1860. O. Madura, March 26, 1873. Ad. *Sevalputti, via Muthakalatur, Madura, Madras P.*

Tracy, James Edward. (Son of Rev. W. Tracy.) B. at Pasumalai, I. July 4, 1850. Graduated at Williams Col. Mass., U. S. A. in 1874 (M. A. in 1877), and at Union Theol. Sem. in May 1877. M. Aug. 1, 1877. A. Nov. 8. 1877. Appointed in Jan. 1878 to Tirupuvanam left vacant, three weeks after his arrival, by the death of his father. Ad. *Tirupuvanam, Madura, Madras P.*

Vathamuttu, D. Professed Christianity Feb. 25, 1855. O. March 10, 1872. Ad. *Palani, Madura, Madras P.*

Vathanaiagum, G. Professed Christianity in 1828. O. Sept. 30, 1863. Ad. *Tirumangalam, Madura, Madras P.*

Washburn, George Thomas. B. at Lenox, Mass., U. S. A.

Sept. 5, 1832. Graduated at Williams Col. Mass., in 1855. Studied theology at Andover three years: was licensed to preach in 1858, and O. in March, 1859. After leaving the seminary, spent a year and-a-half in preaching and in charge of the Congregational Church in East Guilford, Vt, Married Sept. 1, 1859. Embarked for I. Jan. 2, 1860. Reached Madura May 1st, of the same year, and was stationed at Battalagundu, where he was engaged in general missionary work among the heathen and in charge of Christian congregations. In June, 1870, was transferred to Pasumalai and took charge of the theological school then vacant. In 1872, was obliged, by severe illness, to visit America: returned in 1874. Has edited and published an edition of the Tamil Lyrics: is the editor of an Anglo-vernacular Christian mission newspaper, the "*Satthiavartamani*" (True News). Ad, *Pasumalai, Madras P.*

WILLIAMS, C. O. Dec. 8. 1858. Ad. *Periakulam, Madura, Madras P.*

RETIRED MISSIONARIES.

James R. Eckard. Originally appointed to the Ceylon Mission. Removed to Madura in Feb. 1835, where he remained until the middle of 1837, when he R. to Ceylon: In 1843 R. to America where he continued to labor as a pastor and College Professor.

Alanson C. Hall. Entered the Mission Oct. 18, 1835, but remained only till Sept. 1836, when he R. to America.

Ferdinand D. W. Ward, D. D. B. in Rochester, N. Y., U. S. A. E. in Union Col. After pursuing the usual course of Theol. study, he offered himself to the Board and joined the company which sailed from Boston Nov. 23, 1836. He reached Madras the 21st of March following, and after remaining there for several months proceeded to Madura, Oct. 9, 1837. He continued in connection with the Madura Mission until early in 1843, when he was transferred to Madras where he continued to labor until 1846, when he R. to America. While in Madura he prepared with the aid of Mr. Lawrence a work on the "Parables of Christ," which was subsequently published. He also prepared and published in Madras, some smaller books which are now out of print. Since his return to America, Dr. Ward has been engaged in teaching and pastoral labor, and during the war of the Rebellion he served for some time as a chaplain in the northern army.

Henry Cherry. Studied theology at Lane Seminary, Ohio, U. S. A. Reached Madras March 21, 1837, but instead of going to Madura sailed for Ceylon. R. to the continent and was stationed at Shevaganga, and afterwards at Madura. In 1850 R. to America and became disconnected with the Board.

Edward Cope. A. Madura May 10, 1837, and was stationed for a short time at Shevaganga. As the health of both Mr. and Mrs. Cope was feeble, they took a change to Ceylon in Jan. 1840, where they remained until 1849 when they R. to America.

Edward Webb. B. in Yarmouth, England. At a very early age

he went as a missionary to Australia. After a short residence there, he went to America and entered the Andover Sem. where he pursued the usual course of theol. study. After his ordination he was married and sailed for India in company with Messrs. Herrick, Rendall and others, and reached Madura, April 29, 1846. S. Shevaganga and Dindigul. While at Dindigul he compiled a volume of Tamil Lyrics, which has been republished with some additions and is in use by Tamil Christians throughout Southern India. He also edited the "Tamil Repository" which contained much valuable matter on natural science, ecclesiastical history, etc. He revisited America for his health, which failed again soon after his return; and he was obliged to leave the mission field and return to America.

George W. McMillan. Joined the Mission in July, 1846, and remained until Nov. 1854, when he R. to America. S. Dindigul. He published a small work in Tamil, on "The Doctrines of Romanism," which is now out of print.

George Ford. Was a graduate of Harvard University. U. S. A., and studied theology at Andover. Reached Madura in April, 1847, and was stationed at Periakulam and afterwards at Tirumangalam, where he remained until 1853, when he R. to America. Labored for some time as pastor in Falmouth, Mass., and afterwards as missionary among the Indians in the western part of New York.

Charles Little. B. in Colombia, Conn., U. S. A. Graduated at Yale College, and also pursued the usual Theol. course: reached Madura in May, 1848. In 1854, he visited America, and R. to the Mission the same year. S. Tirumangalam and then Tirupuvanam where he continued until sickness compelled his return to his native land in 1859. He has since been engaged in various pastoral and editorial labors.

Charles T. White. Reached Madura, April 4, 1857, and was stationed at Palani. On account of Mrs. White's feeble health, he R. with his family to America in 1869 and left the service of the Board.

Hervey C Hazen. Joined the Mission in Jan. 1868. He was stationed at Palani and entered with zeal upon the study of the language, but on account of the severe illness of Mrs. Hazen he was reluctantly compelled to leave I. which he did in the year following his arrival.

Henry K. Palmer, M D. At the outbreak of the recent war in America joined the army, remained in it till the close of the war, at first as a private soldier, then as a medical assistant, and afterwards as assistant surgeon. When his health was sufficiently restored after the war, he offered his services to the American Board, and was sent out, in 1869, as physician to the Madura Mission. His health proved unequal to the stress laid upon it, and after trying various changes in the country, he left I. in 1874, hoping to recover his strength by a visit to America.

DECEASED MISSIONARIES.

Daniel Poor, D. D. B. in Danvers, Mass., U. S. A., June 27, 1789. He was hopefully converted when he was ten years of age, and soon after joined the church. From a very early period he was deeply interested in the cause of missions. After pursuing his preparatory studies in Philip's Academy, Andover, he entered Dartmouth Col. He pursued his theol. studies in the Sem. at Andover and on the 21st of June, 1815, was O. with several others in the Presbyterian Church in Newburyport. On the 23rd of October he sailed from Newburyport for Ceylon in company with Messrs. Richards, Warren, Bardwell and Meigs, where they arrived March 22, 1816. He commenced his labor in Tillipally and remained there until July, 1823, when he took charge of the Mission Seminary at Batticotta, where he continued to labor until his removal early in 1836, to Madura, to assist in the new mission there. He became deeply interested in the education of the people, and established a large number of schools in the city of Madura, which he visited daily, always preaching to the crowds which gathered around him on these occasions. In 1841, he returned to Jaffna and re-occupied his first station at Tillipally. D. of cholera at Manippay, February 3, 1855.

Henry R. Hoisington. Became connected with the Ceylon Mission Oct. 28, 1833. In July of the following year, in connection with the Rev. William Todd, he commenced the Madura Mission, where he remained until Feb., 1835, when he returned to Jaffna. On the removal of Dr. Poor to Madura, he became Principal of the Mission Seminary at Batticotta which he conducted with much efficiency. He published several valuable works, one of them on Hindu astronomy. Some translations of Hindu philosophical works made by him, were published in the Journal of the American Oriental Society. His health failing, he R. to America in 1850, and engaged in pastoral labor in different places. He D. in the work, having been stricken down in the pulpit by an attack of paralysis from which he did not recover. He was a graduate of Williams Col. and of Andover Sem., Mass.

William Todd. Joined the Ceylon Mission at the same time with Mr. Hoisington, and with him commenced the Madura Mission, July 31, 1834. After laboring for some time in the city of Madura, he commenced a station at Shevaganga. His labors were often interrupted by ill health and early in 1839, he R. to America, where he labored for many years as a faithful home missionary. He retained to the last his deep interest in the foreign mission work, and died in Madura, Kansas, having given to the new town where he labored, the name of his much loved mission field.

John Jay Lawrence. A graduate of Union Col. and Andover Theol. Sem. He was appointed to the Jaffna Mission and became connected with the Madura Mission, October 18, 1835.
He was subsequently stationed at Dindigul, where he labored until 1847. D. at Tranquebar, on his way to America.

Robert O. Dwight. B. in Northampton, Mass., U. S. A., Oct. 31, 1802. In his early years he was engaged in mercantile business in Boston, and subsequently in New York. On giving up his business in New York, he determined to carry out a long cherished plan of studying for the gospel ministry. He studied theology in Andover. He sailed from New

Castle, Delaware, Nov. 1835, in company with the Rev. Dr. Winslow, and also several missionaries for Northern India. He arrived in Madura, April 22, 1836, and was shortly afterwards stationed at Dindigul. On Dr. Poor's return to Jaffna, Mr Dwight removed to Madura, where he labored diligently until his death (by cholera) Jan. 8, 1844

John Steele, M. D. B. Aug. 19, 1804, at Hebron, N. Y., U. S. A. At the age of 20, he united with the church in his native place. After studying medicine in Hebron, he received the degree of M. D., from the Vermont Academy of Medicine After practicing in Hebron for several years, his failing health compelled him to relinquish his practice and he engaged in business as a druggist in Auburn. In Feb 1836, his health having been much improved, he offered himself to the Board as a missionary physician and sailed from Boston for Madras, Nov. 23, 1836. Owing to fatigue and exposure on the journey to Madras, he took a severe cold which finally assumed the form of pulmonary consumption. In compliance with medical advice he went to Jaffna, Ceylon, and from thence to Singapore, deriving some benefit from the voyage, which however, was not permanent. He was able to attend to his duties, to the families of the Mission, and also to his practice among the natives, but in March, 1842, his health began to fail rapidly until Oct. 6th, when he peacefully entered into rest.

William Tracy, D.D. B. in Norwich, Conn., U. S. A., June 2, 1807. Pursued his studies in Williams Col. Mass., and in the Theol. Sem at Andover, Mass, and Princeton N. J. O. at Philadelphia, and sailed from Boston Nov. 23, 1836, A. in Madras March 21, 1837. Remained in Madras until Sept and reached Madura on the 9th of Oct. of the same year. Commenced a new station at Tirumangalam in connection with the Rev. Mr. Muzzy. Removed with the Mission Sem to Pasumalai Sept. 1, 1845, and continued in charge of the Sem. until 1867, with the exception of three years, spent on a visit to America from which he R. in 1854. Revisited America in 1867, and R. in 1870, taking charge of the station at Tirupuvanam. For twenty-five years was engaged in educational work as principal of the Sem., which was established for the education of native pastors, catechists and schoolmasters: was engaged for eight years on the committee for the revision of the Tamil Bible. Prepared and published a work on Theology (mostly a translation from an American work) which is still used in the instruction of the Mission helpers. Received the honorary degree of D. D. from Western Univ., Pittsburg, Pa. in 1870. D. at Tirupuvanam, Nov. 28, 1877.

Clarendon F. Muzzy A graduate of Middlebury Col., Vt., and of Andover Sem. He joined the Mission in Madura May 10, 1837, and was stationed at Tirumangalam. He was subseqently stationed at Tirupuvanam and Madura, and afterwards commenced a new station at Melur. Partly on account of his own health, and partly to provide for his children, he left the Mission and R. to America in 1857. Afterwards labored for several years as missionary among the small remnant of Mohegan Indians near Norwich, Conn D. at Amherst, U. S. A, Jan. 4, 1878.

Nathaniel M. Crane Sailed from Boston, Nov 23, 1836: reached Madura May 18, 1837 He commenced a new mission at Tirupuvanam, where he remained several years, when he was transferred to Madura. R. to America as the only means of saving his life. D. in America after several years of labor.

Alfred North, Esq. Came to Singapore as a printer, and when that field was relinquished by the Board, he proceeded to Madura as an assistant missionary, Jan. 1, 1844. Remained in the Mission until 1847, when he returned to America. Afterwards studied Theology at Auburn, N.Y.. and being O , labored as a home missionary until his death.

Horace S. Taylor. E. at the Western Reserve Col. Hudson, Ohio. O. and appointed to the Madura Mission, which he reached Oct. 10, 1844. Was at first stationed at Tirupuvanam. In 1850, he commenced a new station at Mandapasalai, where, with the exception of a visit to America, he continued to labor until his death, which occurred Feb. 3, 1871.

Charles S. Shelton, M.D. Received his appointment as physician to the Madura Mission, which he joined March 23, 1849. He was engaged in good practice as a physician, but when the want of a doctor at Madura was brought to his notice he offered his services to the American Board. Before leaving for India he was licensed to preach the gospel. In 1856, owing to continued ill health, he returned to America and resigned the service of the Board. D in Jersey City, U. S. A , May 21, 1879.

Nathan L Lord, M. D. Obtained his collegiate education at the Western Reserve Col. Hudson, Ohio, U. S A , of which Inst. he afterwards became the very successful agent. He joined the Ceylon Mission in 1853, and removed to Madura in 1863 where he labored until March 1867. when owing to ill health he R to America and soon afterwards D.

David Coit Scudder. B. in Boston, Mass , U. S. A He graduated at Williams Col. and at Andover. Reached Madura in July, 1861, and was stationed at Periakulam. Returning from a visit to one of his villages, he attempted to swim a stream, swollen by a sudden flood, and was drowned Nov. 19, 1862. His body was recovered after several days' search and was buried at Kodikanal on the Palani Mountains.

Thornton B. Penfield. E. at Oberlin Sem and went to the island of Jamaica as a missionary to the freed blacks. He R. to America on account of the illness of his wife, who shortly afterwards died. He was subsequently married and with his wife reached the Madura Mission in May, 1867. He was stationed, first at Tirupuvanam, and afterwards at Periakulam. D. at Pasumalai, Aug 19, 1871.

William Banfield Capron. B April 14, 1824, at Uxbridge, Mass. U. S. A. O Sept. 1856 M. Oct. 1, 1856. A. at Madras, March, 7, 1857. S. Manamadura, (residing in Madura four years and Tirupuvanam three years): R. to America May, 1872 to Dec. 1874. D. Oct. 6, 1875.

Marshall R. Peck. A. in Madras Dec. 6, 1875. Left I. April 27, 1876 : D. at Brookfield, Vt., U. S. A., Aug. 7, 1876.

———o———

CHAPTER V.

MISSIONARY SOCIETIES OF THE CHURCH OF ENGLAND.

BEFORE proceeding with this chapter it is but proper to remark that the Church of England, through her chaplains and other representatives besides regularly constituted missionaries, has rendered very great assistance to the cause of Protestant Missions in India. The chaplains of Calcutta at the close of the last and beginning of the present century "strove laboriously and long to establish a mission, not for Calcutta merely, but also for the whole of Bengal." Those of Madras and other stations in South India were equally zealous. Bishop Heber delighted in calling himself "the chief missionary in India." As the author of "*Protestant Missions in India*" very truly and gratefully re arks, "All the Bishops of Calcutta, without a single exception, though some more than others, have exhibited their interest in this work; and while preferring, as was natural, their own ecclesiastical organizations, have, in a true spirit of catholicity, extended the right hand of Christian fellowship to missionaries of all denominations. They have been missionary Bishops; and, in their day and generation, have been a spiritual power in the land. Who is there who does not thank God for the earnestness of Middleton, the devoutness of Heber, the practical sense and shrewdness of Wilson, the sweetness and large-heartedness of Cotton? Who is there who does not thank God likewise for the calm wisdom of David Brown, the high enthusiasm of Buchanan, the fiery zeal of Henry Martyn, the unwearied energy of Thomason, the love and labor of Corrie and of Dealtry, the sagacity and self-sacrifice of Pratt, who while discharging faithfully their important duties as chaplains, devoted themselves assiduously to the evangelisation of the heathen around them? May successors to such apostolic men ever be found in the English Church in India!"

The name of Henry Martyn should not be passed without some further mention. This devoted servant of God arrived in India in 1806. He at once engaged in studying

Persian, Sanskrit, and other languages, and in translating the New Testament into Hindustani. His first station was Dinapore, where he opened schools and continued his translations. Completing the Hindustani translation in 1807, he began tho Persian, and, in 1809, the Arabic. From Dinapore he proceeded to Cawnpore, but in 1810 he returned to Calcutta and on account of failing health was obliged to leave India. This he did in January, 1811, bound for Shiraz, where he remodelled and completed his Persian Testament. He thence proceeded to Tebriz near the Caspian Sea. Shattered in health he determined to return to England by way of Constantinople, and commenced his long journey. He travelled about 600 miles to Tohat, 250 miles from Constantinople. Unable to go further he died there on the 16th of October, 1812, at the early age of thirty-one.

I. CHURCH MISSIONARY SOCIETY.

This Society was instituted in London in the month of April, 1799. It was originally designed to operate "in Africa and the East," but has extended its operations beyond these bounds. In 1807 the Society made a grant of £150 for missionary work in India and sent the same to the Rev. Messrs. Brown and Buchanan and Mr. Udny, of Calcutta where it was appropriated to the translation of the Scriptures into the Eastern languages. Grants were also made in behalf of the schools in Tranquebar. A Corresponding Committee of the persons just named was formed in Calcutta in 1814. From these beginnings a great work has grown up, which may be best sketched by considering each Presidency separately.

I. Madras Presidency.—In 1814, the Society with the consent and approval of the College at Copenhagen sent out two missionaries to Tranquebar, the Rev. Messrs. Schnarre and Rhenius. Their stay in Tranquebar was short as the Society had decided to establish a mission of its own in Madras, whither they proceeded in January, 1815. Schnarre soon after returned to the languishing mission at Tranquebar: Rhenius continued to labor at Madras until 1820, when he was transferred. Other missionaries had arrived in the interval and the progress of the mission in Madras has been steady and solid. Meanwhile the Danish mission in Tinnevelly, having been virtually abandoned on account of the scarcity of laborers, was transferred in 1817 to the Church Society, mainly through the efforts of the Rev. Mr. Hough. This energetic chaplain entered heartily into missionary work; he purchased land and erected buildings at Palamcottah, a station which afterwards became the head-quarters of the Society's Tinnevelly missions. Here Rhenius and the Rev. Mr. Schmid began laboring in 1820, with what measure of success may be seen from the fact that by 1825 there had been an increase of 4,300 converts. During the next five years there was a proportionate increase, the total number of Christians in 1830 being 7,500. About 1830, the province was divided into ten missionary districts and the work was energetically carried forward. In 1835, the Christian community consisted of 11,000 persons. In the same year on account of ecclesiastical difficulties Rhenius and others separated from the Society and a sad controversy followed. Rhenius organized a new Society; but died in 1838, and in 1839-40, the separated congregations re-united with the Society. By this time the number of Christians had increased to 17,000.

During the past twenty years, and especially in the past decade the progress in Tinnevelly has been most encouraging. In 1878, there were 58 Native clergymen compared with 9 in 1858, and 53,536 Native Christians, compared with 28,151. There was a large ingathering during the recent Famine, 1877-78.

On the 11th of March, 1877, the Rev. E. Sargent, a missionary of long experience, was consecrated as Suffragan Bishop or coadjutor to the Bishop of Madras.

In the year 1816, the Society sent out the Rev. Messrs. Bailey, Baker and Fenn, with the object of imparting instruction to the Christians of the Syrian faith in Travancore. These missionaries carried out the wishes of the Society and formed a kind of union between their own and the Syrian Church. The scheme worked well and these happy relations continued between the two bodies from 1816 to 1838, when the union was dissolved by the Syrians. Several new stations were at once opened by the Church missionaries; at Cottayam, Mavelikara; and in 1841, at Trichoor. Gradually other stations were formed both in Travancore and Cochin. The missions thus established have been very successful.

In 1873 a notable revival occurred in which thousands of persons were influenced for good. In the years 1858-78 the Native Christian community increased from 5,899 to 17,564. On the 25th of July 1879, the Rev. J. M. Speechly, who had been many years in charge at Cottayam, was consecrated Bishop of Travancore and Cochin.

In 1841, mission work was begun at Masulipatam, in the Kistna district, to the north of the Kistna river. In 1854, Ellore was occupied, in 1858 Bezwada, and in 1859, Dummagudem. Since 1861, there has been a great increase of converts in this field.

II. Bengal Presidency.—In the year 1815 the Corresponding Committee established a school at Kidderpore in the suburbs of Calcutta and another at Dum Dum. The first missionaries sent by the Society to Bengal were the Rev. Messrs. Greenwood and Schroeter, who reached Calcutta in June, 1816. The former engaged in educational work, and the latter proceeded to a station bordering on Thibet where he labored four years and died. Early attention was given to schools in Calcutta, and especially among girls. In 1819 a printing-press was sent out from England to the mission, and in 1822 Mr. Browne arrived as printer, but died soon after. The press did effectual work, until 1843, when it was sold. In September, 1823, a Church Missionary Association was formed which has labored chiefly in establishing schools and erecting chapels. In 1824, the "Ladies" Society for Native Female Education" was established with the patronage of the Marchioness of Hastings. In 1825, Abdul Masih, who had been baptized in 1811, was ordained by Bishop Heber, as was also the Rev. Mr. Bowley afterwards so zealous in preaching. The death of Bishop Heber, in 1827, was an afflictive event to the Calcutta mission. For several years it had comparatively few laborers, but of late years this has been bettered. In 1865, the Cathedral Mission College was established.

In 1816, educational work was begun at Burdwan, but the first missionary did not arrive until 1820. In 1831, the Rev. J. J. Weitbrecht was appointed to the station where he labored many years. A Christian colony was early founded and schools established. Orphanages were also formed.

In 1817, the Rev. D. Corrie was appointed chaplain at Benares, and in the following year secured the transfer to the Society of the Jay Narain School, which afterwards developed into a large and flourishing college, called after the name of its founder, a wealthy Rajah. The first missionary, the Rev. T. Morris, arrived in 1821. The work has since been steadily carried forward by the Rev. Messrs. Smith, Leupolt and others. The mission has at present extensive schools, a normal institution, two Christian villages and two native churches.

Mr. Corrie, who was stationed at Chunar in 1807, took an active interest in missionary efforts and presented the Church Society with premises in that station. Mr. Bowley removed to the place in 1815, and continued to labor there both before and after his ordination. In 1819, Mr. Greenwood arrived from Calcutta, being the first missionary appointed to the station.

In 1823, work was opened in Goruckpore. This contains at present an orphanage, a flourishing high-school and a large Christian village. Calna was occupied in 1825, but was made over to the Church of Scotland in 1842.

In 1816, the Rev. H. Fisher while chaplain at Meerut baptized the celebrated Anand Masih who afterwards labored effectually both at this place and at Delhi. In 1828, the first missionary, the Rev. Mr. Richards, was appointed here.

In 1831, the Society formed a mission at Krishnaghar: the first missionary, the Rev. Mr. Deer, arrived the following year. About 1838, a remarkable movement towards Christianity took place among the natives, and within the course of a few months about 3,000 persons embraced Christianity. In the year 1831, work was also begun at Azimgurh.

As early as 1812, missionary operations were begun at Agra by Mr. Corrie. He was assisted by Abdul Masih, who continued in charge of the work after his departure to England. In 1839, the Rev. T. Hoernle, the first missionary, arrived. A Native Church has been raised up and a well known institution of learning, St. John's College, established. In 1839, immediately after the great famine in North India, a large Orphanage was founded at Secundra near Agra. A printing-press was established in connection with the Orphanage in 1840: and in 1842 a church was built at Secundra: The following stations were occupied in the order mentioned: Bhagalpur, 1850; Jubbulpore 1854: Muttra, 1856: Lucknow, 1858: Allahabad, 1859: Fyzabad, 1862: Aligarh, 1864.

In the year 1843, the Society commenced a mission station at Kotgarh in the Himalayas. Schools were established and the gospel preached. Kangra, north-west of Kotgarh, was occupied in 1854. Other stations in the Punjab were taken up about this time: Amritsar, in 1852: Peshawar and Mooltan, 1855: Dera Ismail Khan, 1861: Srinagar in Cashmere (where a most interesting medical mission has been carried on by the lamented Dr. Elmslie, and his successors Drs. Maxwell and Downes), in 1863; and Lahore in 1867.

In 1862, the Society began its missions among the Santals being the first to enter this interesting field. It has numerous stations which have many schools connected with them, and also a training institution. Taljhari is the headquarters of the Mission.

III. Bombay Presidency.—The Society commenced its operations in the city of Bombay in 1818, when a Corresponding Committee was formed. The first missionary, the Rev. R. Kenney, was sent out in 1820. He organized schools, and preached in the city. An educational institution, the Robert Money School, is located here. Nasik was occupied as a mission station in 1832. For many years, but slow progress was made, but, after the establishment of an industrial school, affairs assumed a better shape, and converts were multiplied. Junir was taken up as a field of labor in 1846; and Mulligaum in 1848. Mission work was begun at Kurrachee in Scindh in 1850, and at Hyderabad in 1857; at Aurungabad in 1860, and at Buldana in 1868.

Including missionaries at home, the Society has at present in connection with its missions in India, 210 missionaries. The following statistics for 1880 show the increase since 1871:—

European missionaries,	...	103	increase	1
Native ordained agents,	...	107	do.	40
Native Christians,	...	75,677	do.	6,663
Communicants,	...	17,294	do.	4,188

MISSIONARY BISHOP.

The Right Rev. Bishop (Edward) Sargent, D.D. Educated at Islington College. Arrived in India in 1842. Labored many years in Tinnevelly, specially at Palamcottah. Author of " A Commentary on the Gospels and Acts," Tamil translation of Paley's Evidences, Elements of Natural Philosophy, Ancient History of Egypt, etc. March 11, 1877, consecrated, at Calcutta, Suffragan Bishop, Co-adjutor to the Bishop of Madras.

MISSIONARIES OF THE SOCIETY.

ABEL, FREDERICK. B. at Agra about 1825. O. in Jan. 1866 : S. Meerut, Goruckpore, Fyzabad. M. Dec. 4, 1846. Ad. *Fyzabad, Oudh.*

ABRAHAM, D. O. 1876. Ad. *Madathupatti, Madras P.*

ABRAHAM, VEDAMUTTU. B. Nov. 1842. O. D. Jan. 3, 1876, O. P. Jan. 11, 1880. Ad. *Santhapuram, Madras P.*

ALEXANDER, FREDERICK WILLIAM NASSAU. B. at Dublin, Aug. 20, 1832. O. D 1855, O. P. 1857. M. in May, 1857. A. in Sept. 1857. S. Ellore : W. ver. as pastor and evangelist. One of the delegates for translating the book of Common Prayer into Telugu. H. to Eng. from Sept. 1869, to March, 1872 ; to Melbourne from July to Nov. 1875. Ad. *Ellore, Madras P.*

ALI, JANI. B. Hydrabad, Deccan. O. D. May 27, 1877. O. P. Dec. 22, 1878. E. at Noble High School, Masulipatam and Christ Col. Cambridge (B.A.) Rt. from Eng. Nov. 29, 1877. Ad. *Girgaum, Bombay.*

ARDEN, ALBERT HENRY. B. May 5, 1841, at Longcrofts Hall, Staffordshire. M. A. Christ Col. Camb. O. D. by Bp. of Lichfield, 1864 ; O. P. by Bp. of Madras, 1866. A. 1864. S. missionary in Telugu country, 1864-73 ; vicar of All Saints Sudbury, Suffolk, 1873-75 ; incumbent of Newhall, Derbyshire, 1875-77 ; Sec. C. M. S. Madras, since 1878. L. " A Progressive Telugu Grammar," Companion " Telugu Reader :" Trubner and Co. Lon., and S. P. C. K. Depot, Madras. Ad. *Egmore, Madras,*

ARULANANTHAM, D. B, in 1831 : O. 1876. Ad. *Piragasapuram. Madras P.*

ARUMANAYAGAM, G. B. 1824 : O. 1876 : Ad. *Sathianagaram, Madras P.*

ARUMANAYAGAM, P. B. 1822 : O. 1859 : Ad. *Asirvathapuram, Madras P.*

ASIRVADHAM, ADITHASAN. B. March 15, 1835 in Tinnevelly : O. D. Oct. 11, 1874, O. P. Jan. 31, 1876 : W. Native Pastor : Ad. *Palamcottah, Tinnevelly, Madras P.*

ASIRVADHAM, S. Ad. *Parapadi, Madras P.*

BAILEY, ARTHUR. A. 1877. Ad. *Dera Ismail Khan, Punjab.*

BAKER, WILLIAM GEORGE. A. 1873. Ad. *Bezwara, Madras P.*

BALL, A. E. A. 1880. Ad. *Kurrachee, Scindh.*

BALWANT, SHANKAR. Ad. *Nasik, Bombay P.*

BAMBORD, J. Ad. 1880. Ad. *Amritsar, Punjab.*

BAMBRIDGE, JOHN. A. 1877. Ad *Kurrachee, Scindh.*

BAPAJI, APAJI. Ad. *Bombay.*

BATEMAN, ROWLAND. A. 1868. Ad. *Kangra, Punjab.*

BAUMANN, AUGUSTUS WILLIAM. O 1876. Ad. *Godda, Bengal.*

BAUMANN, CHARLES A. 1868. Ad. *Calcutta.*

BELL, R. J. Ad. *Calcutta.*

BISHOP, JOHN HUNTER. B at Ostent, Belgium, March 23, 1844 : O. in June, 1867 : A. Dec. 1867. M. Dec. 1868. (Ad). *Trichur, Travancore.*

BISWAS, MATTHEW SARTHOK. B. in 1835 at Gongra, Nadiya. O. D. in 1872, O. P. in 1879 : W. Native Pastor : Ad. *Ratanpur, Nadiya, Bengal.*

BISWAS, MOLAM. Ad. *Kistapur, Bengal.*

BLAICH, J. A. 1877. Ad. *Hiranpur, Bengal.*

BLACKETT, W. B. B in Eng. O. D 1860, O. P. 1861. A. Nov. 1876. S. Principal, Cathedral Divinity Col. C. M. S.—Carried on C. M. S. Theol. class at Krishnaghar 1878-79, and at Christ Church, Calcutta, 1880. L. *Sunday Magazine* Articles ; Pamphlets, &c. Ad. *Calcutta.*

BLUMHARDT, EDWARD KEENE. A. 1871. Ad. *Burdwan, Bengal.*

BOSE, RAJ KISTO. Ad. *Thakurpukar, Bengal.*

BOWER, FREDERICK. A. 1867. Ad. *Mavelikara, Travancore.*

BRIGGS, WILLIAM. B. Bingley, Yorkshire, Eng. Nov. 16, 1837. A. Jan. 4, 1858. W. Educational. S. Multan. L. Author of several Urdu tracts, " Muhabbat náma ;" " Ek Tamsil" &c. Ad. *Multan, Punjab.*

BROWN JAMES. B. at Thorndon, Suffolk, Feb. 2, 1844. Entered Islington Col. in 1866. A 1868. O. D. in Dec. 1870 ; O.P. in Jan. 1873. Ad. *Taljhari, Bengal.*

CAIN, JOHN. A. in 1869. S. Dumagudiem, H. to Eng in May, 1880.

CALEY, JOHN. A. in 1871. *Now in Europe.*

CARSS, THOMAS C. A. 1862. Principal Robert Money School. Ad. *Bombay.*

CHAMPION, ELIAS. A. in 1858. Ad. *Jubbulpur, C. P.*

CHANDY, JACOB. B. Nov. 4, 1852. O. D. Nov. 21, 1875, O. P. March 9, 1879. W. Native Pastor. Ad. *Trichur, Travancore.*

CLARK, ROBERT. M A. Trinity Col. Cam. O. D. 1850, O. P. 1851, A. 1851. S. Amritsar, 1851, Peshawar, 1854. H. 1857, Peshawar, 1858, Cashmire, 1864, Amritsar, 1864. H. 1869. Lahore, 1870, Amritsar, 1872, H. 1876. Amritsar, 1876. H. 1879. Amritsar, 1880. Sec. Punjab Bible and Rel. Book Socy., 1871 : Sec. Cor. Com. C. M. S. Punjab and Sindh, 1878 : Sec. Ch. of Eng. Zenana Missy. Socy. 1880. L. Translated St John's Gospel (Pushtu) ; joint editor of Commentaries on St. Matthew and the Acts of the Apostles, with the Rev. Imad-ud-Din (Persian Urdu) : Rel. Book Socy. Lahore. Ad. *Amritsar, Punjab.*

CLARK, WILLIAM. A. 1848. Ad. *Allepie, Travancore.*

CLAYTON, WALTER. A. in 1869. S. Masulipatam. *Now in Europe.*

Clifford, Alfred. B. in Eng. Nov. 12, 1819. O. D. 1872. O. P. 1874. A. Nov. 1874. S. 1874-78, Calcutta, 1879-80, Krishnaghar, 1880 to present, Calcutta and Agarpara, H. Dec. 1878 to Oct. 1879. Ad. Cornwallis Square, *Calcutta.*

Cole, Frederic Thomas. B. at Dedham, Essex, in 1848. O. by the Bishop of Lon. Dec. 21, 1871. A. April, 1872. S. St. John's Col. Agra: Santhalistan. M. in 1875. Has prepared a few school books in Santhali. Ad. *Taljhari, Bengal.*

Cooksley, Manuel Henry. B. May 26, 1845. O. D. Sept. 22, 1878, O. P. Jan. 11, 1880. W. Native Pastor L. Four original tracts in Tamil. Ad. *Mengnanapuram, Madras P.*

Curean, George. O. 1856. Ad. *Thalawady, Travancore.*

Curean, P. Matthew. O. 1872. Ad. *Trichoor, Travancore..*

Dauble, Carl Gustav. A. 1857. S. Lucknow. *Now in Europe.*

David, Joseph. B. July 18, 1834 in Tinnevelly. O. D. Jan. 31, 1869, O. P. Dec. 24, 1872: W. Native Pastor: L. Translated into Tamil, "The Angel's Message," and "Tales for young Protestants;" has written several tracts. Ad. *Mengnanapuram, Tinnevelly, Madras P.*

David, P. B. 1840. O. 1876. Ad. *Dohnavur, Madras P.*

Davis, Brocklesby. B. at Homerton, Hackney, Lon. E. at Cambridge: B. A. in 1849: M. A. 1852. O. D. by the Bishop of Ely in 1850, O. P. 1854. A. in Nov. 1859. S. Benares, 1859-61, Allahabad, 1861-78, since, Benares. W. Ver. preaching; itinerating: college work at St. Peter's Col.,Allahabad; from 1861-70, Secretary N. I. T. Society. H. two-and-half years from 1870. L. (1) *Aqaid i Faraiz* (translation of Faith and Duty of Christians), in Urdu: obtainable at the North India branch of the C. K. S., Banda. (2) Almanac in Hindee: 1868; North India Tract Society. (3) A Sermon preached at the Jubbulpur Annual Conference: C. M. S. Allahabad. (4) Reportsof North India Tract Society, 1861-70. M. Ad. *Benares.*

Deimler, Johann Gottfried. B. Windstein, Germany, April 2, 1826. O. D. June 11, 1854, O. P. May 1, 1856. A. Feb. 9, 1855. Transferred to East Africa in 1856. Re-appointed to I. in 1858. S. Bombay. H. from 1857-58, 1868-70, 1878-80: L. Translation of "The Heart-book," *Aina e Dil,* (Book Society, Punjab), and "The Judgment" *Insaf ul Qiyamat,* (Tract Society Bombay). Ad. *Girgaum, Bombay.*

Devaprasadham, D. O. 1865. Ad. *Strivilliputhur, Madras P.*

Devaprasadham, Muttuswami. B. Palamcottah in 1820: O. D. Feb. 1851. O. P. Dec. 18, 1859. W. Native Pastor. Ad. *Pannikalam, Madras P.*

Devaprasatham, Muttuswami. B. March 10, 1845 in Tinnevelly: O. D Sept. 22, 1878: Since labored at (Ad.) *Ambasamadram, Madras P.*

Downes, Edmund. B. April 11, 1843, at Horton, Northamptonshire, Eng. Not O. A. Nov. 1866 as Lieut. in Royal Artillery. Joined the Rev. W. Ferguson's Mission at Chumba, Nov. 15, 1869: joined C. M. S. in Jan. 1872. S. Madhopore, Punjab: in Oct. 1872, Peshawar. H. to Eng. in Aug. 1863. While at Home studied medicine at

St. Mary's Hospital, Lon. (L. R. C. P. Lon. in Oct. 1876, M. D. of Brussells in Nov. 1876). Rt. Feb. 28, 1877. Has since labored as Medical missionary in Kashmir, Ad. *Kashmir.*

DOXEY, JOHN SMITH. B. Manchester, Lancashire, Nov. 1839. E. Manchester Grammar School and Dorcester Col. Oxford. O. Manchester, June, 1865. Curate of Milnrow 1865-70, and Minister, Habeyhamlawes 1870-75. A. 1875. Ad. *Multan, Punjab.*

DROESE, ERNEST. A. in 1842, labored in connection with the Berlin Society at Ghazipur until 1849, when he joined the C. M. S. In 1850 was appointed to Bhagalpur, where he has since labored. Ad. *Bhagalpur, Bengal.*

DURRANT, GEORGE. B. A. in 1876. Has since labored at (Ad) *Lucknow, Oudh.*

DYSON, SAMUEL. A. 1855. S. Calcutta. *Now in Europe.*

EALES, HENRY WILLIAM. A. 1878. Ad. *Dumagudiem, Madras P.*

ELLIOTT, ROBERT. A. 1878. Ad. *Taljhari. Bengal.*

ELLWOOD, JOHN PRICE. A. 1871, S Lucknow. *Now in Europe.*

ERHARDT, JAMES. B. at Boennigheim, Wurtemberg, Germany. O 1848. Missionary to East Africa from 1849 to 1856. M. 1859 A. 1857. S. Bhagulpur, 1857-60: Benares, 1861-64 : Lucknow, 1864-67 : H. 1868-69. At Secundra (Agra) since 1870. W. has been both Engl. and ver. L (1), *A Vocabulary of the Masai Language.* (Central Africa) : (2), *Urdu Songs and Hymns* ; translations from Engl and German. Ad. *Secundra Orphanage, Agra.*

FISHER, A. T. A. 1878. Ad. *Amritsar, Punjab.*

GHOSE, BHOLA NATH. Ad. *Narowal, Punjab.*

GMELIN, FRIEDRICH. B. Dec. 23, 1837, at Heidelberg, Germany. Called to mission work, July, 1859. A. Feb. 13. 1860 M. Jan. 2. 1864. O March 5, 1871. S. 1860, Tutor in the C. M. S Training Inst. Santipore ; 1862, Inspector of Mission schools, Ruttanpur : 1863, Supt. Amherst St. Engl. School, Calcutta : 1864. Principal of C. M. S. Training Inst. and Inspector of schools, Krishnaghar. L. Original works : (1) "*The First Instructor in Arithmetic, A Manual for Teachers.*" Parts I and II. (2) "*Introduction to Bengali Composition*" Calcutta School Book Society's Depot Partly translated and partly original : "*Manual of Education for the use of Vernacular Teachers.*" Calcutta, School Book Society's Depot. Compilation : "*First steps to the Church Catechism ; and the Church Catechism with Scripture Proofs.*"—out of print. All these works are in Bengali. H. 1868-71 and in 1880.

GNANAMUTTU, A O 1869. Ad. *Nalumavadi, Madras P.*

GNANAMUTTU, DEVASAGAYAM. B in Tinnevelly, 1818 : O. April 4, 1847 : S. Black Town, Madras, 1847-55, Chindatripet, 1856, Dohnavur, 1857, since, Nelloor District, Tinnevelly. L. Translated into Tamil "Under the Microscope," and "Thornton's Commentary," and wrote in Tamil—"God's Portion :" Ad. *Koviluttu,* Palamcottah, *Madras P.*

GNANAMUTTU, SAMUEL. B. in Tinnevelly, 1822 : O D Jan 8, 1866, O.P. Jan. 31, 1869. W. Native Pastor. Ad. *Anukragapuram, Madras P.*

GNANAMUTTU, V. O. 1876 : Ad. *Nedungulam, Madras P.*

GNANAPRAGASAM, M. O. 1869 : Ad. *Tureiyur, Do.*

GNANAYUTHAM, P. O. 1879 : Ad. *Suveshipuram, Do.*

GNANAYUTHAM, V. O. 1876 : Ad. *Perpulankulam, Do.*

GOLDSMITH, H D. A. 1880. Ad *Madras.*

GOLDSMITH, MALCOLM GEORGE. B. at Woolwich, Kent, Jan. 5, 1849. O. by the Bishop of Lon in May, 1872. A. Nov. 5, 1872. Appointed to Mohammedan work in Madras : transferred to Calcutta in Nov. 1873 : R. to Madras in March, 1875. W. chiefly ver. with occasional Engl. service. Ad *Royapettah, Madras.*

GURUBADHAM, ISAAC. B. in 1843. O. in 1878. W. Native Pastor: Ad. *Palamcottah, Madras P.*

HACKETT, HENRY MONK MASON. A. 1877. Ad. *Madras.*

HANSDA, BHIM. O. 1878. Ad. *Taljhari, Bengal.*

HARCOURT, VINCENT WARD. A. 1867. Ad. *Palamcottah, Madras P.*

HARRINGTON, CHARLES SUMNER A. 1879. Ad. *Palcutta.*

HARRISON, JOHN. A. 1876. *Now in Europe.*

HASTINGS, THOMAS. O. 1878, Ad *Parvathiapuram, Madras P.*

HODGES, EDWARD NOEL. B. in 1849, O. D. in 1873, O. P. in 1874. A Nov 1877. In 1878 appointed Principal of Noble College. Ad. *Masulipatam, Madras P.*

HODGSON, THOMAS ROBINSON. B. in Eng 1850. O. D. St. Paul's Cathedral Lon. 1875. O. P. St. Paul's Cathedral, Calcutta, 1877. A. 1875, S. St. John's College, Agra, 1875, Cathedral Mission College, Calcutta, 1877, St. Saviour's Church, Calcutta, 1878. Jabalpur. 1878 to present. Ad. *Jubbulpur, C P.*

HŒRNLE, CHRISTIAN THEOPHILUS. A. 1838. Ad. *Annfield, N. W. P.*

HŒRNLE, J. G. HERMANN. A 1872. Ad *Meerut, N. W. P.*

HOOPER, WILLIAM. B. Sept. 27, 1847 at East Harptree, Somerset, Eng E. at Oxford : B A. in 1859; M. A. in 1861. O. D. by the Bishop of Lon in May. 1861. A. in Oct. 1861, and was appointed to Benares In Nov. 1862 O. P by the Bishop of Calcutta. M. in Dec. of the same year. Labored at Benares five years, chiefly in connection with the Jay Narain Col. Was transferred to the Cathedral Mission Col, Calcutta at the close of 1866. H. to Eng. at the close of 1868. While in Eng. engaged in pastoral work. In 1872 Rt. and was re-appointed to Benares. La ored there until March, 1874, when he succeeded Mr. French in charge of the Divinity Col., Lahore. In 1879 was transferred to Benares, to open the Divinity School. Ad *Benares.*

HOPPER, RALPH. B in Tinnevelly, Aug. 10, 1838. O, D. Jan. 31, 1869. O P. Jan 30, 1873. W. Native Pastor. Ad. *Anukragapuram, Tinnevelly, Madras P.*

HORSLEY, HUGH. B. at Courtallum, Tinnevelly, Aug. 11, 1849. O. D. 1873. A. Dec. 4. 1873. S. Sachiapuram. *Now in Europe.*

HUGHES, THOMAS PATRICK. O. D, by Bp. of Lon. 1864. O. P. by Bp. of Calcutta 1867. Deg. B D : M. R. A S. S. Peshawar, 1864. H. 6 months in 1875, and one year in 1878. Author :—*Notes on Muhammadanism*

1st Ed. 1875, 2nd Ed. 1877. (W. H. Allen Lon.) *Kalid i Afghani.* or Government Text Book for Pashto Examinations. (Lahore Press.) *Roman Urdu Qurán*, joint Editor with Rev. E. M. Wherry, M. A., (Lodiana) Pashto Tracts. (Peshawar.) Ad. *Peshawar, Afghanistan.*

ILSLEY, JOSEPH. B. Sept. 19, 1855, at Liverpool. O. D. by Bp. of Lon. June 10, 1879. A. March, 1880. Ad. *Sivagasi*, North Tinnevelly, *Madras P.*

IMAM UD DIN. Ad, *Amritsar, Punjab.*

ISAAC, ABRAHAM. O. 1859. Ad. *Panneivilei, Madras P.*

ITTY, CHERIAN. O. 1868. Ad. *Malapally, Travancore.*

JACO, KOLLATTA. Born at Kollatt, Aug 5, 1830: E. in the Cottayam Col. O. D. March 1, 1863, O. P. Dec. 1868: S. Pallam, Melukava, Erumaparn, and (Ad.) *Erecarte, Travancore.*

JACOB, A. J. B. at Cottayam, May 16, 1842. O. Dec. 24, 1871. S. Arpukara, Olesa and (Ad.) *Alleppy, Travancore.*

JAMES, ANTONY. B. in Dec. 1826. E. at Palamcottah and Madras: O. D. in Jan, 1866. S, Ootacamund 1869-73, Since Ukirankotei. Ad. *Ukirankotei, Madras P.*

JEREMY, DAVID. Ad, *Ikla, Meerut N. W. P.*

JOHN, E. V. O. 1879. Ad. *Cottayam, Travancore.*

JOHN, JESUDASEN. B. Tranquebar, Dec. 15, 1819: O. April 4, 1847. S. Palamcottah, 1847, Tavow, 1849, Suviseshapuram, 1850, Dohnavur, 1853, Radatchapuram, 1855, Suvtankulan, 1857, Piragasapuram, 1859, Nalumavadee, 1860, Kadatchapuram 1861, Tinnevelly, 1869, Palamcottah, 1874 to present: *Palamcottah, Madras P.*

JOHNSON, J. J. A. 1879. Ad. *Benares.*

JOSEPH, POTHEN. O. 1872. Ad. *Kannit, Travancore.*

JUKES, ANDREW. B. in Canada West, May, 1847. Medical degrees, M. R. K. S. 1869, L. S. A. 1869, L. R. C. P. 1872. Medical Work in London, 1869-78. A. Dec. 1878. Medical missionary to Biloochees. O. Ad. *Dera Ghazi Khan, Punjab.*

JUKES, WORTHINGTON. B. in Canada, Jan. 1849. M. A. Trinity Col. Camb. O. by Bp. of Lon. in 1872. A. Nov. 1872. S. Amritsar till Oct. 1873, since, Peshawar. L. engaged in the translation of the Pentateuch into Pushtu. Ad. *Peshawar, Afghanistan.*

KEENE, WILLIAM. B. Minety, Gloucestershire, Eng. July 6, 1828. E. Brasenore Col. Ox. (M. A.) O. D. 1852 O. P. 1854. A. March 10, 1854. S. Simla and Kotgur 1854, Amritsar, 1860, H. to Europe March, 1865, Amritsar. Feb. 1868, H. to Europe, Dec. 1872, Amritsar Jan. 1877. L. Translated "Selections from the Book of Common Prayer" in Panjabi and "Essay on the Sikhs" read at Missionary Conference, Lahore, 1862-63. Ad. *Amritsar, Punjab.*

KEMBER, THOMAS. A. 1865. Ad. *Palamcottah, Madras P.*

KORATHA, KUNENGHERI. O. 1868. Ad. *Kedawalaniya, Travancore.*

KOSHI, KOSHI. O. 1856, Ad. *Pallam, Travancore.*

KRISHNAYYA, GANUGAPATI. B Ellore, Sept. 15, 1838: O. D. Dec. 24, 1871, O P. Feb. 1, 1874: W. Native Pastor. Ad. *Ellore, Madras P.*

KURRUWELLA, KURRUWELLA. O. 1860, Ad. *Cochin, Travancore.*

LAL, KATWARI. Ad. *Agra.*

LASH, A. H. A. 1867. S. Palamcottah. *Now in Europe.*

LEVI, AMAN MASIH. B. Benares, Nov. 18, 1850: O. D. Feb. 1, 1878. W. Native Pastor. Ad. Sigra, *Benares.*

LEWIS, ARTHUR B. Clifton, Bristol. June 18, 1854 E. Queen's Col. Oxford. O. D Llandaff, Sept. 28, 1877. O. P Canterbury, Sept. 22, 1878. A. Dec 1878. Ad. *Dera Ghazi Khan, Punjab.*

LLOYD, JOHN ABBOTT. A. 1876. Ad. St. John's Col. *Agra.*

LONG, JAMES. A. 1840. S. Calcutta. *Now in Europe.*

MACARTNEY, FREDERICK GRAHAM. B. Jan. 30, 1850, at Portsmouth, Eng. O. D. May 31, 1874. O. P. Jan. 1, 1878 A. Dec. 1874. S. Nasik, 1875, since, Malegaon. Ad. *Malegaon.* Nasik, *Bombay P.*

MACDONALD, REGINALD CHAMBERS. A. 1859. S. Madras. *In Europe.*

MADDOX, RALPH HENRY. A. 1863. Ad. *Trichur, Travancore.*

MALOBA, LUCAS, Ad. *Nasik, Bombay P.*

MAMEN, OMEN. O. 1856. Ad *Changanacherry, Travancore.*

MANWARING, ALFRED. B. Broadwater, Eng. 1855. O. June 8. 1879 A. Dec. 1, 1879. Ad. *Nasik, Bombay P.*

MASIH, SADIQ. B. about 1850. O. Nov. 2, 1875. Ad. *Batala, Amritsar, Punjab.*

MASILLAMANI, S. O. 1874. Ad. *Sinnamalpuram, Madras P.*

MASILLAMANI, S. O. 1876. Ad. *Paliputtu, Do.*

MAYER, THOS. JNO. LEE. B at Newcastle Staffs, Oct 17, 1844, Called to the ministry in 1866, at Queensland: O.D. 1872 by the Bishop of Canterbury, at Lambeth; O. P. in 1874, by the Bishop of Calcutta, at Allahabad. Was engaged in ministerial labor at Aldershot Hants, before coming to I. A. Feb. 1873. S. Amritsar, and Bunnoo. W. Eng and Ver. (Pushto). M. September 13, 1875. Ad. *Bunnoo, Derajat.*

MEADOWS, ROBERT RUST. B. Feb 10, 1829, near Ipswich. Suffolk. O by the Bishop of Lon, June, 1852. A. 1852. After studying Tamil in Madras for more than a year began the work of itinerating in April, 1854. Continued in this until Sept, H. 1858, to Eng. Jan. 1859 : R. to Madras M. Sept. 1860 ; took charge of the Sivagasi district. H. in Aug. 1870, and reached Madras again in May 1873, resuming the work at Sivagasi. L. (1). A small Greek Grammar in Tamil, procurable at C. M. S. Office, Madras. (2) "History of Sandhai, or the Model Catechist's Wife." (Tamil) C. V. E. S. Depot, Madras. (3). "Advice to educated Women" (by Rev. D. Fenn, and Rev. R. R. Meadows), Tamil Religious Tract Society, Madras. H. To Eng. in Feb. 1877. *Now in Europe.*

MOHUN, DAVID. B at Chunar, 1811. O. 1859. M. 1842. Has labored in preaching and in teaching ; at present pastor of Native Church. Allahabad. Translated two sermons on Infant Baptism ; also several stories from "*Agathos*" and "*Spring Morning*" ; (published in Urdu, and Roman Urdu and obtainable of the translator). Ad. *Allahabad.*

MOUNTFORT, CHARLES. B. Daventry, Feb. 9, 1855. O. D. June. 8, 1879, O. P. Sept. 19, 1880. A. Nov. 17, 1880. Ad. *Nasik, Bombay P.*

NALLATHAMBI, JOHN. O. 1859, Ad. *Achampatti, Madras P,*

NALLATHAMBI, SWAMIDASEN. O. 1874. Ad. *Maruthakulam, Madras P.*

NEEVE, CLEMENT ALFRED. O. in 1879, A in 1879. S. Cottayam: W. Principal, C. M. S. Col. Ad. *Cottayam, Travancore.*

NOWROJEE, RUTTONJEE. B. Oct, 18, 1838, at Ahmednagar, Baptized at Sharanpur, near Nasik, June 26. 1856. M. Oct 22, 1861. O. D by Bishop Douglas, June 12, 1870, O. P, April 1, 1872. Labored as lay pastor at Sharanpur for twelve years: as missionary catechist at Yeola, two years. In charge of the Aurungabad mission since June, 1870. W. chiefly Ver. L. A Translation into Marathi of Bishop Wilsons's "Paraphrase of the Lord's Prayer." Obtainable at the Depository S.P. C. K., Bombay. Ad. *Aurungabad, Deccan.*

NUGENT, CHARLES P. C. A. 1877. *Now in Europe.*

PADFIELD, JOSEPH EDWIN. B. at Bath, Oct. 25, 1843. O. D by the Bp. of Lon., June 7, 1868. A in Dec. 1868. M. Jan. 22, 1870. O. P. by the Bp. of Madras, Feb 5, 1870. S. From Feb. 1878 to the following Oct. in educational work at Ellore: from Oct. 1870 to March, 1872 in charge of the Ellore district: from this time to Oct. 1874, Head Master C. M. S. Anglo-vernacular School at Ellore: from this to the present Principal of the C. M. S. Training Inst. at Masulipatam. W. has been both Engl. and Ver. Ad. *Masulipatam, Madras P.*

PAINTER. ARTHUR FREDERICK. O. D Sept. 1877, O. P. Jan. 1880. A. Nov 1877. S. Kunnankulam, 1877 to Sept. 1880 *Now in Europe.*

PAKIANADHAM JOHN. O 1878 Ad. *Tiruvarangapatti, Madras P.*

PAKIANADHAM, JAMES HARRIS. B. Pragasapuram, Aug 7, 1842. O. D Sept. 22, 1878. O. P. March, 1881. W. Native Pastor: Ad. *Kupapuram, Madras P.*

PARAMANANDHAM. S. O. 1878: Ad *Satankulam, Madras P.*

PARINDAM, D. O. 1869. Ad. *Ananthapuram, Do.*

PARSONS GEORGE HENRY. B in Ceylon Dec 31, 1854. O. D. June 8, 1879 A Dec. 19. 1879. Ad. *Krishnaghar, Bengal.*

PARKER, HENRY PERROTT. A. 1878. Ad. *Calcutta.*

PAUL. SAMUEL B. in Tinnevelly, in 1844. O. Oct. 1874. S. Pastor Tamil Local Mission. Ootacamund. L. (in Tamil) "History of the Church of England." "History of the Book of Common Prayer," "Geography of Madras Zillah," "Geography of Neilgherries," etc, etc; a number of original tracts, pamphlets and hand-bills, and a number of translations for Madras Tract Society and for the C. V. E S. Ad. *Ootacamund, Madras P.*

PERIYANAYAGAM, MADHURANAYAGAM. B. Tuticorin, June 17, 1825. O. D. Dec. 18, 1859, O. P. Dec. 21, 1862: Labored since at (Ad.) *Alvaneri.*

POOLE, ARTHUR WILLIAM: A. 1877. *Now in Europe.*

RAM CHARN. Ad. *Godda, Bengal.*

RAM, MADHO. Ad. *Jubbulpur, C. P.*

RASENTHIRAM, ABRAHAM. O. 1869. Ad. *Kongarayakurichi, Madras P.*

RASENTHIRAM, DAVID. O. 1869. Ad. *Manuriantatu, Madras P.*

RATNAM. MANCHALA. O. 1864, Ad. *Bezwara, Madras P.*

RAZU, I. VENCATARAMA. O. 1872. Ad. *Dummagudem, Do.*

REBSCH, WILLIAM. A. 1853. Ad. *Kotgarh, Punjab.*

REDMAN, JOSEPH. B. Overtown, Swindon, Eng. April 4, 1855. E.C. M. Col. Islington O. June 8, 1879. Curate of Christ Church, Wellington, 1879. A. Dec 5. 1880. Ad. *Hyderabad, Sindh.*

RICHARDS, J. Ad. *Dehra Doon, N-W. P.*

RICHARDS. WILLIAM JOSEPH. A. 1871. *Cottayam, Travancore.*

ROBERTS, WILSON AYLESBURY. B. Feb 12, 1846, at Ledbury. Herefordshire, Eng. Entered Islington Jan. 1866. O D May 23, 1869, by the Bishop of Lon. O. P April 25, 1871, by the Bishop of Bombay. A. Nov. 21, 1869. S. Kurrachee, 1869 : Berhampoor, 1871 : Malligaum, 1872. W. both Engl. and ver. Ad. *Nasik, Bombay P.*

RUDRA, PIYARE MOHUN. Ad. *Calcutta.*

SAMUEL, ABRAHAM O 1870. Ad. *Paneidipatti, Madras P.*

SAMUEL, ISAAC. O. 1869. Ad *Edeiyangulam, Do.*

SAMUEL, PERPETTAN. O 1874. A. 1874. Ad. *Suviseshapuram, Do.*

SAMUEL, SAMUEL. O 1878. Ad *Nallor, Do.*

SANTHOSHAM, S. O. 1876. Ad. *Manarkadu, Do.*

SARKUNAN GNANAMUTTU. O. 1873. Ad *Kylasupuram, D.*

SATTHIANADHAN, WILLIAM THOMAS, B. in Madura Oct, 12. 1830, of heathen parents. Was converted in July 1847. as the result of education received in tho mission school at Palamcottah ; was baptized the same year M. Feb. 16, 1849. After pursuing Theol. studies for a time spent five years as a teacher in the Preparandi Institution Afterwards studied in Madras two years. O. D. Dec. 18, 1859 ; O. D. in Dec. 1862, and in March, 1863. was transferred to Madras, where he has since labored in connection with the Southern Pastorate. W. chiefly Tamil being partly pastoral and partly educational and evangelistic. L (1) A Church History in English (out of print) (2) A large Church History in Tamil, procurable at the Depository of the C K Society, Madras (3.) A Commentary on the N. T. in Tamil, on the basis of the Tract Society's Annotated Paragraph N. T., Religious Tract Society s Depot, Madras. He also edited two monthly Magazines, " The Mission School Magazine," in Tamil for children, for the C. V. E. S. and the " Desabhimani," an Anglo-vernacular periodical. Ad. *Phintadrepettah, Madras.*

SAVARIROYAM, MADURENDHIRAM. O. 1851. Ad. *Nallammalapuram, Madras P.*

SCHAFFTER, HENRY. J. A. 1877. Ad *Palamcottah, Madras P.*

SEAL, MODHU SUDAN. B. of Hindu parents in Calcutta, about 1815. E. partly at the General Assembly's Inst. at Calcutta and partly at Bishop's Col. Howrah. Baptized at Cawnpore in 1836. O. by Bishop Harding in Bombay, 1855. Transferred to Calcutta and appointed to Kidderpore, 1860 : sent to the Krishnaghar district in charge of the congregations at Ratanpur and Joginda in 1862. Re-appointed to Kidderpore in 1865. L. "*English and Hindustani Manual*" : Baptist Mission Press, Calcutta. Ad. *Kidderpore, Bengal.*

SEBAGNANAM, I. Ad. *Palamcottah, Madras P.*

SELL, EDWARD. O. D. 1864, O. P. 1867 A. 1865. S. Madras. W. Head Master, Harris School. L. "The Faith of Islam" (Engl), Addison and Co. Madras; Persian and Urdu Grammar: Persian Idioms with Hindustani translation; and various vernacular School Books. H. from March 1876 to Dec. 1877. Ad. *Madras.*

SHAH, IMAM. B. about 1840 in the Amritsar district. Baptized in 1862 (parents Mohammedans), and appointed to Peshawar as catechist. O. D. Dec. 15, 1872. O. P. Nov. 28, 1875. Pastor of Native church at (Ad.) *Peshawar, Punjab.*

SHAM, BESRA. Ad. *Bahawa, Bengal.*

SHARP, JOHN. A. 1861. Ad. *Massulipatam, Madras P.*

SHELDON, JAMES. A. 1854. Ad. *Kurrachee, Scindh.*

SHIRREFF, FRANCIS ARCHIBALD PATTULLO. B. at Chinsurah, Feb. 7, 1848. O. D. 1872, O P. 1873. A. Dec. 1873. Tutor in St. John's Divinity School, Lahore from 1874-78, since Feb. 1879, Principal of said Inst. L. Translation of Abridgement of the Pastoral Rule of Gregory the Great (Urdu): Punjab Rel. Book Socy. Ad. *Lahore, Punjab.*

SHIRT, GEORGE. B. in 1843 at Cawthorne, Yorkshire. E. Islington and Cambridge Col. O. 1866. A. Dec. 1866. S. Hydrabad 1866-73, Kurrachee. 1875-77, Hydrabad 1877 to present. H. from 1873-75. L. Some original tracts in Sindhi and translated some portions of the Bible and joint Compiler of Sindhi-Engl. Dictionary. Ad. Hydrabad, *Sindh.*

SIDO, WILLIAM. Ad. *Bahawa. Bengal.*

SIMEON, JOHN. O. 1869. Ad. *Tharmanagaram, Madras P.*

SIMEON, VEDAYAGAM, O. 1866. Ad. *Madras.*

SINGH DAUD. Ad. Charkabad, *Amritsar, Punjab.*

SOLOMON, DAVID. Ad. *Lucknow, Oudh.*

SQUIRES, HENRY CHARLES. A. 1870. Ad. *Bombay.*

SQUIRES, ROBERT ALFRED. A. 1870. Ad. *Nasik, Bombay.*

SIMEON, LUKE. B in 1816. O. D. Sept. 25, 1870, O. P. Jan. 30, 1876. W. Native Pastor. Ad. *Puliangudi, Madras P.*

STARK, ALFRED. B. in Calcutta July 11, 1834. M. in 1857. O. in 1870. S Doveton Col. Calcutta, March, 1856 to Dec. 1866; Assistant Secretary, C. M. S. Calcutta, Feb. 1867 to June, 1869; from July, 1869 to Feb. 1872. Taljhari; from March, 1872 to Jan. 1879, Godda. W. is entirely Ver. Ad. *Taljhari, Bengal.*

STEPHEN, DAVID. B. Tinnevelly, 1834. O. D. Jan. 31, 1869. O. P. Dec. 24, 1871. W. Native Pastor. Ad. *Kadutchapuram, Madras P.*

STERN, HENRY. B. at Karlsruke, Germany. O. D. by the Bishop of Lon. in 1850. O P. by the Bishop of Calcutta in 1853. A. 1851. S. Benares 1851-53, since, Gorakhpur. L. Translated "*Religious Anecdotes,*" (Urdu); Benares Medical Hall Press: "*History of the Kings of Judah and Israel*" (Urdu); N. I. Tract Society' Depot, Allahabad. "*Catechism of the Christian Religion,*" (Roman Urdu), to be had from the author. "*Manual for the Holy Communion,*" (Roman-Urdu). Out of print. H. 1860 and 1878. Ad. *Gorakhpur, N-W. P.*

STONE, JAMES A. 1876. Ad. *Raghapur, Madras P.*

STUART, J. A. 1862. Ad. *Aligarh, N.-W. P.*

SWAMIDASEN, SUVISESHAMUTTU. B. Jan. 1836 in Tinnevelly. O. D. Sept. 25, 1870. O. P. Oct. 12, 1874. Ad. *Surandei, Madras P.*

THARIEN, JACOB. O. 1856. Ad. *Mavelicara, Travancore.*

THARMAKAN, V. O. 1876. A. *Pulavanur, Madras P.*

THOMA, AMBARTA. O 1868. Ad. *Olesha, Travancore.*

THOMAS, CHANDIPILLA. O. 1872. Ad. *Ellanthur, do.*

THOMAS, JOHN DAVIS. A. 1863. Ad. *Palaveram, Madras P.*

THOMPSON, CHARLES STEWART. B. Easington. Durham, Eng., June 26. 1851. O. D. June 11, 1880. O. P. Sept. 19, 1880. A. Nov. 19, 1880. Appointed to labor among Bhils. Ad. *Kherwara, Rajputana.*

THWAITES, WILLIAM. A. 1871. *Now in Europe.*

TUNBRIDGE, JAMES. B. at Bath, Eng. 1849. A. 1877. O. D. 1879. S. Godda, 1879, since, (Ad.) *Bhagaya, Bengal.*

VAUGHAN, JAMES. B. at Hall, Yorkshire, in 1826. O. Dec. 25, 1854. A. 1855. S. Calcutta, from 1855-74. H from 1874-77. Krishnaghar, 1877 to present. L. "Pratyahik Upashana," (Daily Devotion) in Bengali; S.P.C K. Depot, Calcutta. "Fulfilled Prophecy: translated the latter into Bengali: "What think ye of Christ?" "The Trident, the Crescent and the Cross;" "Jesus Christ who and what is He?" All obtainable at Tract Society, Calcutta. Ad. *Krishnaghar, Bengal.*

VEDAKAN, S. O. 1876 Ad. *Kallathikinaru, Madras P.*

VETHAMUTTU, A. O. 1869. Ad. *Arumuganeri, Do.*

VETHANAYAGAM, D. O. 1876. Ad *Truvaranganeri, Do.*

VETHANAYAGAM, THOMAS. B. of heathen parents in 1825. Professed Christianity in 1839. O' D. 1869. O. P. 1871. Ad. *Vellalenvilei, Madras P.*

VETHANAYAGAM, V. O. 1859. Ad. *Vageikulam, Madras P.*

VIRAVAGU, DEVANAYAGAM. O. 1859. Ad. *Mengnanapuram, Madras P.*

VORES, S. O. 1880. Ad. *Ellore, Madras P.*

WADE, THOMAS RUSSELL. A. 1863. Ad. *Kashmir.*

WEATHERHEAD, TRENHAM KING. A. 1860 *Now in Europe.*

WEBER, GEORGE HENRY. A. 1861. O. 1879. *Now in Europe.*

WEITBRECHT, HERBERT UDNY. B. Lon. 1851. O. 1874. Curate Christ Church Everton, Liverpool, 1874-76. A. Dec. 1876. S. Divinity School, Lahore 1878. L. Translated Christlieb's "Modern Doubt." (Clark, Edinburgh, 1876). Degree, Ph. D. Tubingen 1873. Ad. *Lahore.*

WILLIAMS, HENRY. B Oct. 4, 1853 at Oswestry, Shropshire. O. D. Lon. Dec. 1876, O. D. Calcutta, Dec. 1878. A. Nov. 27, 1877. S, Ballabpur 1878; Krishnaghar, 1880. Ad. *Ballabpur,* Krishnaghar, *Bengal.*

WILLIAMS, J. Ad. *Dera Ismail Khan, Punjab.*

WILLIAMSON, HENRY DRUMMOND. B. Dec 17. 1851, at Alvaston, Derbyshire. B. A. Christ Col. Camb. O. D, 1877. O. P. 1879, A. Feb. 1878. Ad. *Mandla, Cent. Prov.*

WIRGHESE, MATTHEW. O. 1868. Ad. *Puthupally, Travancore.*

YESUDIAN, GNANAMUTTU. B. 1831, in Tinnevelly. O. D. Jan. 26, 1873. O. P. Jan. 30, 1876. Ad. *Siralasamuthiram, Madras P.*

YESUDIAN, TUCKER. O. 1878. Ad. *Puthukulam, Do.*

DECEASED AND RETIRED MISSIONARIES.

Names.	Arrival.	Field of Labor.	Death, Withdrawal or Retirement.
J. C. Schnarre, ..	1814,	Palamcottah ..	D. Oct. 1820.
C. T. E. Rhenius, ..	1814,	Tinnevelly ..	D June, 1838.
C. G. Schroeter, ..	1815,	Titalya ..	D. July, 1820.
W. Greenwood, ..	1815,	Chunar ..	D. 1839.
T. Norton, ..	1815,	Allepie ..	D. Aug. 1840.
B. Bailey, ..	1816,	Cottayam ..	R. 1850, D. Apr. 1871.
T. Dawson, ..	1816,	Cochin ..	D. Feb. 1828.
D. Schmid, ..	1817,	Calcutta ..	D. Dec. 1829.
L. B. E. Schmid, ..	1817,	Mayaveram ..	R. 1837, D. Oct. 1857.
J. Adlington, ..	1817,	Benares ..	W. 1828.
H. Baker, ..	1818.	Travancore ..	D. July, 1866.
G. T. Barenbruck, ..	1818,	Madras ..	D. May, 1833.
J. Fenn, ..	1818,	Cottayam ..	W. 1826, D. Jan. 1878.
J. A. Jetter, ..	1820,	Burdwan ..	R. July, 1840.
W. J. Deerr, ..	1820,	Do. ..	R Dec. 1842.
T. Morris, ..	1820,	Benares ..	W. Jan. 1829.
B. LaRoche, ..	1820,	Do. ..	D. Aug. 1821.
J. Perowne, ..	1820.	Burdwan ..	W. Sept. 1827.
J. Ridsdale, ..	1820,	Madras ..	D. Aug. 1831.
R. Kenney, ..	1820,	Bombay ..	W. June, 1826.
I. Wilson, ..	1821,	Madras ..	D. Sept. 1828.
W. Sawyer, ..	1822,	Do. ..	D. Jan. 1832.
J. Maisch, ..	1822,	Burdwan ..	D. Aug. 1825.
T. Reichardt, ..	1822,	Calcutta ..	W. July, 1828.
M. Wilkinson, ..	1823,	Goruckpore ..	D. Nov. 1848.
J. F. Beddy, ..	1824,	S. India ..	W. Jan. 1826.
S. Ridsdale, ..	1824,	Cochin ..	D. Oct. 1840.
J. W. Doran, ..	1825,	Cottayam ..	R. 1830, D. 1862,
W. Mitchell, ..	1826,	Bombay ..	R. 1834, D. 1870.
J. Steward, ..	1826,	Do. ..	W. Aug. 1828.
J. Kindlinger, ..	1827,	Pulicat ..	D. Dec. 1829.
J. C. F. Winckler, ..	1827,	Tinnevelly ..	R June, 1834.
P. P. Schaffter, ..	1827,	Do. ..	D. Dec. 1861.
J. Latham, ..	1827,	Calcutta ..	W. May, 1830 D. Nov. 1879.
C. Friend, ..	1828,	Chunar ..	D. June, 1829.
R. Eteson, ..	1828,	Do. ..	R. Nov. 1830.
J. B. Morewood, ..	1828,	Madras ..	W. Apr. 1835.
C. P. Farrar, ..	1829,	Nasik ..	W. May, 1847.
J. B. Dixon, ..	1829,	Do. ..	D. Jan. 1846.
R. V. Reynolds, ..	1829,	Burdwan ..	R. Sept 1836.
T. Sandys, ..	1830,	Calcutta ..	D. Nov. 1871.

NAMES.	ARRIVAL.	FIELD OF LABOR.	DEATH, WITHDRAWAL OR RETIREMENT.
C. Blackman, ..	1830,	Madras ..	R. Feb. 1842.
J. Marsh, ..	1830,	Do. ..	D. May, 1831.
W. Smith, ..	1830,	Goruckpore ..	D. Jan. 1875.
J. J. Weitbrecht, ..	1830,	Burdwan ..	D. March, 1852.
J. C Thompson, ..	1830,	Calcutta ..	R. 1842.
P. Fjellstedt, ..	1831,	Tinnevelly ..	R. July, 1840.
H. C. Kruckeberg, ..	1831,	Krishnaghar ..	D. Feb. 1860.
J. J. Muller, ..	1831,	Madras ..	D. March, 1843.
W. Morse, ..	1832,	N. India ..	R. July, 1836.
J. Haberlin, ..	1832,	Burdwan ..	R. Jan. 1838.
J. C. G. Knorpp, ..	1832,	Benares ..	D. March, 1838.
C. B. Leupolt, ..	1832,	Do. ..	R. April, 1872.
J. T. Lincke, ..	1832,	Krishnaghar ..	D. March, 1868.
C. W. Isenberg, ..	1832,	Bombay ..	D. October, 1864.
J. Peet, ..	1833,	Travancore ..	D. August, 1865.
G. Pettitt, ..	1833,	Tinnevelly ..	W. January, 1855.
J. Tucker, ..	1833,	Madras ..	R. Mar. 1847, D. 1873.
H. Snashall, ..	1833,	Do. ..	R. Jan. 1834.
W. J. Woodcock, ..	1834,	Cottayam ..	R. Nov. 1840.
J. Lechler, ..	1834,	Tinnevelly ..	R. June, 1835.
F. J. DeRozario. ..	1834,	Agurpara ..	R. 1880.
T. H. Applegate, ..	1835,	Do. ..	D. November, 1837.
H. Harley, ..	1836,	Cochin ..	R. 1861.
C. C. Menge, ..	1836,	Bombay ..	R. June, 1874.
C. F. Warth, ..	1836,	Nasik ..	D. May, 1842.
J. Thomas, ..	1836,	Tinnevelly ..	D. March, 1870.
F. Wybrow, ..	1837,	Calcutta ..	D. June, 1840.
J. H. Gray, ..	1837,	Madras ..	R. April, 1847.
J Johnson, ..	1837,	Travancore ..	D. May, 1846.
T. J. Norton, ..	1837,	Madras ..	R. 1840.
J. N. Norgate, ..	1837,	Calcutta ..	W. 1842.
J. J. H. Elonis, ..	1838,	Madras ..	R. January, 1849.
G. M. Valentine, ..	1838,	Bombay ..	D July, 1844.
W. T. Humphrey, ..	1838,	Travancore ..	R. November, 1841.
F. E. Schneider, ..	1838,	Agra ..	R. March, 1875.
J. S. S. Robertson, ..	1838,	Bombay ..	R. May, 1877.
J. C. Barclay, ..	1838,	Madras ..	W. 1840.
C. Stone, ..	1839,	Nasik ..	R. 1840.
C. K. Blumhardt, ..	1839,	Krishnaghar ..	R. April, 1877.
J. Innes, ..	1839,	Do. ..	R. February, 1851.
C. T. Krauss, ..	1839,	Do. ..	D. October, 1849.
C. W. Lipp, ..	1839,	Do. ..	R. January, 1856.
F. Rogers, ..	1839,	Mayaveram ..	R. February, 1841.

NAMES.		ARRIVAL.	FIELD OF LABOR.		DEATH, WITHDRAWAL OR RETIREMENT.
S. Hobbs,	..	1839,	Tinnevelly	..	R. 1880.
A. H. Alexander,	..	1839,	Culna	..	D. 1845.
C. J. Taylor,	..	1839,	Mayaveram	..	D April, 1851.
C. G. Pfander,	..	1840,	Agra	..	D December, 1865.
F. A. Kreiss,	..	1840,	Goruckpore	..	D. June, 1856.
J. P. Menge,	..	1840,	Do.	..	D. September, 1878.
J. Chapman,	..	1840,	Travancore	..	D December, 1862.
J. Hawksworth,	..	1840,	Do.	..	D. January, 1863.
J. F. Osborne,	..	1840,	Calcutta	..	W. February, 1847.
J. Baumann,	..	1840,	Benares	..	D. August, 1843.
J. C. Wendnagel,	..	1840,	Goruckpore	..	D. December, 1846.
R. P. Noble,	..	1841,	Masulipatam		D, October, 1865.
H. W. Fox,	..	1841,	Do.	..	D. October, 1848.
R. Hawes,	..	1841,	Jounpore	..	R. January, 1849.
J. G Symes,	..	1841,	Madras	..	R August, 1857.
J. T. Tucker,	..	1842,	Tinnevelly	..	D. July, 1866.
S. Hobbs,	..	1842,	Do.	..	R. Nov. 1862.
G. Stolzenberg,	..	1842,	Benares,	..	D. 1845.
J. D Prochnow,	..	1843,	Kotgarh	..	R. 1858.
E. Johnson,	..	1843,	N. India	..	R. September, 1858.
H. Baker, Jr.	..	1843,	Travancore	..	D. November, 1878.
H. Mellon,	..	1843,	Bombay	..	R July, 1844.
J. J. Muhlheisen,	..	1844,	Do.	..	R. May, 1848.
P. L Sandberg,	..	1844,	Benares	..	R. January, 1849.
E. Reynolds,	..	1844,	Krishnaghar	..	R September, 1846.
D. Hechler,	..	1844,	Chunar	..	R. 1851, D. 1878.
J. T. G. Barenbruck,	..	1844,	Tinnevelly	..	D. March, 1859.
B. Geidt,	..	1845,	Burdwan	..	R. Feb. 1862.
A. Dredge,	..	1845,	Bombay	..	D. June, 1846.
E Newman,	..	1845,	Tinnevelly	..	R. 1850, D. 1880.
C. J Rhenius,	..	1845,	Do.	..	R. March, 1851.
G. G Cuthbert,	.	1846,	Calcutta	..	D October, 1861.
T. G. Ragland,	..	1846,	Madras	..	D October, 1858.
F. Schurr,	..	1846,	Burdwan	..	T'd. to Mauritius, 1873
C. Bomwetsch,	..	1846,	Santipore,	..	W. July, 1877.
J. Spratt,	..	1846,	Tinnevelly	..	D. September, 1854.
R. L. Allnutt,	..	1846,	Do.	..	R. October, 1847.
R. M. Lamb,	..	1847,	Meerut	..	D. June, 1857.
E Rogers,	..	1847,	Nasik	..	D July, 1865.
A. Acheson,	..	1847,	Goruckpore	..	R February, 1853.
S. Hasell,	..	1847,	Krishnaghar	..	D. June, 1879.
J. Fuchs,	..	1847,	Benares	..	D. March, 1878.

NAMES.	ARRIVAL.	FIELD OF LABOR.	DEATH, WITHDRAWAL OR RETIREMENT.
M. J. Wilkinson, ..	1847,	Benares ..	R. 1854, D. 1873.
T. Jerrom, ..	1847,	Bombay ..	D. May, 1851.
G. F. H. Ansorge, ..	1847,	Krishnaghar ..	R. 1855.
T. Y. Darling, ..	1847,	Masulipatam	R. 1877.
J. Harding, ..	1848,	Travancore ..	R. July, 1854.
W. Clark, ..	1848,	Tinnevelly ..	Trans'd., to Ceylon, 1868.
G. English, ..	1849,	Masulipatam	R. September, 1858.
T. Foulkes, ..	1849,	Tinnevelly ..	R. November, 1860.
W. S. Price, ..	1849,	Nasik ..	R. July, 1876.
C. F. Reuther, ..	1849,	Kangra ..	D. January, 1879.
T. K. Nicholson, ..	1850,	Masulipatam,	R. September, 1854.
G. Candy, ..	1850,	Bombay ...	R. 1857, D. 1869.
C. C. T. Schreiber, ..	1850,	Kurrachee ..	R. 1852.
J. G. Benttler, ..	1850,	Travancore ..	R. 1867.
J. Whitechurch, ..	1850,	Tinnevelly ..	D. January, 1871.
T. V. French, ..	1850,	Agra ..	Bishop of Lahore.
E. C. Stuart, ..	1850,	Agra ..	Trans'd. 1877.
J. N. Merk, ..	1850,	Kotghar ..	D. October, 1874.
S. Bost, ..	1850,	Krishnaghar,	R. February, 1853.
J. J. Meyer, ..	1850,	Do. ..	R. February, 1853.
T. H. Fitzpatrick, ..	1851,	Amritsar ..	D. February, 1861.
W. Wilkinson, ..	1851,	Benares ..	R. 1856.
A. Matchett, ..	1852,	Kurrachee ..	R. August, 1863.
D. Fenn, ..	1852,	Madras ..	D. October, 1878.
C. F. Cobb, ..	1852,	Benares ..	R. 1859.
A. P. Neele, ..	1852,	Burdwan ..	R. March, 1876.
J. Pickford, ..	1852,	Tinnevelly ..	Trans'd. 1854.
N. J. Moody, ..	1852,	Madras ..	D. July, 1858.
H. D. Hubbard, ..	1853,	Benares ..	R. April, 1876.
A. H. Frost, ..	1853,	Nasik, ..	R. 1875.
A. Davidson, ..	1853,	Bombay ..	W. 1866.
E. Trumpp, ..	1854,	Scindh ..	R. November, 1859.
P. Goodall, ..	1854,	Do. ..	D. April, 1861.
C. J. Batstone, ..	1854,	Krishnaghar,	R. January, 1857.
W. Wright, ..	1854,	Agra ..	R. April, 1867.
A. Strawbridge, ..	1854,	Amritsar ..	R. May, 1865.
J. Leighton, ..	1854,	Agra ..	R. February, 1860.
A. Medland, ..	1854,	Meerut ..	W. February, 1861.
C. Every, ..	1854,	Tinnevelly ..	D. August, 1857.
C. F. Schwartz, ..	1854,	Junir ..	D. August, 1878.
R. Collins, ..	1854,	Cottayam ..	R. January, 1880.
L. Craddock, ..	1854,	Madras ..	R. November, 1859.

NAMES.		ARRIVAL.	FIELD OF LABOR		DEATH, WITHDRAWAL OR RETIREMENT.
J. A. L. Stern,	..	1855,	Calcutta	..	R. 1877.
A. Dibb,	..	1855,	Tinnevelly	..	D. October, 1876.
H. Dixon,	..	1855,	Do.	..	W. July, 1871.
S. Dyson,	..	1855,	Calcutta	..	R. March, 1878.
H. Andrews,	..	1855,	Allepio	..	D. October, 1866.
W. J. Ball,	..	1855,	Punjab	..	R. 1875.
R H. Vickers,	...	1855,	Travancore	..	R Feb. 1860.
A. B. Valpy,	..	1855,	Tinnevelly	..	R. Feb. 1861.
G. Walker,	..	1855,	Madras	..	R. Feb. 1866.
P. S. Royston,	..	1855,	Do.		R July, 1871.
A. Burn,	..	1856,	Scindh	..	R. 1871.
F. Goodall,	..	1856,	Masulipatam		R. May, 1868.
W. T. Storrs,	..	. 1856,	Lucknow, etc		R. 1879.
J. Gritton,	...	1856,	Madras	..	R. May, 1866.
R. P. Greaves,	...	1857,	Calcutta	..	D. Nov. 1870.
J. A. McCarthy,	..	1857,	Punjab	..	R. Jan. 1868.
C. Tanner,	..	1857,	Masulipatam.		R. May, 1873.
H. C. Milward,	..	1857,	Calcutta	..	R. Jan. 1860.
T. Tuting,	..	1857,	Punjab	..	D. Oct. 1862.
T. G. Gaster,	..	1857,	Agra	..	R. May, 1863.
H. W. Shackell,	..	1858,	Do.		R. July 1873.
P. G. Ansorge,	..	1858,	North India	..	R. 1880.
D. Fynes-Clinton,	..	1858,	Agra	..	R. 1860, D. May, 1880.
J. H. Wilkinson,	..	1858,	Travancore	..	R. April, 1866.
T. Spratt,	..	1858,	Tinnevelly	..	R. April, 1873.
R. Galbraith,	..	1858,	Bombay	..	R. 1865.
L. Hofer,	..	1858,	Junir	..	R. 1861.
R. Bruce,	..	1858,	Punjab	..	Trans'd, 1869.
J. L Knight,	..	1858,	North India	..	R. 1859.
W. Gray,	..	1858,	Madras	..	R. Oct. 1867.
T. E. Hallett,	..	1859,	Santhalia	..	W. 1860.
A. Lockwood,	...	1859,	Benares	..	R. Jan. 1872.
J. H. Buncher,	..	1859,	Madras	..	R. March, 1860.
W. B. Cole,	..	1859,	Meerut	..	R. 1861.
J. B. Archer,	..	1859,	Do.		R. 1861.
R E. Clark,	..	1859,	Peshawar	..	D. Jan. 1863.
S. Attlee,	..	1860,	Lucknow	..	R. 1860.
G Yeates,	..	1850,	Mooltan	..	R 1873.
W. Ellington,	...	1860,	Masulipatam		D. June, 1878.
W. J. Edmonds,	...	1860,	Do.	...	R. 1863. [1877.
N. Honiss,	...	1860,	Tinnevelly	...	Trans'd. to Mauritius,
J. D. Simmons,	...	1860,	Do.	...	Do. 1874.
J. M. Speechly.	..	1860.	Travancore	..	Bishop of Travancore.

Names.		Arrival.	Field of labor	Death, Withdrawal or Retirement.
R. B. Batty,	...	1860,	Punjab ...	D. June, 1861.
J. B. Wheeler,	...	1860,	Lucknow ...	R. 1861.
J. Barton,	...	1860,	Calcutta, etc...	R. Feb. 1876.
E. S. Puxley,	...	1861,	Santhalia ...	R. 1865.
J. M. Brown,	...	1861,	Punjab ...	R. Apr. 1866.
J. Welland,	...	1861,	Calcutta ...	D. Dec. 1879.
T. Storrs,	...	1861,	Lucknow ...	W. July, 1872.
W. P. Schaffter,	...	1861,	Tinnevelly ...	R. 1880.
J. Sharp,	...	1861,	Masulipatam	R. 1880.
W. Soans,	...	1862,	Derajat ...	D. June, 1862.
J. Cooper,	...	1862,	Do. ...	R. May, 1865.
T. Lane,	...	1862,	Travancore ...	R. Dec. 1868.
H. Bartlett,	...	1862,	Madras ...	D. Dec. 1865.
E. Wynne,	...	1862,	Junir ...	R. Sept. 1863.
H. S. Patterson,	...	1862,	Mooltan ...	R. Mar. 1866.
C. E. Vines,	...	1862,	Agra ...	D. Nov. 1879.
F. Wathen,	...	1862,	Amritsar ...	D. Nov. 1865.
A. Johnson,	...	1862,	Allepie ...	R. Dec. 1871.
J. Wilson,	...	1862,	Travancore ...	R. June, 1871.
J. L. Holbeck,	...	1862,	Scindh ...	R. 1863.
W. Handcock,	...	1863,	Peshawar ...	R. 1867.
J. F. D. Hoernle,	...	1864,	Meerut ...	R. 1878.
J. W. Bardsley,	...	1864,	Scindh ...	D. Feb. 1868.
J. Elmslie,	...	1864,	Kashmir ...	D. Nov. 1872.
R. Warren,	...	1864,	Bombay ...	R. 1865.
W. G. Mallet,	...	1865,	Amritsar ...	R. 1875.
J. Stevenson,	...	1865,	Do. ...	D. Dec. 1865.
C. W. H. Isenberg,	...	1865,	Hydrabad ...	D. Feb. 1870.
H. Croley,	...	1865,	Scindh ...	R. June, 1869.
L. E. W. Foote,	...	1866,	Bombay ...	R. Jan. 1870.
C. S. Cooke,	...	1866,	Do. ...	R. Feb. 1877.
J. C. Mill,	...	1866,	Tinnevelly ...	W. 1872.
E. Sampson,	..	1866,	Bombay ...	R. July 1871.
W. Ridley,	..	1856,	Peshawar ...	R. 1874.
D. Brodie,	..	1866,	Dera Ismail K.	R. 1874.
S. Carter,	..	1866,	Goruckpore ...	D. July, 1871.
W. Johnson,	..	1866,	Travancore ...	R. 1879.
W. Hope,	..	1866,	Do. ...	R. 1874.
C. E. Storrs,	..	1866,	Amritsar ...	R. 1871.
G. M. Gordon,*	..	1866,	Lahore ...	D. August, 1880.
A. B. Spaight,	..	1868,	Mooltan ...	R. 1870.

* Killed in action at Kandahar,

NAMES.		ARRIVAL.	FIELD OF LABOR.	DEATH, WITHDRAWAL OR RETIREMENT.
J. Conn,	..	1868,	Raghapuram	D. Dec. 1871.
W. Smith,	..	1868,	Travancore ...	D August, 1874.
R. F. F. Trench,	..	1868.	Lucknow ...	D. June, 1869.
J. W. Knott.	..	1869,	Lahore ...	D. June, 1870.
J. Shearman,	..	1869,	Madras ...	R. Dec. 1871.
F. Peake,	..	1870,	Tinnevelly ...	R. Jan. 1872.
A. Yarnold,	..	1871,	Hyderabad ...	R. 1878.
W. W. Cox,	..	1871,	Masulipatam	R. 1872.
H. Davis,	..	1871,	Taljhari ...	D. Sept. 1877.
S. T. Leupolt,	..	1871,	Calcutta ...	R. Feb. 1878.
H. R. Kendall,	..	1872,	Madras ...	R 1877.
W. Mitchell,	..	1872,	South India ..	R. 1877.
H E. Jennings,	..	1872,	Tinnevelly ...	R. 1875.
E. Carter,	..	1872,	Allahabad ...	D. Aug. 1872.
A. Morgan,	..	1872,	Masulipatam	R Oct. 1879.
F. H. Baring,	..	1872,	Amritsar ...	R Apr. 1880.
T. Maxwell,	..	1873,	Kashmir ...	R Nov. 1875.
G. T. M. Grime,	..	1873,	Agra ...	D Oct. 1878.
B. H Skelton,	.	1874,	Azimgurh ...	R. 1880.
E. Blackmore,	..	1874,	Tinnevelly ...	D. Oct. 1879.
D. T Barry,	..	1876,	Madras etc. ...	R. Jan. 1879.
F. W. Ainley,	..	1877,	Cottayam ...	R. Feb. 1879.
H. D. Day,	..	1879,	Calcutta ...	R. Nov. 1879.

———o———

II. THE GOSPEL PROPAGATION SOCIETY.

"The Society for the Propagation of the Gospel in Foreign Parts" was organized in June, 1701, when it received a charter from William III. It was designed "to provide for the ministrations of the Church of England in the British colonies and to propagate the Gospel among the native inhabitants of those countries." The Society began its labors in India in 1817.

I. Madras Presidency.—During the early years of the present century the old Danish Missions which were rapidly decaying were transferred as a rule to the Christian Knowledge Society and by this to the Propagation Society. In 1817 the latter Society established missions at Bangalore and in the province of Cuddapah. For many years but little progress was made in these fields: but within the past fifteen years there has been a great ingathering of converts, especially in Cuddapah. For several years prior to 1816 the misson of the Knowledge Society in Madras was sadly disorganized and inefficient: but in this year through the efforts of Bishop Heber while visiting Madras a thorough reformation was made and the mission revived at once. In 1825 a large church was completed; and about this time the mission was made over to the Propagation Society by which it has since been sustained.

The Danish missions in Tanjore and Trichinopoly passed into the hands of the Society about 1820. In these provinces the Society now has nine central missions besides numerous outstations. Cuddalore in the province of Arcot, and several stations in Madura, were also occupied about 1820. The early Bishops of the Church of England manifested peculiar interest in all the Society's missions, and by the erection of the see of Madras in 1835 the interests of these missions were still further advanced.

The first missionary appointed to Tinnevelly was the Rev. D. Rosen in 1829. In 1839 the missions were divided into small districts, which proved an excellent plan. In 1844 at Sawyerpuram and at Christianagram there were general movements towards Christianity and hundreds of accessions: so at Edeyeugoody and Nazareth.

In the same year two Theological Seminaries were established, one at Sawyerpuram in Tinnevelly and the other at Vediarpuram in Tanjore ; a third which had previously existed at Madras, was re-modelled.

In Tinnevelly and Ramnad the number of villages in which there are Christian congregations is 631. There are four Boarding schools, and several orphanages. In every district there is a Local Church Council, in addition to which there is a Provincial Church Council, in which all the clergy, European and Native, and elected lay representatives from each district, have a place and by which all questions affecting the welfare of the Native church are considered. It has been partly through the great increase of voluntary evangelistic effort which has taken place in Tinnevelly for some years past, and partly the influence of the lessons taught by the history of famine relief, that so many thousands of the people have within the last few years abandoned heathenism and placed themselves under Christian instruction. The progress made will be seen from a comparison of the following numbers : persons under Christian instruction, including baptized and unbaptized, in 1877, 1878 and 1879 respectively, 22,886 ; 39,946 ; 44,069.

A Medical mission was opened at Nazareth in 1870. There are also flourishing dispensaries at Erungalore and Madras.

When the Prince of Wales visited India, in 1875, 10,000 Native Christians of Tinnevelly, headed by Drs. Caldwell and Sargent, met His Royal Highness and presented him with an address, to which he made an appropriate reply.

In March, 1877, the Rev. Dr. Caldwell, the founder of the mission at Edeyengoody, was consecrated as Suffragan Bishop, Coadjutor to the Bishop of Madras.

II. Bengal Presidency.—The attention of the Society was directed to Bengal immediately after the foundation of the Episcopate. In 1818 Bishop Middleton proposed the establishment of a College to train Christian agents, and of Schools for Hindoos and Mohammedans. His proposal was favorably received and the foundation-stone of the new Institution at Calcutta was laid December 15th, 1820 : the building was completed about four years afterwards. The Institution has since been known as Bishop's College.

At the suggestion of Bishop Heber, the Society appointed

the Rev. T. Christian to Bhagulpur, in 1825, where he labored a short time and died in 1827. The Rev. W. Morton, who was the first missionary sent to Bengal by the Society, was appointed to Chinsurah, in 1829. The station was abandoned in 1837. Tallygunge was also occupied in 1829. The first missionary, the Rev. Mr. Tweedle, died in 1832, but the work has been successfully and steadily carried forward.

The Society established a station in Cawnpore in 1832, the Rev. J. Carshowe being the first missionary appointed. Tezpur, in Assam, was occupied in 1850. Forty schools have been established and at least nine Christian communities formed. The work at Delhi was begun in 1854. The mission was broken up by the Mutiny and the missionary, the Rev. A. R. Hubbard, and three assistant missionaries, were put to death by the rebels: but the mission was soon renewed, and has been greatly prospered since. Burmah was occupied by the Society in 1863, when a mission was opened at Rangoon. Moulmein and Mandalay were taken up in 1869 and Tounghoo, in 1875. At Rangoon, St. John's College contains about 600 boys. Work is carried on among the Tamils, Chinese and others. Mandalay was given up in 1879. The Chota Nagpore mission dates from 1869, when a number of Berlin missionaries who had been laboring there for years joined the Society. The progress here has been steady. Roorkee was occupied in 1871, Banda, in 1872.

In 1877, the Cambridge mission at Delhi was opened. It is carried on by the Rev. E. Bickersteth and five associates.

III. Bombay Presidency.—Bishop Heber while in Bombay in 1827, formed a committee in connection with the Propagation Society, but it was not until 1859, that a mission was established. A mission at Guzerat was opened in 1830, but was checked in the early death of its first missionary, the Rev. Mr. Pettinger. Kolhapur was occupied in 1870, Ahmednagar in 1872, and Dapoli, in 1878. In 1879 the statistics of the Society were as follows:—

European missionaries,	53,	increase since 1871,	12.
Native do.	62,	do.	25.
Native Christians,	53,842,	do.	8,759.
Communicants,	16,187,	do.	5,583.

MISSIONARY BISHOP.

The Right Rev. Bishop (Robert) Caldwell, D. D., L.L.D, M.R A.S. Born May 7, 1814, near Belfast. Studied at Glasgow. Ordained July 7, 1837. Came to India in 1837 in connection with the London Missionary Society, and labored at Madras until 1841 when he joined the Gospel Propagation Society. In 1842 commenced a station at Edeyengoody where he labored many years. March 11, 1877, consecrated at Calcutta Suffragan Bishop, coadjutor to the Bishop of Madras.

MISSIONARIES OF THE SOCIETY.

ABHISHEKANATHAN, SAMUEL. B. in Tinnevelly, Dec. 18, 1847 O.D. June, 1878. W. Native Pastor. Ad. *Rangoon, Burmah.*

ABRAHAM, G. O. 1879. Ad. *Ramnad, Madras P.*

ABRAHAM, V. O. 1874. Ad. *Nazareth, Do.*

ADAMSON, T. A. 1871. Ad. *Sawyerpuram, Do.*

ADEIKULAM, D. O. 1860. Ad. *Aneycadoo, Do.*

ALI, ABDUL. O. 1879. Ad. *Banda, N.-W. P.*

ALI, ASAD. O. 1880. Ad. *Delhi.*

ALLNUTT, S. S. O. P. 1866. A. 1879. Ad. *Delhi.*

ANTONI, DARI. O. 1875. Ad. *Ranchi, Chota Nagpore.*

ATHANASIUS. O. 1873. Ad. *Do. Do.*

BATSCH, FREDERICK GOTTLIEB. B. Jan. 24, 1820 at Straupitz, Germany. O. Berlin, July 8, 1844. A. Dec. 1844. S. Chota Nagpore, till 1868, in connection with the Berlin Society, since then in connection with the S. P. G. H. in 1860 and in 1874. Ad. *Ranchi, Chota Nagpore.*

BICKERSTETH, EDWARD. O. P. 1874. A. 1877. Ad. *Delhi.*

BILLING, G. A. 1871. Ad. *Ramnad, Madras P.*

BLACKETT, HERBERT F. A. 1878. O. P. at Delhi, 1880. H. to Eng., 1880.

BLAKE, W. H. A. 1875. Ad. *Tanjore, Madras P.*

BOHN, F. A. 1869. Ad. *Ranchi, Chota Nagpore.*

BOWER, HENRY. A. 1844. Ad. *Madras.*

CARLYON, HENRY C. O. P. 1873: A. 1878. Ad. *Delhi.*

CHAND, TARA. B. in Delhi, Nov. 5, 1839. O.D Dec. 1863. O.P. 1864. S. Delhi. L. "Mufta-ul-Iman," a manual of Christian Faith, Gyan Darpan, the same in Hindi character; "The Epistle to Diognetus" (Urdu and Hindi) S. P. C. K. Depot, Cawnpore; "Tazkarat-ul-Mominin, or Christian Life of the First Three centuries"; "Mawaiz-i-Uqba or the Letter of a Jewish convert to her father." Ad. *Delhi.*

CHOWDRY, B. C. O. 1857. Ad. *Howrah, Bengal.*

CHRISTIAN, S. O. 1869. Ad. *Mudaloor, Madras P.*

CLAY, JOHN. B. May 5, 1828 at St. Thomas Mount, Madras. O. D. March 12, 1854. O. P. April 1, 1855. S. Pastor of Engl. congregation at Cuddapah, 1854-56, since missionary among Telugus in Kurnal and Cuddapah Districts. L. "Elementary Catechism." "O. T. Stories:"

Translation of the Gospels and Acts from the original; compendium of "Pearson on the Creed." Ad. *Mutyalapad, Kurnal, Madras P.*

COE, J W. A. 1862. Principal Bishop's Col. Ad. *Calcutta.*

COULBECK, J. A. A. 1874. Ad. *Moulmain, Burmah.*

DEVASAYAM, SWAMIDIAN. B. at Nazareth, Aug. 5, 1832. O. D. March 17, 1867. O. P. Jan. 31, 1869. S. Edeyengoody 1867, Mudalur 1869, Ramnad 1871, Puthiamputhur 1878, Tuticorin 1879. W. Native Pastor. Ad *Tuticorin, Madras P.*

DEY, G. C. O. 1875. Ad. *Mograhat, Bengal.*

DREW, WILLIAM. B. at St. Columbo, Cornwall, in 1840. A. 1865, Ad. *Barripore, Bengal.*

DUNNE, D. H. G. A. 1868. Ad. *Cawnpore, N.-W.P.*

DUTT, ROGER. B in Calcutta, Nov. 9, 1847. O. April 4, 1874. S. 1868. Christ Church School, Cawnpore: 1869, Bishop's Col., Calcutta: 1870, Ranchi. Has been engaged in both Engl. and ver. W. L. Two small pamphlets, (1) A Compilation: "*Questions and Answers on the order for Morning and Evening Prayer.*" (2) "*The Church Catechism.*" Both are in Hindi and procurable at the S. P. C. K. Depot, Cawnpore. Ad. *Ranchi, Chota Nagpore.*

ELEAZER, J. O. 1862. Ad. *Salem, Madras P.*

ELLIS, PERCY ANSLEY. B. Kensington, Jan. 19, 1855. A. Dec. 14, 1877. O. D. Poona, June, 1879. S. Poona, Kolhapur, Ahmednagar. Ad. *Ahmednagar, Bombay P.*

ENDLE, SIDNEY. A. 1864. Ad. *Tezpore, Assam.*

FAIRCLOUGH, J. A. 1866. Ad. *Rangoon, Burmah.*

FLEX, OSCAR THEODOR. B. Aug. 27, 1840, at Dubrau, Prussia. A. in connection with Gossner's Society, in March, 1861. O. in 1869. M. 1869. S. Ranchee. W. in charge of mission schools, and engaged in other ver. L. Uraun Grammar (in Engl.) translations of Scripture portions into Uraun: several works in German. H. 1871-72. In 1877 joined the S. P. G. *Now in Europe.*

GADNEY, ALFRED. A. 1872. Ad. *Dapoli, Bombay P.*

GHOSE, B. C. O. 1875. Ad. *Ranchi, Chota Nagpore.*

GILDER, CHARLES. A. 1860. Ad *Bombay.*

GNANADHIN, JOSEPH. B. in Tinnevelly, Oct. 17, 1846. O. D. Jan. 30, 1876. O. P. March 17, 1878. E. Sawyerpuram Col. S. Pathiamputhur 1876, Ramnad 1878. W. Native Pastor. Ad. *Ramnad, Madras P.*

GNANAKKUN, G. M. B at Nazareth, Dec. 18, 1830. E. Sawyerpuram Inst. and Madras Sem. O. D. Dec. 24, 1871. O. P. Oct 11, 1874. S. Naugoor and Tranquebar. Ad. *Tranquebar, Madras P.*

GNANAMUTTU, ABRAHAM. B. in Tinnevelly, Feb. 14, 1839. O. D. March 9, 1879. E. Sullivan's Gardens, Madras. W. Native Pastor. Ad. *Daviputam, Ramnad, Madras P.*

GNAPRAGASAM, PARANJOTHY. B. at Nazareth, Sept. 10, 1837. O. D. Palamcottah, Jan. 26, 1873. Ad. *Ramnad, Madras P.*

GNAYAYUTHUM, P. O. 1879. Ad. *Ramnad, Madras P.*

HARRISON, HENRY JOSEPH. B Allahabad, Nov. 10, 1824, E. Bishop's Col. Calcutta, O. D. Nov. 1, 1848. O. P. May 1, 1851. S. Khari, 1848; Barripore, 1855, Tollygunge, 1871 to present. Ad. *Tollygunge, Bengal.*

HERZOG, A. A. 1869. Ad. *Ranchi, Chota Nagpore.*

HILL, J. R. A. 1862. Ad. *Banda, N.-W. P.*

HOPPNER, FREDERICK HENRY THEODORE. B. Prisaunewitz, Germany, April 10, 1829. O. June 26, 1853, and O. to full orders Oct. 4, 1864. A. Dec. 27, 1853 S. Buxar 1853, Ghazipore 1854-64, Muzafferpore 1864-74. H from 1874-75: Rt. in connection with S. P G in Oct. 1875. S. Roorkee. O. D Dec. 19, 1875. O. P. Feb. 6, 1876. Ad. *Roorkee, N.-W. P.*

HUNTER, T. W. A. 1876. Ad. *Calcutta.*

IGNATIUS, J. O. 1863. Ad. *Christianagram, Madras P.*

INMAN, A. A. 1877. Ad. *Mutialpad,* *Do.*

JONES, W. E. A 1879 Ad. *Tounghoo, Burmah.*

JOSEPH, D. O. 1879. Ad. *Puthiamputhur, Madras P.*

JOSEPH, S. O. 1869. Ad *Do.* *Do.*

KAY, W. H. A. 1875. Ad. *Tanjore,* *Do.*

KENNET, CHARLES ROBERT. B. at Madras, Sept. 21, 1826. O. D. Feb. 2, 1851. O P July 25, 1853. S Tinnevelly, 1848-65, Madras 1865 to present. C. K. S. Secretary from July, 1865 to April, 1880. Incumbent of St. John's Church from Oct. 1868. Divinity Lecturer in Theol. Sem. 1872-78. Principal of S P. G. Theol. Col. Oct 18, 1878 to present. H. from March 1860 to July 1861 and from April 1875 to Oct. 1875 Ad. Sullivan's Gardens, *Madras.*

KOHLHOFF, CHRISTIAN SAMUEL.* B. in Tanjore, May 14, 1815. O. D. Jan. 6,1839. O. P. Jan. 6, 1840. S. Mudaloor 1839, Dindigal, 1840, Trichinopoly, 1841. Erungalore 1843, Vepery, Madras, 1846. H. 1853-56. Rt. Jan. 19, 1856. S. Madras 1856, Erungalore 1858, Trichinopoly 1859, remaining at Erungalore. Founded in 1862, a Fund for the pension of widows. Served as a Delegate for the Revision of the Tamil Bible. and the Book of Common Prayer S. P. C. K. in Tamil. L. Compiled a Hymn-book in Tamil. (Depository at Madras). Ad. *Erungalore, Madras P.*

KRISTNA, J. O. 1879. Ad *Tounghoo, Burmah.*

KRUGER, FREDERICK. B. in Germany, Apr. 2, 1837. A. 1863. O. as S. P. G. Missionary in 1874. S. Purulia, 1863-66, since, Chaibassa. L. Translated Book of Common Prayer into the Lorka language: compiled First Reader in the same. H. 1873. Ad. *Chaibassa, Chota Nagpore.*

LATEWARD, H. E G. B. at Boulogne, France, June 1, 1849. A. 1876. O. D. 1877. O. P. 1878. S Kolhapur, Ahmednagar, Poona. Ad. *Poona.*

LAZARUS, G. O. 1862. Ad. *Bangalore.*

LEDGARD, G. A. 1863 Ad. *Bombay.*

LEEPER, F. J. A. 1857. Ad. *Cuddalore, Madras P.*

---

* It is a singular fact that in the family of Kohlhoffs, the missionary succession has been preserved 146 years, from father to son, and to the grandson, all laborers in India.

LEFROY, G A. O. D. 1878. A. 1879. Ad. *Delhi.*

LUTHER, W. O. 1869. Ad. *Ranchi, Chota Nagpore.*

MANUEL, A. O. 1875. Ad. *Tanjore, Madras P.*

MARGOSCHIS, A. A. 1877. Ad. *Nazareth, Do.*

MARKAS. O. 1873. Ad. *Ranchi, Chota Nagpore.*

MARKAS, MARSA. O. 1875. Ad. *Do. Do.*

MARKS, J. E. A. 1863 Ad. *Rangoon, Burmah.*

MARDWAI. O. 1879. Ad *Taunghoo, Do.*

MASIH DAS. O. 1873. Ad. *Ranchi, Chota Nagpore.*

MASILAMANI, A. O. 1856. Ad. *Puthiamputhur, Madras P.*

MITTER, P. L. N. O. 1869. Ad. *Jhanjra, Bengal.*

MURRAY, J. D. M. A. 1877. O. P. at Lahore, 1879. H. to Eng. 1880.

NATH, K M. O. 1870. Ad. *Calcutta.*

NORMAN, HARRY BATHURST. B. Havre, France. O. D. March 14, 1880. A March, 1879. W. Bishop Caldwell's Chaplain and assistant in the evangelistic department of his work. Ad. *Edeyengoody, Palamcottah, Madras P.*

OSWELL, G. D. Ad. *Calcutta.*

PAKKIAM, D. O. 1876. Ad. *Edeyengoody, Madras P.*

PARENJOTHY, G. O. 1874. Ad. *Do. Do.*

PARNPERSHED, KASCHAH. O. 1875. Ad. *Ranchi, Chota Nagpore.*

PAUL, B. N. O. 1862. Ad. *Meerpore, Bengal.*

PERIANAYAGAM, J. O. 1879. Ad. *Puthiamputhur, Madras P.*

PERIANAYAGAM, R. O. 1874. Ad. *Nazareth, Do.*

PRABHU DHANG. O. 1873. Ad. *Ranchi, Chota Nagpore.*

PRIESTLY, J. J. A. 1877. Ad. *Kolhapur, Bombay P.*

SAMUEL, D. O. 1859. Ad. *Edeyengoody, Madras P.*

SANDEL, H. N. O. 1857. Ad. *Calcutta.*

SAVARIMUTTU, D. O. 1851. Ad, St. Thome, *Madras.*

SEBASTIAN, ANTHONY. B. Madras, Sept. 5, 1837. E. Madras Training Inst. M. Jan. 19, 1859. O. D. Madras, March 17, 1867. O. P. Bangalore, Sept. 19, 1869. S. Oossoor, 1867-71 ; since, Secunderabad. W. Native Pastor. Ad. *Secunderabad, Deccan.*

SHARROCK, J. A. A. 1877. *Now in Europe.*

SHEPHERD, RICHARD DENDY. B. April 10, 1855, in Tenterden, Kent. A. Dec. 1. 1877. O. D. March 9, 1879. O. P. March 14, 1880. S. Mulyalapad 1877-80, since, Kalasayad. Ad. *Kalasayad, Madras P.*

SHWAY NYO. O. 1878. Ad. *Taunghoo, Burmah.*

SINGH, YAQUB KISHAN. B. near Agra, Dec. 15, 1826. O. Nov. 19 1871. Ad. *Rohtak, Punjab.*

SOLOMON, P. O. 1879 Ad. *Puthiamputhur, Madras P.*

SUNDOSHAM, D. O. 1879. Ad. *Do. Do.*

SUVESASHAMUTTU, A. O. 1879. Ad. *Do. Do.*

STRACHAN, J. M. A. 1862. Ad. *Madras.*

ST. DIAGO, J. A. 1866 Ad. *Bombay.*

SWAMIDASEN, A. O. 1865. Ad. *Trichinopoly, Madras P.*

SWAMIDASEN, S. O. 1871. Ad. *Ramnad, Do.*

TAUBIE. O. 1878. Ad. *Tounghoo, Burmah.*

TARYNAH. O. 1878. Ad. *Do. Do.*

TAYLOR, A. A. 1860. Ad. *Eastern Erungalore, Madras P.*

TAYLOR, J. A. 1866. Ad. *Kolhapur, Bombay P.*

VEDAKKAN, ARUMANAYAGAM. B. at Nazareth, 1836. O. D. March 9, 1879. E. Madras Diocesan Sem. Ad. *Paumben, Madras P.*

VETHAMUTHU, DEVAPINAM. B. at Nazareth, 1833. E. Diocesan Sem. Madras. O. D. 1866, O. P. 1869. W. Theol Tutor, at Sawyerpuram 1866-72, since 1872, Native Pastor. Ad. *Sawyerpuram, Madras P.*

WHITLEY, J. C. A. 1862, Ad. *Ranchi, Chota Nagpore.*

WILLIAMS, T. A. 1869. Ad. *Ahmednagar, Bombay P.*

WINDLEY, T. W. A 1875. Ad. *Tounghoo, Burmah.*

WINTER, R. R. A. 1860. Ad. *Delhi.*

WYATT, J. L. A. 1866. Ad. *Trichinopoly, Madras P.*

YESADIAN, GUMBATHAM. B. May 12, 1830. O D. Jan. 31, 1869. O. P. Jan. 30, 1876. W. Native Pastor. Ad. *Pettakulam, Madras P.*

YESADIAN, MADURANAYAGAM. B. Nazareth, 1833: O. D. 1867, O. P. 1869. W. Native Pastor. Ad. *Nazareth, Madras P.*

YESUDIAN, S. O 1879. Ad. *Puthiamputhur, Madras P.*

YESUDIAN, S. G. O. 1865. Ad. *Do. Do.*

YESUDIAN, V. B. Nazareth, Aug. 20, 1835. O. March 9, 1879. L. " Christian's duty of preaching to the Heathen" (in Tamil, Original. Ad *Eral, Tinnevelly, Madras P.*

RETIRED MISSIONARIES.

A. F. Cammerer. O. 1835. Ret. Ad. *Madras.*

John Guest. B. at Quilon, Oct. 11, 1812. E. at the C. M. S. Inst. and labored a short time with that Society. In 1832 joined the Wesleyan Society and labored in the Engl. school at Black Town. In March, 1836 transferred to Melnattam Tanjore, and thence in Feb. 1838, to Madras. In Jan. 1850 rejoined the Church of England and was appointed as catechist to Black Town. O. D. by the Bishop of Madras Feb. 27, 1842, after which time he labored at Pulicat until Oct. 1842, when he was O. P. and appointed to Cuddalore. In Jan. 1866 appointed to Erungalore ; in Oct. 1847 to Tanjore ; in June, 1851 to the Vepery mission, Madras, where he labored until April, 1864 : then re-appointed to Tanjore where he continued until Oct. 1872 when he was transferred to Trichinopoly and placed in pastoral charge of the Fort congregation. Ret. 1879. Ad. *Poonamallee, Madras.*

Thomas Phillip Adolphus. B. at Tranquebar, April 14. 1820. O. D June 18, 1848, O. P. Feb. 2, 1851. S, Sawyerpuram 1848, Ramnad and Paumben 1854, Pallamcottah, 1855, Trichinopoly 1864, Canadagoody, 1879. Ret. 1880. Ad. *Trichinopoly, Madras P.*

Balavandram David. B. in Tanjore, Dec. 1823. E. in S. P. G. Theol. Sem. Madras. O. D. March, 13, 1854. O. P. June 7, 1857. S, Ootacamund 1854-57, Madras 1858-74, W, Native Pastor. Ret. in 1874 on account of failure of sight. Ad. *Vepery, Madras.*

———o———

CHAPTER VI.

THE WESLEYAN MISSIONARY SOCIETY.

THE attention of the Wesleyan Church was directed to India by the venerable Dr. Coke, the "Father of Methodist Missions," in the year 1813: prior even to the formal organization of the Missionary Society. His heart was so set upon establishing a Mission to India that he offered to defray the expenses of beginning the same himself to the extent of £ 6,000. Accordingly at the Liverpool Conference in August, 1813, Dr. Coke and six young ministers, the Rev. Messrs. Ault, Lynch, Erskine, Harvard, Squance and Clough were appointed to proceed on a Mission to the East Indies. Judging that he would meet with less opposition from Government by beginning operations in Ceylon rather than in continental India, Dr. Coke with the party sailed for the former place, at the close of December, 1813. He died on the voyage; of apoplexy as was supposed, he being found dead in his cabin on the 3rd of May, 1814. (He was at this time sixty-six years of age.) The other members of the party committed the body of their leader to the deep, and proceeded on their way, arriving at Bombay May 21st. After spending a month here they (with one exception) embarked for Ceylon, where they arrived and began the work which has been carried continuously forward since.

From Ceylon the work spread to Madras. The Rev. Mr. Lynch was the first missionary of the Society here: he arrived in 1817, and labored successfully, especially among the English-speaking population. A chapel was erected in Black Town: subsequently work was begun among the Hindoos and Mohamedans. In 1859 a commodious Tamil chapel was built near the English church which is now the centre of the North Tamil circuit. The centre of the South Tamil circuit is at Royapettah, where a large native chapel has been erected and a flourishing Anglo-vernacular school established. Soon after the commencement of the work in the city of Madras, stations were formed and schools established at St. Thomas' Mount.

Stations were also formed at Trichinopoly (1818), at Negapatam, Manargudi, and Melnattam (1821); and (in 1861) at Warriore, Trivalur and Carur. In 1862 it was proposed to open a station at Hyderabad, and two missionaries visited the country about the Godavery, but several causes led to a postponement of operations. Hyderabad was taken up in 1879. These places are all included in the "Madras District." A "Children's Home" was commenced in 1877. It has four branches at Madras and elsewhere, and contains upwards of 300 children.

In 1817, the Rev. J. Horner was appointed to Bombay, and was joined in 1818 by the Rev. J. Fletcher, but from various causes the mission was relinquished in 1821, and the missionaries transferred to other places.

In 1820 the Rev. Messrs. Mowat and Hoole were appointed to Bangalore, but suffering shipwreck just before reaching Madras, they remained for a time at the latter place. In May, 1821, Mr. Hoole proceeded to Bangalore, and was soon after joined by Mr. Mowat. They began to preach at once, but before the work was fairly organized were called away to other stations. During the following three years Bangalore was visited only occasionally by the missionaries. In 1826 it was once more occupied; by the Rev. J. F. England, who preached in both English and Tamil and laid the foundation of a Native Church which has continued to the present. In 1836 the Rev. Thomas Hodson who was familiar with Canarese was appointed to the station aud began at once to preach in that tongue. Subsequently schools were opened, buildings erected, and an active printing establishment formed. Seringapatam was occupied in 1821, the Rev. T. Close being the first missionary to visit the place. A resident missionary was not appointed until some years later. Stations were formed at Gubbi in 1837, at Mysore and Ootacamand in 1839, at Tumkur in 1857, and at Shimoga in 1863. In 1853 the inhabitants of the city of Mysore petitioned the Society to establish in their city a first class English school, which was accordingly done: the school has continued in successful operation ever since. In 1873 Hassan became a regular station. The stations just named together with Bangalore form the "Mysore District." In the Famine of 1877 a new orphanage was formed at Hassan, and those at Bangalore and Tumkur were enlarged. In all, 500 orphans were received.

In 1829 the Rev. Messrs. P. Percival and Thomas Hodson were appointed to commence missionary operations in Calcutta. They arrived early in 1830, and entered upon their assigned work. They preached, built a native chapel and established schools: but after three or four years the station was abandoned and the laborers transferred to other places. After the lapse of about thirty years the way opened for the re-establishment of the mission, and in 1862 the Rev. Messrs. Broadbent and Highfield were appointed to the station. They arrived in September, 1862, and the work has since been carried steadily forward.

In 1864, the Society commenced operations at Lucknow by appointing the Rev. D. Pearson as chaplain to the garrison, and missionary. In 1869 a "Calcutta District" was formed, embracing Lucknow and Calcutta. Benares was occupied in 1880. This station, together with Lucknow and Fyzabad, constitute the "Benares District." It will thus be seen that the work of the Society in India is divided into four Districts, the Madras, the Mysore the Calcutta and the Benares.

The Society now occupies 24 stations in India. It has 44 foreign missionaries, 8 Native ordained agents and upwards of 2,000 Native Christians, of whom 1,000 are communicants.

MISSIONARIES OF THE SOCIETY.

ARNOLD, SAMUEL. B. Spalding, Lincolnshire, July 8, 1853. O. Sept. 11, 1879. A. Oct. 30, 1879. Ad. *Rungpur, Bengal.*

ARUMANAYAGAM, R. B. in Tanjore, May 25, 1842. E. Diocesan Inst. Madras. O. Jan. 13, 1878. S. Manargudi, 1878, Trichinopoly, 1879 Black Town, 1880. Ad. *Black Town, Madras,*

BARLEY, A. F. A. 1867. Ad. *Madras.*

BAUGH, G. A. 1861. Ad. *Calcutta.*

BOULTER, R. S. A. 1871. Ad, *Madras.*

BROADHEAD, J. R. A, 1875. Ad. *Calcutta,*

BURGESS, WILLIAM. B. Stockport, Sept. 12, 1845. A. 1866. S. Manargudi, 1866-71. Madras, 1871-74. H. to Eng. 1875-76. Madras, 1876-78, since, Hyderabad. Ad. *Secunderabad, Deccan.*

CARMICHAEL, THOMAS. A. 1879. Ad. *Fyzabad, Oudh.*

COBBAN, G. M. K. A. 1872. Ad. *Madras.*

COOLING, J. A. 1871. Ad. *Madras.*

DIXON, JOHN. A. 1863. Ad. *Madras,*

ESLICK, ELISHA ROBERT. B in S. Wales, Aug. 30, 1852. O. at Birmingham, Oct. 4, 1878. A. Nov. 15, 1878. Ad. *Bangalore.*

EVERS, PETER JAMES. B. Arcot, Jan. 23, 1831. O. 1857. S. Negapatam, 1857-58, Madras, 1859-62, Manargudi, 1863-66, Madras, 1867-72, Negapatam, 1873-75, Trichinopoly, 1876-78, Madras 1879 to present. W. Tamil and Engl. L. Prize Hand-bill (Tamil) on "the Throne of Grace," Tract Society. Translated in Tamil, "Englishwoman in India;" Higginbotham and Co. Madras, and "Life of Rev. John Wesley, M.A,": Eclipse Press, Negapatam. Ad. *Madras.*

FENTIMAN, ALBERT. A. 1864. Ad. *Benares.*

FRYAR, GEORGE. B. Wrekenton, Eng. Jan. 17, 1835. A. 1861. O. Jan. 15, 1865. S. Negapatam, 1861-66, Manargudi, 1866-79, since at Madras. H to Eng. 1874-75. L. "Tamil Proverbs." (incorporated with the Rev. P. Percival's work, published by Henry S. King and Co. in 1875.) "The Hill stations of South India," 1880: Messrs. Higginbotham and Co. Madras. Ad. *Madras.*

GLORIA, E. E. A. 1854. Ad. *Madras.*

GOSTICK, F. W. A. 1878. Ad. *Mysore.*

GULLIFORD, HENRY. B. Wheddon Cross, Somersetshire, Eng., Nov. 15, 1852. O. in Sept. 1877. A. Oct. 1877. S. Bangalore 1877, since at Mysore. W. educational. Ad. *Mysore.*

HAEGH, H. A. 1874. Ad. *Mysore.*

HALIDAY, F. A. 1874. *Now in Europe.*

HOBDAY, G. A. 1857. Ad. *Madras.*

HOBDAY, J. A. 1852. Ad. *Do.*

HOCKEN, C. H. A. 1871. Ad. *Mysore.*

HUDSON, JOSIAH. B. Westmoreland, 1840. Entered the ministry 1862. E. Lon. 1863. A. March, 1864. S. Bangalore 1864-65, Mysore (High School) 1866-67, Bangalore (High School) 1867-76. H. to Eng. from May, 1876 to June, 1878, since, Bangalore, in charge of Theol. Inst. and Chairman of Mysore Dist. Ad. *Bangalore.*

JOHNSON, JOSEPH A. *Now in Europe.*

KALYANA, RAMAN. O. 1869. Ad. *Madras.*

KENDALL. W. C. A. 1877. Ad. *Calcutta.*

LITTLE, H. A. 1872. Ad. *Madras.*

LUKE, S. A. 1878. Ad. *Mysore.*

MACDONALD, JAMES ALEXANDER DONALD JOHN. B. Banbury, Oxon, Oct. 1855. O. Birmingham, Oct. 4, 1878. A. Nov. 1878. Ad. *Barrackpore, Bengal.*

MALE, A. H. A. 1874. Ad. *Lucknow.*

PATTERSON, G. A. 1875. Ad. *Madras.*

PICKEN, WILLIAM HENRY JACKSON. B. Lincoln, Eng. July 15, 1855. O. Bradford, York, Sept. 13, 1880. E. Theol. Inst. Richmond. A. Nov. 1880. Ad. *Bangalore.*

PRATT, BENJAMIN. B. Bradford, Eng. 1853. O. 1880. A. Oct. 1880. S. *Secunderabad, Deccan.*

REES, D. H. A. 1875. Ad. *Mysore.*

RIDDETT, A. P. A. 1871. Ad. *Do.*

Roberts, Ellis. B. Clocaenog, N. Wales, Aug. 11, 1850. E. Didsbury Col. A. Nov. 1875. O. Bangalore, 1878. S. Chikballapur. Ad. *Bangalore.*

Row, Cooraswami. O. 1875. Ad. *Madras.*

Samuel, Jacob. O. 1874. Ad. *Mysore.*

Sawday, G. W. A. 1875. Ad. *Do.*

Slater, J. R. A. 1877. Ad. *Madras.*

Spencer, William Marshman. B. Draycott, Somerset, March 9, 1856. O. Bradford, York, Sept. 13, 1880. A. Nov. 13, 1880. Ad. *Raneegunge, Bengal.*

Sulivan, H. O. A. 1838. Ad. *Madras.*

Symons, Silas Edward. B. Cornwall, Eng. Nov. 20, 1831. O. Lon. Sept. 1858. A. Feb. 1859. S. Madras, 2 years, St. Thomas' Mount 3 years, Bangalore 14 years. H. to Eng. from 1869-71. Ad. *Bangalore.*

Thompson, J. M. A. 1876. Ad. *Madras.*

Vanes, James Alfred. B. in 1853. E. New Kingswood, Bath. (B. A. Lon. 1873). O. Jan. 1876. A. March, 1876. S. Bangalore, 1876-77 Gabbi, 1878, since, Bangalore, in charge of Wesleyan High School. Ad. *Bangalore.*

Wannal, R. D. A. 1874. Ad. *Mysore.*

Whitney, Joseph. B at Grendon, Eng. in 1857. O. at Lon. in Oct. 1876. A Dec. 3. 1876. Has labored since at Calcutta. W. ver. Ad. *Calcutta.*

———o———

CHAPTER VII.

THE GENERAL BAPTIST MISSIONARY SOCIETY.

THE General Baptists of England formed a Missionary Society in 1816, the leader in the movement being the Rev. J. G. Pike. In May, 1821, the Rev. William Bampton and the Rev. James Peggs were appointed as the Society's first missionaries to India. After remaining two months at Serampore and Calcutta they proceeded to Cuttack, where they arrived February 12, 1822. Mr. Bampton removed to Pooree in 1823, where he labored until his death in 1830. The first mission chapel at Cuttack was opened in November, 1826, on the site of a heathen temple. The first converts were made in 1828. In 1836 orphanages were established at Cuttack. Many children saved by the Government from the Meriah sacrifices were made over to the missionaries. The mission press was established at Cuttack in 1838, and has done much to promote the enlightenment of Orissa.

Stations were formed at Balasore in 1827, and at Midnaporo in 1836, which were made over to the American Free Baptists.

The Society has now four principal stations, Cuttack, Berhampore (Ganjam) Piplee, and Sumbulpore, C. P., with several important out-stations.

The following were the statistics for 1880 :—

Foreign missionaries,			8
Native ordained agents,	...	...	10
Native Christians,	...	...	2,722
Communicants,	...	...	997

MISSIONARIES OF THE SOCIETY.

BAILEY, THOMAS. B. April 11, 1837, at Barton Fabis, Leicestershire, at which place he was subsequently called to the ministry. E. at General Baptist Col. at Sherwood Rise, Nottingham: O. at Ashley-de-la-Zouch, Sept. 17, 1861. A. Nov 30, 1861. M. 1873. Has labored at Berhampore, Russelcondah, Cuttack and Piplee, mainly in the ver. but partly in Engl. H. to Eng. Jan. 1, 1872 to Oct 24, 1873. Ad. *Cuttack*, *Orissa.*

BARRICK, THOMA SANTRA. B. in 1837, at Byalli, Orissa. E. in the mission asylum, and the Col. at Cuttack. M. April 18, 1855. O. Jan 1, 1863. Has labored at Cuttack, Berhampore, Piplee, Choga, and Sumbulpore. Ad. *Sumbulpore, C. P.*

BROOKS, WILLIAM, ESQ. B. in 1819, at Ticknall, Derbyshire. M. in 1841. A. Nov. 27, 1841. H, in 1860 and in 1867, five years and ten months in all. Has labored at Piplee and Cuttack: as Supt. of the mission press, in charge of asylum, orphanages, and engaged in ver. preaching. Has edited "Introduction to the study of Oriya," compiled a new edition of "Oriya and English Dictionary," revised Bunyan's "Holy War," etc : Cuttack Mission Press. Ad. *Cuttack, Orissa.*

BUCKLEY, JOHN. A. Sept., 1844, Labored at Cuttack. H. 1875-76. Ad. *Cuttack, Orissa.*

DAS, HARAN. O. 1867. Ad. *Macmillanpatra, Cuttack, Orissa.*

DAS, MAKANDA. O, 1849. Ad *Piplee, Orissa.*

HEBERLET, PERCIVAL EDWIN. B. at Benares, July 21, 1854. A. 1879. Ad. *Sumbulpore, C. P.*

MAHANTY, DAMODAR. O. 1844. Ad. *Berhampore, Ganjam, Madras P.*

MILLER, WILLIAM. B. April 7, 1824, at Douglas, Isle of Man. O. May, 1845. A. Sept. 1845. S. Piplee, Pooree and Cuttack. L. Two Dictionaries, Engl. and Oriya; and Oriya Synonyms: translations, "Pictures and Sketches of Church History," "Fulfilled Prophecy," Tract on Mahomedanism, (Oriya); Tract "Praise to God" (Oriya and Sanskrit): Cuttack. H. 1857, 1870, 1879. Ad. *Cuttack, Orissa.*

NAIK, GHANU SHYAM. B. in 1824, in Orissa. Baptized June 30, 1839. E. at the mission school and college at Cuttack. O. in 1856. Ad. *Cuttack, Orissa.*

NAIK, KUMBHU. O. 1849. Ad *Khundittur, Orissa.*

PIKE, JOHN GREGORY. B. March 23, 1845, at Wisbech, Eng. E. at Regents Park Col. Lon. O. Jan. 5, 1869. Labored as pastor of Baptist Church, Commercial Road, Lon. 1868-73. A. Dec. 20, 1873. S Cuttack 1874-77, Berhampore, 1877-78, Cuttack, 1879, since, at (Ad.) *Sumbulpore, C. P.*

PATRA, SEBO. O. 1841. Ad. *Cuttack, Orissa.*

PATRA, TAMA. O. 1849. Ad. *Russelconda, Ganjam, Madras P.*

SAHOO, SHEM. B. Dec. 9, 1840, at Cuttack. Baptized Aug. 3, 1856. E. in the Mission Col. at Cuttack. M. May 24, 1859. O. Feb 26, 1869. Has labored since at Khoordah, as the agent of the "Auxiliary Missionary Society," formed at Cuttack in 1867. Has written a tract and several hymns: translated into Oriya "Pilgrim's Progress," Part First: Bunyan's "Dying Sayings: and "Sweet Story of Old": Mission Press, Cuttack. Ad. *Cuttack, Orissa.*

SINGH, PAUL. O. 1856. Ad. *Choga, Athgur, Orissa.*

VAUGHN, J. A. 1878. Ad. *Piplee, Orissa.*

WOOD, HENRY. B. June 26, 1843 at Stalybridge, Cheshire, Eng. O. Sept. 1872. A. Dec. 1876. Ad. *Berhampore*, Ganjam, *Madras P.*

DECEASED MISSIONARIES.

Names.	Date of Arrival.	Death.
William Bampton, ...	Feb. 12, 1822, ...	Dec. 17, 1830.
James Peggs, ...	do. do. do.	Jan. 5, 1850.
Charles Lacey, ...	Dec. 19, 1823, ...	Jan. 8, 1852.
Amos Sutton, ...	March 11, 1825, ...	Aug. 17, 1854.
Joshua M. Cropper, ...	Dec. 1827, ...	Dec. 8, 1828.
Thomas Grant, ...	Dec. 19, 1841, ...	Feb. 4, 1843.
John Orissa Goadby, ...	Dec. 1857, ...	July 27, 1868.
Bonamalee....		
Bamadabe, ...		Oct. 1, 1850.
Doitaree Naik, ...		May 31, 1852.
Deenabundhu Mahanty, ...		Sept. 1857.
Sebo Sahoo,...		Dec. 25, 1860.
Ram Chandra Jacheck, ...		Oct. 20 1863.
Jajannath Mahanty, ...		1864.
Gunga Dhor Sarangee, ...		Nov. 4, 1866.
Jagoo Roul,...		June 18, 1870.
Pursooa Rout, ...		1873.
William Bailey, ...		1880.

RETIRED MISSIONARIES.

Names.	Date of Arrival.	Retirement.
William Brown, ...	Dec. 1830,...	1837.
John Goadby, ...	Dec. 17, 1833,... ...	1837. To America.
John Brooks, ...	April 1, 1835, ...	June, 1845.
Isaac Stubbins, ...	Feb. 1837, ...	March, 1865.
Henry Wilkinson, ...	March 30, 1839, ...	1859.
William Hill, ...	Dec. 29, 1855,... ...	———
George Taylor, ...	do. do. do.	———
J. H. Smith, ...	Nov. 7, 1874, ...	March, 1877.

———o———

CHAPTER VIII.

CHURCH OF SCOTLAND MISSIONARY SOCIETY.

IN the month of February, 1796, two Missionary Societies were formed in the Church of Scotland; they were called the Glasgow and the Scottish Missionary Societies. In 1822 the latter Society sent to Western India the Rev. Donald Mitchell, who arrived in January, 1823, but died about eight months subsequently. Shortly before his decease there arrived three other laborers, the Rev. Messrs. John Cooper, James Mitchell and Alexander Crawford: and these were joined in February, 1824 by the Rev. John Stevenson. These missionaries labored first in the Southern Concan: but this field not proving very eligible it was abandoned and the Mission was transferred.

About 1825-26, the Church of Scotland became more throughly awakened in the cause of missions, and in the latter year a general missionary collection was made. The interest increased in 1827, and the Church began looking about for a missionary. The Rev. Alexander Duff was eventually chosen, and is generally spoken of as the first missionary of the Church of Scotland. He embarked for India in October, 1829, and arrived in Calcutta, in May, 1830.

In August, 1835 the Rev. Messrs. James Mitchell, R. Nesbit and John Wilson (of the Bombay mission) were on their own application amicably transferred from the Scottish Missionary Society to the Church of Scotland. Between 1829 and 1835 a flourishing educational institution had been established at Bombay, chiefly through the efforts of Mr. Wilson.

During the next few years the Church sent a number of missionaries to India, among them the Rev. Mr. Anderson, who proceeded to Madras to establish an institution of learning similar to those already in existence at Calcutta and Bombay.

The Disruption occurred in May, 1843, and materially lessened the number of foreign missionaries of the Church of Scotland, those in India universally adhering to the Free

Church; and this of course caused a temporary cessation of the missionary operations of the Established Church. The Society's educational institutions were re-opened soon after the Disruption; that in Calcutta by the Rev. Dr. Ogilvie who spent more than 25 years laboring in connection with it. At Calcutta and Bombay, buildings had been erected and these with libraries, furniture, etc., remained in the hands of the Church of Scotland. In 1871 these schools, contained in all near 2,000 pupils. While the Society has in the main confined its operations to the Presidency seats it has also taken up other stations. Sealkote in the Punjab was added in 1858; Secunderabad and Vellore were occupied in 1861: Guzrat, (Punjab), in 1868; Darjeeling, in 1870; while in 1873 the Chamba mission, founded in 1863 by the Rev. Mr. Ferguson of the Scotch Kirk, was made over to the Society.

The Society now occupies 10 stations in India and has 17 foreign missionaries and 4 native ordained agents: with 681 native Christians, and 326 communicants.

Reference may here be made to the "Presbyterian Alliance of India."

"Indian missionaries of various Presbyterian Societies anxious for unity, have formed themselves into a Confederation in order that while retaining connection with their own distinctive denominations, they may act together in India as one undivided community. The importance of the organization will be seen in the fact that missionaries of the following societies are associated with it: the Church of Scotland, the Free Church of Scotland, the United Presbyterian Church of Scotland, the American Presbyterian Church and the Reformed Church in America." The Confederation held its first conference in Allahabad in November, 1873, and another at the same place in December, 1875, at which time an organization called "The Presbyterian Alliance of India" was formed, which is to meet in Council ordinarily once in three years. The first Council was held in Dec. 1877, the second (at Allahabad) in Dec. 1880.

MISSIONARIES OF THE SOCIETY.

Bailey, Wellsley Cosby. B. at Abbeyleix, Ireland, in 1846 Came to India in 1869 in search of Government employment. Afterwards joined the Lodiana Mission (American Presbyterian) as head master of the Amballa mission school in Dec. 1869. M. in Oct. 1871. Was appointed Supt. of the Lodiana mission school in Nov. 1872: went home in 1873 on account of wife's health. Sent out as an evangelist to Chamba in Nov. 1874 by the Church of Scotland. W. both Engl. and Ver. In Oct. 1879 transferred to Wazirabad. Is Indian Hon. Sec. to the Mission to Lepers in India: author of several pamphlets on Mission work among Lepers. Ad. *Wazirabad, Punjab.*

Bourquin, A. A 1871. Ad. *Bombay.*

Chuckerbutty, Bipro Churn. B. near Calcutta, in 1823. Forefathers were Kulin Brahmins, and priests by profession. His mother burned herself as a *suttee.* Was brought up in the Government Sanskrit Col., Calcutta. Was baptized in 1843: began teaching and preaching in Bengali. Licensed in 1868, and O. in 1872, by the Presbytery of Calcutta, as pastor of St. Andrew's Bengali Church, Boitakhana: L. Six Tracts on "*The Hindoo gods and goddesses:*" a tract on "*The True Guide:*" and two small Christian hymn-books: published by the Calcutta Tract and Book Society. Also a Bengali Grammar; a series of Bengali books, and two elementary Sanskrit books for the use of the missionary schools in Bengal. All except the tracts and Grammar now out of print. Some years ago was editor for more than two years of a bi-monthly Bengali periodical, called the "*Aurunodaya.*" Ad. *Calcutta.*

Coomarappen, D. Ad. *Vellore, Madras P.*

Edwards, James. O. Sept 15, 1874. S. Bombay, two years; since, General Assembly's Inst, Calcutta. W. Educational. Ad. *Calcutta.*

Harper, William. B. Aberdeenshire, Scotland, 1845. O. Sept. 1873. A. Nov. 1873. S. Gujrat, 1873, Sealkote, 1874 to present. L. "Religious Ritual," both in Engl. and Urdu," "Prayer Books" in Engl. to be had of the author. Ad. *Sealkote, Punjab.*

Hastie, William. Principal, General Assembly's Inst. Ad. *Calcutta.*

Hutcheson, John. (L. R. C. P. and S. E.) B. Dumfriesshire, Scotland, 1847. A in April 1870: S. Sealkote, 1870, to Nov. 1873, since at Chamba. H. 1877. Ad. *Chamba, Himalayas.*

Lal, Sohan. Ad. *Chamba, Himalayas.*

Legate, G. W. Ad. *Arconum, Madras P.*

Macfarlane, William. B. in Dunkeld, Perthshire, Scotland, Jan. 5, 1840. Licensed to preach in St. Andrews in May 1862, and O. in Glasgow, Jan. 1865. Labored in Glasgow in connection with St. Columba's church 1862-65. A. March, 1865. Labored in Gya from March, 1865, till June, 1870, when the mission of the Church of Scotland in that place was removed to Darjeeling, where he was transferred and where he has since labored. W. both Engl. and Ver.; both teaching and preaching. Has written and translated two or three simple Primers and tracts in Nepaulese and Lepcha: Darjeeling Mission Press. Ad. *Darjeeling, Bengal.*

MELVIN, WILLIAM FOTHRINGHAM. B. St. Cyrus, Kincardineshire, Nov. 26, 1842. A. Feb. 22, 1867. W. Principal, General Assembly's Inst., Bombay. H. from April, 1874 to May, 1875. Ad. *Bombay.*

PATERSON, CHARLES ALFRED, ESQ. B. Glasgow, Feb. 22. 1847. E. at Glasgow Univ. (M. A., LL B.) A. March 15, 1880. Not O. W. Educational. A. *Vellore, Madras P.*

RICE, HENRY. B. at Bangalore, Jan. 4, 1846. E. at Blackheath, Lon., Cheshunt Col. and the Missionary Col. at Highgate, Lon. O. Aug. 15, 1869. A. Madras. Oct. 8, 1869. S. Coimbatoor. Transferred in Nov. 1870 to the L. M. S. Inst, Madras. In Jan. 1873 appointed to the charge of Salem and Tripatoor. From March, 1875 to Nov. 1876 labored at Tripatoor. H. from Nov. 1876 to Feb. 1879. M. Jan. 17, 1879. Rf. in March, 1879. S. Madras. Labored in evangelistic work in Madras in connection with the L M. S. until Nov. 30, 1880, when he transferred his services to the Church of Scotland Mission. Madras. At present evangelistic W. in Engl. and Ver. with the oversight of schools. L. "Helps to truth seekers, or current objections to Christianity considered," (Engl.) Bangalore Tract and Book Society. Ad. *Madras.*

RUNGANATHUM, C. Ad. *Vellore, Madras P.*

SAMUEL, W. Ad. *Madras.*

SINCLAIR, D. B. East Lothian, in 1844. E. Edinburgh Univ. (B. A. 1866). A. 1869: has labored since at Madras. W. Educational. L. History of India: Addison and Co. Madras. Ad. *Madras.*

SUTHERLAND, WILLIAM SOMERS. B. Fraserburgh, Aberdeenshire, Jan. 4, 1856. E. Aberdeen. (graduated in 1876; M. A.) O. in Dec. 1879. A. Feb. 1880. Ad. *Darjeeling.*

THOMSON, JAMES. B. Aberdeen, Scotland, 1854. O. 1878. A. 1878. Professor in General Assembly's Inst., Calcutta Ad. *Calcutta.*

TURNBULL, ARCHIBALD. B. Kirkliston, July 26, 1855. E. Educational Univ. (M. A., B. D.) O. Edinburgh, Nov. 1880. A. Jan. 12, 1881. Ad. *Darjeeling.*

WILSON, JAMES. B. at Glasgow in 1836. E. at the High School and Univ. of that city. Engaged for several years in commercial employment in Glasgow. A. as a lay missionary in 1862, and has labored in connection with the Assembly's Inst., Calcutta. M. in 1864. H. 1870-71. *Now in Europe.*

YOUNGSON, JOHN WHITE. B. in Rosehearty, Scotland, March 6, 1852. O. July 28, 1875. A. Oct. 10, 1875: has labored since at Guzrat. L. "Haqiqi Qurbani" in Urdu. Ad. *Guzrat, Punjab.*

RETIRED AND DECEASED MISSIONARIES.

James Ogilvie, D. D. B. in Keith in Banffshire in 1811. E. at the Univ. of Aberdeen. He was appointed to India, and A. at Madras in Jan. 1845. In 1846 he was transferred to Calcutta where the rest of his life was spent. By him as Principal and his colleagues, the General Assembly's Inst. was re-opened in 1846. In 1867 the degree of Doctor of Divinity was conferred upon him by his Alma Mater. During the 26 years of his

Indian career he never went on furlough. Towards the close of 1870 he was seized with fever; he was ordered to Singapore; but as he grew weaker he had to be landed at Penang, where he D. Jan. 25, 1871.

James Charles Herdman, D. D. Labored for several years in the Assembly's Inst. at Calcutta. Afterwards obtained a chaplaincy, then became minister of a parish church in Melrose. Is now the Convener of the Foreign Mission Committee of the Church of Scotland.

John Anderson. Labored for several years in the Assembly's Inst. at Calcutta. Upon taking furlough was appointed to the parish of Culter in Lanarkshire, Scotland.

William White. Labored for a few years in the Assembly's Inst. at Calcutta: then obtained charge of Presbyterian Church, Manchester.

Charles James Cameron. E. in Canada. Labored for about two years in Bombay. Left about 1869 from ill health, and proceeded to Australia. Is now in Canada.

Charles Munro Grant. O. by the Presbytery of Glasgow. Was for about two years in charge of a church in Halifax. Labored for two years amongst the educated Natives of Calcutta. In 1871 Ret. from ill health, and is now minister of St Mary's church, Partick, Glasgow.

William Ferguson. O. (about) 1852. A. in 1853, as a missionary of the Church of Scotland: appointed to Bombay. Rt. home the same or following year on account of wife's health. Was appointed chaplain in the army, and served through the Crimean War and the Indian Mutiny, being present at the siege and capture of Lucknow. Served in I. till 1863, when he resigned his chaplaincy with the view of beginning an independent mission in Chamba. Labored in Chamba till 1870, when he went home. R. in 1872. Ret. in 1873, when his mission was made over to the Church of Scotland.

Jacob Isaac David. Son of the Rev. Isaac David. B. at Salem, Feb. 23, 1838. E. in the L M. S. Inst. at Madras. Joined the Church of Scotland in 1858. O. 1859 S. Madras until his death, Aug. 19, 1869.

Joseph David. Son of the Rev. Isaac David. B. at Salem in 1830. E. in the L. M. S. Inst. at Madras. Joined the Church of Scotland in 1849: in 1860 was licensed by the Presbytery of Madras and appointed to Vellore, where he continued to labor until his death, early in 1865.

Thomas Hunter. B. in Aberdeen, Dec. 4, 1827. A. at Bombay in 1855 Labored here some months: in Oct. 1856 proceeded to the Punjab, and began a station at Sealkote, where, with his wife and child, he perished at the hands of the rebels in July, 1857.

R. Jardine. B. in 1840, at Brockville in Canada. E. at Queen's Col. Kingston. (B A. and B. D. 1866). Afterwards proceeded to Scotland and attended the Univ. of Edinburgh, where he obtained the degree of Doctor in Science in 1867. In the same year was appointed Professor in the Univ. of New Brunswick where he remained two years. Was appointed to India. and O. by the Presbytery of Glasgow. A. at Bombay in Feb. 1870, where he remained one year, when he accepted the Principalship of the General Assembly's Inst. Calcutta, which he filled till June, 1879 when he Ret. L. "The Psychology of Cognition."

CHAPTER IX.

Free Church of Scotland Missionary Society.

No history of the Free Church of Scotland Missions in India would be complete without prominent reference to the work done prior to 1843 at Calcutta and elsewhere. Immediately on his arrival in Calcutta, Dr. Duff established an educational Institution for the godly training of non-christian young men in English Literature, Science, etc. He had specially in view the conversion of souls to Christ and thereafter the training of such for the Christian ministry, not only for the Church of Scotland, but also for other Missions and Churches co-operating with him. As regards the latter part of his scheme he sought and obtained the sympathy and promise of co-operation from the members of the Calcutta Missionary Conference. The idea seems, however, to have been premature then, and nothing came of it for many years, but it is now largely carried out in the Christian College of South India at Madras. The Institution soon became a great success, and the names of upwards of a thousand boys were on its rolls. The education, as tested by the most experienced, was pronounced thoroughly efficient, and the Governor General of the day, Lord William Bentinck, publicly declared the result as "unparalleled." From the beginning the teaching of the Bible and public prayer occupied the most important place in the daily work of the Institution. Dr. Duff says that, "while from the very first the Bible itself was made a school and class-book it was so made *distinctly, avowedly and exclusively for religious and devotional exercises.*" Form the beginning Dr. Duff also, in addition to the work in the institution, carried on outside it evangelistic and missionary services of various kinds. In these his colleagues and successors also engaged, but the work both in the Institution, as far as carried on directly by the European missionaries in Bengal, has been by means of the English language. The first converts of the mission were the fruit of these extra labours. They were Mohesh C. Ghose and the now well-known Sanskrit scholar, the Rev.

K. M. Bannerjea, LL. D. They were led to the Lord in 1832. The first convert from the Institution was baptized the following year. Dr. Duff had in the meantime been joined by other laborers, and when in 1834, his health had so completely broken down through over exertion that he was forced to leave the country for a few years, the work was left under the charge of Dr. Mackay, Dr. Ewart, and others.

The Mission was also extended by the opening of branch schools in the neighbourhood; but more especially by the enlargement of the work in Bombay and Poona. In the Bombay Presidency the missionaries gave themselves much more to the vernacular languages and the study of oriental thought and religious systems. Among their first converts were the Parsee Dhunjeebhoy Nowrojee and the Brahmin Narayan Sheshadri, both still labouring as honored ministers, and the Rev. Hormasdjeo Pestonjee now in the Baptist mission, Poona. The western Mission laboured among Jews, Parsees, Mahomedans, Portuguese and Africans, as well as Hindoos, speaking various languages. Dr. Wilson was also largely helpful in the establishment of the Irish Presbyterian Missions in Gujerat and Scindh and of the United Presbyterian Church Missions in Rajpootana. The work at Madras was carried on also on the same educational plans as the Bombay and Calcutta Missions. Among its most distinguished converts were the late Rev. A. Venkataramiah and the Rev. J. Rajahgopal. The work here also extended not only in the capital but also in the surrounding towns and villages, by means of branch schools and schools for girls.

When the Disruption took place in the Church of Scotland, all the missionaries without exception, fourteen in number, adhered to the Free Church party, believing that it better than the other party represented the Church which had sent them out. The work went on, as far as they were concerned, without any change of plan, agency, locality or sphere of labour, save that additional men were sent out and new fields occupied. The Madras Institution continued in the same building, being only hired, but the Calcutta and Bombay Institutions had to vacate the old buildings and to obtain new ones, which they soon did. Immediately after the Disruption the Free Church opened a new mission in Nagpore under the Rev. S. Hislop, by means of money left for that purpose by the wife of Captain, now Sir William Hill, K. C. S. I. Other missions soon followed in the rural districts of Bengal, Bombay and Madras.

The rural missions at Mahanad in Bengal under the Rev. J. D. Bhuttacharjea, and that at Indapore and Jalna in Bombay under the Rev. Narayan Sheshadri, are of especial interest, but carried on on two different plans, the first being chiefly educational and consequently for the young. The other is more purely evangelistic, and remarkable as the only Free Church mission in a feudatory State. Near the place where Dr. Wilson was forbidden to preach in 1832, the Nizam's Government has granted a free site for a Christian Church and renewed, on favourable terms, a lease of the land on which a Christian village has been built professedly as a centre of evangelistic operations in His Highness' dominions. This village had only two Christians in it in 1864. Now there are 600.

Pachamba, near the Kurhurballi coal mines about 210 miles N.-W. of Calcutta, is the centre of missionary operations among the Santals. In addition to smaller branch stations there are two larger ones. This mission was opened in 1871.

The Rev. James Dawson commenced work in 1869, among the 300,000 Gonds in and around Chindwara, some 70 miles north of Nagpore, and has laboured among them ever since, assisted by catechists, evangelists and teachers.

With greater or less persistency, the Bombay missionaries have laboured to evangelize the Waralis a jungle tribe in the Northern Concan, from 1834 to the present time, but not with such encouraging results as have followed labours given to the aboriginal tribes in other parts of India and Burmah.

Besides these Indian Missions, the Free Church of Scotland carry on missionary operations on the continent of Europe, in Syria, in Central and South Africa and in the islands of the New Hebrides in Melanesia. Altogether since the Disruption £586,828 have been subscribed towards the Foreign Missions of the Free Church alone, and there are now in connection with them 3,384 communicants, of whom 891 are in India; there are also in India 1,476 baptized adherents in connection with them.

The present staff in charge of 10 principal stations, and

43 branch stations are, 22 European and 8 native ordained missionaries, 9 licentiates, 5 unordained medical missionaries, 12 European missionary teachers, and 12 other teachers, 144 native teachers, 2 European lay evangelists, 36 native catechists and 40 other Christian agents, making in all 286 Christian agents.

This includes the work carried on by the Ladies' Society for Female Education in India and South Africa, commenced in 1837 by Mrs. Margaret Wilson the wife of Dr. John Wilson of Bombay. It works chiefly by means of orphanages, Boarding and Normal schools for the growing native Christian community, Hindu day schools and Zenana teaching. This Society works side by side with the Foreign Missions of the Free Church and is really an integral part of them. [K. S. M.]

MISSIONARIES OF THE SOCIETY.

ALEXANDER, ALEXANDER. A. 1877. Ad. *Madras*.

ANDREW, ADAM. B. Dailly, Scotland, June 7, 1854. O. June 19, 1879 at Glasgow. A. Sept. 23, 1879. S. Chingleput. W. Ver. Ad. *Chingleput, Madras P.*

BANERJEA, P. K. O. 1879. Ad. *Bansberia, Bengal.*

BANERJEA, SHIB CHANDRA. Ad. *Calcutta.*

BAUBOO, R. M. Ad. *Madras.*

BEAUMONT, J. S. A. 1855. Ad. *Poona.*

BHUTTACHARJEA, JAGADISHWAR. B. about 1823. Baptized at Calcutta by Dr. Duff, in Nov. 1841. O. Sept. 1855. Ad. *Mahanad, Bengal.*

BLAKE, BUCHANAN, A. 1876. Ad. *Bombay.*

BOSE, P. C. Ad, *Calcutta.*

CAMPBELL, ANDREW. A. 1871. Evangelist among the Santhals. Ad. *Pachamba, Bengal.*

COOPER, CHARLES. B. Oct. 26, 1831, in the parish of Kincardine O'Neil, Aberdeenshire, Scotland. Licensed, 1864. O. Jan. 23, 1866. Was pastor of the United Presbyterian congregation, Holm of Balfron, Sterlingshire, Scotland from Jan. 23, 1866 till Nov. 1868. A. Feb. 27, 1869. Head Master, Doveton Protestant Col., Madras five years. Joined the Free Church Col. Madras, in April, 1874, where he still labors. W. Engl. H. 1879-80. Ad. *Caseemode, Madras.*

COOPER, JOHN G. O. in Nov. 1855, and A. at Madras in the following month. In 1856 he proceeded to Nagpore, where he has since labored. H. 1870-72. Ad. *Nagpore, C. P.*

DANIEL, S. A. Ad. *Calcutta.*

DAWSON, JAMES. B Dunblane, Perthshire, Scotland, Sept, 29, 1832. O. Edinburgh, Oct. 6, 1864. A. Nov. 1864. S. Nagpore 1864, Chindwara, 1866 to present. L. Original: "Gondi Words and Phrases;" "Additional Gondi Vocabulary;" "A Skeleton Grammar in Gondi;" "Gondi

First Book," C. V. E. S. Allahabad. Translated Gospels according to St. Matthew and St. Mark in Gondi, N. I. B. Society, Allahabad. H. to Scotland, 1875-76. Ad. *Chindwara, C. P.*

DAY, LAL BEHARI. B. 1826, at Palasi, Burdwan, Bengal. E. at the General Assembly's Inst, then under the superintendence of Dr. Duff. Baptized in 1843. O. in 1855 by the Free Presbytery of Calcutta and appointed to Calna. In 1859 travelled through North-west and Central I. M. in 1860, at Gogo, Guzerat. On returning to Calcutta was elected pastor by the congregation of Native Christians at Cornwallis' Square, and inducted minister of that church in Oct. 1860. Resigned this charge in 1867, and was appointed Head Master of the Government Col. at Berhampore. In 1872 transferred to the Hooghly Col. as Assistant Professor; is now Professor of Engl. Literature and History in the same. Though not now formally connected with any mission he holds every Sunday with the sanction of the Free Presbytery of Calcutta at the mission church at Chinsurah a service in Engl. for the benefit of the Europeans and others of that station. L. (1.) In Bengali, for the Calcutta Christian Tract Society, a tract on "Vedantism," which has since been translated into Engl. (2,) Edited in Bengali for the Tract Society a fortnightly illustrated periodical, "*The Aurunodaya.*" (3.) Started successively two weekly newspapers in Engl. "*The Indian Reformer,*" and "*The Friday Review.*" (4.) Published in 1867, "An Antidote to Brahmoism, in Four Lectures:" (5.) Has written several pamphlets, such as "Searchings of Heart in connection with Missions:" "Literary Beauties of the Bible:" "Primary Education in Bengal," etc. Is the author of "Govinda Samanta:" Macmillan and Co., Lon.; and "Recollections of Alexander Duff;" 1879, Nelson and Sons, Edinburgh. Is at present Editor of the *Bengal Magazine*, a monthly periodical in Engl. Ad. (Hooghly College.) *Chinsurah, Bengal.*

DE, BAIKANTHA NATH. Ad. *Calna, Bengal.*

DE, KEDAR NATH. O. 1880. Ad. *Chinsurah, Do.*

DOUGLASS, JOHN. A, 1878. Ad. *Nagpore, C. P.*

DYER, JAMES ALEXANDER. (L. R. C. S. Ed.) B. Leslie, Scotland, July, 1848. A Dec 1875 H. Oct. 1877 to Nov. 1878. Unordained Medical missionary. Ad. *Pachamba, Bengal.*

ELDER, WILIAM. (L. R. C. S Ed.) B. Dec. 23, 1845, at Buckie, Banffshire, Scotland. Home mission work in the Cowgate, Edinburgh for five years during Col. course. Appointed to I. in June, 1871. A. Nov. 11, 1871. Has labored at Madras; ver. and Engl. preaching; dispensary work and teaching. M. Dec. 29, 1874. Ad. *Madras.*

FYFE, WILLIAM CRICHTON. Appointed to Calna as a teacher Nov. 15, 1841. Licensed to the ministry Nov. 18, 1856, and O. April 29, 1860. S. Calna and Calcutta. H. 1871: since returning has served as Principal of the Free Church Inst. Ad. *Calcutta.*

GRIEVE, ALEXANDER CHRISTIE. B Portobello, Edinburgh, May 9, 1847. O. Edinburgh, Nov. 30, 1876. A. Feb. 10, 1877. Ad. *Bombay.*

HECTOR, JOHN. O. at Aberdeen, Dec. 14. 1871, and A. at Calcutta early in 1872, where he has since labored. Ad. *Calcutta.*

Macdonald, D. (M. B.) A. 1878. Ad. *Bombay.*

Macdonald, Kenneth Somerled. B. April 18, 1832, at Glen-Urquhart, Inverness, Scotland. Licensed, Oct. 9, 1861, O. Jan. 8, 1862: A. March 1, 1862. M. April 7, 1863. Has labored at Calcutta. From Nov. 1, 1873 to Feb. 1. 1875 was minister of the Free Church congregation. W. has been Engl. L. Annotated a number of Engl. Classics; edited and annotated Reid's "Enquiry"; edited the periodicals, *Indian Student*, 3 vols.; *Calcutta Christian Advocate*, etc: author and compiler of a number of school and college text-books, and of Lectures on Instinct and Intelligence" and "Auguste Comte, the Positivist" (translated into Bengali): "Rome's Relation to the Bible"; "The Vedic Religion," etc. the most of which are obtainable at Thacker, Spink and Co., Calcutta or at the Bible Society's House. H. from Dec. 1871 to March, 1873: Is Hon. Secretary of the Calcutta Bible Society: Editor of *Indian Evangelical Review*. Ad. *Calcutta.*

Macdonald, Roderick N. A. 1876. Ad. *Calcutta.*

Mackichan, Dugald. O. in 1874, and proceeded to Bombay, where he has since labored. Ad. *Bombay.*

Mahatekar, L. R. Ad. *Indapoor, Deccan.*

Maitra, Guru Das. B in Bengal Sept. 6, 1826. O. Nov. 6, 1864 by the Lodiana Presbytery at Umballa. S. Calna, 1852-57, Bansberia 1857-59, Lahore 1859-69, since 1869, Calcutta, W. Pastoral. Ad. *Calcutta.*

Miller, William. B. at Thurso in 1838. O. in 1862. A. in 1862. Has been since, Principal of the Madras Mission Inst. of the Free Church. H. during 1862. Has published a number of Lectures, chiefly historical. especially, "The Plan of History." Ad. *Madras.*

Misal, Sidoba Bapoojee. B. Sholapur, Sept. 1829. E. Ahmednagar and Sirur. O. in connection with the Am. Board in 1859. S. Sirur 1859-68, Berar 1868. In 1870 joined the Free Church Mission; has labored since at Amroati, Berar. L. several original tracts in Marathi. Ad. *Amroati, Berar.*

Navalkar, Gunpatrao. Ad. *Bombay.*

Nowroji, Dhanjibhai. B in Gujrat, 1822. Went to Europe with Dr. Wilson, in 1843. E. Free Church Col. Edinburgh. O. Edinburgh, 1846. Rt. 1847. S. Gujrat 1847-75. Bombay 1875 to the present, L. A tract, "Polytheism of the Parsis," Bombay Tract and Bible Society. Ad. *Bombay.*

Rae, George Milne. B. Udny, Aberdeenshire, Scotland. Sept. 2, 1840. O. Aberdeen, June 27, 1867. A. 1867. S. Madras. W. Professor in Free Church Inst. and Madras Christian Col. H. Feb. 1875 to Sept. 1876. Ad. *Madras.*

Rajahgopal, P. B about 1823. Baptized at Madras June 20, 1841. Licensed in 1846. In April, 1849 went to Eng. Rt. to Madras in Dec 1850. O. Nov. 26, 1851. In July, 1858 called to the pastorate of the Madras Native church. In 1863 labored for a time at Nellore: since at Madras. Ad. *Madras.*

Robertson, James. O. June 8, 1871. A. in Calcutta the same year, where he labored until Jan. 1877, when he resigned. Rejoined Jan. 1881. Ad. *Calcutta.*

SCOTT, ROBERT. B. Banffshire, Scotland, Sept. 29, 1853. O. Aberdeen, June 24, 1879. A. Dec. 1879. Ad. *Bombay.*

SHESHADRI, NARAYAN. A Mahratta Brahman: baptized at Bombay, Sept. 13, 1843. O. Oct. 11, 1854. He labored at Bombay until 1862, when he re-opened the stations of Indapur and Jalna, where he has since been actively engaged. In 1873-74 he visited Europe and America. In 1880 went to America by way of China and Japan. Ad. *Jalna, Nizam's Territory.*

SMALL, JOHN. B. Arbroath, Scotland, Dec. 4, 1833. A. Dec. 1863. O. Poona, Dec. 1869. S. Bombay and Poona. W. Educational and Evangelistic. H. from July, 1874 to Jan. 1876. Ad. *Poona.*

SMITH, CHARLES MICHIE. B. Keig, Aberdeenshire, July 13, 1854. A. Jan. 1877. S. Madras. W. Professor of Physical Science. L. A few Scientific papers in the proceedings of the Royal Society of Edinburgh. Ad. *Madras.*

STEVENSON, WILLIAM. B. Sept. 26, 1839. Licensed, Oct. 1863. O. Oct. 1864. Engaged in ministerial labor half a year before coming to India. A. Dec. 9, 1864. S. Professor in Central Inst. and (at present) Secretary, Free Church Mission, Madras. Engaged in Engl. W. M. Nov. 1867. H. May, 1873 to Feb. 1875. L. "Hinduism and Christian Education"; Two Lectures: published in Edinburgh. Translated from the German, Bech's Outlines of Christian Doctrine; C. E. V. S.: edited South India Missionary Conference Report, Addison and Co., Madras: "The Claims of Christ on the Human conscience;" Bombay Tract Society. Ad. *Madras.*

STEVENSON, WILLIAM H. B. Dundee, Scotland, March, 16, 1853, A. Feb. 14, 1877. Not O. W. educational and evangelistic. S. *Pachamba, Bengal.*

STOTHERT, RICHARD. O. Jan. 5, 1860 and A. at Bombay in the following month. Labored two years at Nagpore, and was then transferred to Bombay. H. in 1871. Since 1872 has labored at Bombay. Ad. *Bombay.*

WHITTON, DAVID. O. July 13, 1869. A. shortly after, and has since labored at Nagpore. Ad. *Nagpore, C. P.*

DECEASED AND RETIRED MISSIONARIES.

James Mitchell. B. near Stirling in 1800. O. in Aug. 1822, and A. at Bombay in the following year. Labored for a time in the Southern Concan. In Aug. 1835, was transferred to Poona, where he subsequently labored. On the Disruption in 1843 he joined the Free Church. H. in 1853, and in 1860. He D. at Poona, March 28, 1866.

Robert Nesbit. B. at Bowsden, County of Durham, March 22, 1803. O. Dec. 15, 1826, and A. at Bombay Sept. 19, 1827. Labored in the Southern Concan until Aug. 1831, when he removed to Poona. In 1834 he visited the Cape of Good Hope and returned, recruited, to

Bombay, where he labored until May, 1848, when he went to Eng. Rt. in May, 1851, continued his labors at Bombay until his death (from cholera) July 27, 1855. L. (1) Discourses on Doctrinal Subjects," (English): (2) "Essays and Reviews": (3) "Analysis of the Bhagwad Gita" (Marathi); (4) "On True A tonement," (5) "On Elemental Worship" (Marathi).

John Wilson, D. D., F. R. S. B. in Lauder, Dec. 11, 1804. O. June 24, 1828, A. at Bombay, Feb. 13, 1829. In Aug. 1835 he was transferred to the Church of Scotland, and in 1843 he went over to the Free Church. In Dec. 1835 he established the Engl. School, which subsequently became the Free Church Inst. In Jan. 1843 he visited Palestine and proceeded to Eng. where he remained until 1847. He returned to Bombay in Nov. 1847, and labored steadily until 1870 when he returned to Scotland and was chosen Moderator of the General Assembly. In 1871 he was again at his post in Bombay, where he labored until his death, December 1, 1875 He was at one time President of the Bombay Branch of the Royal Asiatic Society, and at another Vice Chancellor of the Bombay University. For many years he was Editor of the *Oriental Chistian Spectator.* Among his literary works may be mentioned the following: "*Exposure of Hinduism*" (which has been translated into many languages);" "*Refutation of Mahomedanism*"; "*The Lands of the Bible:*" "*India Three Thousand Years Ago*": "*The Parsi Religion as contained in the Zend Avesta*": "*Memoirs of Mrs. Margaret Wilson*": "*History of the Sect of the Maharajas:*" *A Work on the Aboriginal Tribes of this Country*": *A work on the Religious Excavations of Western India:*" "*A Work on Caste*" (not completed and not published): a number of tracts in different languages: and other works.

Alexander Duff, D. D., LL. D. B. April 25, 1806, near Pitlochrie, Perthshire, Scotland. E. at the Univ. af St. Andrews and the Divinity School of St. Mary's College. In 1829 he was appointed a missionary to India, and was O. at Edinburgh August 12, of the same year. In the following Oct. he sailed for Calcutta, where he arrived (after having been twice shipwrecked) May 27, 1830. He at once set to work in accordance with his instructions to open an English School. A beginning was made in the following Aug. His health failing he was obliged to leave India in July, 1834, but returned to his post, recruited, in May 1840. With the other India missionaries, when the Disruption occurred in 1843, he united with the Free Church, and was thenceforth identified with the Free Church Inst. He left I in 1850 and visited the Home Church in the interests of missionary work. In 1851 he was Moderator of the General Assembly. In 1854 he paid a visit to America, where he received a hearty welcome. The Univ. of New York conferred upon him the degree of LL. D. By the autumn of 1855 finding his health sufficiently improved he again sailed for India and reached Calcutta Feb. 16, 1856. In 1863 his health again failing he was compelled to take his final departure from I. which happened Dec. 20, 1863. On the way home he visited Caffraria and other mission fields. On arriving in Scotland assumed by the voice of the General Assembly the office of Convener of the Foreign Mission Committee, and in 1867 he was called to the professorship of evangelistic theology. Besides other literary labors was the author of "India and India Missions";; (1840); and "The India Rebellion: its Causes and Results"; (1858). D. Feb. 12, 1878. *Vide* "Life" by Dr Smith.

William Sinclair Mackey, D. D. B. at Thurso in Caithness, in 1807. A. in Calcutta near the close of 1831. In 1838 his health failed and he visited Van Dieman's Land. R. in Aug. 1839. In 1855 he was obliged to proceed to Scotland for his health, but R. to Calcutta early in 1857. He Ret. in Feb, 1862, and D. in Scotland in Sept. 1865.

David Ewart, D.D. B. near Alyth, Sept. 24, 1806. A. at Calcutta in 1834, and labored here continuously until Sept. 1856, when he took furlough. R. in Dec. 1858, but D. of cholera Sept. 9, 1860.

John Anderson. B. May 23, 1805 at Kirkcudbrightshire. O. in Edinburgh July 13, 1836, and A. at Madras Feb. 22, 1837. He founded the Free Church mission at Madras and continued to labor at its head until April, 1849, when failing health compelled him to return to Europe. In Dec. 1850 he was again at his post in Madras, where he continued to labor until his death, March 25, 1854.

John Macdonald. B. in Edinburgh, Feb. 17, 1807. O. March 17, 1831 and served as pastor six years or more. A. in Calcutta Feb. 17, 1838. He labored here until his death Sept. 1, 1847.

J. Murray Mitchell, M. A., LL. D., B. in Aberdeen, in 1815. E. at Marischal Col., Aberdeen, and at Edinburgh. O. in July, 1838. A. at Bombay, Nov. 1838. H. 1846-47. In Jan. 1857 failing health compelled him to leave I. Rt. in 1859. S. Poona, 1860-61; Bombay 1861-63. On account of ill health went home in 1863. His health improved and he Rt. A. at Calcutta in Jan. 1868. Labored chiefly as Principal of the Free Church Inst. till Jan. 1873. Ret to Scotland in 1873. W. mainly educational, with ver. preaching, in Marathi. L. Memoir of the Rev. Robert Nesbit: "Letters to Indian Youth on the Evidences of the Christian Religion" (translated into several languages). "The conflict of Ancient Paganism and Christianity": "The elements of Christian Truth"; and several smaller books—all in Engl. Also wrote about twelve Marathi tracts, and a trilingual tract in metrical Sanskrit with translations in Marathi and Engl.: editor of the Engl. edition of the Report of the Evangelical Alliance held at Basle, Switzerland in 1879. As convener of the European Committee on Missions gave in a Report to the General Presbyterian Council at Philadelphia in Sept. 1880. On his return to Scotland in 1873 became Secretary of the Foreign Mission Committee of the Free Church. Resigned this office in 1878. and became Honorary Secretary. R. to India by way of China and Japan in Feb. 1881.

Thomas Smith. O. May 8, 1839, and A. in Calcutta Aug. 18, the same year. Visited the Cape of Good Hope, 1841-43. H. to Eng. in 1856. R. to Calcutta early in 1857. His health failing he was compelled to leave I in 1858. At present has a charge in *Edinburgh.*

Robert Johnson. B. Dec. 16, 1807, near Moffat. Licensed in 1835, became a home missionary in 1837. O. Sept 5, 1838. A. at Madras Jan. 24, 1839. He was compelled by ill health to leave I. in Feb. 1851, and D. at Edinburgh, March 23, 1823.

John Braidwood. O. Aug. 6, 1840. A. at Madras, Jan. 15, 1841. After laboring a number of years at Madras he went on H. Rt. Jan. 28, 1856. His health failing he Ret. to Scotland July 9, 1860, where he D. April 30, 1875.

Stephen Hislop. O. Sept. 4, 1844. A. at Bombay Dec. 13, 1844, and Nagpore Feb. 13, 1845. He founded the Nagpore mission in which he labored the greater part of the time. He visited Eng. from 1858-60, when he again repaired to Nagpore, where he labored until his death; he was drowned Sept. 4, 1863. He was noted as a geologist.

James Aitken. A. 1844. Labored in West India. D. in 1870.

William Henderson. Formerly a Professor in the Elphinstone Col. at Bombay. Resigning his position he joined the mission and labored in it from Jan. 1846-49, when he was compelled by ill health to return to Europe. He D. at Barnstable in May, 1850.

Robert Hunter. O. at Aberdeen, Oct. 22, 1846, and A. at Nagpore March 27, 1847. He was obliged to leave I. on account of ill health, May 17, 1855, and Res. Sept. 3, 1857. Has written a "History of the Missions of the Free Church" (1873): and other books.

David Sinclair. B. in 1822. A. at Calcutta Nov. 10, 1848, where he labored until his death, Dec. 29, 1852.

Ebenezer Miller. Took charge of the mission at Chinsurah in Aug. 1850. In 1857 started for Australia to recruit his health but D. of cholera at Galle, in the same year.

James Drummond. O. Sept. 5, 1850, and A. at Madras May 24, 1851. His health being poor he was obliged to leave I, R. to Scotland the same year, 1851.

A. Venkataramiah. Professed Christianity, June 20, 1841 at Madras. O. Nov. 26, 1851. Labored at Nellore and Madras. D. 1876.

S Ettirajulu. Professed Christianity at Madras, and was baptized in Aug. 1841. O. Dec. 12, 1851: labored at Madras and Vellore until 1863, when he Res.

Robert B. Blyth. O. July 26, 1852. A at Madras in the following Nov. Labored here until compelled by ill health to return to Scotland, July 6, 1858.

Alexander B. Campbell. O. and A. in 1842. H. from Jan. 1862 to the close of the same year. R. to Madras and labored a few months when he was compelled to retire, May 10, 1863. At present a minister in *Markinch, Fife, Scotland*

William Kincaird Mitchell. Son of the Rev. James Mitchell. O. Aug. 10, 1852, and arrrived at Poona, Jan. 20, 1853. He labored here until compelled by failing health to leave I., in March 1857.

Thomas Gardiner. A. at Calcutta May 29, 1853, where he labored until failing health compelled him to Ret. in May 1859. D. in Aberdeen in 1877.

James Miller Mackintosh. O. Dec. 13, 1853, and A. at Madras Jan. 26, 1854. He labored here until compelled by failing health to leave I. April 5, 1869. D. in 1879.

William Moffat. A. in 1854. S. Madras. D. 1859.

John Pourie. B. Oct. 9, 1824, near Dundee. O. by the Presbytery of Glasgow, Nov. 28, 1854, and A. at Calcutta Jan. 15, 1855. He labored here until April, 1867, when he was obliged to proceed Australia, for his health, where he D. in the same year.

Prasana Kumar Chatterjee. B of Kulin Brahmin parents about 1822, near Calcutta, Baptized in 1840. E. at the General Assembly's Inst, Calcutta, under Dr. Duff. O. in 1855 by the Presbytery of Calcutta. Labored at Chinsurah, both in Engl. and Bengali, L. original: (I) "*Chandiamukshee*," (in Bengali), (2.) "*Gyanchandra*," (3.) "*Gyanaroon*: written in Bengali for school children. Translated three books from Engl. into Bengali for the Calcutta Tract Society; (1) "Theological Lectures for the Illiterate :" (2) "Knowledge of Animals: (3) God's Way of Peace;" Calcutta Tract Depository. D. 1879.

Alexander McCallum. O. Oct. 16, 1855. A. at Madras Dec. 2, 1855: D. at Bangalore whither he had gone for his health, June 11, 1862.

Joseph Frost, Esq. Licensed in 1855 at Madras: when about to receive ordination he was stricken down by cholera, and D. at Wallajabad, July 11, 1860.

Adam White. B. in Aberdeen, May 19, 1829. O. Nov. 29, 1855. A. at Bombay early in 1856. He labored here until Jan. 1859, when he was transferred to Nagpore. He left the Free Church in 1860, and labored near Poona until his death, caused by cholera, May 16, 1864.

David H. Paterson. (F. R. C. S, Ed.) Appointed Dec. 18, 1855. A. at Madras in 1856, and was engaged in general medical missionary work. Left I. in 1870. and D in Edinburgh Feb. 14, 1871.

James Wardrop Gardner. O. Oct. 1, 1856, and proceeded to Poona. He labored here until his health failed, when he Ret. to Scotland, in 1871.

James Houston, Esq. Appointed as a teacher to Madras Oct. 19, 1859. Labored here until compelled to resign on account of ill health, in Jan. 1863.

Joseph Dewar. Appointed a Professor Oct. 10, 1859. A. at Bombay early in 1860, and labored here until his death, Jan. 23, 1862.

Alexander Blake. A. 1859. S. Madras. Ret. in 1868.

Behari Lal Singh. Baptized at Calcutta Aug. 1843. Visited Eng. and was O. at Edinburgh, July 18, 1861. L. at Calcutta and Rampore Bauleah. D. in Dec. 1874.

S. Ramanoojum. O. in Feb. 1862. Labored at Wallajabad. Left the mission in 1866. D. in 1867.

William Robson, M. D. A. 1862. Ret. 1867. D. 1878.

John Davidson Don. O. Oct. 16, 1862, and A. at Calcutta the same year. Took charge of the Free Church congregation in 1868. Resigned in 1874. Is now minister and missionary, King Williamstown, South Africa.

William Carslaw, M. D. Appointed to I. July 22, 1863. A. in Madras the same year. Transferred to Syria, 1876.

G. F. Metzger. Formerly connected with the Basel Mission. Joined the Free Church Mission in 1863, and labored at Chinglepat and Madras until 1871, when he Ret. to Europe.

William Young. A. 1864. S. Nagpore. Res. 1875.

John Macmillan. O at Aberdeen, Oct. 10, 1864, and A. at Madras in the same year. Subsequently removed to Nellore. Res. 1879.

John Dalziel. Appointed as a teacher to Nagpore in Nov. and reached his station Dec. 31, 1864. H. 1874-75. D. 1876.

Robert Angus. O. July 10, 1865, and A. in India a few months later. Labored at Poona, until 1872, when he Res. and R. to Scotland. At present laboring in Victoria.

Baba Padmanji. B. about 1821. Baptized at Belgaum in 1855. O. Aug. 7, 1867. Labored chiefly at Bombay and Poona. Res. in 1873.

William Stephen. O. July 6, 1869, and A. at Bombay shortly after. Labored here until 1873, when he Ret. to Scotland.

William Ross. B. on the Island of Islay in Scotland May 8, 1844. A. Nov. 1871. Labored as Professor of Mathematics and Natural Philosophy in the Free Church Col. Madras. D. 1876

Archibald Templeton. B. in Glasgow, Dec. 26, 1844. Licensed and O. in 1871. A. Nov 1871. Appointed to Giridi, Pachamba, where he labored until 1876, when he Ret.

———o———

CHAPTER X.

AMERICAN PRESBYTERIAN MISSIONARY SOCIETY.

THE Presbyterian Church in the United States began its missionary operations in India in the year 1834, under the auspices of the Western Foreign Missionary Society. The Lodiana Mission thus commenced was afterwards, on the establishment of the Board of Foreign Missions of the General Assembly of the Presbyterian Church, made over to that body. The first missionaries appointed to India by the Society, were the Rev. Messrs. John C. Lowrie and William Reed, who, with their wives, arrived in Calcutta in October, 1833. Their instructions were to select a station in some part of the northern provinces if expedient. As the result of enquiries made at Calcutta, Lodiana was selected as the station to be first occupied. Before setting out for this field, Mr. Lowrie was called to part with his companions, and proceed to the work alone. Mrs. Lowrie died at Calcutta, of consumption. Mr. Reed was attacked by the same disease; and was advised to return at once to his native land. He accordingly embarked, but died before leaving the Bay of Bengal, and his body was committed to the deep near the Andaman Islands.

Mr. Lowrie arrived at Lodiana November 5, 1834. He was disabled for some time on account of severe illness, and was obliged to repair to Simla. The Mission was thereby suspended almost a whole year immediately after it began to exist.

In the meantime the Rev. Messrs. James Wilson and John Newton had arrived at Lodiana in December, 1835, and entered upon their work. Besides the school and other duties they took charge of a printing-press established in 1836. The third company of missionaries reached Calcutta in March, 1836. Here they were met by Mr. Lowrie, who on account of failing health was proceeding home (having left Lodiana in January, 1836). The new missionaries proceeded on their journey to Lodiana, but Mr. McEwen was led to stop at Allahabad which, though at that time isolated from the chosen sphere of the Society's operations, has ever since been occupied. Upon the arrival of this reinforcement at Lodiana two new stations were occupied, Messrs. Campbell and Jamieson being appointed to Saharanpur, and Messrs. Wilson and Rogers to Sabathu.

A church was organized at Lodiana in 1837: schools were opened and extensive itinerations made. Other laborers arrived in 1838 and in following years, and the Society commenced operations in other stations as follows: Futtegurh, in 1838: Mainpuri, 1843: Furrukhabad, 1844: Agra, 1845: Jalandhar, 1846: Amballa, 1848: Lahore, 1849: Futtehpore, 1852: Dehra, 1853: Rawal Pindi, 1856: Roorkee, 1856: Peshawar, 1857: Kapurthala, 1859: Etawah, 1863: Hoshyarpore, 1867: Muzafarnagar, 1869: Jagrawan and Ferozepore, 1870: Rupar and Jagadari, 1872: Morar (Gwalior), 1875: and Morinda, in 1876. For various reasons Agra, Peshawar and Kapurthala were afterwards abandoned. In most of the stations churches were formed. The Presbytery of Lodiana was organized in 1837, that of Lahore in 1869: that of Furrukhabad in 1842: and that of Allahabad, in 1842. The two latter Presbyteries constitute what has since about 1843 been called the "Furrukhabad Mission." The Synod of North India held its first meeting at Futtegurh in November, 1845. It may be remarked that some of the missionaries at Saharanpur and Dehra belong to the "Reformed Presbyterian" Church, but all the stations alike are under the control of the General Assembly's Board of Foreign Missions.

In the Mutiny of 1857 the missions of this Society like those of other Societies in North India, were greatly interrupted and met with heavy losses and bereavements. In the Cawnpore massacre the Rev. Messrs. Freeman, Campbell, Johnson and McMullin, their wives and the two youngest children of Mr. and Mrs. Campbell fell victims to the cruelty of Nana Sahib: a devoted company who thus went up "out of great tribulation."* Compared with the loss of life and the endurance of great suffering during the Mutiny, the loss of mission property was of small account: and yet it was a serious loss, the destruction of houses, school-rooms, chapels, etc., being estimated at about

* Memorial of Missionaries of Futtehgurh, killed at Cawnpore in the Sepoy Mutiny. By J. J. Walsh: Philadelphia, Joseph M. Wilson. 1858.

£24,000. A part of this pecuniary loss was afterwards made good to the Mission by Government.

Two other missionaries of this Society met with violent deaths. One was the Rev. Dr. Janvier of Sabathu who was killed at a mela at Anandpur by a Sikh fanatic in October, 1863: the other was the Rev. J. Loewenthal, of Peshawar, who was shot by his watchman in April, 1864.

The missionaries of the Society have from the beginning devoted much attention to the preparation of books, both original and translations, and a large number of popular tracts have been written by them. The Lodiana press since its establishment in 1836 has sent forth millions of pages which have had a wide circulation throughout Northern and Central India. Its issues during the year 1880 were 91,395 copies, with 6,088,000 pages: in at least four languages, and for eight different Societies. The Allahabad press was established in 1838 and continued in active operation until 1857 when it was entirely destroyed by the mutineers. After the lapse of several years it was re-established but on a smaller scale, and under Native Christian management.

Educational work has been vigorously and successfully carried forward. In 1879 the boarding and day-schools of the Society in India contained 7,798 pupils, 1,882 of whom were in the schools at Lahore. A flourishing boarding school for Christian girls (established in 1858) is in operation at Dehra. A boarding school for Christian boys was opened in 1875 at Lahore, but afterwards suspended. It is to be re-opened on a solid base.

The mission at Kolhapur (Bombay Presidency) was commenced by the Rev. R. G. Wilder under direction of the American Board in 1852. Being the first missionary to enter this field, Mr. Wilder experienced considerable opposition, and the people petitioned the British Government to banish him from the kingdom, failing, however, in their efforts. In a few years there was a marked change in their bearing towards the missionary, and many children were gathered into the mission schools. In 1857 Mr. Wilder returned to America on account of broken health and in 1859 the mission was relinquished by the American Board. In 1861 the founder of the mission returned to Kolhapur, and with the aid of funds supplied by friends of the mission in India prosecuted his work until 1869 when illness again compelled him to visit America. In 1870 the mission was taken up by the American Presbyterian Board and Mr. Wilder returned to Kolhapur the same year. In December, 1870 the Rev. G. W. Seiler arrived from America and joined the mission. Other laborers subsequently arrived and a Presbytery has been formed. Several Marathi books have been prepared by members of this mission, including two Commentaries. Schools and churches have been organized, and some converts have been gained.

It will be thus seen that the Society is represented in India by the five Presbyteries, Lodiana, Lahore, Furrukhabad, Allahabad and Kolhapur, all uniting to form the Synod of North India. In 1879, 21 stations and 16 sub-stations were occupied.

The following statistics of the Society (for 1879) show the progress since 1871:

Foreign missionaries,	29,	decrease	3
Native Ordained Agents,	15,	increase	7
Native Christians,	2,100,	do.	766
Communicants,	971,	do.	408

MISSIONARIES OF THE SOCIETY.

Alexander, James M. A. 1866. S. Mainpuri. H. 1874-76. Ad. *Mainpuri, N.-W.P.*

Basten, William. Joined the Society in 1865. Ad. *Amballa, Punjab.*

Bergen, George Spofford. B. Nov. 1, 1844 at Jersey Prairie, Ill., U. S. A. O. in 1865, A. the same year. S. Lahore, one year; Lodiana, six: Amballa, six. M. in 1869. W. chiefly ver. H. 1879-81. Ad. *Amballa, Punjab.*

Bose, Jogendra Chandra. B. about 1838, at Hooghly, Bengal. Served for a time as head-master of the Rawul Pindi high school. O. at Lodiana in Nov. 1868. Ad. *Ferozepore, Punjab.*

Calderwood, William. B. Dec. 20, 1822, in the Parish of Lochwinnoch, Renfrewshire, Scotland. Removed to America in 1823. Graduated in 1847 at Union College, Schenectady, N. Y. Was connected for same years with the Reformed Presbyterian Church, laboring as an agent of the American Tract Society. Graduated in 1853, at the Theol. Sem. of the above named Church in Philadelphia: in May, 1854, appointed missionary to India. M. A. Nov. 7, 1855, and was appointed to Saharanpur, where he has labored nearly all the time since, with the exception of the years 1870-72, when he was on H. to Germany and America. W. has been chiefly ver. Ad. *Saharanpur, N.-W. P.*

CALEB, JOHN JAMES. B at Bajhera in the Bareilly district. O. at Allahabad. in Jan. 1871. Has since labored as pastor of the Kuttra church, Allahabad. L. translations ; "*Intikhab Tarikh-i-Kalisiya*" ; Hodge's Commentary on the "Confession of Faith" (both in Roman-Urdu) : original ; "Sharir aur Rastbaz ka Anjam," and "Risala dar bab-i-Taslis :" N. I. T. Society's Depot, Allahabad. Ad. *Allahabad.*

CARLTON, MARCUS M. A. in 1855. At present engaged at Santokh Majra and Kulu Valley (as itinerant missionary). Ad. *Amballa, Punjab.*

CHARN, ISA. B. in 1828 at Kuluwal, Punjab. M. in 1851. O. in Dec. 1869. S. Ferozepore and Lahore. Ad. *Lahore.*

CHATTERJEE, KALI CHARN. B. near Calcutta, Aug. 23, 1839 : parents were Kulin Brahmins. E in the C. M. S. school at Augurpara and in the Free Church Col. Calcutta : while attending the latter, was baptized. Nov. 8, 1854. Remained here until 1861, then became head master of the mission school at Jalandhar. In Jan. 1866, transferred to the Lahore Mission Col as professor of Logic and Mental and Moral Sciences: continued here until the close of 1867, when he was licensed to preach, and in June, 1868, was appointed to Hoshyarpur, where he has since labored. O at Lodiana Dec. 24, 1868. Ad *Hoshyarpur, Punjab.*

EWING, J. C.R. B. June 23, 1854 in Armstrong Co, Pa., U. S. A. O. Sept. 4, 1879. A Dec 1, 1879. Ad. *Futtegurh, N.-W. P.*

FERRIS, GEORGE HENRY. B Hillsdale, Mich., U. S. A., Dec. 1853. O. April, 1878, A. Jan. 13, 1879. S. Kolhapur, 1879, Panhala, 1880. M. Ad. *Panhala, Bombay P.*

FORMAN, CHARLES WILLIAM. B March 3, 1821, in Ky., U. S. A. O. July 7, 1847. A. in Jan. 1848. M. July 3, 1855. S. Amballa, Nov. 1848 : Lodiana, Jan. 1849 : Lahore, Nov. 1849. W. has been chiefly ver. L. : 26 Urdu Tracts ("Justice and Mercy" : "The Brazen Serpent," etc) : "Bible Passages" : "Christian Sword and Shield," (in Urdu) : printed and obtainable at the Mission Press, Lodiana. H. from Nov. 1866 to Nov. 1869. and from March to Nov. 1880. Ad, *Lahore.*

GOHEEN, JOSEPH MILLIKEN. B. in Feb. 1847, at Rock Spring, P. U. S A. E. at Princeton Col. (1872.) and at Princeton Theol. Sem. (1875) O. in June, 1875. A. in Dec. 1875. S. Kolhapur. Ad. *Kolhapur, Bombay P.*

GOLUKNATH. Joined the Society in 1843. Author of several Ver. tracts (Punjabi and Urdu.) Ad. *Jalandhar, Punjab.*

GRAHAM, JOSEPH PATTERSON. B. at New Lisbon, Ohio, U. S. A., June 12. 1847. E. at Washington and Jefferson Col. Pa. (1869) and at Princeton Theol. Sem. (1872) O. June 14, 1872 A. Nov 18, 1872. M. S. Panhala, 1875-79, since, Ratnagiri. W. Ver. Ad. *Ratnagiri, Bombay P.*

HERRON, DAVID. B. Aug. 31, 1820, in Rathfriland, County of Down, Ireland. O. in Nov. 1849, and installed pastor at Shenango, Pa. U. S. A. Appointed to I. in May 1854, by the Reformed Presbyterian Church,

A. Nov. 10, 1855, and reached Dehra, Dec. 31, 1855. S. Lodiana from May to Nov. 1856; then at Dehra until Jan. 1864. H. from 1864 to April 1868. S. Amballa from the latter date to Jan. 1869, Dehra 1869-78. W. has been both Eng. and Ver. Has written a few pamphlets in Engl. H. to America 1878-79. Ad. *Dehra, N.-W. P.*

HEYL, FRANCIS. A. in 1867. Ad. *Allahabad.*

HOLCOMB, JAMES FOOTE. A. in 1869. S. Allahabad. H. to U. S. A. in 1880.

HULL, JAMES JOHNSON. B in Ohio, U. S. A. in 1847. Graduated (A. B.) at Washington and Jefferson Col., Pa., in 1869, entered the Western Theol. Sem the same year. O. 1872. A. in Dec. 1872 M. in Dec. 1874. H. to America in 1879. Ad. *Cannonsburg, Penn., U. S. A.*

JOHNSON, WILLIAM F. B. Cadiz, Ohio, March, 1838. O. 1860. A. 1860. S. Allahabad, 1860, Futtehpore, 1861, Futtegurh, 1865. H. to America 1872-74, Mainpuri 1875, Allahabad, 1866. L. Editor of "*Makhzan i Masihi*," a monthly Magazine in Roman-Urdu; Commentaries on Haggai, Zechariah and Malachi, in Roman-Urdu; "Prem Dohawali," couplets in Hindi on the love of Christ, with an Engl. translation; "Stuti Prakash," a book of Hindi hymns to native tunes; "Guru Pariksha." or Search after the Divine Teacher; "Des Chitr Mala," Pictures of many lands, "Pratima Pariksha," and many others N. I. Tract S., Allahabad. Ad. *Allahabad.*

KANWARSAIN. B. in 1830. E. at Saharanpur. Baptized in 1856. O. in 1867. Has labored since at (Ad.) *Muzaffarnagar, Punjab.*

KELSO, ALEXANDER. P. Joined the Society in 1870. H. to America in 1881.

LAL, MOHAN. B. near Hurdui, Oudh, in the year 1822. Baptized in Futtegurh in 1860. O. as pastor of the Furrukhabad city church. in 1874. Ad. *Gwalior.*

LUCAS, JAMES JOSEPH. B. in 1847 at Dublin, Ireland. O. in Danville, Ky., U. S. A., in 1870. A. the same year. W. Ver. M. S. Futtegurh. H. to America in 1881.

MCMASTER, GILBERT. B. in Persia. A. about 1833. O. Feb. 8, 1867. S. Dehra. W. educational and evangelistic. L. several tracts in Hindi and Urdu. Ad. *Dehra, N.-W. P.*

MORRISON, JOHN HUNTER. B. June 29, 1806, in Orange County, N. Y., U. S. A. O. in Sept. 1837, and A. in April, 1838. S. Allahabad from June, 1838, to Jan. 1841: Sabathu and Simla to Oct. 1842, H. to America from 1843-46, returning to Agra, 1847: Sabathu Dec. 1849; Amballa to 1853: Lahore to 1855: Rawal Pindi to Dec. 1860. H. 1862-64: Rawal Pindi 1864-67—Amballa until Sept. 1874: at Simla until April, 1875: then at Sabathu. W. has been both Engl. and Ver., chiefly preaching. Has written two Urdu tracts republished at Lodiana. M. Ad. *Dehra, N.-W. P.*

MORRISON, WILLIAM J. PHILLIP. B. in India. E. in America: R. to India in 1866. Ad. *Saharanpur, N.-W. P.*

NABIBAKSH, ELLIOT. B. at Lucknow. 1834. O. Etawah, 1870. S. Etawah: W. Native Pastor. Ad. *Etawah, N.-W. P.*

NEWTON, CHARLES BEATTY. B. at Lodiana, Feb. 2, 1842. E. in America, graduating at Washington Col. Pa., and at the Western Theol. Sem., Alleghany, Pa. O. in 1867. R. to India March 10, 1868. M. April 13, 1871. Has labored at Lahore, engaged in educational W. Engl. and ver. preaching. Ad. *Lahore.*

NEWTON, EDWARD PAYSON. B. at Lahore, in July, 1850. E. in America, graduating at Princeton and studying theology at the Western Theol. Sem. Alleghany, Pa. O. in 1873. R. to India Dec. 20, 1873, and has labored since at Lodiana. W. Engl. and ver. Ad. *Lodiana, Punjab.*

NEWTON, FRANCIS JANVIER. B. at Sabathu, Punjab, July 14, 1847. Graduated at Washington Col., Pa. After a three years' course in Presbyterian Theol. Sem. at Alleghany, Pa. O. in 1870. M. Sept. 27, and A. Dec. 10 of the same year. Has labored since at Lahore. W. chiefly Ver. Has written an Urdu tract, "Tahqiq ul Waqiat ul Injil:" obtainable at the Mission Press, Lodiana. Ad. *Lahore.*

NEWTON, JOHN. B. Oct 1, 1810, at Griggstown, N. J., U. S. A. Graduated at Jefferson Col. Sept. 30, 1830. Studied theology at the Western Theol. Sem. Alleghany, Pa. O. Oct 26, 1834. M: A. at Calcutta Feb. 25, 1835. S Lodiana, Sabathu, Lahore. W. preaching in Hindustani, Punjabi, and in Engl., superintending the press, etc. L (1) a Punjabi Grammar: (2) a Punjabi and Engl. Dictionary in connection with the Rev. L. Janvier: (3) translation of the N. T. into Punjabi: (4) a number of tracts and small books in Punjabi, chiefly translations: (5) two tracts in Urdu, "The Day of Judgment," and "The Integrity of the Scriptures": (6) a brief Commentary on the Epistle to the Ephesians (Urdu) with a revised translation. (7) some small tracts in Hindee: Lodiana Mission Press. H. 1851-54; 1870-71, and in 1881.

RUDOLPH, ADOLPH. B Berlin, 1815. A. in connection with Gossner's Mission, 1849. S. Tirhoot, 1839-42, Kotegurh 1842-45. O. in connection with A. P. M. in 1845: labored at Lodiana 1845-80, had charge of the High School 10 years, of Girls' Orphange 11 years, of the Press, 12 years. H. 1856, 1870, 1877. L. Several tracts in Urdu. M. Ad. *Sabathu, Punjab.*

SEELEY, GEORGE AUGUSTUS. B. at Calcutta in 1847. O at Princeton, N. J., U. S. A. A. in 1870. S. Futtegurh. H. to America 1876-79. M. 1879. Ad. *Futtegurh, N.-W. P.*

TEDFORD, LYMAN BEECHER. B. Maryville, Tenn., U. S. A. Sept. 1851. O. Sept. 12, 1880. A. Nov. 17, 1880. M. Ad. *Kolhapur, Bombay P.*

THACKWELL, REESE. A. in 1859. Ad. *Rawal Pindi, Punjab.*

TRACY, THOMAS. B. March 15, 1842, at Jewett City, Ct., U. S. A. O. June 11. 1868. A. Nov. 6, 1869: S. Futtegurh. W. Engl. and ver. M. April 2, 1862. H to America, 1880.

ULLMANN, JULIUS FREDERICK. B. Berlin, May, 22, 1817. A. in connection with Gossner's Mission Nov. 1839 S. Chapra, 1841, Benares, 1844-48. In 1848 joined A. P. M, and was O. by the Furrukhabad Presbytery, 1849. S. Futtegurh, Mainpuri, Etawah. H. 1850, 1858, 1866. L. "Majmuai-Manzuma," Songs for children, in Rom-Urdu (out of print): "Dharmtula," "Religion weighed," in Hindi, Persian Urdu, and Engl.; "Gurugyan," a Catechism in Hindi, for Bazar schools and Zananas; "Sreshth Mulkatha," or "the Old, old story," translated into Hindi verse, Persian Urdu and Roman-Urdu; "Larkon ki Gitmala," Hymns and songs for children, in Rom-Urdu, with music, and in Persian Urdu; "Qaid Kusha," or Deliverance from Bondage, in Persian Urdu; "Nazmi Sawal-o-Jawab," a short Catechism, in verse, in Persian Urdu; "Preshnuttar" and Mulkatha," "Catechism" and Old old story," in Hindi. "Zabur aur Git," with and without music, Rom-Urdu (of the 516 hymns 313 are Mr. Ullmann's): "Bible stories"—O. T. and N. T; "Gitawali," songs and Hymns for children, Persian-Urdu, and Rom-Urdu; Catechism in Rom-Urdu. Ad. *Etawah, N.-W. P.*

WHERRY, ELWOOD MORRIS. B. in 1843, at South Bend, Pa., U. S. A. Called to the ministry in 1864. O. in 1867. M. in 1867. A. March 20, 1868. S. 1868, Rawal Pindi; 1870, Lodiana. W. chiefly Ver. L. "What think ye of Christ?" and a number of small tracts, in Urdu. Edited Rom.-Urdu Quran, and wrote Index to the same in Urdu: "The Sinless Prophet of Islam" (Urdu): is preparing a comprehensive Commentary on the Quran, (Engl., the first Vol. to appear in 1881): principal editor of "*Nur Afshan*" 7 years. H. 1878-79. Ad. *Lodiana, Punjab.*

WOODSIDE, JOHN SIMMS. B. in Ireland, Sept. 2, 1824. Licensed in January, 1848. M. April 18, 1848. O. in July, 1848, A. Nov. 25, 1848. S. Saharanpur, 1849: Dehra, 1853: Kapurthala, 1859: Dehra, 1865: H. 1873-75. W. both Engl. and Ver. Ad. *Futtegurh, N.-W. P.*

WYLIE, THEO. W. J. B. about 1826. Baptized in 1841. M. in 1846. O. in 1859. Associate pastor of the church at Saharanpur. Translations: (1) *Talim-ul Iman*; Persian-Urdu: (2) *Kalam Ilahi ka Qissa*; (3) *Masihi Jawab Dahi* (Christian Responsibility): (4) Several tracts: obtainable at the Mission Press, Lodiana. Ad. *Saharanpur, N.-W. P.*

DECEASED AND RETIRED MISSIONARIES.

John C. Lowrie. A. in 1833. One of the founders of the Mission. Labored at Lodiana until 1836 when on account of failing health he Ret. Is now Secretary of the Board of Foreign Missionaries of the Presbyterian Church in America.

William Reed. One of the first two missionaries. Graduated at Jefferson Col., pursued his Theol studies at Alleghany. A. at Calcutta in Oct. 1833. While here his health began to fail, and he was advised to return home at once. He embarked in July, but his health rapidly declined and he died at sea, Aug. 12, 1834.

James Wilson. A. in 1835. Labored at Lodiana and Allahabad: Ret. in 1851.

James R. Campbell, D. D. A native of Ireland. Went to America in his youth. He was a member of the Reformed Presbyterian Church, and pursued his studies under its direction. A. in 1836. Was home once, about 1852. Labored chiefly at Saharanpur. D. at Landour, Sept. 18, 1862.

James McEwen. A. at Calcutta in March, 1836. On the way to Lodiana he was led to stop at Allahabad where he founded the mission and organized a church. He was compelled from failing health to leave I. in 1838; served as a pastor in New York until his death, in 1845.

Jesse M. Jamieson, D. D. A. in 1836. Labored at Amballa. Ret. in 1857.

Joseph Porter. B. in Derby Plains. Ohio, U. S. A.. Jan. 5, 1808. Graduated at Oxford. Reached Lodiana in Dec. 1836. O. Oct. 1837. H. in 1848-49. Labored at Lodiana: for several years previous to his death as Supt. of the press. D. Nov. 21, 1853.

William S. Rogers. A. and O. with Mr. Porter. Labored at Sabathu and Saharanpur. Ret. to America in 1843. D. in 1873.

James Craig, Esq. B. in 1800. A. in 1838. Was a member of the Reformed Presbyterian Church. Labored as a teacher at Saharanpur. D. Aug. 16, 1845.

Reese Morris, Esq. A. in 1838. Labored as missionary printer at Lodiana. Ret. 1845.

Henry R. Wilson, D. D. A. in 1838. Labored at Futtegurh. Ret. in 1846. Is now Secretary of the Board of Church Extension of the Presbyterian Church, (U. S. A.)

Joseph Caldwell. B. April 20, 1810, at Pittsburg, Penn., U. S. A. E. at Western Univ. Pittsburg. O. in 1837, A. May 1, 1838. S. Roorkee. No H. D. at Mussoorie, May 29, 1877.

Joseph Warren, D. D. A. in Feb. 1839. Established the mission press at Allahabad, and superintended it twelve years. Wrote and translated and superintended translations by native assistants. Left I. in 1854. Remained at home through family affairs. Was Chaplain in the army, Assistant in charge of Freedmen, and Superintendent of Education in the service of the Freedmen's Bureau. four years. Rt. in Dec. 1872: labored at Futtegurh and Morar until his death, March 7, 1877.

John Edgar Freeman. B. in 1809 in N. J., U. S. A. Was a graduate of Nassau Hall and Princeton Theol. Sem. O. in Aug. 1838. A. with his wife in 1839, and was stationed at Allahabad. His wife died in 1849, and in 1850 he went to America for his health. R. in 1851. Labored at Mainpuri until 1856, when he removed to Futtegurh, where he remained until the Mutiny of 1857 led to his violent death at Cawnpore.

James L. Scott. A. in 1839. Labored at Futtegurh and Mainpuri. Ret. in 1867. Afterwards D. at Dehra, Jan. 2, 1880.

William H. McAuley. A. in 1840. S. Futtegurh. Ret. in 1851.

John C. Rankin. A. in 1840. Labored at Futtegurh Ret. in 1848.

Joseph Owen, D. D. A. in 1840. Labored chiefly at Agra and Allahabad. Wrote a new translation of the Book of Psalms, and also several commentaries, besides other works. D. in Scotland, in 1865.

Levi Janvier, D. D. B. April 25, 1816, at Pitt's Grove, N. J., U. S. A. Graduated at Princeton. A. at Lodiana early in 1842. His time was divided between preaching and translating, and throughout his course his labors were connected with the press. Together with Mr. Newton he prepared a Punjabi Dictionary which was published in 1854. He met his death March 24, 1864 at a mela, being killed by a fanatic.

Willis Green, M. D. A. in 1842. Labored at Lodiana. Ret. in 1843.

John Wray. A. in 1842. Labored at Allahabad. Ret. in 1849.

John Johnston Walsh. A. in 1843. S. Futtegurh, Mainpuri, etc. Author of "Memorial of Missionaries of Futtegurh." Ret. in 1872.

Royal Gould Wilder. B. Oct 27, 1816 at Royalton, Vt., U. S. A. Graduated at Andover Theol. Sem. in 1845. O. soon afterwards. M. in 1846. A. at Bombay Sept. 20, 1846. Was engaged six years, teaching and preaching in the Ahmednagar mission until 1852, when he was directed to start a mission at Kolhapur, where he labored until 1875. L. (1) Original; "Scientific Errors of Hinduism": Commentary on Matthew and Mark; and on Luke (2) Translations; "Jane the young Cottager": "The Shepherd of Salisbury plain:" The School Boy": "Theol. Class-book." H. 1857-61; 1869-70. Ret. to America in March, 1875. Is editor of the "Missionary Review" (Bi-monthly.) Ad. *Princeton, New Jersey, U. S. A.*

David Irving, D. D. A. in 1847. S. Futtegurh. Ret. in 1849.

Augustus H. Seeley. A in 1847. S. Futtegurh. Ret in 1854.

Robert M. Munnis. A in 1847, Labored at Allahabad. Res. in 1861, and afterwards D. in India.

Gopeenath Nandi. B. in Calcutta about 1807. Professed Christianity in 1832. In the following year removed to Futtegurh and took charge of an English school. O. in 1844, and was stationed at Futtegurh. Futtehpore having become vacant he was transferred to that station in 1853 where he remained until his death. During the Mutiny he fled to Allahabad, but afterwards returned to Futtehpore. An operation for Hernia to which he submitted proved fatal, and he D. March 14, 1861.

Archibald A. Hodge, D. D. A. in 1848. Labored at Allahabad. Ret. in 1850. Now Professor of Theology at Princeton, N. J., U. S. A.

Horatio W. Shaw. A. in 1850. S. at Allahabad. Ret. in 1855.

Lawrence Gano Hay. A. in 1850. Labored as Missionary printer at Allahabad. Ret. in 1857.

David Ellliott Campbell. B. June 7, 1825, at Mercersburg, Pa., U. S. A. Graduated at Marshall College in 1846, and spent three years at the Theol Sem. at Alleghany, Pa., graduating in 1849. O. June 5, 1850; M. June 29, 1850. A. in 1851 and labored in Futtegurh until the Mutiny broke out. He, his wife and two youngest children in company with three other missionaries and their wives left Futtegurh and attempted to reach Allahabad, but they were taken prisoners and put to death at Cawnpore, by order of Nana Sahib, June 13, 1857.

Robert Stewart Fullerton. B in Ohio. E. at Athens College, Ohio, and Alleghany Theol Sem. A. in 1850 and labored a short time at Futtegurh and Mainpuri, but within a year proceeded to Agra where he established two schools, and labored until the Mutiny broke up the mission at this place. He afterwards labored at Futtegurh until 1864, when he removed to Dehra. D. in 1865.

James H. Orbison. A. in 1850. Labored at Lodiana, Amballa, and Rawal Pindi. Went to America in 1868: D. in 1869.

Robert Elliott Williams. A. in 1852. S. at Agra: Ret. in 1861.

William Pratt Barker. B. Feb. 18, 1822, at South Wales, Erie Co., N. Y., U. S. A. Converted in 1840 in Ohio. Entered New York Univ. 1844; entered Union Theol. Sem. New York, in 1848; O. 1851; took two courses of lectures (1851-2) in Crosby St. Medical Col. Was appointed to Ahmednagar by the American Board in April, 1851, and A. in Bombay in Dec. 1853. Labored at Ahmednagar. Khokar and Pimplus. Joined the Kolhapur mission in 1872 and labored chiefly at Ratnagiri. His health failing he went to America in April, 1865, and Rt. in Dec. 1872. Proceeded to America invalided in 1876. Has since labored as a missionary among the Seneca Indians in Western New York. Ad. Versailles, N. Y., U. S. A.

George O. Barnes. A. in 1855. Labored at Lahore Ret. in 1860.

Albert Osborne Johnson. B. June 22, 1833, at Cadiz, Ohio, U. S. A. Graduated at Jefferson Col. in 1852 and at the Alleghany Theol Sem. in 1855. A. in 1855. S. Futtegurh, where he labored about eighteen months: perished at Cawnpore in June, 1857.

Edward H. Leavitt. A. in 1855. Labored at Lahore. Went to America in 1857. D. recently.

Isidor Loewenthal. B. in the year 1827 at Posen, Prussian Poland, of Jewish parents. He emigrated to America in 1846. In 1847 he secured a position as teacher in La Fayette College. In the autumn of the same year he made a profession of Christianity. He graduated at the College and taught several years. In 1852 he entered Princeton Theol. Sem. where he afterwards graduated. While engaged as a tutor, he received an appointment to the new mission to the Afghans. He was licensed in 1856 by the Presbytery of New York, and sailed for India in August of that year. When he arrived, near the close of the year, he went to Peshawar which was his field of labor. He translated and published the New Testament in Pushto, and, at the time of his death, had nearly completed a Dictionary of that language. He was noted for his linguistic and other literary labors. At the early age of 38, in 1864, he came to his death by violence at the hand of his watchman, who it is said mistook him walking in his garden at night for a robber and shot him.

Robert McMullin. B. in Philadelphia, U. S. A., Nov. 30, 1832. Graduated at the Univ. of Pennsylvania in 1850, and three years afterwards at Princeton Theol. Sem. M. July 14, 1856, O. the same month. A. at Calcutta in Jan. 1857. Labored for a few months at Futtegurh and was called to his reward at Cawnpore in June, 1857.

John Newton, Jr. B. at Lodiana, March 4, 1838. E. in America, graduating with B. A. at Princeton and with M. D. at the Univ. of Pa. A. in 1858. S. Lahore: Kapurthala: Lahore: Sabathu. Besides medical practice engaged in preaching in ver. and Engl. and in teaching. L several tracts in Urdu and Punjabi, and a Commentary on Colossians ; procurable at Allahabad and Lodiana. Also a treatise on "Leprosy" (Engl.) M. in 1861. O. in 1868. H. to America in 1875-76. Ret. and Labored at Sabathu until his death, July 29, 1880.

Augustus Brodhead, D. D. B. May 13, 1831, at Milford, Penn., U. S. A. O. in 1858. A. April 4, 1859. S. Mainpuri, Furrukhabad, Allahabad. W. ver. L. original, Miscellany (Urdu); Hymns (Urdu and Hindee) : translations, several works in Urdu and Hindee ; and Hymns in the same. H. 1869, and in 1876-77. Ret. in 1876. Ad. *Newark, N.J., U.S.A.*

Benjamin Wyckoff. A. in 1860. S. Futtegurh. Ret. in 1876.

Edward H. Sayre. A. in 1863. S. Etawah. Ret in 1869.

Alexander Henry. A. in 1864. Labored at Lodiana. D. in 1869.

Joseph H. Myers. H. about 1838, in Ohio. O. in May, 1865, and A. the same year. Labored at Lodiana until his death, in Nov. 1869.

Ishwara Das. B. about 1827. He was one of the Futtehpore orphans (of 1837). He became a Christian and a teacher in the high school at Furrukhabad. During the Mutiny he was obliged to flee for his life with other Native Christians. L. a Manual of English and Urdu ; a series of Urdu text books for schools, etc. After his return from America he published a small volume of his impressions and experiences in that land. He also wrote in English, "Domestic Manners and Customs of the Hindoos :" a useful work. He took the prize for the best essay on "Female Education in India," and also for the best treatise on Theology, the latter being a volume of over 400 pages. After the Mutiny he was licensed to preach by the Furrukhabad Presbytery. At the close of 1865 he was O. and appointed to Futtehpore. His health, however, soon began to fail, and at the end of a year he was sent back to Futtegurh where he D. in 1866.

Theodore Stephen Wynkoop. B. Nov. 22, 1839, at Wilmington, Del. U. S. A. O. in Oct. 1864. Pastoral work at Huntingdon, Long Island 1865-68. A. Dec. 31, 1868. W. ver. S. Allahabad. Ret. to America 1877. Ad. *Washington, D. C., U.S.A.*

Samuel Henry Kellogg, D. D. B. Sept. 6, 1839, at Quogur, L. I., U.S. A. O. April 20, 1864. M. May 3, 1864. A. June 3, 1865. Labored at Futtegurh until April, 1871 : H. till Nov. 1872 : at Allahabad until March, 1876, when he proceeded to America. W. chiefly ver. L. A tract, "A Living Christ" (Presbyterian Board Publication, Philadelphia) : A Hindee Grammar ; obtainable at Allahabad, and also at Calcutta and Lon. Is now Professor of Theology at Alleghany City, Pa., U. S. A.

Galen Wilkins Seiler. B. Grantville, Pa , U. S. A., Jan. 1844. E. at Princeton Col. (1864) at Princeton Theol. Sem. (1869): O. in 1870. A. in Dec. 1870. S Kolhapur, 1870-75 : Ratnagiri, 1875-79. L. translation (Marathi) of "The Woodcutter of Gutech": 1876 : Bombay Tract and Book Society. R. to America in July, 1879. Ad. *Harrisburg, Pa., U. S. A.*

John Neil McLeod. B. near Agra in 1826. O. 1873. S. Roorkee. D. 1878.

———o———

CHAPTER XI.

THE BASEL EVANGELICAL MISSIONARY SOCIETY.

THIS Society has its name from the city of Basel (or Basle or Bâle) in Switzerland, quite close to the German frontier, and may at present be considered as the Missionary Society for the Southern part of Germany (Württemberg, Baden, Alsace) and the whole of Switzerland. Württemberg has been the chief seat of this mission in the history of its foundation as well as in the contributions of money and men, whilst the other provinces mentioned have also had their honest share in the work, and especially the city of Basel has proved worthy of being the centre of this German-Swiss Society.

The Society was founded in the year 1815, not at first with a view to begin foreign missions of its own, but only to educate Christian youths for misson work and to give them over to other Societies to be sent out to foreign countries. Especially with the Church Missionary Society a close connection was kept up. As many as 88 missionaries passed from the Basel College to this Society and amongst them are some well-known names, the Rev. Messrs. Pfander, Weitbrecht, Leupolt, Schmid, Reuther, Rhenius, Schaffter, and many others. At present it is chiefly the Bremen Missionary Society in Western Africa, which draws missionaries from the College in Basel, whilst the majority are sent out in the service of the Basel Missionary Society itself. The number of students who have from 1815-76 been received into the Mission College amounts to 1,010. It is impossible to give the total number of missionaries that have been sent out in the service of the Basel Mission, but the number of ordained and unordained European Agents of the Basel Society in China, India, and Africa amounts at present to more than 100.

In ecclesiastical matters the name "Evangelical" is meant to show the stand-point of the Society. The missionaries are members of different Churches at home and ordained by the authorities of the established Churches of different countries in

Germany. (They therefore cannot be called "Dissenters"). But the Churches to which they belong are of different creeds and constitutions, which differences, however, are not by this Society considered important enough to prevent common work. Lutherans, Calvinists and Zwinglians work together in one Society and are also represented in the Home-Committee, and the endeavor is not to plant any particular church form from home, but to plant Christ and sound Christian principles in the hearts of the Hindoos.

In 1833, on the renewal of the Charter to the East India Company, India being opened to settlers from foreign countries, the Basel Missionary Society at once resolved to establish a Mission there, and in 1834 sent out three missionaries, the Rev. Messrs. Hebich, Lehner and Greiner, who arrived in Mangalore in South Canara on the Western Coast, the 30th of October, 1834. The Mission was reinforced in 1836 by four, and in 1839 by five new arrivals. In 1837 Dharwar in the South Mahratta country was taken up as the second station, and in 1839 Tellicherry in Malabar was added as the third station. Thus, three stations at great distances from each other, in three different districts with as many different languages, Tulu, Canarese, Malayalam, had been occupied, and from these centres the surrounding country was more and more put under regular systematic work and also dotted with stations and out-stations. North Canara was also drawn within the extent of the operatians by the opening of a station at Honore. In 1846 another district, the Nilagiri was taken up in consequence of Mr. Casamajor's legacy for this purpose, and is now occupied by two stations. In 1853 the operations of the Society were extended to the Coorg country, by Dr. Mögling, with two stations. The missions of the Society thus extend over a strip of country about 400 miles in length, and occupy six districts with 10 stations and about 64 out-stations.

Care of the congregations is considered one of the prime tasks of the missionaries, but preaching to the heathen and itineracy are therefore not neglected.

Much work is bestowed on the training of a futuro ministry. The Catechist Seminary receives its pupils from the districts of the Basel Mission through the Proparandi schools. The boys commonly at the age of 14 enter these schools with the knowledge that can be acquired in the common elementary schools and remain four years, after which some enter the Training classes to become school masters, others the Catechist Seminary to study there for four years more and to become grounded in the Bible and theology. Greek is taught but not Hebrew. The lessons are in the vernacular, but English is taught as a study. The day-schools contain altogether 2,303 pupils.

Among the characteristic features of this Mission are the Industrial and Mercantile Establishments. Their purpose is not to gain money, although they are intended to be self-supporting, which has been the case of old Establishments, but not always with new ones. They are meant to train the Christians, especially boys from the boarding-schools or Orphanages, and other men without livelihood, to honest and Christian trade and to raise people from pauperism to a decent Christian life. Many people now earn their rice in a healthy way by honest labor, and the European Superintendent, together with the whole expense of the Establishment, is no burden on the Mission funds. There are now twelve Establishments in the different stations, three Mercantile, six Weaving, two Tiling, and one Carpenter. Besides the above there is in Mangalore a printing-press and a book and tract depository, the first turning out books and tracts in Canarese, Tulu, Malayalam, and English, the latter selling them all over the country by a thoroughly organized system of sub-depôts and other agencies of sale, and by a staff of 10 or 12 colporteurs. The consequence of these Establishments is that there are quite a number of lay brethren in the Mission especially at Mangalore, who are placed in their sphere on a footing of equality with the ordained missionaries. The number of ordained missionaries now in the field is 54 that of lay missionaries, 20. [W. S.]

The following statistics (January, 1880) indicate the progress since 1871:

Foreign missionaries,	74	increase,	16
Native ordained agents,	8	do.,	2
Native Christians,	6,805	do.,	2,193
Communicants,	3,572	do.,	1,300

MISSIONARIES OF THE SOCIETY.

AARON, DANIEL. B. in 1830, in Bangalore. O. in 1872. Ad. *Udapi, Madras P.*

ALTENMULLER, H. Esq. B. 1851 in Prussia. A. 1877. In charge of Balmatta Weaving Establishment. Ad. *Mangalore, Madras P.*

BACH, L. B. 1856 in Alsace. A 1880. Ad. *Bettigherry, Gadak, Bombay P.*

BACHMANN, H. B. 1853 in Switzerland. A. 1880. Ad. *Chombala, Mahe, Madras P.*

BAUMANN, JACOB, Esq. B. Jan. 29, 1849, in Switzerland. A. in 1874. M. Supt. of Tiling works at (Ad.) *Mangalore, Madras P.*

BENNER, G. B. 1850 in Württemberg. A. 1877. M. Ad *Calicut, Madras P.*

BRASCHE, J. ANDREAS. B. Jan. 22, 1846, in Prussia. A. 1869. W. educational, and Ver. preaching. M. Ad. *Udapi, Madras P.*

BUHRER, ADAM. B. Jan. 29, 1815, in Switzerland A. in 1842. W. ver preaching. One of the translators of the New Testament in Tulu and author of some Christian books in the same language. M. Ad. *Kotagherry, Madras P.*

BURCKHARDT, ADOLF, Esq. B. Dec. 8, 1848, in Switzerland. A. in 1872. Is Assistant to the General Agent of the Mission. Ad. *Mangalore, Madras P.*

CHANDREN, PAUL. B. in 1810 in Chombala, Malabar. O. in 1867. Ad. *Tellicherry, Madras P.*

DAIMELHUBER, HEINRICH. B. Sept. 17, 1844 in Württemberg. A. in 1870. W. Ver. preaching. M. Ad. *Mercara, Coorg.*

DIEZ, K. A. ERNST. B. Dec. 24, 1826, in Württemberg. A. in 1851. W. has been Ver. preaching and literary work. One of the revisers of the Malayalam Bible. M. Since 1880 Theol. teacher in the Sem. at (Ad.) *Mangalore, Madras P.*

DIGEL, THOMAS, Esq. B. July 28, 1840, in Württemberg. A. in 1872. M. Supt. of the Weaving Establishment at (Ad.) *Mangalore, Madras P.*

DILGER, W. B. 1855 in Württemberg. A. 1880. Ad. *Tellicherry Madras P.*

EBLE, G. B. 1852, in Württemberg. A. 1876. M. W. Ver. preaching. Ad. *Udapi, Madras P.*

ELSASSER, THEODORE, Esq. B. April 18, 1844 in Württemberg. A. in 1867. M. Is the head of the Mercantile Branch at (Ad.) *Calicut, Madras P.*

FERNANDEZ, DIEGO. B. in 1831, in Kalamundkur, South Canara O. in 1872. Ad. *Gudde, Udapi, Madras P.*

FEUCHTER, CARL, Esq. B. Sept. 25, 1842, in Württemberg. A. in 1876. Supt. of Tiling Works at (Ad.) *Calicut, Madras P.*

FIEG, I. Esq. B. 1851 in Baden. A. 1879. Ad. *Calicut, Madras P.*

FROHNMEYER, J. B. 1850 in Württemberg. A. 1876. M. W. educational, and Ver. preaching. Ad. *Tellicherry, Madras P.*

FURTADO, SEBASTIAN. B. 1830, in Mangalore. O. in 1866. Ad. *Utshila, Madras P.*

GANGNAGEL, LUDWIG. B. in Crumstadt, Grand Duchy Hessen, Germany, Dec. 12, 1845. O. in 1875. A. in 1875. M. W. chiefly itinerating in the district. Ad. *Honore, Bombay P.*

GOJAR, CHARLES. B. 1845, in Mangalore. O. in 1878. Ad. *Shirva, Udapi, Madras P.*

GRAETER, J. BENIGNUS. B. May 12, 1838, in Württemberg. A. in 1863. Is Chairman of the Mission, and Principal of the Theol. Sem. M. Ad. *Mangalore, Madras P.*

GROSSMANN, GOTTLIEB. B. Nov. 30, 1848, in Switzerland. A. in 1874. W. Ver. preaching, and educational. M. Ad. *Hubly, Bombay P.*

HAFNER, JOHANNES. B. May 3, 1845, in Switzerland. A. in 1871. M. W. Ver. preaching. Ad. *Basrur, Kundapur, Madras P.*

HALBROCK, E. B. 1856 in Prussia. A. 1876. Ad. *Calicut, Do.*

HANHART, LEONHARD GOTTL. B. May 25, 1831, in Switzerland. A. in 1857. W. chiefly Ver preaching: also charge of schools. M. Ad. *Cannanore, Madras P.*

HARLIN, EMMERICH. B. Nov. 5, 1843, in Württemberg. Pastoral work several years before coming to I. A. 1873. W. educational, and Ver. preaching. M. Ad. *Mangalore, Madras P.*

HARTMANN, RUDOLF. B. April 1, 1831, in Switzerland. A. in 1859. M. Formerly in charge of the orphanage at Udapi: now engaged in Ver. preaching at (Ad.) *Karkal, Madras P.*

HASENWANDEL, WILHELM. B. Oct. 20, 1843, in Württemberg. A. in 1872. W. Ver. preaching. M. Ad. *Dharwar, Bombay P.*

HAURI, RUDOLF, Esq. B. Dec. 25, 1852, in Switzerland. A. 1878. M. In charge of Mercantile Branch at (Ad.) *Mangalore, Madras P.*

HERMELINK, JAN. B. July 18, 1848, in Hanover. A. in 1872. W. Ver. preaching. M. Ad. *Mulky, Madras P.*

HIRNER, GOTTLOB, Esq. B. Aug. 2, 1846, in Württemberg. A. in 1871. Supt. of the Mission Press. M. Ad. *Mangalore, Madras P.*

HOCH, M. B. 1854 in Switzerland. A. 1876. W. educational; teacher in Theol. Sem. Ad. *Mangalore, Madras P.*

HUBNER, NATHANAEL. B. March 21, 1848, in Prussia. A. in 1871. W. educational, and Ver. preaching. M. *Now in Europe.*

HUTTINGER, CARL, Esq. B. Dec. 5, 1846, in Baden. A. in 1871. Supt. of Mechanical Workshop. M. Ad. *Mangalore, Madras P.*

JACOBI, JOSEPH. B. in 1829, in Madras. O. in 1868. Ad. *Calicut, Madras P.*

JAUS, I. B. 1855 in Württemberg. A. 1879. W. educational. Ad. *Palghat, Madras P.*

KAMSIKA, J. B. in 1818 at Mangalore. O. in 1878. Ad. *Karwar, Bombay P.*

KAUNDINYA, HERMANN ANANDRAO. B. March 20, 1825, at Mangalore. E. at Basel: O. in 1851. W. charge of congregation. Translator and author of some Christian works, and one of the translators of Canarese Commentary on the N. T. M. Ad. *Anandapur, Madras P.*

KEPPLER, C. B. 1849 in Württemberg. A. in 1879. W. Ver. preaching. Ad. *Karkala, S. Canara, Madras P.*

KITTEL, FERDINAND. B. March 17, 1832, in Hanover. A. in 1853. W. literary; and Ver. preaching. Author, translator and editor of several philological, Christian and school books, in classical and modern Canarese. M. *Now in Europe.*

KNAUSENBERGER, I. B. 1853 in Württemberg. A. 1878. W. Ver. preaching, and schools. Ad. *Bettighery, Gaduk. Bombay P.*

KNOBLOCH, JULIUS. B. in Baden, South Germany, Sept. 14, 1838. A. Oct. 1865. M. W. has been Ver. preaching, and educational. L.. edited a Children's Hymn-book; and a few smaller tracts: one of the revisers of the Malayalam Bible. Ad. *Calicut, Madras P.*

KRAPF, I. B. in 1858 in Switzerland. A. 1878. In charge of Basel Mission Book and Tract Depository. Ad. *Mangalore, Madras P.*

KUHNLE, G. B in 1850 in Württemberg. A. 1878. W. ver. preaching. Ad. *Calicut, Madras P.*

LAUFFER, JAKOB. B. Jan. 4, 1834, in Württemberg. A. in 1856. W. ver. preaching. M. Ad. *Cannanore, Madras P.*

LAYER, JOHANNES. B. Nov. 11, 1846 in Württemberg. A. in 1873. W. educational; and ver. preaching. M. Ad. *Mangalore, Madras P.*

LIEBENDORFER, EUGEN. B. Feb. 16, 1852, in Wuttemberg. A. 1875. W. educational, and congregation. M. Ad. *Tellicherry, Madras P.*

LINDER, CARL. B. June 20, 1840 in Baden. A. in 1868. W. ver. preaching. M. *Now in Europe.*

LUTZE, WILHELM. B. May 15, 1849, in Württemberg. A. in 1875. W. educational and ver. preaching. Ad *Hubly, Bombay P.*

MACK, JOHANNES. B. May 18, 1834 in the Grand Duchy of Baden. A. in 1858. W. educational and ver. preaching. Has written several school-books in Canarese. M. *Now in Europe.*

MANNER, J. FR. B. in Württemberg. A in 1857. W. literary, and ver. preaching. Chairman of the Dists. of Canara and Coorg. Ad. *Mangalore, Madras P.*

MATTHISSEN, FRANZ J., ESQ. B. Aug. 18, 1839, at St. Petersburg, Russia. A. in 1867. Secular agent for the Malabar district; and educational work. Has written several tracts in Malayalam. Ad *Calicut, Madras P.*

MIEG, M. B. in 1855 in Württemberg. A. 1878. M. W. educational and ver. preaching. Ad *Kotagherry, Neilgherris, Madras P.*

MULIL, A. B. in 1822. O. 1875. Ad. *Taliparambu, Do.*

MULLER, J. FRIEDRICH. B. in Württemberg. A in 1861. W. educational. M. Ad. *Kaity, Neilgherris.*

NUBLING, WILHELM. B in Denzlingen, Baden, Germany, May 25, 1846. O. 1871. A. 1871. W. chiefly ver. preaching. M. Ad. *Honore, Bombay P.*

OSTERMEIER, JOHANNES S. K. ESQ. B. June 22, 1855, in Bavaria. A. in 1873. M. W. Mercantile Branch at (Ad.) *Calicut, Madras P.*

OTT, PAUL. B. Nov. 1, 1845 in Württemberg. A. 1871. W. educational and ver. preaching. Ad. *Mulki, Madras P.*

Pfleiderer, Carl, Esq. B. April 8, 1850, in Württemberg. A. 1874. General Agent and Treasurer of the Mission. Ad. *Calicut, Madras P.*

Ritter, Gustav. B. March 20, 1844, in Württemberg. A. in 1869. W. ver. preaching. M. Ad. *Udapi, Madras P.*

Roth, Wilhelm. B. in Baden. A. in 1857. M. W. ver. preaching. Ad. *Guledgud, Bombay P.*

Ruhland, A. B. 1851, in Bavaria. A. 1876. W. ver. preaching. Ad. *Palghat, Madras P.*

Schauffler, Th. F. B. in Württemberg. A. in 1860. M. *Now in Europe.*

Schenkel, Rudolph. B. July 28, 1845, in Baden, Germany. A. 1874. W. ver. in charge of orphanage. M. Ad. *Hubly, Bombay P.*

Schmolck, Wilhelm. B. Sept. 12, 1839, in Baden. A in 1869, M. *Now in Europe.*

Schonthal, W. P. Esq. B. in Baden. A. in 1870. M. Supt. of Weaving establishment at (Ad.) *Cannanore, Madras P.*

Sikemeier, Willem E. B May 27, 1843, in Holland. A. in 1870. M. In charge of Basel Mission Press. Ad. *Mungalore, Madras P.*

Stierlen, F. Esq. B. 1853 in Württemberg. A. 1880. Ad. *Cannanore, Madras P.*

Stokes, William. B. Feb. 18, 1837, at Shemoga, Mysore. O. in 1860. W. charge of an orphanage; and ver. preaching. Has written several Canarese tracts. M. Ad. *Kaity, Madras P.*

Thumm, J. J. B. in Württemberg. A. in 1860. W. ver. preaching. M. Ad. *Bettigherry, Gadak, Bombay P.*

Veil, Johannes, Esq. B. Dec. 14, 1853, in Württemberg. A. in 1875. M. Manager of Mercantile Branch at (Ad). *Mercara, Coorg.*

Veil, J. Friedrich. B. July 16, 1849, in Württemberg. A. in 1872. W. ver. preaching. Ad. *Mercara, Coorg.*

Wagner, Gottlieb. B. March 28, 1846, in Baden. A. in 1872. W. ver. preaching. M. Ad. *Codacal, Madras P.*

Walter, Simeon. B. March 3, 1841, in Switzerland. A. in 1866. W. charge of orphanage; and ver. preaching. Has written several tracts in Malayalam. Ad. *Chombalu, Madras P.*

Walz, Theodore M. B. Jan. 26, 1843, in Württemberg. A. in 1866. W. educational and ver. preaching. Editor of a Canarese monthly for Christians, and author of several tracts. M. Ad. *Udapi, Madras P.*

Warth, C. B 1853, in Württemberg. A. 1878. W. ver. preaching. Ad. *Guledgud, Bagulcote, Bombay P.*

Weismann, T. B. 1855, in Württemberg. A. 1878. Ad. *Cannanore, Madras P.*

Welsch, Jakob. B Aug. 22, 1848, in Alsace, Germany. A. 1871. W. educational; and ver. preaching. M. Ad. *Guledgud, Bombay P.*

Ziegler, Fr. Esq. B. Württemberg. A. in 1862. M. W. educational; and ver. preaching. Ad. *Dharwar, Bombay P.*

Ziegler, Gustav Adolf. B, March 12, 1848, in Württemberg. A. in 1872. W. charge of orphanage and training class. M. Ad. *Udapi, Madras P.*

RETIRED AND DECEASED MISSIONARIES.

Samuel Hebich. B. April 19, 1803, in Wurttemberg. O. and appointed to I. in 1834. Was engaged in ver. preaching and was the means of many conversions. Ret. in 1859. D. in 1868. (*Vide* Memoir, obtainable at Mangalore.)

C. Greiner. B. in Württemberg. A. in 1834. Labored at Mangalore and in the South Canara District. Ret. in 1855. Has labored since as pastor of a German Colony in North America.

H. Lohner. B. in Württemburg (or Baden). A. in 1834 along with Rev. Messrs. Hebich and Greiner. Was engaged in ver. preaching in South Mahratta and North Canara. Ret. in 1848.

H. Mogling, Ph. D. B. May 29, 1811, in Württemberg. O. and A. in 1836. Labored chiefly in South Canara and Coorg. The author and editor of several works in Canarese, philological, theological, and Bible translations; and tracts. Ret. in 1860. After his retirement served as a minister in the State Church of Württemberg: since 1868 has been engaged in literary work for the Basel Mission.

Hermann Gundert, Ph. D. B. Feb. 4, 1814, in Württemberg. O. and A. in 1836 in connection with Mr. Norris Groves' Mission. Joined the Basel Mission in 1838. Labored chiefly in Malabar; in ver. preaching, school and literary work. Author of several works in Malayalam, linguistic, theological and practical. Translator of the N. T. and Poetical Books of the O. T. which form the basis of a new revision now in progress of the Malayalam Bible. Since returning to Europe he has been actively engaged in editing Missionary and other literature.

A. Loesch. B. in Switzerland. O. and A. in 1838. Ret. in 1840, on account of failing health.

J. Dehlinger. O. and A. in 1838. Ret. in 1840 with broken health.

H. Frey. B. in Württemberg. O. and A. in 1838. Labored at Hubly. Ret. on account of ill health in 1843. Was shipwrecked at Mauritius, and proceeded in another vessel which had scarcely reached St. Helena when it was demolished. He remained there as Chaplain until his death, about 1871.

G. F. Sutter. B. in Württemberg. O. and A. in 1838. Labored at Mangalore. Ret. in 1846 on account of failing health.

Johannes Layer. B. Wurttemberg. O. and A. in 1838. Labored in South Mahratta and North Canara. The author of two popular tracts in Canarese. Ret. in 1849. Has since served as pastor of a free congregation in Württemberg.

J. M. Fritz. B. June 6, 1815, in Alsace, Germany. A. in 1839. W. chiefly ver. preaching. One of the revisers of the Malayalam Bible and author of some Malayalam tracts. Was Chairman of the Basel Mission in India, and of the Malabar District. M. Ret. in 1880. Now in Germany.

H. Mengert. O. and A. in 1839. After some years joined the S. P. G. Mission in Guzerat.

C. Essig. B. in Württemberg. O. and A. in 1839. Labored in South Mahratta. D. of cholera, in 1843.

C. Hiller. B. in Württemberg. O. and A. in 1839. Labored in South Maharatta. Ret. in 1852. Afterwards labored as pastor of German colonists in North America.

G. Supper. B in Württemberg. O. and A. in 1839. Labored in South Mahratta. Ret. in 1843 on account of ill health.

Johannes Muller. B Jan 15, 1813, in Württemberg. O. and A. in 1839. Labored at Hubly; ver. preaching and care of congregations. After twenty-three years of uninterrupted labor D. at his post, Dec. 28, 1864.

G. Weiglo. B. in Württemberg. O. and A. in 1839. W. educational and literary. D. June 7, 1855.

Jacob Ammann. B. July 6, 1816, in Switzerland. O. and A. in 1839. One of the founders of the Tulu Mission. Labored in North and South Canara: ver. preaching, and literary work. Translated the N. T. and the Psalms into Tulu. D. January 2, 1865.

Ch. Irion. B. July 6, 1812, in Württemberg. O. and A. in 1841. Labored at Tellicherry: ver. preaching and literary work. Author of several school-books and tracts in Malayalam. Ret. in 1860. Has since served as Missionary Secretary in the Grand Duchy of Baden.

T. G. Stanger, Esq. B. in Württemberg. A. in 1841. Labored as Manager of the Christian colony at Malasamudra, South Mahratta until 1849, when he joined the L. M. S. at Bellary. Afterwards went to North America.

M. Hall. O. and A. in 1841. Labored at Bettigherry, until his death, in 1845.

J. Huber. B. in Switzerland. O. and A. in 1841. Labored at Calicut: ver. preaching; and school work. Ret. in 1855. Has served since as traveling agent of the Society for Switzerland.

G. F. Muller. B. in Württemberg. O. and A. in 1842. Labored at Tellicherry: in charge of the orphanage, congregation, and engaged in literary work. Author of several tracts. Ret. in 1855. Has served since as Missionary Secretary for Württemberg.

F. H. Albrecht. B. in Saxony. O. and A. in 1842. Labored at Dharwar and Honore. From 1855 to 1861 acted as traveling agent of the Society for Middle Germany. Ret. in 1865. D. 1866.

Christian Muller. B. Jan. 21, 1819, in Württemberg. A. in 1842. W. literary, educational; and ver. preaching. The author of a number of tracts and school books in Malayalam, editor of Malayalam periodicals; and one of the revisers of the Malayalam Bible. Ret 1878.

J. Friedrich Metz. B. in Württemberg. A. in 1843. Ret. in 1873.

Carl Moericke. B. Feb. 10, 1822. in Württemberg. After several years of pastoral work at home was appointed to I. in 1845. Labored in South Mahratta, but chiefly on the Neilgherries, where he gathered together the first congregation. Ret. in 1865, and D. a year or two thereafter.

G. Wurth. B. Sept. 18, 1820, in Württemberg. O. and A. in 1845. Labored in South Mahratta: Ver. preaching. An accomplished Canarese scholar. D. in Dec. 1869.

J. G. Kies. B. Feb. 25, 1821, in Württemberg. O. and A. in 1845. Labored in South Mahratta: literary work, care of congregations and schools. Author of a number of Canarese school-books and tracts. Ret. in 1866, and proceeded to North America as a pastor, where he D. about 1870.

M. Buhler. B. about 1816, in Württemberg. O. and A. in 1846. Labored on the Neilgherries: Ver. preaching, and educational work. Noted as a linguist. D. of cholera, July 7, 1854.

B. Deggeler. B. April 27, 1822, in Switzerland. O. and A. in 1846. Labored in South Canara: Ver preaching and school-work, Ret. in 1858. Has served since as pastor of a German colony near the Caucasus.

W. Hoch. B. May 6, 1821, in Switzerland. O. and A. in 1846. Was principal of Mission (Engl.) school at Mangalore. Ret. in 1860. Was traveling agent of the Society in and about Frankfort until his death, in 1865.

F. Lehmann. B. Oct 20, 1823, in Bavaria. O. and A. in 1848 Labored in North and South Canara. Ret. in 1859: afterwards went to North America as pastor of a German Colony, where he D. in 1874.

J. Leonberger, Esq. B. Jan. 6, 1822, in Württemberg. A. in 1849. Labored as manager of Christian Colony at Malasamudra. Ret. in 1861. Afterwards went to North America, where he is engaged in evangelistic work.

S. Muller, Esq. B in Württemberg. A. in 1849. Labored as superintendent of Clock-making workshops in Mangalore, until 1854, when he entered the Public Works Department.

G. Boesinger, Esq. B. in Württemberg. in 1849. Supt. of Workshops at Mangalore, until 1851, when he resigned the mission service. Is now at Ootacamund.

J. Haller, Esq. B. Feb. 15, 1825, in Württemberg. A. in 1851. Supt. of Weaving Establishment at Mangalore until 1865, when he resigned the mission service. Now in Coorg.

G. Plebst, Esq. B. Aug. 16. 1823, in Württemberg. A. in 1851. Labored as Supt of the Mission press. which had previously been a lithographic one. He added a typographical press, and made many other improvements, including an Engl. department. Also established the tiling works at Mangalore. Ret. in 1867, and has since labored as traveling agent of Young Men's Association for South Germany.

S. Kullen. B. in Württemberg. After several years of pastoral work at home was appointed to I. in 1851. Labored in the Catechist school at Mangalore. Ret. in 1855. Afterwards went as a missionary to the Jews at Beyrout, where he D.

O. Kaufmann. B. Oct. 19, 1828, in Baden. O. and A. in 1853. Labored at Mahratta and Coorg in Ver. preaching. R. to Europe in 1869, and D. just after arriving at Stuttgart.

G. Camerer. B. Jan. 22, 1831, in Württemberg. O. and A. in 1854. Labored at Udapi. D. in 1858.

Gottlob Pfleiderer, Esq. B. Sept. 28, 1829 in Württemberg. A. in 1854. Treasurer and general agent in secular affairs of the Mission;

head of the Mercantile Branch at Mangalore. M. Ret. in 1880. Agent of mercantile and industrial establishments of the Mission. Ad. *Basel.*

F. Sauvain. B. Dec. 26, 1829, in Switzerland. O and A. in 1854. Labored at Chiracal: in charge of the orphanage. Ret. in 1858: has labored since as pastor in North America.

G. Richter. B May 4, 1829, in Baden. O. and A. in 1855. Principal of the Central school in Mercara, as a missionary, until 1863, since as a Government official.

Ch. Aldinger. B. Jan. 4, 1826, in Württemberg. O. and A. in 1855. Labored in the schools and in charge of the congregations. Ret. in 1866: has labored since as traveling agent of the Society in Württemberg.

J. Handrich. B. Aug. 18, 1830, in Bavaria. O. and A. in 1856. Labored in Dharwar. D. in 1858.

G. Hauser. B. May 7, 1829, in Württemberg. O. and A. in 1856. Labored at Mulky. D. in 1858.

Friedrich Keuler. B. Feb. 8, 1834, in Württemberg. O. and A. in 1856. Labored at Mangalore, in charge of the Engl school. D. in 1858.

J. Strobel. B Feb. 19, 1832, in Frankfort. O. and A. in 1856. W. Ver. preaching. Ret. in 1863. Labored until 1874, as traveling agent of the Society in and about Frankfort, since as a minister.

J. Bosshard, Esq B. Dec 27, 1827, in Switzerland. A. in 1856. Labored as manager of the colonies Codacal and Chowa. Ret. in 1866. D. Nov 21, 1874.

J. Hunziker, Esq. B. May 20, 1831, in Switzerland. A. in 1856. Labored as Supt. of the press, at Mangalore. Ret in 1863. Labored afterwards as town missionary in Zurich: since 1870, as an evangelist in North America.

P. A Convert B. Sept. 17, 1832, in Switzerland. O. and A. in 1857. Labored at Calicut: W. ver. preaching and educational. Ret. in 1867. French minister in Schaffuausen until his death in 1871.

Ch J. Wurtele. B. Nov. 21, 1833, in Württemberg. O. and A. in 1857. Labored in South Canara and Neilgherries: ver. preaching and educational work. D. Feb. 2, 1863.

J. Huber. B. Feb. 28, 1834 in Switzerland. O. and A. in 1857. Labored at Hubly: ver preaching. Was Chairman of the Mission. Ret. in 1869. Since 1871 has labored as a pastor in North America.

C. F. R. Hahn, Esq. B. Feb. 17, 1833, in Württemberg. A. in 1857 Manager of the Colony Anandapur: also labored at Bettigherry. Ret in 1871. Was principal of a home for destitute children at Württemberg until his death, March 28, 1875.

H. Hauff. B. Sept. 8, 1825, in Wurttemberg. O. and A. in 1857. Labored at Mangalore. Was chairman of the South Canara district. Ret. in 1865. Is now a minister in the State Church of Württemberg.

A Finkh. B. Nov. 30, 1831, in Württemberg. O. and A. in 1857. Labored in the catechist seminary at Mangalore. Ret. in 1865: D. on the way home, and was buried at Corfu.

Samuel Gottlieb Schoch, Esq. B. Dec. 13, 1835, in Switzerland. A. in 1857. M. S. Cannanore. D. 1876.

Johann J. Brigel. B. in Württemberg. A. in 1858. S. Mangalore. Ret. 1875. Now minister in Württemberg.

J. G. Burckhardt. B. Nov. 20, 1829, in Württemberg. O, and A. in 1858. Labored at Tellicherry: and at Mangalore. Ret. in 1869. Is now a minister in Württemberg.

C. Schlunk, Esq. B. Jan. 31, 1831, in Prussia. A. in 1858. Was Treasurer of the Mission. Ret. in 1864. D. in 1870.

J. Fr. Traub. B. July 30, 1834, in Württemberg. O. and A. 1859. Labored at Shirva, South Canara: Ver. preaching. Ret. in 1868. D. from consumption Oct. 27, 1868.

L. Ph. Reinhardt. B. Sept. 12, 1836, in Baden. O. and A. in 1859. Labored at Tellicherry: educational work, and Ver. preaching. Ret. in 1871.

K. Brunner. B. in Nov. 1831, in Switzerland. O. and A. in 1860. Ret. in 1866. Has since served as a pastor in North America.

Chr. F. Krauss. B. May 3, 1835, in Württemberg. O. and A. in 1860. Labored at Neilgherries and at Dharwar. D. July 6, 1871, from an attack of fever caught on his last tour, and which became fatal as he was returning home chiefly by the uncharitableness of the people who refused him even drinking water.

E. H. Bergfeldt. B. in Prussia. A. in 1860. Ret. 1874. Traveling Agent for the Society in Germany.

R. Riehm Esq. B. March 8, 1833, in Baden. A. in 1860. Was Treasurer of the Mission, and of the mercantile branch, Mangalore. Ret. in 1872 on account of poor health. D. 1872.

T. Costa. B. in 1834, at Shemoga, Mysore. O. in 1861. Labored in the Anglo-ver. school, Dharwar. Left the Mission in 1876.

Albert Wenger. B. May 9, 1837, in Switzerland. O. and A. in 1861. Labored in Neilgherries and Coorg. Ret. in 1874. Now Prin. of the Miss. Girls' Home, Basel.

H. C. Schmidli, Esq. B. May 11, 1830, in Switzerland. A. in 1861. D. 1865.

Fr. Schlunk, Esq. B. March 21, 1841, in Prussia. A. in 1862 Labored at Calicut in the mercantile department. Ret. in 1864. Now in Calicut.

Samuel Gundert. B. Aug. 4, 1840, in Württemberg. A. in 1863, Labored chiefly in Malabar, and from 1874 at Mangalore. D. in May. 1819.

C. Stolz, Esq. B. in Switzerland. A. in 1863. S. Mangalore. Ret. in 1874.

Chr. Roeck. B. Nov. 6, 1836, in Baden. O. and A. in 1864. Labored at Codacal and at Chowa. Ret. in 1867. Now in North America in charge of a German congregation.

Joh. Buchmuller. B. March 9, 1841, in Switzerland. O. and A. in 1865. Labored at Calicut, until his death, Nov. 13, 1866.

Edward Schweizer. B. July 28, 1840, in Switzerland. O. and A. in 1866. Labored in Udapi and Mangalore. Ret. in 1870: has served since as pastor to a German colony in North America.

Z. Deuber. B. May 21, 1842, in Switzerland. O. and A. in 1866. Labored at Honore and Hubly. Ret. on account of ill health in 1871: has labored since as city missionary in Alsace.

Wilh. Schnepf. B. Dec. 29, 1842, in Wurttemberg. O. and A. in 1866. Labored at Mangalore and Anandapur. Ret. on account of ill health: has since served as city missionary in Alsace.

Johannes Muller, Esq. B. March 7, 1845 in Wurttemberg. A. in 1866. M. Ret. 1878.

Christian G. Weigele. B. Oct. 6, 1845, in Wurttemberg. A. in 1877. W. ver. preaching. D. 1877.

Jabbo Kittet. B. Hanover. A. in 1867. S. Tellicherry. Ret. in 1876. Now minister in North Germany.

Chr. Reuter, Esq. B. July 12, 1833, in Wurttembrg. A. in 1867. Supt. of the Mission Press. D. in Mangalore. March 6, 1871.

Carl Schober, Esq. B. Dec. 8, 1841, in Württemberg. A. in 1867. Was in charge of the mercantile branch in Calicut. Ret. on account of ill health, in 1872.

Andreas Stoll. B. April 15, 1843, in Switzerland. O. and A. in 1867. Labored in South Mahratta and North Canara. Ret. in 1871: has since served as pastor to a German Colony in North America.

Louis Langell. B. Dec. 7, 1840, in Switzerland. O. and A. in 1868. Labored in South Canara. Ret. in 1873: has since been engaged in evangelistic work in Canada.

Friedrich Gundert, Esq. B. March 7, 1847, in Wurttemberg. Was manager of the book and tract depository at Mangalore. Ret. in 1870, on account of poor health.

G. Spillmann, Esq. B. in Switzerland. A. in 1869. Ret. in 1876.

Johannes Hesse. B. June 2, 1847, in Esthland, Russia. O. and A. in 1869. Labored in the Neilgherries and at Mangalore. Ret. on account of ill health: has since been engaged in literary labors for the Society at Württemberg.

Gustav Schmid, Esq. B. Oct. 21, 1840, in Württemberg. A. in 1870. Was connected with the mercantile branch at Mangalore until his death, June 22, 1870.

A. Bourquin. B. April 8, 1848, in Switzerland. O. and A. in 1871. Labored in Malabar. Left the Mission at the close of 1875. Now in Bombay.

J. L. Grieshaber. B. June 13, 1847, in Wurttemberg. O. and A. in 1871. Labored at Guledgud. Ret. in 1874 to enter the ministry at home.

Nathanael Weitbrecht, Esq. B. in Württemberg. A. in 1871. Ret. in 1876.

August Dobler, Esq. B. Sept. 24, 1845, in Surinam. A. in 1872. Ret. 1879. Now pastor in Newark, North America.

A. Merkle. B. July 31, 1845, at Baden. O. and A. in 1872. Labored in Chowa. Ret in 1875: is now pastor in America.

Andreas Kohler. A. 1873. D. early in 1876.

———o———

CHAPTER XII.

THE AMERICAN BAPTIST MISSIONARY UNION.

THIS Society, one of the oldest of its kind in America, was organized May 18, 1814, in the city of Philadelphia. The Rev. Adoniram Judson (who had arrived at Calcutta in 1812 under the auspices of the American Board, and, changing his views somewhat, had united with the Baptist missionaries at Serampore and had proceeded to Rangoon in July, 1813) was in May, 1814, appointed the first missionary of the Society. From Burmah the operations of the Society were extended in 1836 to Assam: and about the same time the Telugu Mission was commenced. As these fields are widely separated, they can be best described by taking them up one by one.

I. THE BURMESE MISSION.

In 1816 Mr. Judson was joined by the Rev. G. H. Hough, who had been a printer and who brought from Serampore a printing-press and a fout of Burman types. A Catechism and the Gospel of Matthew in Burmese were at once printed. In September, 1818 the Rev. Messrs. Colman and Wheelock arrived: the latter, a year later, was compelled by failing health to withdraw from the Mission and was drowned at sea on his passage to Bengal. In 1819 the first house for public worship and teaching was opened. In June of the same year the first Burman convert, Moung Nau, was baptized. In 1821 the Rev. J. Price, a physician as well as a minister, arrived at Rangoon, and in 1823 the Rev. J. Wade joined the Mission.

The war of 1824-26 suspended all the operations of the Mission: it compelled Messrs. Hough and Wade to retire from the country, while upon Messrs. Judson and Price and their families at Ava it brought the severest calamities and sufferings. After the war the Mission was removed to Amherst (in 1827) and thence, in 1828, to Maulmain. Tavoy was also occupied, by the Rev. G. D. Boardman, in 1828: at Rangoon, a small Native church was still maintained under a Native Pastor.

By the year 1831 several other missionaries had arrived

from America, increasing the number to seven: another station, Mergui, had been occupied: the Press had printed 200,000 tracts and books, among which were the New Testament and several books of the Old Testament: schools had also been established.

Work among the Karens had been begun by Mr. Boardman at Tavoy, and at his death, in 1830, was carried on most successfully by Mr. Mason. The Karens in all parts of Burmah have received the Gospel with far greater readiness than the Burmans themselves. The language of this people was in 1832 reduced to writing by the Rev. Mr. Wade.

In the two years, 1833-34 nine other missionaries arrived and the work was proportionately extended : during this period Mr. Judson completed his translation of the Bible into the Burman tongue. "It had been his daily task amid the vicissitudes of many years. It had been his solace in grief, his companion in solitude, his support in weariness and depression."

In 1835 a branch of the Mission was opened in the province of Arracan : in 1840 Akyab and Sandoway were occupied. Missionaries from America continued to arrive, and the number of converts, especially Karens, was multiplied. In 1840 Mr. Judson finished the revision of his Burman translation of the Bible. In 1843 the persecution of the Christian Karens was renewed with increased violence ; ill treatment and imprisonment however were endured with heroic Christian fortitude, by the simple dwellers among the mountains of Arracan. In the same year the New Testament was translated into the Karen languages.

In 1845 Dr. Judson visited America, returning to his work in December, 1846. He made an effort to establish himself at Ava or at Rangoon, but being unsuccessful returned to Maulmain, where he continued to labor until 1849, when his health failed: in April, 1850, he took passage on a French ship bound for the Isle of France, but died when four days out, April 12th.*

About this time the Burman and Karen departments of the work at Maulmain and in Arracan were separated from each other, a measure which led to greater efficiency and larger success. The war between Burmah and Great Britain, in 1852,

* See Wayland's "Memoir of Dr. Judson."

greatly altered the condition of the missions in Burmah. The missionaries together with a deputation from America, assembled at Maulmain, to discuss the leading subjects connected with the organization and conduct of the missions. The convention continued from April 4th, to the 17th of May, 1853. Several important modifications were made in the missions already existing, and five new missions were established: Rangoon, Bassein, Shwaygyeen, Prome, and Tounghoo. There were at this time thirty-one missionaries in the field.

In 1854, a new station was formed at Henthada, and in 1855 another was opened at Thongzai: Zeegong was occupied in 1876, and Bhamo, in 1877.

At present, work is carried on in the larger stations in several languages, Burmese, Karen, (Pgho and Sgau) and Shan. The Bassein Karen Churches support four missionaries among the Kakhyens in the mountains beyond Bhamo. The growth and liberality of the Karen Churches are so well-known that they need only this word of mention.

There are now (1881) 21 Burman, and 431 Karen Churches. The number of Native Christians is about 60,000; communicants, 21,594.

MEMBERS OF THE MISSION.

BENNETT, CEPHAS. B. Homer, N. Y., U. S. A., March 20, 1804. A. in Madras, Sept. 1829, in Maulmain, Jan. 13, 1830. H. to America 1840. O. in Utica, N. Y. 1840. R. to Maulmain, 1841. S. Maulmain, Tavoy, and Rangoon. H. 1871-72. Has labored chiefly as Supt. of Mission Press: has printed in five languages the first books printed in those languages. Ad. *Rangoon.*

BRAYTON, D. L. Ad. *Rangoon.*

BUNKER, A. Ad. *Tounghoo, Burmah.*

BUSHELL, WALTER. B. Charlton Kings, Gloucestershire, Eng. July 4, 1850. E. Crozer Theol. Sem. (1878) O. July 30, 1878. A. Dec. 5, 1878. Ad. *Maooben, Thonkwa, Burmah.*

CARPENTER, C. H. Ad. *Bassein, Burmah.*

CUSHING, JOSIAH NELSON. B. North Attleboro, Mass., U.S.A. May, 1840. O. July 1865. A. March, 1867. S. Rangoon. H. to U. S. A. from May, 1874, to Oct. 1876 and to Eng. 1879. L. Translated into the Shan language: The New Testament, "Grammar," "Manual," Shan and Eng. Dictionary, Small Astronomy, and Geography, several Tracts and a Hymn-book: Mission Press, Rangoon. Ad. *Rangoon.*

CROSS, E. B. Ad. *Tounghoo, Burmah.*

CRUMB, A. V. Ad. *Do. Do.*

ELWELL, JACOB THOMAS. B. Philadelphia, U. S. A., May 10, 1844. E. at Lewisburg Univ. (1871) and at Crozer Theol. Sem. (1874). O. July, 1876. Pastoral work at home. 1875-78. M. May 14, 1879. A. Dec. 5, 1878. Ad. *Bassein, Burmah.*

EVELETH, FREDERIC HOWARD. B. Durham, Me., U. S. A. March 21, 1843. O. at Portland, June, 1873. A. Jan. 12. 1874. S. Tounghoo. H. March 28, 1879 to Dec. 1, 1880. Ad. *Toungkoo, Burmah.*

FREIDAY, J. A. Ad. *Bhamo, Burmah.*

HANCOCK, R. B. Ad. *Zeegong, Burmah.*

HARRIS, NORMAN. B. Becket, Mass., U. S. A., Feb. 19, 1813. O. Oct. 9, 1844. A. Dec. 1. 1846. S. Maulmain, 1846-53, Shwaygyeen, 1853 to present. H. 1857-59 ; 1862-66 : 1867-68. Ad. *Shwaygyeen, Burmah.*

HASCALL, W. H. S. Ad. *Maulmain, Burmah.*

JAMESON, MELVIN. B. Lyons, N.Y., U.S.A. March 3, 1836. O. April, 1860. S. Alton, Ill., U. S. A., 1860-1869. A Feb. 22, 1870. S. Bassein, 1870-80. H. to America 1881. Ad. *Bassein, Burmah.*

KO-SHOAY. Ad. *Maulmain, Burmah.*

MIX, B. J. Ad. *Toungkoo, Do.*

MORROW, HORATIO. B. St. Peter's Bay, P. E. Island. April 24, 1843. O. Nov. 11, 1871. A. Dec. 27, 1876. Ad. *Tavoy, Burmah.*

MYA-MAI. Ad. *Rangoon.*

NICHOLS, CHARLES ALVORD. B. Westport, Conn., U. S. A., Aug. 16, 1853. O. Aug. 19, 1879. A. Dec. 9, 1879. Ad. *Bassein, Burmah.*

NORRIS, JAMES FREDERIC. B. Danbury, N. H., U. S. A. March 10, 1838. O. July, 1865. A. March, 1866. S. Maulmain, 1866, Tavoy, 1869, Maulmain, 1879. H. to America 1871-79. Ad. *Maulmain, Burmah.*

PACKER, JOHN. Ad. *Rangoon.*

PRICE, W. J A 1879. Ad. *Shwaygyeen, Burmah.*

ROBERTS, W. H. Ad. *Bhamo, Burmah.*

ROSE, A. T Ad. *Rangoon.*

SAIR-TAY. Ad. *Do.*

SHWAY-NOO. Ad. *Do.*

SMITH, D. A. W. Ad. *Do.*

STEVENS, EDWARD ABIEL. B. near Riceboro, Ga., U. S. A. O. at Ruckersville, Ga. A. Feb. 19, 1838. S. Maulmain, 1838-57 ; since, Rangoon. H. 1854 and 1876. L. Translations, (in Burmese) "History, Ancient and Modern" ; Barth's "Church History" ; Headings to Chapters and References to N. T.; Hannay's Concordance ; several Tracts : original, several Tracts ; editing a monthly Newspaper in Burmese. Ad. *Rangoon.*

STEVENS, EDWARD OLIVER. B. at Maulmain, Burmah, Dec. 17, 1838. O. Newton, U. S. A. Oct. 23, 1864. A. Feb. 22, 1866. S. Prome. L. Editing second edition Judson's Burmese and Engl. Dictionary. H. to America 1875. Ad. *Prome, Burmah.*

TAY-TOY. Ad. *Rangoon.*

THOMAS, W. Ad *Henthada, Burmah.*

VINTON, J. B. Ad. *Rangoon.*

WEBSTER, DAVID. Ad. *Maulmain, Burmah.*

II. THE ASSAM MISSION.

The Rev. Messrs. Brown and Cutter, from Burmah, arrived at Sadiya, March 23, 1836, having been four months on the journey from Calcutta. A school-house was built in May and a school opened in June, 1836. The Rev. Messrs. Thomas and Bronson with their wives sailed from Boston, October 17 1836, taking presses and printing materials, and arrived at Sadiya, July 17, 1837,—except Mr. Thomas, who was killed below Sadiya by a tree falling from the river-bank across his boat. Several translations were made and books printed both in Assamese and Khamti. Sadiya was relinquished in May, 1839, a disturbance having arisen in which several Khamti chiefs were killed and the Khamtis entirely dispersed. The first Assamese convert was baptized in 1841. Jaipur had been previously occupied by Mr. Bronson, who, in 1840 removed to the Naga Hills where he opened work. Sibsagor was adopted as a station in May, 1841 by the Rev. Messrs. Brown and Barker, and Nowgong in October, 1841, by Mr. Bronson.

Gowhatti was occupied in 1843. In the same year an orphanage was formed at Nowgong ,afterwards discontinued. In 1847 two other missionaries arrived and the work was carried forward more vigorously. In 1848 the second edition of the New Testament in Assamese was printed : and in 1850, the third. In 1851 each of the three stations was re-inforced and three separate churches were formed. There were at this time five Native assistants of whom two had visited the United States. Converts were added from time to time, numbering in 1855, 62. About 1857 sickness compelled several of the missionaries to return home, and the churches were somewhat weakened. Other missionaries arrived soon after and new converts were gained. The first Garo convert was baptized in February, 1863, and the first Mikir convert in the following September. In April, 1864, two Garos, who had been baptized at Gowhatti, were sent to preach to their own people ; in 1867 the Garos were first visited by the missionaries, and a church of 40 members was organized, at Goalpara. Schools were established and itinerations made. This field has proven an interesting one : by October, 1874 no less than 446 Garos had been baptized in various parts of the Mission; and the work has continued with increasing interest since.

The "Orunodoi," a monthly religious newspaper in Assamese, was begun in January, 1846 and continued to 1880. A monthly newspaper in Garo was begun in 1880.

In 1877 a new mission was opened among the Nagas beyond British territory, and in 1878 a station was formed at Tura, the head quarters of the Garo work. In 1879 a new mission was begun among the Angami Nagas.

There are now in connection with the Assam Mission of the Union six missionaries, and 11 ordained Native preachers. The Native Christian community exceeds 4,500: communicants 1,933.

MEMBERS OF THE MISSION.

CHOKIN. Ad. *Rangjubie, Assam.*

CLARK, E. W. A. 1869. Ad. *Amguri, Assam.*

DEDING. Ad. *Rangshipura, Assam.*

GANGA RAM Ad. *Rajasimla, Do.*

GODHULA. Ad. *Amguri, Do.*

GURNEY, A. K. A. 1874. Ad. *Sibsagor, Do.*

KING, CHARLES. D. B. Mexico. N. Y., U. S. A, May 25, 1847. O. Sept. 11, 1878. A. Dec. 10, 1878. S. Naga Hills. Ad. *Kohina, Naga Hills, Assam.*

MALJONG. Ad. *Resu, Agia, Assam.*

MASON, MARCUS CLARK. B. Wales, Eric Co., N. Y., U. S. A, June 6, 1844. E. Madison Univ. (June, 1872) and Hamilton Theol. Sem. (June, 1874). M. June 18, 1874. O. July 29, 1874. A. Dec. 19, 1874. S. Goalpara, 1874-78; since, Tura. Ad. *Tura, Garo Hills, Assam.*

MENDRO. Ad. *Rangjubie, Assam.*

MOORE, PITT HOLLAND. B. Akyab, Dec. 4, 1853. O. July 23, 1879. A. Dec. 14, 1879. Ad. *Nowgong, Assam:*

OMED. O. 1864. Ad. *Rajasimla, Assam.*

PHILLIPS, ELNATHAN G. B Dec. 6, 1845, in East Bloomfield. N. Y., U. S. A. E. Madison Univ. (B. A. 1872, M. A. 1874). O. July 8, 1874. M. June 18, 1874 A. Dec. 19, 1874. S. Goalpara, 1874-77; since, Tura. Ad. L. revision of Garo hymn-book, etc. Ad. *Tura, Assam.*

RAMKHE. Ad *Rangjubie, Assam.*

RUNGKHU. Ad. *Tura, Do.*

SMITH, KANDURA ROLLIN. B. at Nowgong, in 1837. O. Aug. 1, 1877. Ad. *Gowhatti, Assam.*

THOMAS, SONIRAM CHARLES. Ad. *Nowgong, Assam.*

III. THE TELUGU MISSION.

In the year 1835 the Society decided to establish a mission to the Telugus. The Rev. S. S. Day and wife, the first missionaries sent out, arrived in India in 1836. In 1840 Mr. Day established the present Telugu mission at Nellore. In March of the same year he was joined by Rev. S. Van Husen and wife, and in the following September the first Telugu convert was baptized. Four years later a church was organized, but the following year failure of health compelled the missionaries to retire from the field. In April, 1849, Mr. Day returned to Nellore accompanied by the Rev. L. Jewett. During the ensuing five years the progress of the mission was so discouraging that for the second time the question of abandoning the field was agitated in America. However, it was decided to let the "*Lone Star*," as the mission came at that time to be called, "shine on;" and in 1855 the Rev. F. A. Douglass came out to assist Mr. Jewett, who had been left alone a second time.

In December, 1861, Kanakiah, the first native pastor, was ordained. Still the progress of the work was so slow and unsatisfactory that the question of abandoning the mission was again discussed by the Missionary Union. At the earnest appeal of Mr. Jewett, who arrived in America at that time in quest of health, it was once more decided to let it live; and in April, 1865, he again arrived at Nellore accompanied by the Rev. J. E. Clough and wife. In September of the following year Mr. Clough removed to Ongole and began a mission there. On the 1st of January, 1867, he organized a church of 18 members, which very soon commenced to grow and from this time the work among the Telugus began to assume a more encouraging appearance. In February, 1870, the Rev. A. V. Timpany began work at Ramapatam, and in the following March, organized a church of 35 members. In the year 1872 a Theological Seminary was opened at this place, for which Mr. Clough, while in America, in 1872-73, secured an endowment of £10,000. Other missionaries continued to arrive from America, and the work was rapidly extended. The Rev. R. R. Williams took charge of the Seminary at Ramapatam in 1874. The next year a new station was opened at Secunderabad by the Rev. W. W. Campbell.

In theyear 1877 work was begun at Kurnool by the Rev. D. H. Drake. The following year Dr. Jewett opened a station in Madras. In 1879 a new station was opened at Hanamaconda by the Rev. A. Loughridge.

During the terrible famine of 1876-79 everything was done by the missionaries that could be to alleviate the distress of the people. In addition to the distribution of more than £40,000 at Nellore and Ongole, Mr. Clough took a contract to cut several miles of the Buckingham canal. He appointed his native preachers, colporteurs, etc. as overseers, and to read and preach to the workmen as opportunity offered. In this way from three to four thousand coolies at a time from all parts of the country were brought under the influence of the Gospel, at the same time that they were afforded the means of keeping themselves and families from starving. Before the famine the people in great numbers had begun to embrace Christianity; and before its close indications of much greater ingatherings began to appear. This was chiefly in the Ongole district, though it was not confined to it. For fear of being deceived Mr. Clough rejected all applications for baptism until all relief operations had been suspended, and he felt that he could no longer refuse. Between June 16th, 1878, and December 31st, of the same year, 9,606 were baptized. Since then the work has gone steadily forward, though not on so large a scale, and more than two years of trial and persecution have demonstrated its genuineness.

In addition to evangelistic work, that of educating and enlightening the converts has received all the attention possible under the circumstances. A bi-monthly magazine in the vernacular, "The Telugu Baptist," has reached its fifth volume. The Theological Seminary is well attended. A High School has been established at Ongole.

The following are the statistics of the Telugu Mission, December 31, 1880: stations occupied, 7; missionaries, 12; native preachers ordained, 40; schools, 166; pupils, 2,891; baptisms for the year 1880, 3,027: Native Christians, 17,020.

[W. R. M.]

MEMBERS OF THE MISSION.

Batum, Gooraviah. B. 1847. O. 1850. Ad. *Ongole, Madras P.*

Bezwara, Paul. B. 1842. O. 1872. Ad. *Do. Do.*

Boggs, William Bambrick. B. Nova Scotia, Canada, May 8, 1842. O. at Sydney, Sept. 24, 1865. A. Nov. 1874 under the Baptist For. Miss. Board of the Maritime Provinces of Canada. H. to America from 1876-78. Rt. under appointment of A. B. M. U. Jan. 18, 1879. S. Ongole, 1879-80: in Jan. 1881 transferred to Ramapatam to take charge of Theol. Sem. Ad. *Ramapatam, Madras P.*

Buddepoddy, Abraham. B. 1846. O. 1872 Ad. *Ongole, Madras P.*

Bullard, Edwin. (Son of the Rev. E. B. Bullard). A. Nov. 1870. S. Nellore, 1870, Alloor, 1872. H. to America. Ad. *Rutland, Vt., U. S. A.*

Bundare, Laban. B. 1852. O. 1880. Ad. *Ongole, Madras P.*

Bundare, Luke. B. 1851. O. 1880. Ad. *Do. Do.*

Bundare, Presunge. B. 1852. O. 1880. Ad. *Do. Do.*

Campbell, Woodley W. B. Busti, N. Y., U. S. A. July 31, 1843. O. Oct. 22, 1873. A. Jan. 31, 1874. M. S. Ongole, 1874-75, Secunderabad June, 1875. L. Editor of "Telugu Baptist" two and-a-half years Ad. *Secunderabad, Deccan.*

Cavore, Yellamundu. B. 1850. O. 1880. Ad *Ongole, Madras P.*

Cavore, Zechariah. B. 1839. O. 1880. Ad. *Do. Do.*

Clough, John Everett. B. July 16, 1836 near Shrewsbury, Chautauqua Co. N. Y., U. S. A. Government employment in Minnesota four years. Entered Burlington (Iowa) Collegiate Institute in 1857. M. Aug. 15, 1861. Graduated at Upper Iowa Univ. at Fayette, in 1862. Taught one year and labored one year as missionary colporteur in Eastern Iowa. Appointed to I. Aug. 8, 1864; O. Nov. 20, 1864. A. March 26, 1865. Labored for more than a year at Nellore: in Sept. 1866 proceeded to Ongole where he opened a new station. W. has been chiefly ver. L. Two tracts, "Where are you going": "Messages for All." H. from March 5, 1872 to Jan. 18, 1874. While in America secured an endowment for the Theol. school at Ramapatam. Ad. *Ongole, Madras P.*

Cola, Moses. B. 1826. O. 1872. Ad. *Ongole, Madras P.*

Derashe, Obadiah. B. 1841. O. 1880. Ad. *Do. Do.*

Douthalure, Yellamundu. B. 1844. O. 1880. Ad. *Do. Do.*

Downie, David. Graduated at Brown Univ. (R. I.) in 1869 and at the Theol. Sem. Rochester, N. Y. in 1872. O. in Monneville, Ohio, 1872. A. at Nellore, Dec. 10, 1873, where he has since labored W. Anglo-vernacular. Is Treasurer of the Mission. Ad. *Nellore, Madras P.*

Drake, D. H. B. in N. J., U. S. A. E. Shurtliff Col. and Chicago Union Theol. Sem. A. Dec. 25, 1874. S. Ramapatam, Kurnool. H. to America. Ad. *Danville, N. Y., U. S. A.*

Goodoore, Yerriah. B. 1851. O. 1880. Ad. *Ongole, Madras P.*

Goombarde, Ramiah. B. 1848. O. 1880. Ad. *Do. Do.*

Gundum, Pediah. B. 1825. O. 1873. Ad. *Do. Do.*

Gungasapu, Peter. B. 1850. O. 1880. Ad. *Do. Do.*

Indla, Philip. B. 1853. O. 1880. Ad. *Do. Do.*

JEWETT, LYMAN. B. March 9, 1813, at Waterford, Me., U. S. A. Graduated at Brown Univ. and Newton Theol. Sem. Pastoral work several years in Mass. O. at Boston, Oct. 6, 1848. M. 1848. A. at Madras Feb. 21 1849, S. Nellore. H 1862-65: and 1874-76. L. Translated several tracts into Telugu: also the Gospel of Matthew, upon which he wrote a Commentary. Was a member of the Telugu Bible Revision Committee several years. Ad. *Madras.*

JONALAGEDDA, ENOCH. B. 1852. O. 1880. Ad. *Ongole, Madras P.*

KANAKIAH, N. O. in 1861. Ad. *Nellore, Madras P.*

KELLEY, K. Ad. *Ramapatam,* *Do.*

KONDAPALE, VENKATIAH. B. 1844. O. 1880. Ad. *Ongole, Do.*

KUNDLA, VENKIAH, B. 1844. O. 1880. Ad. *Do. Do.*

LOUGHRIDGE, ALBERT. B. at Oskaloosa, Iowa, U. S. A., June 12, 1845. E. State Univ. of Iowa, (B. A. 1871, M. A. 1877). M. Aug. 20, 1874. O. Sept. 20. 1874. A. Nov. 19, 1875. S. Ongole, 1875-78; since Jan. 1879, Warongal. Ad. *Hanamaconda, Hyderabad, Deccan.*

MADECONDA, EZRA. B. 1830. O. 1873. Ad. *Ongole, Madras P.*

MANLEY, W. R B. in Pa., U. S. A. June 13, 1850. O. in March 1879. M. Aug. 31, 1879. A. at Rangoon, Dec. 3, 1879, at Ongole Aug. 26, 1880. Ad. *Ongole, Madras P.*

MORGAN, FREEMAN ELDER. B. Batavia, Ill, U. S. A. Feb. 9, 1850. O. Sept. 18, 1879. A. Dec. 8, 1879. M. Ad. *Kurnool, Madras P.*

MUCKIN, REUBEN. B. 1841. O. 1880. Ad. *Ongole, Do.*

MULLELA, ISAAC. B. 1844. O. 1872. Ad. *Do. Do.*

NAGAPOGU, YOSAPU. B. 1832. O 1880. Ad. *Do. Do.*

NARSU, K. Ad. *Nellore, Madras P.*

NEWHALL, ALFRED AUGUSTUS, JR. B. in Cambridgeport, Mass., U. S. A., Jan. 7, 1844. E. Univ. of Rochester, N. Y. (1872) and Rochester Theol. Sem., (1875) O. Sept. 2, 1875. A. Nov. 19, 1875. S. Ramapatam. H. to America. Ad. *Morgan, Park Co, Ill., U. S. A.*

NOMALA, NARSU. B. 1830. O. 1880. Ad. *Ongole, Madras P.*

ONGOLU, ABEL. B. 1824. O. 1880. Ad. *Do. Do.*

PEDATE, PAMIAH. B. 1828. O. 1873. Ad. *Do. Do.*

PERASHAPOGU, AYANAH. B. 1848. O. 1880. Ad. *Do. Do.*

POOLAKOORE, BALIAH. B 1842. O. 1880. Ad. *Do. Do.*

POOLAKOORE, PIXLEY. B. 1852. O. 1880. Ad. *Do. Do.*

RAGAPATE, YAKOBU. B. 1848. O. 1880. Ad. *Do. Do.*

RANGIAH, TUPELE. O. 1872. Ad. *Ramapatam, Madras P.*

STERAM, SOLOMON. B. 1833. O. 1872. Ad. *Do. Do.*

TALURE, DANIEL. B. 1834. O. 1872. Ad. *Do. Do.*

TEATU, B. Ad. *Ramapatam, Madras P.*

VEDADELLA, JONAH. B. 1841. O. 1880. Ad. *Ongole, Do.*

WILLIAMS, R. R. B. in Ohio, U. S. A. E at Granville Col. and at the Chicago Union Theol. Sem. Appointed to I. in May, M. July 3, and sailed Oct. 5, 1873. A. at Ramapatam in Jan. 1874. H. to America in 1881. Ad. *Ramapatam, Madras P.*

YOHON. Ad. *Ramapatam, Madras P.*

DECEASED MISSIONARIES.

Samuel Stearns Day. B. in 1808, in Ontario, Canada. Graduated at Madison Univ. (N. Y.) in 1831. O. Aug. 24, 1835. A. in Calcutta in Feb. 1836. Proceeded to Vizagapatam and afterwards to Nellore where he laid the foundation of the Telugu Mission. H. from Oct. 1845 to Feb. 1849. R. to America in June, 1853. Ret. in Feb. 1863. Served as a pastor several years in N Y. and Mich. D. in 1871.

Steven Van Husen. B. Dec. 5, 1812, at Catskill, N Y., U. S. A. E. at Madison Univ. Appointed to I. Aug. 23, 1838. O. Aug. 29, 1839 A. at Nellore, March 21, 1840. R. home on account of poor health in Oct. 1845. D. at Brattleboro, Vt., U. S. A.

Jacob Thomas. B. at Elbridge, N. Y., U. S. A. E at Madison Univ. Appointed to Assam April 29, and sailed Oct. 17, 1836. Was killed by a falling tree on the Brahmaputra river, near Sadiya, July 7, 1837.

Cyrus Barker. B. March 27, 1807, at Portsmouth, R. I., U. S. A. E. at Madison Univ. Appointed to I. in July, and O. in Sept. 1839. A. at Calcutta Feb. 20, 1840. Labored at Jaipur from May, 1840 to May 1841, when he removed to Sibsagor: labored here and at Gowhatti. Left India with broken health Oct. 29, 1849. D. at sea (in the Mozambique channel) Jan. 31, 1850.

G. Dauble. Came to I. under the auspices of the Basel Society and labored at Dacca. Joined the Baptist Mission in 1850 and was appointed to Nowgong. D. of cholera, March 21, 1853.

William Ward. E. at Madison Univ. Appointed to I. in 1849. Sailed July 25, 1850 : arrived at Gowhatti, April 29, 1851. R. home on account of his wife's health in Nov. 1857. Rt. Dec 10, 1860. Labored here until his death in 1873.

Edward Payson Scott. B. in 1832 at Greensboro, Vt., U. S. A. E. at Knox Col. Ill. and at Madison Univ. Appointed to I. May 8, 1860: A. at Nowgong, Nov. 1862 : and labored here until his death.

Appleton Howe Danforth. B. July 8, 1817, at Pelham, Mass., U S. A. E. at Madison Univ. Appointed to I. June 28, O. Oct. 22, and sailed Nov. 3, 1847. A. at Gowhatti in May, 1848. R. home on account of Mrs. Danforth's health in 1858. D. in America.

S. W. Nichols. A. 1878. D. at Madras, Dec. 8, 1880.

———o———

CHAPTER XIII.

THE AMERICAN FREE BAPTIST MISSIONARY SOCIETY.

THE Rev. Amos Sutton, D. D. may be called the founder of the Society and of its Mission in Northern Orissa and Southern Bengal. After nine years of labor in Orissa in connection with the General Baptist Society, his health failed and he repaired to America. While recruiting his health, he made earnest appeals to the Baptist churches in behalf of the perishing heathen of Orissa: and aroused and assisted by his labors the Free Baptists were led to form in 1834 a Foreign Missionary Society, of which Mr. Sutton was Secretary and Traveling Agent for more than a year. In September, 1835, he left America as the leader of a party of twenty missionaries male and female, being the largest missionary company which had up to that time ever left America for the Eastern hemisphere.

The first two missionaries to enter Orissa for the Society were the Rev. Messrs. J. Phillips and Eli Noyes, who spent six months in connection with the English General Baptist missionaries. At the expiration of that time it was mutually agreed that they should enter a separate field, and Sambhalporo was selected: this was soon abandoned, however, and the station Balasore was occupied. The missionaries in addition to other labors formed the nucleus of a boarding-school. Early in 1840, Mr. Phillips formed a new station at Jellasore, where schools were organized and subsequently a hospital established. About 1842 a dispensary was opened at Balasore and a medical class formed. This agency has been highly useful in the Mission. Midnapore was occupied in 1844, but was after a time abandoned: it was subsequently permanently occupied and is now the centre of an interesting work. About 1852 work was opened at Santipore, near Jellasore. A farm of two hundred acres has been brought under cultivation and affords means of support to a number of Christian families. The Mission has at present nine separate native Christian communities occupying thirteen villages. A number of schools have been opened, about half of which are for Santali children.

The Mission has now eight churches in the districts of Balasore and Midnapore. There are schools at all the stations, mostly of a primary character. At Bhimpore, there is a Santal Training school, and there are about seventy primary schools in the Santal country. There is a high grade vernacular school at Balasore and an orphanage for girls at Jellasore. In 1879 a Bible School for training native helpers was opened at Midnapore. There is a Mission Press at Midnapore, where Scriptures, tracts, and school books in Bengali, Oriya and Santal are printed.

The Society has at present ten missionaries and ordained native agents. There are in the Mission 534 communicants and a Native Christian community of nearly a thousand souls.

[J. L. P.]

MISSIONARIES OF THE SOCIETY.

BACHELER, OTIS ROBINSON, (M. D.). B. Andover, N. H., U. S. A. Jan. 17, 1817. O. Lowell, Mass. April, 1840. A Sept. 1840. S. Balasore, 1840-52, H. 1852-62. S. Midnapore, 1862-70. H. 1870-73; since, Midnapore. L. "Medical Guide" (in Oriya), 1848; "Medical Guide" (in Bengali), 1852. Ad. *Midnapore, Bengal.*

BASU, PURNA CHANDRA. B. at Dacca, 1847. O. 1875. S. Midnapore, Dantoon. Ad. *Dantoon, Bengal.*

BURKHOLDER, THOMAS WESLEY. B. 1850. O. 1877. A. 1878. S. Bhimpore. W. ver. Ad. *Midnapore, Bengal.*

COLDREN, MILO JONES. B. in La Grange Co., Ind., U. S. A., June 8, 1850. O. March, 1875. E. Hillsdale Col. Mich., graduating in classical course, 1876, Theol., 1878. A. Dec. 24, 1879. Ad. *Balasore, Orissa.*

LAWRENCE, RICHARD M. B. Dover, Eng. Feb. 29, 1848. E. Hillsdale Col., Mich. (B. A. 1873.) A. Dec. 12, 1874. S. Midnapore. W. Supt. of press. Ad. *Midnapore, Bengal.*

MARSHALL, ALBERT JOSIAH. B. in Shelby, N. Y., U. S. A. Nov. 3, 1847. O. April 24, 1872. A. Nov. 15, 1873. Ad. *Balasore, Orissa.*

MISHRA, JACOB. B. at Balasore, 1850. O. 1873. Ad. *Midnapore, Bengal.*

PHILLIPS, JAMES LIDDELL, (M.D.) B. at Balasore, 1840. O. 1862. A. 1865. S. Midnapore, 1865-73, Bhimpore, 1874, Midnapore, Principal of Bible School since 1879. H. 1875-78. Ad. *Midnapore, Bengal.*

DECEASED AND RETIRED MISSIONARIES.

Jeremiah Phillips, D. D. B. in 1812, at Plainfield, N. Y., U. S. A. O. 1835. A. 1856. S. Sambhalpore, Balasore, Jellasore, Santipore, Dantoon. W. ver. L. "Manual of Geography" in Oriya, (1850); and "Introduction to the Santal Language" (1853); and a volume of "Scripture selections" in Santal. H. 1855-65. R. to America 1879. D. at Hillsdale, Mich., Dec. 9, 1879.

Eli Noyes, D. D. B. in 1814 in Me., U. S. A. O. in 1835, A. (one of the first missionaries of the Society) in Feb. 1836. S. several months at Cuttack, and then Sambhalpore for one year. From March, 1838 to June, 1841, Balasore. On account of failing health left I. in June, 1841. R. to America and traveled for a time as agent for the Mission. Was afterwards engaged in pastoral work at Boston, and Providence, R. I. About 1851 he removed to La Fayette, Indiana, where he D. about 1852.

B. B. Smith. B. March 17, 1820, in Sandwich, N. H., U. S. A. O. in June, 1852. A. 1852. S. Balasore. H. 1862-67. D. at Balasore, Nov. 22, 1872.

James C. Dow. Of Livermore, Me., U. S A. A. in March, 1844, S. Midnapore until early in 1847 when his health failed and he R. to America. Labored for a time as pastor: is now residing in one of the Western States, U. S. A.

Ruel Cooley. Of New York, U. S. A. E. at Oberlin, Ohio. A. in Jan. 1850. S. Balasore where he labored ten years, preaching in Oriya and in Engl. and in charge of an orphanage and schools. On account of ill-health R to America in 1861. Labored for a time as Home missionary; for several years has had charge of a church as pastor in Johnstown, Wis. Ad. *Lima Center, Wis., U. S. A.*

Robert D. Frost. B. at Sugar Grove, Ill., U. S. A. in 1846. O. 1874. A. 1874. S. Midnapore. W. ver. Ret. 1876. Ad. *Lewiston, Me., U. S. A.*

———o———

CHAPTER XIV.

GOSSNER'S MISSIONARY SOCIETY.

FATHER or Pastor Gossner, the founder of this Society, was originally a Romish priest, but afterwards became a director of the Berlin Missionary Society. Differing from his brethren of the directorate in his views of a missionary's qualifications he withdrew, and in 1836, constituted himself into a Committee for the education and supply of foreign missionaries. His candidates were all to be mechanics and cordially willing to engage in missionary labors, and to earn their livelihood by manual labor. His first missionaries to India were sent in 1838 and 1840, part to Bengal and the others to Central India. Of six who attempted to establish an agricultural colony among the Gonds, four were cut down by death within five days of each other, only a few months after reaching their field of labor. The others repaired to Nagpore, but were not spared long and the mission was thus a failure.

The first station occupied in Bengal was Muzaffarpore, in 1840. Missionary operations were commenced at Chapra in 1842: at Buxar, in 1852, and at Durbungah in 1863.

The Society was organized in 1842. In 1844 it sent to India four missionaries, the Rev. Messrs. Schatz, Batsch, Brandt, and Fancke. Arriving at Calcutta they sought the advice of the missionaries there, as to the most eligible field of labor and were advised to proceed to Chota Nagpore, and open a Mission among the Kols. They reached Ranchi early in 1845 and began missionary operations, laboring with their own hands, and preaching to the people. They labored patiently five years without seeing any return. On the 9th of June, 1850, the first fruits were gathered, four men from among the Kols receiving baptism. Other converts were gained and the work began to spread from place to place. In 1848 a station had been formed at Lohardugga, in 1850 another was opened at Govindpore, and in 1853, a third at Hazaribagh. Year by year the churches increased in number until at the time of the breaking out of the Mutiny, they numbered upwards of 700 souls. Along with other Europeans the missionaries were driven from their homes by the rebels. The bungalows at Ranchi were set on fire. "The mission-houses being tiled were stripped of their furniture and books: the church was gutted and the organ pulled to pieces; cannon-balls were fired into the tower, but disfigured without harming it. The converts were hunted from their houses and lost all their property of every kind: all their village chapels were unroofed and stripped; and at last when nothing else remained, a price was set upon the converts' heads. A few were killed and their persecutors had seriously planned to exterminate the Christians from the province, when the English soldiers marched up from Hazaribagh, put an end to disorder, and captured the rebel delinquents. The missionaries speedily returned, work was resumed; the congregations were regathered; and a strange measure of prosperity was henceforth granted." *

By 1863 the church in Chota Nagpore had increased to 1,286 members. In this year a new station was formed at Purulia in Manbhoom. In 1864 missionary operations were commenced at Chaibasa in Singbhoom. The number baptized up to the end of the year 1868 was 11, 108. In December of this year six of the missionaries with about 4,000 Christians withdrew from the Society, and on their own application were received by the Society for the Propagation of the Gospel.

Since the schism, the pioneer Society has re-occupied two old and taken up two new, stations. In 1869, a station was formed at Burju in the Lohardugga district, which was called Patrasburj (Petersburgh); a Russian gentleman having presented to the Society at Berlin 3,000 silver roubles, with the request that a station might be founded in Chota Nagpore to be called Petersburgh in commemoration of the blessing which was received in St. Petersburgh by the preaching of Pastor Gossner. In 1870, Govindpore, which had been unoccupied since the Mutiny, was taken up: and in 1871 Lohardugga was also re-occupied. In 1874 a new station was established at Takarma in the Lohardugga district, is called Mathauspur.

* Dr. Mullens' "Ten Years' Missionary Labour in India," pp.41, 43.

Much attention has been given to the subject of education in Chota Nagpore. Eighty village schools have been established and are attended by 1,300 pupils of both sexes. The most promising students are transferred from these to the boarding-schools. From these (which contain on an average 200 pupils) the ablest students are sent to the normal school at Ranchi and trained to become schoolmasters, Bible readers or preachers. Those qualified for the ministry are transferred after a period to the theological department of the Ranchi institution, where they pursue theological studies for three or four years.

In the Chota Nagpore Mission only, there are now 28,283 Native Christians (an increase of 14,000 since 1871) and 10,000 communicants (an increase of 5,300 or more).

In March, 1855, Ghazipore, in the North-West Provinces, was occupied for the Society by the Rev. W. Ziemann, who had already paid several visits to the place in his preaching tours. Previously, in 1844, three missionaries of the Berlin Society had established a mission here, but after a few years, the mission was discontinued. The field has proved a good one, and a flourishing church has been established, numbering 642, in 1880.

The following statistics (for 1880) show the rapid progress made since 1871 by this Society: —

Foreign missionaries,	...	21 ...	increase,	9
Native ordained agents,	...	7 ...	do.	6
Native Christians,	...	29,285 ...	do.	14,481
Communicants,	...	11,091 ...	do.	6,455

MISSIONARIES OF THE SOCIETY.

Bartsch, Ferdinand. B. June 9, 1850, at Konigsberg, Prussia. A. in 1875. Ad. *Burju, Ranchi, Chota Nagpore.*

Beyer, Wilhelm Lebrecht Albert. B. Nov. 24, 1848, at New-stettin, Prussia. O. Stettin Dec. 31, 1873. Pastoral work at Belkow until Oct. 1874. M. Nov. 19, 1874. A. Dec. 29, 1874. S. principal of the mission school at Ghazipore, until 1878, since, (Ad). *Govindpore, Ranchi, Chota Nagpore.*

Bransfeld, Chr. A. in Oct. 1880. Ad. *Ranchi, Chota Nagpore.*

Bruske, Julius. B. Ausche, Germany, Sept. 5, 1853. A. Dec. 26, 1879. Not O. Ad. *Ranchi, Chota Nagpore.*

Cristochit. O. in 1880. Native pastor. Ad. *Ranchi, Chota Nagpore.*

Didlaukies, David. B. June 6, 1836, at Klein-Wannagupchen, Prussia. A. in 1863. O. in 1872. H. March, 1877, to Oct. 1878. S. Ghazipore, 1878-80, since, at (Ad). *Purulia, Chota Nagpore.*

Dodt, Frederick Charles. B. Halle, Westphalia, March 28, 1830. O. A. March 6, 1854. M. in 1859. S. Muzafferpore, 1855-63, Darbangah, 1863, afterwards, Muzafferpore. H. March, 1876 to Dec. 1877. W. Supt. of Mission Press. Ad. *Muzafferpore, Chota Nagpore.*

Gemsky, Otto. B. Nov. 29, 1852. at Rahmed, Prussia. A. in 1875. S. Ranchi, 1875-80, since at (Ad.). *Govindpore, Ranchi, Chota Nagpore.*

Hahn, Carl Heinrich Philip Ferdinand. B. Ketzin, Prussia, Feb. 15, 1846. O. March 26, 1876. A. Sept. 1868. S. Ranchi, 1868-76 in connection with Theol. Sem. ; Chaibasa, 1876-77 ; Lohardugga, 1878, to present. L. a Small Hindi Reading Book; Bibical History in Urau (in Press). Ad. *Lohardugga, Chota Nagpore.*

Hembroom, Ainb. O. in 1876, Native pastor at (Ad). *Marcha, Ranchi, Chota Nagpore.*

Kampfhenkel, Carl. B. Niemegk, Prussia, July 6, 1835. A. April, 1865. M. in 1873. O. March 5, 1874. S. Govindpore, 1865-77, since, Takarma. Ad. *Takarma, Ranchi, Chota Nagpore.*

Kiefel, Wilhelm. B. at Striese, Germany, March 30, 1856. A. Oct. 19, 1880. Not O. Ad. *Ranchi, Chota Nagpore.*

Kroecher, William. B April 14, 1844, at Nadrense, Pomerania. O. M. 1876. A. in Sept. 1871. S. Govindpore, 1871-77, since April, 1877 principal of Theol. Sem. at (Ad). *Ranchi, Chota Nagpore.*

Lakra, Hanukh. E. in the Ranchi boarding-school, and Theol. Sem. 1869-73. O. in 1875. Ad. *Tapkara, Lohardugga, Chota Nagpore.*

Lakshman, Anand Masih. E. in the Ranchi boarding-school, and Theol. Sem. 1869-73. O. in 1875. Ad. *Burju, Ranchi, Chota Nagpore.*

Lorbeer, August William Henry. B. Wippra, Saxony, Dec. 14, 1840. O. A. 1865. M. in 1867. S. Ghazipore, 1865-71, Ranchi, 1871. Lohardugga, 1872-76, Muzafferpore, 1876-78. H. to Germany Oct. 1878-80. Ad. *Ghazipore, N.-W. P.*

Nemo, Paulus. Formerly a zamindar. O. in 1869, and appointed to his adjacent villages. Ad. *Jargo, Manbhoom, Chota Nagpore.*

Nottrott, Carl Alfred. B. Oppershaushen, Prussia, Aug. 19, 1839. E. at Halle, Wuttemberg, 1860-64. O. 1867. A. 1867. M. L. (1.) Dictionary of the Kolh Language (not yet finished). (2.) Hymn-book in Kolh. (3.) Bible History (Old Testament) in Kolh. (4.) Translation of St. Mark's Gospel into Kolh. (5.) Catechism and several small works in Kolh. Ad. *Burju, Ranchi, Chota Nagpore.*

Nowack, Wilhelm. B. Oct. 15, 1842, at Preussisch Eylau, Prussia, A. 1873. S. Ranchi, 1873-74, Ghazipore, 1874-75, Ranchi, 1875-77, since Jan. 1878, at (Ad.) *Chapra, Bengal.*

Onasch, Johann Herman Carl. B. Sept. 3, 1836, at Schœnwalde, Pomerania. A. in 1861. O. in 1866. M. in 1866. S. Purulia, 1871-74. H. March, 1874 to Oct. 1875. Since (Ad.) *Ranchi, Chota Nagpore.*

Reinert, Edward. B. Oct. 30, 1839, at Elbing, Prussia. A. in 1872. Ad. *Ranchi, Chota Nagpore.*

Sommer, Fritz. A in 1877. Ad. *Ranchi, Chota Nagpore.*

Tugu, Andrias. B. in 1840. O. in July, 1875. Pastor of the congregation in (Ad.) *Bandgaun, Singbhoom, Chota Nagpore.*

Tugu, Nathanael. B. in 1836. O. in July, 1872. Pastor of the congregation in (Ad.) *Piring, Singbhoom, Chota Nagpore.*

Uffmann, Peter Henry. B. Feb. 15, 1831, at Theenhausen, Westphalia. A. in 1865, O. in 1874. M. H. to Europe in May, 1880.

Voss, Withelm Lutheri. B. at Uetersen, Holstein, June 14, 1842. A. Sept. 1868. O. 1877. M. S. Ranchi, and Chaibasa. Ad. *Chaibasa, Singbhoom, Chota Nagpore.*

Werth, Oscar. A. in 1877. S. Ranchi, 1877-80; since Nov. 1880, at (Ad.) *Takarma, Ranchi, Chota Nagpore.*

Ziemann, George William. B. Nov. 22, 1806, at Gross-Wudike, Saxony. O. and A. in 1842. Labored at Chapra, Muzafferpore and Buxar from 1842-55. Began the mission station at Ghazipore in March, 1855, and has since labored there. In Feb. 1875. H. to Germany, visiting Palestine on the way. Rt. at the close of 1875. Ad. *Ghazipore, N.-W. P.*

DECEASED AND RETIRED MISSIONARIES.

Names.	Station.	Death or Retiral.
——Paproth, ...		D. 1840.
——Kluge, ...		D. 1841.
——Stulpnagel, ...		D. 1842.
——Maass, ...		D. 1842.
——Schorisch, ...	Kamptee,	D. 1845.
——Bartels, ...	Do.	D. Aug. 16, 1845.
——Voss, ...	Nagpore,	Ret.
——Apler, ...		D. May 27, 1848.
——Brandin, ...		D. 1862.
——Ribbentropp, ...	Ghazipore,	D. 1863.
A. Sternberg, ...		D. 1864.
——Ott, ...	Chaibasa,	D. 1866.
Paul Strive, ...		D. Aug. 20, 1866.
V. Gerpen, ...		D. 1868.
T. Jellinghaus, ...	Patrasburj,	Ret. 1870.
C. Haeberlin, ...	Ranchi,	Do. 1873.
W. Sternberg, ...	Ghazipore,	D. July 30, 1874.
C. Baumann, ...	Chapra,	D. at Benares 1878.
F. Hepp, ...	Ranchi,	D in Germany 1877.
E. W. Huss, ...	Chota Nagpore,	D. June, 1878.
C. F. Sternberg, ...	Ranchi,	Ret. 1877.

CHAPTER XV.

LEIPZIG EVANGELICAL LUTHERAN SOCIETY.

THIS Society was established at Dresden on the 16th of August, 1819 and worked during the first years in connection with the Missionary Society at Basel. A preparatory School for Missionary candidates was opened in 1832, and in 1836 the Society began missionary operations by itself. In 1848, the central seat was removed from Dresden to Leipzig in order that the Mission students might have the benefit of a University education, and the Society received, at the same time, its present organization and its title was changed from "Dresden" to "Leipzig" Society.

In 1840, the Society sent the Rev. H. Cordes as its first missionary to India. He landed at Madras December 27, 1840, and arrived at Tranquebar March 20, 1841 where he began his labours in connection with the Danish Mission. The Rev. C. Ochs arrived in December, 1842, and the Rev. J. M. N. Schwartz in December, 1843. In consequence of the return of the Danish missionary the Rev. H. Knudson to Denmark in 1843 and of the cession of the Danish Indian Colonies to the British in 1845, the charge of the Tranquebar Mission devolved entirely upon the missionaries of the Leipzig Society, and in June, 1847 the Danish Mission Board on an order of His Majesty, King Christian VIII, entrusted the management of its affairs in India to the Leipzig (Dresden) Society and transferred to it in October, 1849 its landed property in India together with about 1,200 Christians, 5 Catechists and 16 teachers. More labourers were in the course of time sent out from Leipzig and the work which was carried on vigorously enjoyed the blessing of the Lord. In 1845 the Society occupied, Mayavernm: in 1847-1849 two small stations near Tranquebar: in 1848, Madras: in 1849, Puducottah which was transferred to it by the American Madura Mission. Trichinopoly was taken up in 1850: Tanjore, in 1851: Manikramam in 1852. Combaconam, Coimbatore, Cuddalore and Sadras were occupied in 1856:

Negapatam in 1862: Mottupatty in 1864: Yercaud in 1865: Chidambaram in 1866: Sheally in 1868: Aneikadu in 1869: Bangalore, in 1873: Madura and Villupuram in 1874: Rangoon in 1878.

In the year 1856 the third "jubilee year" of the Tranquebar Mission was celebrated. By this time there were 4,166 Christians living in 142 villages belonging to the mission. In 1860, an ordination of native ministers, the first since 1817, took place at Tranquebar. Since 1841, when the Society began its work here to this time (the end of 1880) there have been carefully instructed in the fundamental truths of Christianity according to Luther's Smaller Catechism and received holy baptism about 12,000 heathen. There are now 20 European and 8 Native ordained ministers labouring in 19 stations: 11,081 Christians, living in 460 towns and villages: 60 Catechists, 127 schools with 180 teachers and 2,438 scholars. In 1880 the congregations contributed Rs. 3,220 for their church and poor funds.

[J. M. N. S.]

MISSIONARIES OF THE SOCIETY.

Amurdam, Pakiam. B. at Tanjore, Jan. 8, 1843. O. Dec. 16, 1877. Ad. *Poreiar, Madras P.*

Asirvadam, Manikam. B. at Tranquebar, Dec. 10, 1833. O. June 7, 1874. Ad. *Negapatam, Madras P.*

Baierlein, Edward Raimand. B. April 29, 1819, in Germany. E. at the Dresden Sem. 1843. O. in 1847, and sent as a missionary to America: labored among the American Indians in Michigan. M. in 1848. A. in Dec. 1853. S. Sadras, Cuddalore, Bangalore. W. Ver. L. two works in German (published at Leipzig): "The Land of the Tamulians and its Missions" (Engl.): Higginbotham and Co., Madras; 1875. H. 1860-62, and 1871-72. Ad. *Bangalore.*

Beisenherz, Heinrich Daniel Lodovig. B. Sachsenberg, Waldeck, Feb. 1, 1844. E. at Leipzig. O. at Sachsenberg, 1870. A. Nov. 19, 1870. S. Nagapatam, 1872-74, Villupuram, 1874-78, Poreiar since Dec. 1879. H. to Europe, 1878-79. Ad *Poreiar, Tranquebar.*

Bergstedt, Diedrich. B. March 30, 1846, at Hilgermissen, Hanover. E. at Leipzig. O. at Hanover in 1875. A. Aug. 20, 1875. Ad. *Trichinopoly, Madras P.*

Blomstrand, Anders. B. Wexio, Sweden, Dec. 19, 1822. E. Lund Univ. (M. Ph. 1844). O. 1849. Lecturer in Lund Univ. 1846-55. A. Jan. 12, 1858. S. Tranquebar. Degree of D. D. in 1879;

W. Educational. L. Editor of "*Arunodayam*" (Missionary Newspaper) 1863-77. Translated into Tamil. (1) "Concordia," (2) "Scripture History," (3) "Sacred History," (4) "Church History," (5) Spencer's "Catechism," (6) Graul's "Doctrinal differences." (7) Lohe, "Prayer book," (8) Arndt, "Garden of Paradise," (9) Arndt, "True Christianity." Ad. *Tranquebar.*

BRUNOTTE, JOHANN HEINRICH CHRISTOPH. B. in Hanover, Oct. 2, 1834. E. at Hermannsburg O. Mar. 19, 1866. A. Sept. 2, 1866. Labored in the Hermannsburg Mission until Sept. 1878, when he joined the Leipzig Society. M. Ad. *Villupuram, Madras P.*

CHRISTIAN, VARAPPEN. B. Sept. 5, 1832. O. Feb. 19, 1865. Ad. *Motupatty, Madras P.*

DAVID, DANIEL. B. June 30, 1845. O. Oct. 8, 1876. Ad. *Coimbatore, Madras P.*

DEVASAYAGAM, K. B. in 1840. O. Oct. 31, 1878. Ad. *Aneikadu, Tanjore.*

GEHRING, FR. C. ALWIN. B. in Thuringia Feb. 9, 1853. E. at Leipzig 1872-76. O. 1877. A. Oct. 9, 1877. S. Combaconum and Yerkaud. Ad. *Combaconum, Madras P.*

HANDMANN, HEINRICH RICHARD. B. at Oschitz near Schleitz Feb. 27, 1840. E. Leipzig and Erlangen. O. May 25, 1862. A. Oct. 8, 1862. S. Tranquebar, Manikramam, Trichinopoly, Poreiar, and since 1878, Madras. M. in 1867. H 1876-78. Ad. *Pursewaukum, Madras.*

HERRE, WILHELM HEINRICH GUSTAV. B. in Wurttemberg, Sept. 27, 1831. O. Aug. 10, 1856. A. in connection with the Basel Society, Dec. 15, 1856. S. Tellicherry, 1856-60. H. 1860-61: Palghaut, 1861-63, Yerkaud, 1863-66. In 1865, joined the Leipzig Society. Coimbatore, 1866-73; H. 1873-75; Cuddalore since Jan. 1876. Ad. *Cuddalore, Madras P.*

HOBUSCH, FRIEDRICH. A. Sept. 27, 1860. Established the Mission press which he has since superintended: is also treasurer of the Mission. H 1868-69, and 1878-79. Ad. *Tranquebar.*

IHLEFELD, KONRAD ADOLPH ANTON. B. at Ruhn, Germany, Feb. 21, 1837. E. Erlangen, Tubingen and Rostock. O. Oct. 1862. Pastoral work at home, 1862-72. A. Sept. 16, 1873. S. Tanjore, 1874-75, Madras, 1875-78, since, Poreiar. L. short Essay on the Engl. Reformation and the Anglo-Episcopal Church; Tranquebar B. Depot. Translated in Tamil, German Catechism; Tranquebar: Editor of "Arunodayam." Ad. *Poreiar, Tranquebar.*

KABIS, JOHANNES RUDOLPH CARL FERDINAND. B. at Rudolstadt, Germany Aug. 1, 1853. E at Leipzig. O. April 22, 1877. A. Oct. 9, 1877. M. in 1879. S. Mayaveram. W. Supt. of Press. Ad. *Mayaveram, Madras P.*

KREMMER, CARL FRIEDRICH. B. Sept. 8, 1817, in Hesse-Cassel, E. at the Dresden Sem. A. March 5, and O. at Tranquebar Oct. 18, 1847. S. Madras from 1848 to 1858: since at Poreiar. M. in 1853. H. Jan. 1861 to Jan. 1863: Aug. 1875 to May, 1877. Ad. *Madura, Madras P.*

MAYR, ANDREAS. B. May 20, 1838 in Bavaria E. at Erlangen and Leipzig. O. April 5, 1861. A. Oct. 4, 1861. S. Cuddalore, 1862, Madras, 1863, Coimbatore, 1864-66, Negapatam, 1867-70, Mayaveram, 1870-76, Trichinopoly, 1876-78, Rangoon since April, 1880. H. March to Nov. 1870. Ad. *Rangoon.*

OUCHTERLONY, CARL ALEXANDER. B. Oct. 12, 1826, at Stockholm. E. at Lund where he was O. in 1852. A. Dec. 9, 1853. Left the Mission in Aug. 1854: rejoined in May, 1855. M. Sept. 3, 1859. H. 1865-67 and from Aug. 1879 to present. Ad. *Sotanas, Sweden.*

PAESLER, LUDWIG TRANGOTT. B in Silesia, Jan. 1, 1850. E. Leipzig, 1866-74. O. May 2, 1875. A. Aug. 20, 1875. M. 1878. Ad. *Paducottah, Madras P.*

PONAPPEN, SAND. DEV. B. at Tranquebar, March 23, 1843. E. at Tranquebar, O. June 6. 1874. M. Ad. *Mayaveram, Madras P.*

SAMUEL, N. NJANAPRAGASAM. B near Tanjore, Sept 18, 1850. O. Oct. 31, 1878. L. Composed several poetical tracts. Has written in Tamil a short sketch of the Life of Martin Luther; Tranquebar. Ad *Tranquebar.*

SANDEGREN, CARL JACOB. B. Nov. 1, 1851, at Næsinge, Sweden. E. and O. in Sweden. A. Nov. 17, 1869. M. in 1872. S. Coimbatore. *Now in Europe.*

SCHAFFER, HEINRICH AUGUST EDWARD. B. June 27, 1872, at Erfort, Prussia. E. and O. (in 1864) at Leipzig. A. Oct 13, 1864. M. in 1868. W. educational. H April, 1878 to Dec. 1879. Ad. *Tranquebar.*

PAKIAM, MADUR. B. at Tranquebar March 11, 1835. E. at Tranquebar where he was O. Feb. 19, 1865. M. Ad. *Shcally, Madras P.*

PAMPERRIEN, KARL HEINRICH FERDINAND LUDWIG. B. in Mecklenberg, Aug. 11, 1845. E. at Berlin and Rastock. O. Rudolstadt, April 22, 1877. A. Oct. 9, 1877. M. in 1879. S. Tranquebar, 1878-80, since at (Ad.) *Tanjore.*

PERIANAYAGAM, T. P. B. at Madras, July 25, 1851. O. Oct. 31, 1878. S. Tranquebar, 1878, Madura, 1879, Madras, 1880. (Ad.) *Madras.*

SCHWARTZ, JOHANN MICHAEL NICHOLAUS. B March 21, 1813, at Hagenbuchach in Bavaria. E. at Dresden. O. April 27, 1842 A. Dec. 25, 1843. M L. several school-books; a prose translation of the first and second books of the Kural; Explanation of Luther's "Smaller Catechism"; reviser of the newly edited "Golden Treasury" of Bogatsky, the church Liturgy; editor of Fabricus' N. T; Hymn-book. Has never taken furlough. Is Senior and Secretary of the Mission. Ad. *Tranquebar.*

WANNSKE, JOHANN HEINRICH. B. May 11, 1835, in Lissa, Prussia, E. at Leipzig. O. in 1863. A. Dec. 19, 1863. M. in 1870. H. March. 1880 to present. Ad. *Uelzen, Germany.*

WOLFF, AUGUST FRIEDRICH. B. Jan. 19, 1819, at Wittlohe in Hanover. E at the Dresden Sem. A. March 5, 1847. O. at Tranquebar Oct. 18, 1847. M. in 1848. H. from Jan. 1864 to Dec. 1865. L. a Tamil tract "Duty of searching the Scriptures"; and "Letters on the Apocalypse" (Engl.) to be had of the author. Ad. *Challambram, Madras P.*

ZIETZSCHMANN, JULIUS FRIEDRICH. B. in Saxony, March 13, 1852. A. Oct 1877. M. In charge of Industrial school. Ad. *Tranquebar.*

DECEASED AND RETIRED MISSIONARIES.

Johann Heinrich Carl Cordes. B. March 21, 1813, in Hanover. E. at the Dresden Sem. O. at Greiz Feb. 26, 1840. A. Dec. 27, 1840, at Tranquebar March 20, 1841. H. March, 1848 to Sept. 1849: Aug. 1857 to Aug. 1858. Was Senior and Secretary of the Mission while in I. for some time had charge of the training Inst. Edited a small Engl. hymn-book for the Lutheran congregation at Tranquebar, and the Liturgy for Tamil churches. Ret. in 1870 and joined the Home Committee in 1872. Ad. Mission House, *Leipzig, Germany.*

K. H. Schmeisser. B. July 19, 1819, at Furth, Bavaria. E. at the Dresden Sem. A. March 5, 1847. O. at Tranquebar Oct. 18, 1847. D. at Madras, June 3, 1848.

Ernst David Appelt. B. Dec. 30, 1810. E. at the Dresden Sem. A. Sept. 6, 1845. O. at Tranquebar Oct. 18, 1847. H. in Jan. 1859. Left the Mission in Oct. 1860, and went to South Australia where he obtained a pastorate.

Julius Glasell. B. in Sweden in 1821. O. A. March 9. 1849. Left the Mission in July, 1850. R. home in 1851: is now chaplain in Sweden.

Johann C. George Speer. B. in 1824 at Hohndorf, Silesia. E at the Dresden Sem O. Aug 23, 1852. A. Dec. 26, 1852. R. home, sick, in May, 1853, and D. at Hohndorf. April 22, 1855.

Gustav Emanuel Lundgren. A. in Dec. 1853. Left the Mission in Aug. 1854 and R. home. Pastoral work in Sweden.

Johann Friedrich Meischel, B. Feb. 10, 1812, at Augsburg, Bavaria. E. in the Basel Sem. Sent in 1846 to Africa. R. home and in 1854 come to I. in connection with the Leipzig Society. Left the Mission in Feb. 1860 : is now in Australia

Wilhelm Stahlin. B. July 1, 1831, at Westheim, Bavaria. E. at Erlangen. O. at Munich Nov. 5, 1854. A. Jan. 12, 1858. Labored at Tranquebar in charge of the Mission high school. H. in July, 1866. Relinquished Mission service and remained at home as chaplain.

Heinrich Wilhelm Wendlant. A. Jan. 12, 1858. Left I. to join the Hermannsburg Mission in Africa in Sept. 1859: D. at Emlazi, Africa, June 21. 1861.

George Christian Kelber. B. May 29, 1828, at Krautostheim, Bavaria. E. at Erlangen. O. at Anspach in 1857. A. Jan. 12. 1858: labored at Madras Left for Europe on sick leave in the "Cleveland." which sailed from Madras in March, 1860 and was never heard of afterwards.

Swen Ryden. B. Dec. 24, 1825, at Hestra, Sweden. E at Lund, where he was O. in 1855. A. Jan. 12, 1858. H. from June, 1862 to Oct. 1864, and again in Feb. 1866. On his way home D. in Lon. June 1, 1866.

Max Ludwig Julins Doderlein. B. Aug. 22, 1829, at Erlangen in Bavaria. E. at Erlangen and Halle. O. at Anspach in July, 1853. A. Sept. 27, 1860. H. in Feb. 1870. Was not able to return on account of poor health : obtained a chaplaincy at home.

N. Nallathambi. B. (of Christian parents) in 1801. Baptized at Tanjore: licensed May 31, 1849: O. June 27, 1860. Ret. in June, 1869. Ad. *Tanjore, Madras P.*

Aaron Maduravasagam Samuel. B. at Madras Feb. 10, 1827, O. June 27, 1860. Translated from the German Gerhard's "Holy Meditations" (Tamil.) D. at Poreiar, in May, 1880.

Hugo Schanz. B. Nov. 8, 1834, in Voigtland, Saxony. E. at Leipzig where he was O. May 22, 1862. A. Oct. 8, 1862. Edited two collections of sermons (in Tamil); Spiritual Lyrics, etc. Left I. on furlough Feb. 16, 1872, and remained at home as chaplain.

Friedrich Ahner. B. Aug. 8, 1841, at Roda, Saxony. E. at Leipzig. O. in 1863: A. Dec. 12, 1863. D. at Madras May 25, 1864.

Wilhelm German. E. at Erlangen and Leipzig. A. Dec. 18, 1865. He wrote the Lives of the first missionaries, Ziegenbalg, Gründler, Fabricius, and Schwartz (in German): edited Ziegenbalg's "Genealogy of the Malabar Gods" (German): Fabricius' "Sermons on the Sunday Epistles"; and Schultz's Translation of the Apocryphal Books, in Tamil. Ret. Sept. 13, 1867: is now chaplain in Germany.

Sand Swamidasen. B. at Tranquebar in July, 1817. E. at Tranquebar where he was O. Feb. 19, 1865. D. at Madura, Oct. 25, 1877.

M. R. Nanendiram. B. at Tanjore in 1816. E. at Tranquebar, where he was O. Feb. 19, 1865. Labored at Tanjore, where he D. Dec. 27, 1870.

Ludwig Otto Kahl. B. April 17, 1843, at Kleinhenbach. Bavaria. E at Erlangen. O. at Bavaria in 1867. A Nov. 29, 1867. D. at Trichinopoly, July 28, 1874.

Johann Friedrich Zucker. B. Sept. 2, 1842, at Breitenau, Bavaria, E. at Erlangen. O. in 1870. A. Nov. 19, 1870. Ret. in March, 1876, to Missouri, U. S. A.

Heinrich Alfred Grubert. B. Oct. 29, 1848, at Arensburg, Russia. E. at Leipzig. O. at Erlangen in May, 1871. A. July 8, 1871. M. in 1873. Ret. in March, 1876. D. in Germany in 1877.

Carl Manthey-zorn. B. March 18, 1836, in North Germany. E. at Kiel, Erlangen and Leipzig: O. at Erlangen in May, 1871: A. Aug. 7, 1871. S. Tranquebar and Paducottah. Ret. in March, 1876, to Missouri, U. S. A.

Otto Heinrich Theodor Willkomm. B. Nov. 30, 1847 at Ebersbach, Saxony. E. at Leipzig where he was O. March 25, 1873. A. Sept. 17, 1873. Ret. in March, 1876, to Missouri, U. S. A.

Karl Ernst Grahl. B. Jan. 1, 1838, at Mugeln in Saxony. E. at Leipzig. O. in 1870. A. Nov. 19, 1870. S. Poreiar: established Industrial school. D. at Tranquebar, July 15, 1879.

CHAPTER XVI.

THE IRISH PRESBYTERIAN MISSION.

As has already been seen, the London Missionary Society occupied Surat (Gujerat) in 1815, by sending out the Rev. Messrs. Fyvie and Skinner. (It may be remarked that the first to enter this field was the Rev. C. C. Aratoon, an Armenian, a convert of the Baptist Mission in Bengal. He came to Surat in 1812 and continued to labor here until 1821, when he returned to Bengal). The London missionaries early devoted themselves to the work of translating the Scriptures.* A press established by Mr. Skinner still exists, and is know as the "Surat Mission Press." For sixty years it has sent forth in continual issue, hundreds and thousands of tracts and Scriptures. The missionaries just named were the founders of the Mission in Gujerat. They were the first to translate and publish the whole Bible and were the authors of a goodly number of useful tracts, some of which are still in circulation. One of their number wrote a volume of sermons, prepared a book of prayers, and translated from Hindustani a small volume of hymns. They were joined from time to time by other laborers, among them the Rev. J. V. Taylor, who arrived in 1846, and who subsequently connected himself with the Irish missionaries. Besides occupying Surat the London missionaries labored with varied success at Baroda, Central Gujerat, Jambusir, Divan, Borsad, and in the Mahi Kanta Mission.

In the year 1840, the Presbyterian Church in Ireland formed a Board of Foreign Missions. The peninsula of Kathiawad (which had not yet been occupied) was chosen as a special field of labor in India. In 1841, the Rev. James Glasgow and the Rev. Andrew Kerr (both of the Theological Institution at Belfast) arrived in the country, and proceeded to Rajkot. Within six months of their arrival, Mr. Kerr was removed by

---

* There have been several translations of the Scriptures into Gujerati :

1. By Dr. Carey. Serampore : New Testament. 1820.
2. By Rev. Messrs. Fyvie and Rev. J. Skinner : Entire Bible. 1820 23.
3. By Rev. Messrs. Clarkson and Flower : Gospels and Acts, 1845-44.
4. By the Irish Missionaries : Entire Bible. 1857 58.

death, and Mr. Glasgow was left alone. In March, 1842, he was joined by his brother Adam and the Rev. R. Montgomery, and in December of the same year by the Rev. Messrs. McKee and Speers. The two brothers remained at Rajkot, Mr. Montgomery proceeded to Porbandar on the western coast of Kathiawad, and Mr. McKee to Gogo, on the eastern coast.

At Porbandar, a learned and influential Mohamedan after visiting the missionaries and enquiring the way, was convinced of the truth of the Christian religion, and in October, 1843, was baptized, as were his father, brother and other members of the family. The excitement was so great among the people, that the native government refused to allow the missionaries to remain any longer in the place: and they were obliged most reluctantly to withdraw from it.

About 1846, arrangements were entered into for the transfer of Surat from the London Society to that of the Irish Presbyterians. Mr. Montgomery was appointed to this place, and occupied it (furloughs excepted) till his retirement in 1877. The work in Surat had not been fruitful in converts. Much labor had been bestowed upon the city by earnest men, but, at the time of its transfer, no congregation of converts had as yet been formed.

The Mahi Kanta mission, which had been established about 1844 by the Rev. Messrs. Clarkson and Flower, and which was proving a most important field, was transferred in 1859 by the London Society to the Presbyterians; the former Society having decided to withdraw from Gujerat altogether. This mission, which was first called the "Baroda mission," and afterwards (the Guikwar having refused to allow the missionaries to prosecute their labors in his territories) the "Mahi Kanta," is now generally known as the "Borsad mission."

Meanwhile, the Propagation Society having withdrawn from Ahmedabad, this station was taken up in 1861 by the Presbyterian Mission. The resources of Borsad as to land being exhausted, (the converts being as a rule agriculturists) a new settlement was founded at Shahwadi, about four miles from Ahmedabad. At first 64 persons removed here, and others rapidly followed, so that Borsad was almost deserted: it was soon replenished, however, by converts drawn from the Dheds. In a few years the

Dheds in the Borsad and adjoining districts, began to show a disposition to embrace Christianity. It was not possible nor indeed desirable any longer to bring the converts together to form a distinct settlement: they were becoming numorous enough to hold their own in their homes and villages. The work in these districts has been steadily carried forward.

About 1860, a Christian village was formed near Gogo named after one of the missionaries, Wallacepur. It is in a flourishing condition.

The zenana Mission, dating from 1874, occupies Surat and Borsad and has two departments, medical and educational. At Surat a school for girls, chiefly Parsis and Hindus, with an attendance of 50, is conducted on the *Kinder Garten* system. In the medical work the number of patients ranges from 50 to 130 a day, at the dispensary, besides many private cases: work is daily begun by the reading and exposition of Scripture and prayer. A card with a text of Scripture printed on one side and the medical prescription written on the other is given to each patient.

In the last five years this Mission has made considerable advancement, in the number of converts, formation of congregations and church erection. Churches have been built at Nariad, Anand, Bhalaj, Brookhill (near Borsad) and Amode. Christian colonies have been formed at Bhalaj and at Brookhill. The following statistics of the Society (for 1880), show the increase since 1871:

Foreign missionaries,	...	9 :	increase,	1
Native Christians,	...	912 :	do.	380
Communicants,	...	198 :	do.	49

MEMBERS OF THE MISSION.

Beatty, William. E. at the Queen's Univ. Ireland (B. A.) A. in 1865, and was appointed to Gogo. Had special charge of Wallacepur the Christian settlement near Gogo, 1877-78. H. 1877: R. 1878. Ad. *Ahmedabad, Gujerat, Bombay P.*

Brown, William Wallace. E. at the Queen's Univ, Belfast. (M. A.) A. in Nov. 1874. S. Surat, 1874-76, since Borsad. Ad. *Borsad, Gujerat, Bombay P.*

Gillespie, Robert. E. at the Queen's Univ., Ireland (B A.) A. in 1868. S. Rajkot and Ahmedabad. Had charge of the Christian settlement at Shahwadi. H. 1879. *Now in Ireland.*

JERVIS, A. S. Principal, Mission High School. Ad. *Surat, Gujerat, Bombay P.*

MACAFEE, F. L. Principal, Mission High School. Ad. *Ahmedabad, Gujerat, Bombay P.*

REA, G. T. B. Antrim Co., Ireland, 1837. E. at the Queen's Univ. Ireland. (M. A.) O. 1866. A. in 1866. S. Borsad. R. home in ill health in July, 1872. Rt. 1876. S. Gogo, then, Surat. L. Several original stories in Engl., "Ramdas," "Kassibai," "Lee. Fang," etc: to be had of the author: Editor of "*Satyodya*" (Gujerati). Supt. Mission Press. Ad. *Surat, Gujerat, Bombay P.*

SHILLIDY, J. E. at the Queen's Univ. Ireland (M. A.) A. in Nov. 1874. S. Ahmedabad, Gogo, and Anand Ad. *Anand, Gujerat, Bombay P.*

TAYLOR, JOSEPH VAN-SOMEREN. Son of Rev. Joseph Taylor of the L. M. S. Belgaum. E. at Glasgow Univ. (B. A). O. in June, 1845, for the Tamil country, and was appointed to Madras, but was transferred to Gujerat to take the place of the Rev. Mr. Flower. Arrived at Baroda in November, 1846. In 1850 removed to Borsad. Early in 1856 was obliged to take furlough for a few years. On the transfer of the stations to the Irish Mission, he requested to be allowed to resign his connection with the L. M. S. and join the Irish Mission. This arrangement was made and he returned to his former field of labor early in 1860, where he has since remained. Is the author of a Larger and a Shorter Gujerati Grammar, of several tracts, original and translated, and of "*Kavyarpana*" (a collection of metrical compositions), and an enlarged version of Barth's Church History. H. 1880. Ad. *Edinburgh.*

TAYLOR, GEORGE PRITCHARD. B. Cambay, Bombay P., Jan. 1854. O. at Belfast, Ireland, Sept. 1877. A. Nov. 1877. S. Surat, 1878-80, since April, 1880, Gogo. Ad. *Gogo, Gujerat, Bombay P.*

DECEASED AND RETIRED MISSIONARIES.

Andrew Kerr. E. at the Theol. Inst. Belfast. A. in company with Mr. Glasgow in 1841, and proceeded to Rajkot. D. the same year.

James Glasgow, D. D. E. at the Theol. Inst. Belfast. A. in 1841, one of the first missionaries of the Society. For some time previous he had held a pastoral charge at home. Began laboring at Rajkot, where he remained some time. For some years before he retired he labored at Surat. He engaged largely in the work of translating the Scriptures: he wrote also some educational works, a short system of scripture theology, and a metrical version of the Psalms. He retired in 1866, and is residing in Portadown, near *Belfast.*

Adam Glasgow. E. at the Theol. Inst. Belfast. A. in March, 1842. S. Rajkot. After a few years of labor he resigned and R. home. He afterwards proceeded to New Zealand, where he D.

Robert Montgomery. E. at the Theol. Inst Belfast. A. in March, 1842. S. Porbandar, 1842-45: in 1846, Surat which he long occupied. He assisted in revising and re-translating the Bible: translated two volumes of Barth's "Bible Stories;" prepared a large English and Gujerati Dictionary. Was pastor of the Native church at Surat and also Supt. of the press. H. 1877. D. 1880.

James Speers. E. at the Theol. Inst. Belfast. A. in Dec. 1842. Labored for a short time at Surat. R. home, and Ret. from the Mission.

James McKee. E. at the Theol. Inst. Belfast. A. in Dec. 1842. S. Gogo: afterwards Surat, and Rajkot. The author of several tracts and of a compendium of the Bible. Ret. in 1865 with broken health. D. in 1878.

James Wallace. E. at the Theol. Inst. Belfast. He had served as a pastor for a short time at home. A. in 1845. S. Gogo: afterwards Surat. Besides engaging in re-translating the Scriptures, he was the author of an educational book and of several Gujerati tracts. Through his efforts mainly a training school for teachers and catechists was opened at Ahmedabad. H. 1870, but, shortly after his arrival at Belfast, D. from heart disease.

Dunlap Moore. A in 1855. S. Rajkot. and Ahmedabad: at the latter place he opened the Engl. school. Translated several tracts into Gujerati. He left I. in 1866, and after spending some time at home joined the Jewish Mission and was appointed to Vienna. Afterwards R. home. *Now in America.*

William Dixon. M. A. of the Queen's Univ. Belfast. A. in 1864. Was Supt of the Engl. school at Surat. After several years of faithful labor, he D. in 1871.

T. L. Wells. E at the Queen's Univ. Ireland. (B. A.) A. in 1864. S. Rajkot: in 1869 Ahmedabad: in 1872. Surat. The author of several educational books. H. 1874, R. 1876. D. at Surat, 1877.

William McMordie. E. at Queen's Univ. Ireland. (M. A) A in 1867. S. Ahmedabad. The author of "Studies in English." H. in 1874. R. in 1877. Resigned in 1879.

John Hewitt. E. at the Queen's Univ. Ireland, (M. A and LL. B) A. in Nov. 1874. S. Borsad. D. in 1876.

---o---

CHAPTER XVII.

THE AMERICAN EVANGELICAL LUTHERAN MISSIONS.

I. GENERAL SYNOD.

THE Foreign Missionary Society of the American Evangelical Lutheran Church was organized May 30th, 1837. One of its first efforts was to support the Rev. Mr. Rhenius in Tinnevelly: upon his death the Society resolved to establish a Mission of its own in India, and in May, 1840, appointed the Rev. C. F. Heyer to carry out the object. Mr. Heyer arrived at Guntur, July 31, 1842. Subsequently a Board of Foreign Missions of the General Synod of the American Evangelical Lutheran Church was formed to take the place of the Missionary Society. All the Foreign Mission business is now transacted by this Board.

Mr. Heyer was joined in 1844 by the Rev. W. Gunn. In 1849 a mission was commenced in the Palnad District. In 1851, on account of financial difficulties Rajahmundry (occupied by the North German Missionary Society in 1845) was transferred to the Lutheran Society, and until 1869 was under the control of the General Synod.

In 1858 three additional missionaries arrived, and in 1859 a new station was formed at Samulcotta. In 1874, the Rev. A. D. Rowe, the "Children's Missionary to India" arrived. His support is derived exclusively from the Sunday-schools of the Church. In 1877 two Native pastors were ordained. Very encouraging progress has been made. Since 1871 the number of Native Christians has increased from 2,470 to 5,423: communicants, from 731, to 2,193. The following are the statistics for 1880:—

Stations occupied, 4: Foreign missionaries, 4: Native ordained agents, 2: villages where Christians reside, 222: Native Christians, 5,423: communicants, 2,193: baptized in 1880, adults, 679, children, 518, total 1,197: scholars in day-schools, 1,129; in Sunday-schools, 1,822.

MEMBERS OF THE MISSION.

JOHN, B. O. Jan. 7, 1877. Has charge of the eastern part of the Palnad District. Ad. *Dachepalli, Madras P.*

NATHANIEL, M. O. Jan. 7, 1877. Has charge of the western part of the Palnad District. Ad. *Macherla, Madras P.*

ROWE, A. D. O. at York, Pa., U. S. A., Aug. 19, 1874. A. Dec. 11, 1874. H. 1880. *Now in America.*

SCHNARRE, CHARLES. A. 1881. Ad *Guntur, Madras P.*

UHL, L. L. O. at Wooster, O., U. S. A. Oct. 14, 1872. A. March 26, 1873. Has since had charge of the Mission High school. Ad. *Guntur, Madras P.*

UNANGST, E. E. at Gettysburg, Pa., U S. A. A. March 15, 1858. At various times has had charge of the entire Mission. H. May, 1871 to April, 1872. Ad. *Guntur, Madras P.*

DECEASED AND RETIRED MISSIONARIES.

C. F. Heyer, D. D. B. about 1791. A. in 1842. H. to America, 1846-47. Ret. in 1856. Accompanied Mr. Schmidt to I. in 1869. R. in 1870. D. in America, in 1873.

Walter Gunn. A. June 18, 1844. Labored at Guntur until his death, July 5, 1851.

O. Martz. A. in 1850. Ret. in 1851.

C. W. Gronning. Came to I. in connection with the North German Missionary Society. Joined the Lutheran Mission in 1851. H. to Europe in 1858. Rt. Feb. 25, 1861. Ret. to Europe in 1865.

W. E. Snyder. A. in 1858. H. to America from 1856 to March, 1858. D of cholera, March 5, 1859.

W. J. Cutter. A. in 1852. Ret. in 1855.

A. Long. E. at Gettysburg, Pa., U. S. A. A. March 15, 1858. S. Samulcotta, and Rajahmundry. D. at Rajahmundry, March 5, 1866.

J. H. Harpster. A. April 1872. R. to America, March 22, 1876.

II. GENERAL COUNCIL.

IN 1869, Dr. Heyer, the first missionary at Guntur and the Rev. H. C. Schmidt went to America from Europe, for the purpose of attending a meeting of the Pennsylvania Synod. This Synod, on hearing that the Rajahmundry Mission was about to be transferred, at once appointed Mr. Schmidt as their missionary to Rajahmundry. Accompanied by Dr. Heyer he arrived at his station August 4th, 1870. Itinerating and other work was at once begun.

There has been encouraging progress. Since 1870, 536 have been baptized. There are now 4 Foreign missionaries, two Native ordained agents, and 216 communicants.

MEMBERS OF THE MISSION.

ARTMAN, HORACE G. B. B. Zionsville Pa., U. S. A. Sept. 23, 1857. E, Philadelphia (A. B.) O. May 26, 1880. M. June 8, 1880. A. Oct. 18, 1880. Ad. *Rajahmundry. Madras P.*

CARLSON, AUGUSTUS B. B. in Sweden Aug. 16, 1846. O. June 16, 1878, at Princeton, Ill., U. S. A. A. Jan. 14, 1879. Ad. *Rajahmundry. Madras P.*

JOSEPH, TOTA. B. at Guntur, 1839. O. Dec. 25, 1878. L. assisted Mr. Gronning in translating into Telugu, the "Heart Book" Ad. *Jagtimpad, Godavery, Madras P.*

PAULUS, NALAPROALU. B in the Kristna District, 1842 O. Rajahmundry Dec. 25, 1878. W. Native Pastor. Ad. *Valepore, Godavery, Madras P.*

POULSEN, IVER CHRISTIAN. B in Denmark, in 1847. O. and A. 1871. S. Rajahmundry. H March 1880. Ad. *Copenhagen, Denmark.*

SCHMIDT, HANS CHRISTIAN. B. in Flensburg, Denmark, May 25 1840. O 1869. A. 1870. Has labored since at Rajahmundry. Ad. *Rajahmundry, Madras P.*

CHAPTER XVIII.

THE WELSH CALVINISTIC METHODIST MISSION.

The Missionary Society of the Welsh Calvinistic Methodist Church was organized in May, 1840. In November, 1840, it sent the Rev. Thomas Jones as its first missionary to India, who began work at Cherrapoonjee in Assam. Sylhet was occupied in 1850 and the missionary stationed here labored among the Bengalis until 1872 when the mission was discontinued, the Society resolving to confine its labors to the aborignes among the Hills: at present its only fields of labor are the Khassi and Jaintia Hills.

The Society carries on its work of civilizing and evangelizing these tribes by means of education and preaching. The Mission now has 78 day and night schools, attended by 1,843 pupils, of whom 388 are girls. Government gives an annual grant of £500 for these schools, all of which are under the care of and controlled by the missionaries. Government appoints a deputy inspector to visit them, and one of the missionaries is appointed Secretary to the schools, who is the medium of communication between the Government and the Mission. There is also a normal school for training teachers of which one of the missionaries is appointed head-master by Government which also pays his salary.

The converts are quite independent of the Mission, not one of them receiving any support in any shape: a good number of them fill government offices in different parts of the Hills. They contributed in 1880 Rs. 1,244 for evangelistic purposes, besides contributing towards building chapels, etc.

There were (in December 1880), 64 churches, 7 foreign missionaries, 2,458 pupils in the Day-schools, 2,698 scholars in Sunday-school; and 1,659 Native Christians of whom 920 were communicants. The returns for 1871 were imperfect: hence no comparison can be drawn; steady progress, however, has been made.

[T. J. J.]

MEMBERS OF THE MISSION.

EVANS, ROBERT. Ad *Shangpoong, via Jawai, Assam.*

GRIFFITHS, GRIFFITH. (M. B. and C. M. Glasgow Univ.) B Caernarvonshire, North Wales. Dec. 19, 1852. O. 1878. A. 1878. W. Medical missionary. Ad. *Mawphlang, Assam.*

HUGHES, GRIFFITH. B. Llanddeiniolen. North Wales, March 4, 1840. O. Liverpool, Oct. 4, 1865. A. Feb. 22, 1866. S. Cherrapoonjee, Khasi, Jaintia Hills. Shillong, Jawai, Khadsawprah. L. Revised "The Christian Instructor," and translated the Bible in Khasi language (in connection with the other missionaries). H. one year, 1875-76. Ad. *Khadsawprah, Assam.*

JONES, JOHN. B. Holywell, North Wales. March 8, 1847. O. Beaumaris, Nov. 3, 1875. A. Feb. 29, 1866. S. Shellapoonjee, 1876-80, since, Jawaipoonjee. Ad. *Jawaipoonjee, Jaintia Hills, Assam.*

JONES, THOMAS JERMAN. B. Aug. 10, 1832, at Leangristidlus, Anglesea, Eng. Called to the ministry in 1860. O. in 1865. M. 1868. Labored in the North of Eng among colliers and iron-workers before coming to I. A. in Feb. 1870. Has labored since at Jawaipoonjee in charge of the mission district of Jaintia Hills. W. chiefly ver. Ad. *Shillong, Assam.*

ROBERTS, JOHN. O. in 1870. A. the same year. S. Shellapoonjee until 1876, since Cherrapoonjee. Ad. *Cherrapoonjee, Assam.*

STEPHENS, CELEUS LEON. B. Westminster, Lon. Jan. 11, 1847, E. Trevecca Col. O. at Pembroke, Aug. 1870. Pastor at Tenly, Pembrokeshire, 1870-72, Lon. 1872-78. A. Nov. 1880. Ad *Shella, Khasia Hills, Assam.*

DECEASED AND RETIRED MISSIONARIES.

Thomas Jones. A. in 1841 as the first missionary of the Society. He translated some portions of the N T. and also some other books which were the first books printed in the Khassi language. His connection with the Mission ceased in 1849, and he D. soon after at Calcutta.

William Lewis. A. in 1842. After twenty years of labor he proceeded on H. but on account of poor health was unable to return and resigned. He has since continued his literary labors: revising the portions of the N. T. translated by Mr. Thomas Jones, and translating the others, besides some other books. Is now Ret.

Daniel Jones. A. in 1845 and entered upon his work, but was removed by death about nine months afterwards, in 1846.

Hugh Roberts. O. in 1865. A. the same year. S. Sylhet and Cherrapoonjee. H. in 1876. *Now in Europe.*

CHAPTER XIX.

THE ARCOT MISSION OF THE REFORMED CHURCH IN AMERICA.

THIS Mission was formed in the year 1851, when the Rev. H. M. Scudder of the American Madras Mission was appointed to Arcot. He opened a dispensary, which he carried on for two years in connection with other mission labors and then closed. In 1853 he was joined by two of his brothers, the Rev. W. W., and Joseph Scudder, and the three occupied the stations Vellore, Chittoor and Arnee: having at that time about 170 nominal Christians of whom 26 were communicants. The field had previously been worked to some extent by Norris Groves, Esq., who labored in Chittoor, and by the Society for the Propagation of the Gospel, whose agents had occupied Vellore and Chittoor. As they desired to retire from this locality, the Presbyterian missionaries took possession, purchasing the mission property: thus securing the nucleus embraced in the figures given above. The dispensary was re-opened in 1865 by Dr. S. D. Scudder.

This Mission was formed under the auspices of the American Board, through which the Reformed Protestant Church then carried on its foreign work. An amicable separation, however, was effected in the year 1857, since which time the Mission has been directly responsible to the Home Church. Steady growth has followed the labors put forth, and 89 different points are now occupied, 8 of which are principal stations. In addition to the missionaries and zenana workers the Mission has 18 catechists, 33 Bible-readers, and 30 teachers.

[E. C. S.]

The following statistics (December, 1880 show the progress since 1871:—

Foreign missionaries,...	5:	decrease, 1
Native ordained Agents, ...	4:	increase, 1
Native Christians, ...	3,199:	do. 721
Communicants, ...	1,322:	do. 610

MEMBERS OF THE MISSION.

Chamberlain, Jacob, (M. D.) B. 1835. E. at Western Reserve Col. (M. A. 1856), and at New Brunswick Theol. Sem. (1859). O. 1859. M. 1859. A. 1859. S. Palamanair 1860-63, Madanapalle since 1863. Established Hospital and Dispensary at Madanapalle, 1868. L. Translated into Telugu, "Liturgy of Reformed Church:" engaged in revision of Telugu Bible since 1869. Published (1) "The Bible Tested"; Bible Socy. New York: (2) "Tract Work in India"; Tract Soc. New York; (3) "Winding up a Horse" or Christian giving; New York: (4) "Native Churches and Foreign Missionary Societies," (in Bangalore Conference Reports); Addison and Co., Madras. H. 1874-78. W. Telugu and Tamil. Ad. *Madanapalle, Madras P.*

Conklin, John Woodruff. B. in 1851. E. at Rutgers Col., N. J. (1871) and New Brunswick Theol. Sem. (1876). Pastoral work, 1876-80. Sailed for I. Jan. 1, 1881. Ad *Chittoor, Madras P.*

John, Zechariah. B. in Jaulna in 1832. Converted in 1849. Baptized 1853. M. in 1854: O. 1867. S. 1867-75 pastor at Coonoor; 1875-79, Arcot, since at (Ad.) *Arnee, Madras P.*

Nathanael, Moses. B. about 1830. O. Jan. 1880, as Native pastor. Ad. *Arcot, Madras P.*

Sawyer, Andrew. B. of heathen parents about 1810. Baptized when a youth. Labored in Palamcottah eight years and at Chittoor 21 years O. in 1859. Native pastor at Arcot, 1859-65: Gnaniodiam, 1865-75: since, at Chittoor. Ad. *Chittoor, Madras P.*

Scudder, Jared Waterbury, (M. D.) B. in 1830 in the Neilgherries. E. at Western Reserve Col. (1850) and at New Brunswick Theol. Sem. (1855): O. and M. the same year. A. 1856 S. Arnee, 1856-59: to America, in 1859. R. in 1862. Chittoor, 1862-75; to America, in 1875. Rt. Oct. 1878. S. Chittoor. Labored in Tamil and Telugu. Translated into Tamil part of the "Heidelberg Catechism." Ad. *Chittoor, Madras P.*

Scudder, John, (M. D.) B. in 1835, at Chavagacherry, Ceylon. E. at Rutgers College, New Brunswick, (1857), and at New-Brunswick Theol. Sem. (1860) O. in May, 1860. M. in 1861. A in 1861. S. Chittoor. 1861-63: Palamanair, 1863-65: Arcot, 1865-75. Was in charge of hospital and dispensary at Arcot, 1872-75. Vellore, 1875-78. Labored in Tamil. To America, in 1878. Ad. *Creston, Neb., U. S. A.*

William, Abraham. B. about 1835, of heathen parents. E. at Vellore Sem. O. Jan. 1880 as Native pastor at (Ad.) *Kattupadi, Madras P.*

Wyckoff, John Henry. B. in 1851, at Somerville N. J., U. S. A. E. at Rutgers Col. New Brunswick (1871) and at New Brunswick Theol. Sem. (1874) O. 1874. A. in 1874. S. 1875, at Vellore: since, at Tindivanam; W. in Tamil. Ad. *Tindivanam, Madras P.*

DECEASED AND RETIRED MISSIONARIES.

Henry Martyn, Scudder, M. D., D. D. B. Feb. 5, 1822, at Panditeripo, Ceylon. Graduated at New York Univ. in 1840, and Union Theol. Sem. in 1843. Pastoral work at New Rochelle, 1843. M. 1844. A. 1844. S. Madura, 1844-46: Madras, 1846-51: Arcot, 1851-53: Vellore, 1853-57. To America in 1857. Rt. in 1860: Coonoor and Ootacamand, 1860-64. Ret. to America in 1864. Pastoral work at Jersey City, 1865: San Francisco, 1865-71: Brooklyn, 1871 to the present. L. (Tamil); "Spiritual Teaching": "Jewel Mine of Salvation": "Sweet Savor of Divine Truth": "Bazar Book." (Telugu); "Spiritual Teaching": "Jewel Mine of Salvation." Translations: "Heidelberg Catechism" (in part): "Liturgy of the Reformed Church". Ad. No. 29 Ormand Place, *Brooklyn, U. S. A.*

William Waterbury Scudder, D. D. B. Sept. 17, 1823 at Panditeripo, Ceylon. Graduated at the Col of N J., in 1841, and at Princeton Theol. Sem. in 1844. M. in 1846. A. in 1846 Labored at Batticotta, Ceylon until 1851 when he went to America: Rt. in 1852. Labored at Arcot and Chittoor, 1852-56. To America in 1856. Rt. 1858. Chittoor, 1859-60: Vellore, 1860-72. Ret. to America in 1872. Since 1873 has had pastoral charge at *Glastonbury, Conn., U. S. A.*

Joseph Scudder, D. D. B Jan. 14, 1825, at Panditeripo, Ceylon. Graduated at Rutgers Col. New Brunswick, N. J. in 1848, and at New Brunswick Theol. Sem in 1851. A in 1853. S. Arcot, 1853-56: Coonoor, 1856-59: to America 1859-60: chaplain in U. S. Army, 1861-63: Secretary American and Foreign Christian Union, 1863-69: pastoral charge at Glenham, 1872-75: Upper Red Hook, 1875 D. 1876.

Ezekiel Carman Scudder, M. D B. in 1828 at Panditeripo, Ceylon. Graduated at Western Col. in 1850, and at New Brunswick Theol. Sem. in 1855. O. and M. the same year. A. 1856. S. Chittoor, 1856-59: Palamanair, 1859-61: Chittoor, 1861-63: Vellore, 1863-68. To America in 1868. R. in 1870. Arnee, 1871-73: Vellore, 1873-76. Proceeded to America in 1876. Ad. *Upper Red Hook, N. Y., U. S. A.*

Joseph Mayou. Graduated at Rutgers Col. New Brunswick, in 1855, and at New Brunswick Theol. Sem. in 1858. O. in 1858. A. in 1858. S. Arnee, 1859-62: Ginjee, 1862-63: Arnee, 1863-71. Ret. to America in 1871. Pastoral charge at *Somerset, Kansas, U. S. A.*

Silas Downie Scudder M D. B. November 1, 1833, at Panditeripo, Ceylon. Graduated at Rutgers Col. New Brunswick, N. J. in 1856: at 13th Street Medical College in 1858. Medical practice in New York 1858-60. A. in 1860. O. in 1862. In charge of dispensary and hospital at Arcot, 1865-72. R. to America in 1872. D. 1877.

Enne Jahusen Heeren. B. 1842, in Eastfriesland, Hanover, Europe. Went to America in 1855. Graduated at Hope College, Michigan, in 1867 and in the Theol. department of the same in 1870. O. 1872. A. in 1872. S. Vellore, 1872-73: Palamanair, 1873-77. R. to America, 1877 D. in 1878.

---o---

CHAPTER XX.

THE MORAVIAN MISSIONARY SOCIETY.

THE Missionary Society of the Moravians, or United Brethren, began its operations in India in 1855 by establishing a mission station at Kyelang in British Lahoul. The first missionaries were the Rev. Messrs. Hyde and Pagell, who are still in the field. Thus far not many converts have been gained, but the missionaries have made long preaching tours, have established schools which are in a flourishing state, and have laid the foundations for a great work. A second station was formed in 1865 at Poo in Upper Kunawur, near the Chinese-Tibetan frontiers. A third station it is hoped will soon be established at Ladak. A Lithographic printing-press has been established at Kyelang and by its aid the missionaries have been enabled to send forth in Tibetan portions of the Holy Scriptures, religious works, like Barth's "Scripture Stories," "History of the Christian Church," several tracts, and school-books of various kinds. A Tibetan-German Dictionary has been completed and a Tibetan-English Dictionary is in course of preparation. At the request of the Government a mission farm has been opened near Kyelang which bids fair to be a success, by increasing the food-supply of the district and by giving employment to the native converts. In 1870 a new church was erected at Poo, and it is generally well filled at the time of service. Here as at Kyelang the snow and intense cold of the winter months interfere to a considerable extent with missionary operations.

Two churches are now in existence: in 1871 there were 17 Native Christians of whom 8 were communicants. There are now 35 Christians and 17 communicants. There are at present three missionaries in the field.

MISSIONARIES OF THE SOCIETY.

Heyde, Augustus William. B. Feb. 16, 1825, in Prussian Silesia. Called to be a missionary of the Moravian Church in 1852. O. in 1853, A. Nov. 23, of the same year. Went to Kotgarh in 1854, where he spent one year. In 1855 in company with Mr. Pagell, established the Moravian mission station of Kyelang in British Lahoul, where he has since labored. A. *Kyelang*, (Kangrā District) *via Kullu, Punjab.*

Pagell, Johan Louis Edward. A. in 1855. S. Kyelang: since 1865, at Poo. Ad. *Poo, Upper Kunawar, Punjab.*

Redslob, Fritz Adolph. B. June 10, 1838, at Konigsfeld, Baden, Germany. Called to the ministry in 1860. O. as a Deacon of the United Brethren Church in 1867. M. in 1872. A. in 1872 and has since labored at Kyelang. A. *Kyelang*, (Kangra District) *via Kullu, Punjab.*

RETIRED MISSIONARIES.

Heinrich August Jaeschke. A. in——. S Kyelang: W. chiefly translating. Owing to failing health he was obliged to leave I. in Sept. 1868. Has since carried on the work of translating at home.

J. Theodore Rechler. A. in 1864. Labored at Kyelang until failing health caused him to return home, in 1871.

CHAPTER XXI.

The Sealkote Mission of the United Presbyterian Church in America.

The Sealkote Mission was begun by one of the two branches which afterward united, in 1858, to form the United Presbyterian Church of North America. The first missionary was the Rev. A. Gordon, who, with his wife and sister, sailed from New York, September 28, 1854, and arrived at Calcutta early in February, 1855. His general commission was to select a field in Northern India after conferring with missionaries already in the country. Accordingly he repaired to Saharunpur, where he arrived March 23, 1855, and where he remained with the Presbyterian missionaries four months. Sealkote was visited in the following August, and being an eligible and unoccupied field it was decided to make it the centre of the new Mission. Shortly afterwards Mr. Gordon removed thither and purchased property for the Mission. The first missionary work was amongst the inmates of the poor-house near the station, several of whom afterwards became Christians.

Early in 1856 the Mission was reinforced by the arrival of the Rev. Messrs. Stevenson and Hill. Mr. Stevenson having an inclination to educational work, a vernacular school, formerly sustained by the residents of the station, was made over to the Mission, and became a recognized branch of the work. Immediately after the rainy season of 1856 multitudes of village people died: numbers of children were left orphans: and the missionaries were enabled to form the nucleus of an orphanage.

The work was interrupted by the Mutiny of 1857: the missionaries taking refuge in June of that year in the fort at Lahore. One of the mission-houses was plundered and destroyed: the other two escaped. In July, Mr. Gordon returned to the work, and in October following the other missionaries and their families also returned. On the 25th of October the first converts, two men, were baptized. During the three or four years that followed several persons were baptized; and an industrial school was established to assist the converts in supporting themselves. In 1866, Mr. J. W. Gordon was sent from home to take charge of this as a branch of mission work. Land was also purchased at Zaffarwal in the eastern part of the Sealkote district, upon which Christian families were settled.

In 1863 Gujranawala was occupied, and in the following year the boys' department of the orphanage was removed here. In 1866 a branch station was established at Zaffarwal. In 1868 schools were opened at Gujranawala and in 1870 girls' schools were begun at Sealkote. Gurdaspur was taken up early in 1872, and Jhelum in 1873. The industrial school, not proving a great success and not being longer demanded, was closed in 1871: and the orphanages being left comparatively empty, were also closed in 1872. The school work has been carried forward with success. The total number of pupils in the schools is 1,922. A Theological school was opened at Sealkote in April, 1877: in 1880 there were 12 students in attendance. A Girls' Boarding school was begun at Sealkote in 1878.

In September, 1880 a Zenana Hospital was opened at Gurdaspur, which bids fair to do a good work.

[A. G.]

The following statistics (for 1880) indicate the progress since 1871:

Foreign missionaries,	5:	increase,	2
Native Ordained agents,	2:	do.	2
Native Christians,	534:	do.	414
Communicants,	335:	do.	272

MEMBERS OF THE MISSION.

BARR, JAMES SWIFT. B. Dec. 22, 1832, in Washington Co., N. Y., U. S. A. O. June 25, 1861. M. two days later. A. Calcutta March 20, 1862. S. Gujranawala. W. Ver. and Engl. R. to America March, 1873 to Dec. 1875. Ad. *Gujranwala, Punjab.*

GORDON, ANDREW. B. Sept. 17, 1828, in Washington Co., N. Y., U. S. A. O. in New York, Aug. 31, 1854. A. at Calcutta, Feb. 13, 1855. In the same year founded the mission at Sealkote. In 1864, R. to America on account of sickness: was re-appointed, and A. Dec. 10, 1875. W. Ver. and Engl. teaching and preaching. Ad, *Gurdaspur, Punjab.*

MARTIN, SAMUEL. B. Dec. 9, 1836, in Jefferson Co., O., U. S. A. O. at Wellsville, Ohio, July 3, 1866. M. Sept. 27. 1866. A. in May, 1867. S. Sealkote. W. Engl. and Ver. Ad. *Sealkote, Punjab.*

McKEE, J. P. B. in Laughaghary, Ireland, in 1843. M. in 1869. O. at Jamestown, Penn.; U. S. A., in 1870. A. Feb. 11, 1871. S. Gujranawala: W. preaching and teaching in Engl. and ver. Ad. *Gujranawala, Punjab.*

SCOTT, THEODORE L. B. Nov. 21, 1847, in Butler Co., Penn., U. S. A O. at Camp Run. Aug. 26. M. Sept, 1, and A. Nov. 28. 1874. S. Gujranawala one year, teaching and preaching in Engl. In Jan. 1876, appointed to Jhelum. H. to America in 1881.

SWIFT. E. P. B. of heathen parents near Gwalior, in 1829. Labored as a catechist at Lahore for some time. Went to Sealkote in 1856 where he was O. in 1859. S. Sealkote, Gujranawala, and, since 1873, Jhelum. M. in 1864. Ad. *Jhelum, Punjab.*

THAKUR, GEORGE LAWRENCE. B. at Lucknow (parents Brahmins) in 1852. O. Dec. 28, 1877. L. "Izhar-i-Iswi (Urdu.) Ad. *Pasrur, Sealkote, Punjab.*

RETIRED AND DECEASED MISSIONARIES.

Robert A. Hill. B. about 1820 in U. S. A. Was engaged in pastoral work a number of years before coming to I. A. in Jan. 1856: S. Sealkote until 1863, when he Ret. to America. Was pastor in Jersey City for several years, and is now pastor at *Princeton, (near Schenectady) N. Y., U. S. A.*

Ephraim H. Stevenson. B. about 1820. in Penn , U. S, A. O. by the Ohio Presbytery Nov. 4, 1852. Labored as a pastor in Ohio for some time. A. in Jan. 1856. S. Sealkote until the close of 1864, when he R. to America on account of sickness. Is now Principal of a Female Sem. at *Oxford, Penn., U. S. A.*

George Washington Scott. B. of heathen parents in Nidhara, near Gwalior, about 1832. E. in the Orphanage of the Lodiana Mission. Labored as a catechist in the Sealkote Mission from 1856 to 1859, when he was O. by the Sealkote Presbytery. Labored faithfully until his death, in 1869.

CHAPTER XXII.

Methodist Episcopal Church Missions.

I.—NORTH INDIA MISSION.

The Methodist Episcopal Church (whose Missionary Society was organized in the year 1819) was late, comparatively, in entering the India mission field. It was not till the year 1854, that, at the suggestion of the Rev. Dr. Duff, who was then visiting the United States, the project of establishing a Mission in India was seriously entertained, and two years more elapsed before the first missionary arrived in the country. The Rev. William Butler, D. D., who was sent out to locate and superintend the new Mission, arrived in Calcutta on the 23rd of September, 1856, and after consulting the leading missionaries of the city with regard to the best part of the country in which to plant the Mission, proceeded to Benares where he attended the Missionary Conference then convened in that city, and after taking further counsel with the missionaries assembled there, finally selected Oudh and Rohilkund as the best and most needy field for his work. He proceeded at once to Bareilly and entered upon his work, but the Mutiny of 1857 soon swept over the country, and Dr. Butler with his family sought a refuge at Nynee Tal. Meanwhile two other missionaries from America joined him, as did two Englishmen in India, so that the new Mission at the close of the Mutiny had five men in the field ready for active work. Thus reinforced it was determined to establish a station at Nynee Tal, to occupy Moradabad and Lucknow, and to re-occupy Bareilly. This was accordingly done, and, about the close of 1858, the active work of the Mission was fairly commenced.

Reinforcements from America were sent out somewhat rapidly, six men coming in 1859, four in 1861, three in 1862, and four in 1863. Meanwhile additional stations were occupied in the following order: Bijnour, Shahjehanpore, and Budaon, in 1859, Sitapur, 1861, Roy Bareilly, 1864, Gonda, 1865,

Paori, in Gurhwal, 1866, Bahraich, 1867, Cawnpore, 1871, Pithoragarh, in Eastern Kumaon, 1873; while various other stations were occupied by Native missionaries.

Orphanages were formed at Lucknow in 1858: in 1859 the boys were removed to Bareilly and in 1862, the boys' orphanage was finally located at Shahjehanpore, at which time the girls' orphanage was transferred from Lucknow to Bareilly. Both have continued to flourish, and contained, in 1880, 519 orphans, of whom 269 were boys and 250 girls. In connection with the boys' orphanage is the Christian village of Panahpore near Shahjehanpore. It embraces 900 acres of land, and contained in 1880 a Christian community of 335.

A Mission press was established at Bareilly in 1860, which was removed to Lucknow in 1866, and has since continued its useful work: its issues for the year 1880 were 57,000, containing 4,000,000 pages.

A Theological School was founded at Bareilly in 1872 by the Rev. D. W. Thomas one of the missionaries: he gave the institution about £4,000, and through his efforts this was subsequently increased as an endowment fund by donations made in America to £12,000. The first class graduated in 1874: the class of 1880 numbered 13; in all, 57 have graduated.

There are several Boarding-schools in connection with the Mission. Two of these are at Lucknow, one for girls, the other "The Centennial School," for boys. The "Memorial School" at Cawnpore and the "The Cawnpore Girls' School" were established in 1874. In 1880 a High School (for boys) was opened at Nynee Tal, and in 1881, one for girls. The number of day-schools is 344, with 8,338 pupils: there are 222 Sunday-schools attended by 8,952 scholars. For many years much attention has been given with most encouraging results to Sunday-school work both among Christian and heathen children.

Four of the Mission staff are medical missionaries; and there are also two medical ladies with a dispensary at Moradabad and a large hospital and dispensary at Bareilly.

The Woman's Foreign Missionary Society, through its regular agents, including the wives of the missionaries, is carrying on an extensive and most encouraging work among the women and girls. Since 1870 this Society has sent out 19 ladies, most of whom are still in India.

A moderate degree of success attended the labors of the missionaries in some parts of the field, almost from the first, but the chief part of the fruit has been gathered among the lower castes of Rohilkund and more recently among some of the villages of Kumaon and Gurhwal. In Oudh the visible success has, thus far, been much more limited. A large number of Native preachers, of various grades, has been raised up, some of whom are men of personal worth and marked spiritual power. During the past decade (1871-81) the number of Native Christians has trebled.*

The following statistics (for 1880) indicate the progress since 1871 :

Foreign missionaries,	25 :	increase,	4
Native Ordained Agents,	14 :	do.	8
Native Christians,	5,495 :	do.	3,660
Communicants,	2,597 :	do.	1,523

MISSIONARIES OF THE SOCIETY.

ADAMS, HORACE J. B, at Malangapore. 1847. O, by Bishop Harris in Lucknow Jan. 11, 1874. Pastor of the Native Church at (Ad.) *Panahpore, Oudh.*

BADLEY, BRENTON HAMLINE. B. April 27, 1849, at Monmouth, Ind , U S. A. E. at Simpson Col., Indianola, Iowa, (B A. 1870 : M. A. 1873), and at Garrett Biblical Institute, Evanston, Ill, (B. D 1872). Began preaching in 1868. O. D. at Aurora, Ill. by Bishop Ames in Oct. 1871 ; O. E. at Chariton, Iowa, by Bishop Andrews in Sept. 1872. M. Aug. 8, 1872. A. Dec. 19. 1872 S 1873, Lucknow, 1874-77, Gonda and Bahraich, since, Lucknow. L. " Sunday-school Manual:" Translation of "Missionary among Cannibals ;" " Flavia ;" " Glaucia" " Seed Thought;' " Bible Question Book" (the last three in press) : edited Roman-Hindee N T. M. E Church Press, Lucknow. Ad. *Lucknow.*

BARE, CHARLES LYSANDER. B. July 7, 1849, in Clark Co , Ind.,U.S.A. O. D. and O. E New York, Nov 9, 1879, A. Jan. 1, 1880. Has labored since at (Ad). *Shahjehanpore. N.-W. P.*

BUCK, PHILO MELVIN. B. May 15,1846, at Corning, Steuben Co. N.Y. U. S. A. Entered the ministry in March, 1865. O. D. March 17, 1867, O. E. March 28, 1869. Preached five years in the Kansas Conference before coming to I. A Nov. 11, 1870. S. Shahjehanpore ; in charge

* For fuller particulars *vide* Mudge's " Hand-book of Methodism."

of the Boys' orphanage and the Christian village, Panahpore, 1871-76. M. May 22, 1872. W. chiefly ver. H. to America in April, 1876. Rt. Dec. 1878. Has since labored as Presiding Elder of Kumaon District. Ad. *Dwarahath, Kumaon, N.-W. P.*

CHENEY, NATHAN G. A. in Feb. 1876, and has labored since at Nynee Tal. W. chiefly Engl. preaching. Ad. *Nynee Tal, N.-W. P.*

CRAVEN, THOMAS. B. March 28, 1846, in Buckley, County of Flint, North Wales. Removed to America in June, 1864. E. at Evanston, Ill. graduating at North-Western Univ. June 22, 1870, (M. A. 1873), and at Garrett Biblical Institute (B. D. 1872). O. D. and O. E. by Bishop Janes in Aug. 1870: A in Oct. appointed to Lucknow in Jan. 1871, where he has since labored as Supt. of schools and the Mission Press. L. Compiler of several dictionaries, Roman-Urdu and Engl.; and Engl. and Roman-Urdu. M. E. Church Press, Lucknow. Ad. *Lucknow.*

CUNNINGHAM, EDWARD. B. Aug. 13, 1840, at Searsmount, Me., U. S. A. Converted in 1849: licensed as an exhorter in 1863, as a local preacher in 1864. Joined the New York East Conference in April, 1867. Graduated at Wesleyan Univ. Middletown, Ct., in July, 1867. O. D. by Bishop Thomson in 1869; O. E. by Bishop Scott, in 1871. S. Cheshire, Ct., 1867-69, and at Durham, Ct., 1869-71. M. in 1871. A. in Dec. 1871. S. 1872, Seetapore: 1873-77, Lucknow: 1878-79, Presiding Elder, Rohilkund District. H. to America, in Jan. 1880. W. has been both Engl. and ver. Ad. *Belfast, Me., U. S. A.*

CUTTING, HIRAM ADOLPHUS. B. near Moradabad in 1849. E. at Moradabad, where he was converted in 1869. Began preaching in 1870. O. at Lucknow, by Bishop Harris, Jan. 11, 1874. S. Amroha, 1874-80, since at (Ad) *Bijnour, N.-W. P.*

DEASE, STEPHEN S. A. 1881. Ad. *Bareilly, N.-W. P.*

DUTT, ANTONE. O. D. by Bishop Merrill, Jan. 9, 1881. Ad. *Bilsi, Budaon, N.-W. P.*

FIELDBRAVE, ISAAC. B. at Delhi in 1848 of Christian parents. Was converted in 1869 and commenced preaching soon after. O. at Lucknow by Bishop Harris, Jan. 11, 1874. S. Khera Bajhera, 1874-76; since, Lucknow. L. translated a Commentary on the Revelation: has written a Prize Essay in Urdu on the use of Tobacco: M. E. Church Press, Lucknow. Has written and translated a number of hymns. Ad. *Lucknow.*

GILL, JOSEPH HAMILTON. B. March 27, 1844, in Strabane, Co. Tyrone, Ireland. Converted in March, 1854. Removed to America in Sept. 1862. E. at Evanston, Ill. graduating (with B. A.) at the North Western Univ. June 22, 1870, and (with B. D.), at the Garrett Biblical Institute June 29, 1871. M. Sept. 6, O. in Brooklyn, by Bishop Janes, Sept. 24, sailed for I. Oct. 4, A. Dec. 14, 1871. S. from Jan. 1872, to Aug. 1873 at Moradabad: since, at Paori: ver. W. H. to America in Jan. 1881. Ad. *Quincy St. Brooklyn, N. Y., U. S. A.*

GOWAN, THOMAS. O. D. by Bishop Bowman, in Jan. 1879. O. E. by Bishop Merrill, Jan. 9, 1881. Ad. *Nynee Tal, N.-W. P.*

GRAY, RICHARDSON, (M. D.) B. in the United States, in June, 1852.

A. Oct. 20, 1873. O. Jan. 1874, at Lucknow by Bishop Harris. Has labored since in Eastern Kumaon. W. ver. M. in June, 1875. Ad. *Pithorahgarh, Kumaon, N.-W. P.*

GREENWOLD, FREDERIC, W. O. D. by Bishop Merrill, Jan. 9, 1881. Ad. *Paori, Garhwal, N.-W. P.*

HAQQ, ZAHUR-UL. B. in 1833, near Shajehanpore. Called to the ministry in 1859. M. Aug. 19, 1862. O. Jan. 23, 1870, by Bishop Kingsley. S. Bareilly, Nynee Tal, Moradabad, Bijnour. Ad. *Sumbhal, N.-W. P.*

HOSKINS, ROBERT. B. May 7, 1843, in Bennington, Vt., U. S. A. Converted in 1859: called to the ministry in 1860. Graduated at Williams Col. in 1866. O. in 1867. M. in 1867. A. Feb. 1, 1868. S. Bijnour, 1868-69: Budaon, since 1870. H. to America 1876-77. ver. W. L. Urdu and Roman-Urdu Concordances of the Bible; Allahabad, and Lucknow; an Urdu Commentary on the Gospel of St. John. M. E. Church Press, Lucknow. Ad. *Budaon, N.-W. P.*

JANVIER, JOEL THOMAS. B. about 1834, at Banda, Bundelkhund, of Hindu parents. E. in the Presbyterian mission at Allahabad. Assisted Dr. Butler in founding the Mission, in 1857. O. D. Dec. 11, 1864, by Bishop Thomson. O. E. Jan. 23, 1870, by Bishop Kingsley. S. Bareilly, Nynee Tal, Lucknow, Barabanki, Cawnpore. M. Ad. *Bareilly, N.-W. P.*

JOEL, ENOCH. B. Rampore, Moradabad, Dec. 23, 1853. E. Bareilly Theol. Sem. O. D. by Bishop Merrill, Jan. 9, 1881. Ad. *Barabanki, Oudh.*

JOHNSON, THOMAS STEWART, (M. D.) B. Monmouth Co., N. J., U. S. A. Sept. 28, 1833. M. 1855. O. D. 1861. O. E. 1862. A. 1863. S. Shahjehanpore, 1863-73. Kumaon, 1873-75. H. 1876. Budaon, 1877, Shahjehanpore, 1878 to present. L. Translated in Urdu and Hindi (1) "True Repentance," (2) "Gospel Servers," (3) "Bible not of Man:" M. E. Church Press, Lucknow. Ad. *Shahjehanpore, N.-W. P.*

KASTENDIECK, HENRY FRANCIS. B. Brooklyn, N. Y., U. S. A., Oct. 13, 1857. O. Akron, Ohio, Sept. 1879, by Bishop Foster. A Nov. 1879. S. Calcutta, 1880, Nynee Tal, 1881. Ad. *Nynee Tal, N.-W. P.*

KHAN, MAHBUB. O. D. Jan. 9, 1881, by Bishop Merrill. Ad. *Kakrala, Budaon, N.-W. P.*

KNOWLES, SAMUEL. B. in Eng. Joined the Mission in 1858 then in its commencement. S. 1858-64, Nynee Tal, Budaon, Lucknow: 1864-69, Gonda: 1870-71, Seetapore, 1872-73. H. to England: 1874-76, Shahjehanpore, 1877-79, Cawnpore; since, Gonda. L. "Misbah-ul-Iman" (Lamp of Faith): "Tawallud-i-Jadid" (the New Birth): "Ilm-i-Mantiq" (Elements of Logic): M. E. Church Press, Lucknow. Ad *Gonda, Oudh.*

LAWSON, JAMES CHAPEL. B. Platteville, Grant Co., Wis., U. S. A. Oct. 15, 1856. E. at Garrett Biblical Institute, Evanston, Ill., graduating in 1880. O. D. Platteville, Sept. 26, 1880, by Bishop Harris O. E. at Brooklyn, by the same Dec. 1, 1880. A. Jan. 24, 1881. Ad. *Cawnpore, N.-W. P.*

MANSELL, HENRY. B. Nov. 11, 1834, in Trumbull Co., Ohio, U. S. A.

Converted Nov. 7, 1851. Called to be a missionary at seven years of age by reading "Little Henry and his Bearer." Joined the Pittsburgh Conference in March, 1859. O. by Bishop Janes, in July, 1860. A. Jan. 21, 1863. S. Moradabad, April, 1863 to December, 1866: Bijnour, 1867: Paori, Garhwal, 1868-71, (serving during 1870-71 as Presiding Elder of Moradabad District): H. to America from Feb. 1872, to Oct. 1873: Presiding Elder of Oudh District, 1874-75: Cawnpore, 1875-76. Lucknow, 1877; Gonda, 1878-79; since, Moradabad. W. both Ver: and Engl. E. at Alleghany Col. Meadville, Pa., in 1859, (B. A.: M. A. in 1862). L.: (1) Miftah-ul-Majlis (Rules for Deliberate Bodies): (2) Masihi Kamiliyat (Wesley on Christian Perfection): (3) Ahwal i Padri Wasli Sahib (Abridgement of Watson's Life of Wesley): (4) Kitab Muqaddas ke Qawanin i Tafsir (Rules of Biblical Exegesis): (5) Bhugol Bidya ka Parshan Uttar (Hindee Catechism of Geography): (6) Millat i Tashbihi (Butler's Analogy, abridged): (7) Kutub farosh ki Sarguzasht, "Five Years in the Alleghanies") (8) Tazkira e Lizzie (Mrs. Mansell's Biography): (9) Several small illustrated books: (10) Josephus' Histories. M. E. Church Press, Lucknow. Ad. *Moradabad, N.-W. P.*

McGrew, George Harrison. B. Kingwood, Va., U. S. A. May 19, 1846. Served as a scout in the Union army, 1863-64: E. Wesleyan Univ. Middletown (B. A. 1870: M. A. 1873), at Harvard Col. (L L. B. 1873), and at Drew Theol. Sem. (B. D. 1876). O. D. and O. E. Nov. 1875. A. Jan. 5, 1876. M. Sept. 11, 1876. S. Moradabad, 1876-77, Bareilly, 1878-79; since, Cawnpore. L. "Ilm-i-Ilahi ka Khulasa" (in press). Ad. *Cawnpore; N.-W. P.*

McHenry, Albert Deaves. B. Feb. 21, 1846, in Tuscarawas Co. Ohio, U. S. A. Licensed to preach in 1871 while attending Mount Union Col. M. July 27,1873. A. Oct. 20, 1873. O. at Lucknow, Jan. 11, 1874, by Bishop Harris. S. Moradabad, 1874: Bijnour, 1875; Shahjehanpore, 1876, Bijnour, 1877-80. H. to America in 1881. Ad. *Mayfield, Cuyahoga Co., Ohio, U. S. A.*

McMahon, John T. O. in 1870. A. in Nov. 1870. S. Roy Bareilly, 1871-80; since, Paori. M. W. ver. and Engl. Ad. *Paori, Garhwal, N.-W. P.*

Messmore, James Hagar. B. Jan. 15, 1836, in Brant Co., Ontario, Canada. O. and appointed to I. 1860. M. in 1861. S. Lucknow, Shahjehanpore, Lucknow. H. one and a half years, 1873-74; and 1880. Ad. *Brantford, Ontario, Canada.*

Mudge, James. B. April 5, 1844, in West Springfield, Mass., U. S. A. Graduated from the Wesleyan Univ. Middletown Ct., in July, 1865 (with B. A.): and from the School of Theology of Boston Univ. in May, 1870 (with B. D.) O. in 1868. Preached two years in Cambridge, Mass., and three years in Wilbraham, Mass. M. April 29, 1873. A. in Oct. 1873. S. Lucknow, where he has since remained, as editor of the *Lucknow Witness*, an Engl. religious weekly. Pastor of M. E. Church (Engl.) Lucknow, 1880-81. L. "Handbook of Methodism;" "History of Methodism;" "Good stories for the Leisure Hour" (selected and edited); "Good Stories and Best Poems" (selected and edited): "Spiritual Songs" (revised edition edited); "Suwalat-i-Ilm-i-Ilahi" (a simple catechism translated into Urdu). Ad. *Lucknow*.

NEELD, FRANK L. E. at Western Univ. Pa., (B. A. 1878) and at Drew Theol. Sem. (B. D. 1881). A Jan 24, 1881. Ad. *Cawnpore, N.-W. P.*

PARKER, EDWIN WALLACE. B. Jan. 21, 1833, at St. Johnsburg, Vt. U. S. A. Converted in 1853, and commenced preaching in 1856. M. in 1856. A. Aug. 21, 1859. S. Bijnour, in Oct. 1859 : Luckimpore, Oct. 1861: Moradabad, Jan. 1863 : Nynee Tal, Oct. 1863 ; Moradabad, Jan. 1864. H. from April, 1868 to Nov. 1870 : since, Moradabad, most of the time Presiding Elder of Rohilkund District. Ad. *Moradabad, N.-W. P.*

PAUL, AMBICA CHARN. B. in 1841, in Bengal. Converted Oct. 8, 1861. M. 1863. O. 1870, by Bishop Kingsley. S. Luckimpore, Seetapore Sambhal, Chandousi, Bijnour, Hurdui, and (Ad.) *Roy Bareilly. Oudh.*

SCOTT, JEFFERSON ELLSWORTH. B. May 21, 1851, near Steubenville, Ohio, U. S. A. Studied at Newmarket and Mount Union Col. Taught one year. Entered ministry in July, 1871 and preached two years. Appointed to L. Aug. 12, 1873, sailed Aug. 20 and A. at Bombay Oct. 20, 1873. O. D. and O. E. by Bishop Harris at Lucknow, Jan. 11, 1874. S. Moradabad, 1874-75, since Jan. 1876, Seetapore. M. at Bombay Dec. 14, 1877. W. chiefly ver. Ad. *Seetapore, Oudh.*

SCOTT, THOMAS JEFFERSON. B. Oct. 4, 1835, at New Alexandria, Ohio, U. S. A. Licensed to preach in 1855. O. D. by Bishop Ames, in March, 1861 ; O. E. in July, 1862. M. June 26, 1862. Preached five years while attending the Ohio Wesleyan Univ. and two years in the Pittsburgh Conference. A. Jan. 20, 1863. S. six years at Budaon, and ten years at Bareilly. W. chiefly ver. Presiding Elder of the Bareilly District four years. Taught six years in the Bareilly Theol. Sem. five of them as Principal. L. (1) *Waz Banane ki Tariqa* (On the "Preparation of Sermons"): (2) A Work on Logic ; diglott, Urdu and English *(Kuwaif ul mantiq)*: (3) Bible Dictionary, *(Taqdis ul Lugat)* Urdu translation and compilation from Barr's "Index" : (4) Urdu Commentary on Matthew and Mark : (5) Revision and re-translation in Hindee, on Committee, of the Catholic Epistles and the Revelation : (6) A small Urdu work on Natural Theology : (7). A Work in Urdu on Homiletics. M. E. Church Press, Lucknow. H. to America 1875-76. Ad. *Bareilly, N.-W. P.*

THOMAS, DAVID WESLEY. B. Jan. 1, 1833, in Sherbrooke, Lower Canada, where his parents were temporarily residing : native town, Malone, Franklin Co.. N. Y. E. at the Franklin and Ogdensburgh Academies and in the New York State Normal School, graduating in 1855. Taught several years. O. D. June 6, 1858, and two days later joined the Black River (now Northern New York) Conference ; S. Nicholville, N. Y. O. E. by Bishop Baker in Boston Aug. 14, and sailed Aug. 17, 1861. A. Jan. 17, 1862. Has labored since at Bareilly, in charge of the Girls' orphanage from 1862 to 1871 : since, as Agent and Principal of the Theol. Sem. Received the honorary degree M. A. in 1868 from Geneseo Col. L. A Commentary on Genesis : A Work on the Trinity and a pamphlet on Miracles (Roman-Urdu) M. E. Church Press, Lucknow. H. to America, 1873-74. Is Treasurer of the Mission. Ad. *Bareilly, N.-W. P.*

WAUGH, JAMES WALTER. B Feb. 27, 1832, at Mercer, Penn., U. S. A. Began to preach in 1857. E. at Alleghany Col., and at Garrett Biblical Institute, Evanston, Ill. O. in April, 1859. After one year of pastoral work, was appointed to I. A. at Calcutta in Aug. 1859. S. Shahjehanpore, 1859: Bareilly, 1860-65: Lucknow, 1866-71: Lucknow, 1874: Bareilly, Theol. Sem., 1875-76. W. almost exclusively Ver. In charge of the Mission press for ten years from its founding: Supt. for a time of Boys' orphanage: Presiding Elder of Oudh District for five years. Principal Memorial School, Cawnpore, 1877-79. Principal Boys' High-School, Nynee Tal, 1880. L. edited *Kaukab i Iswi*, ("The Christian Star") four years. Translated the three Catechisms of the M. E. Church, and some small books: *Intikhab i Sabaq*, (Scripture Lessons) in Roman and Lithograph Urdu. Hymns in Urdu: "Indian Temperance Singer," etc. M. E. Church Press, Lucknow. H. 1871-73; and in Feb. 1881. M. Ad. *Evanston, Ill, U. S. A.*

WILSON, PEACHY TALIAFERRO, (M. D.) B. Christian Co., Ky., U. S. A. Oct. 26, 1832. E. at Garrett Biblical Institute, Evanston, Ill. (M. A. and B. D.) O. D. and O. E. Youngstown, Ohio, 1862. A. Jan. 20, 1863. S. Luckimpore, 1863: Roy Bareilly, 1864-70: Paori, 1870-73: H. to America, 1873-78: Roorkee, 1878: Gurhwal, 1879. L. Translated into Hindustani, (1) Binney's Theol. Compend. (first Ed.) (2) "Michael the Miner." (3) "Mary Lathrop" (4) "Grandfather Ormand's Stories to his grand-children. Ad. *Paori, Garhwal, N.-W. P.*

RETIRED MISSIONARIES.

William Butler, D. D. B. in Ireland in 1820. Attended the Wesleyan Theol. School, Didsbury, Eng. Removed to America in 1853. Engaged in pastoral work several years, contributing largely to Newcomb's "Cyclopedia of Missions." In May, 1856, was appointed by the Methodist Episcopal Church as its first missionary to I. A. at Calcutta in Sept. 1856, and proceeded to Oudh and Rohilkund where he founded the Mission. In May, 1857, he was obliged to flee with his family to Nynee Tal where he remained until 1858. His house and library at Bareilly were burned by the mutineers. From 1858-64 he labored as Supt. of the Mission, having his residence at Bareilly. In Jan. 1865, R. to America. In 1869 he was appointed Secretary of the American and Foreign Christian Union. In 1872 he published "The Land of the Veda;" including Personal Reminiscences in India. In 1873 appointed to open and superintend the Mission of the Methodist Episcopal Church in Mexico. R. to America in 1879. Ad. *Melrose, Mass, U. S. A.*

James Lorenzo Humphrey, M. D. B. in 1828, in the State of N. Y. U. S. A. Was engaged as pastor for a time before coming to I. A. during the Mutiny in 1857. S. Moradabad, Bareilly, Budaon, and Shahjehanpore. In 1864, R. to America and during his stay there studied medicine and received the degree of M. D. at the Albany Medical Col. Rt. in 1868, S. Nynee Tal until 1874, when he Ret. on account of ill health. Established a dispensary and taught native students (male and female) in medicine; also published a small work in Hindi, on Practice and Materia Medica. Ad. *Utica, N. Y., U. S. A.*

Ralph Pierce. B. in 1827, in U. S. A. E. at Dickinson Col. Pa. A. in 1857. S. Lucknow till 1863: then at Bareilly. R. to America in 1864. Ad. *Knoxville, Tenn., U. S. A*

James A. Cawdell. B. in Eng. Joined the Mission in 1858. S. Lucknow, 1858-62, Bareilly, 1863-64, Sambhal, 1865-68. In 1868 left I. for Australia.

James Baume. B. in Eng. in 1824.. Removed to U. S. A. in 1846. Pastoral work for some years in and near Chicago, Ill. A. in July, 1859. S. 1859, Lucknow, Engl. work: 1860, Shahjehanpore: 1861-63, Lucknow: 1864-66, Nynee Tal: R. to America in 1866, and resumed pastoral work near Chicago. While in India edited "*Samachar Hindustani:*" wrote several Urdu hymns and tracts: published a small Temperance hymn-book. Ad. *Princeton, Ill., U. S. A.*

John Talbot Gracey. B. in 1830, in Philadelphia, U. S. A. E. in that city: was there O. and engaged for some time in pastoral work. A. in 1861. S. Seetapore until 1865: then at Bareilly: at Nynee Tal, 1866-67. Engaged in both Engl. and Ver. W. Prepared one or two tracts on the Mahommedan controversy. R. to America in 1868. At present engaged as Presiding Elder in N. Y. and as missionary editor of the *Northern Christian Advocate.* Ad. *Rochester, N. Y., U. S. A.*

Henry Jackson. E. in Canada. A. in April, 1861. S. 1861-63, Luckimpore, Bareilly, Budaon; 1864-67, Lucknow: 1866, H. to America, 1869, Budaon: 1870-73, Bijnour: in Jan. 1874 was appointed to open the Memorial School at Cawnpore where he labored, as Principal, 1874-76: 1877, Shahjehanpore: 1878, Ranee Khet. In 1879, R. to America and engaged in pastoral W. Ad. *Port Ewen, N. Y., U. S. A.*

Isaiah L. Hauser. B in 1836, in U. S. A. E. at Appleton, Wis. A. in 1861. S. Bijnour, 1861-66: then at Shahjehanpore. Translated the Methodist Discipline into Urdu. R. to America in 1867. Is editor and proprietor of a weekly journal, the *Christian Statesman.* Ad. *Milwaukee, Wis. U. S. A.*

William W. Hicks. B. in Eng. Removed in boyhood to America. A. in 1862. S. Luckimpore, and Budaon. R. to America in 1863. Ad. *Jacksonville, Florida, U. S. A.*

Frank A. Spencer. B. in 1842, in Ohio, U. S. A. E. at Ohio Wesleyan Univ. A. in Dec. 1865. S. Shahjehanpore, 1866; Bareilly, 1867. Translated a small volume into Urdu. R. to America in 1867. On the way spent two years in mission work in Genoa and one year at Bologna in Italy. Ad. *Pt. Harman, Ohio, U. S. A.*

Samuel Sexton Weatherby. B in 1840, in Baltimore, U. S. A. E. at Pennington Sem. N. J. A. in Dec. 1865. S. 1866, Moradabad: 1867-68, Bahraich: 1869-72, Gonda: 1873, Paori. In 1873 R. to America. Has labored since as Supt. of the Minard Mission Home at Morristown, N. J. Now engaged in pastoral work. Ad. *Tuckerton, N. J, U. S. A.*

Francis Marion Wheeler. B. Oct. 14, 1842, at Dix, Schuyler Co. N. Y., U. S. A. Entered the ministry in 1866. O. April 11, 1867, at Newark, N. J. M. July 22, 1867. A. Jan. 31, 1868. S. Lucknow, Moradabad, Budaon, Calcutta, (temporarily). H. from March, 1872 to Dec. 1875. R. to America in 1878. Ad. *Varna, N. Y., U. S. A.*

Fletcher Bailey Cherington. B. April 14, 1850, at Patriot, Gallio Co. Ohio, U. S. A. O. in 1871. Preached in the Iowa Conference one year. M. Oct. 2, 1872. A. Dec. 19, 1872. S. Seetapore, 1873-75. R. to America on account of wife's illness, in Jan. 1876. Ad. *Anamosa, Iowa, U. S. A.*

DECEASED MISSIONARIES.

Joseph R. Downey. B. Dec. 15, 1836, at New Albany, Ind. U. S. A. E. at Garrett Biblical Institute, Evanston, Ill. M. in Feb. 1859. A. in Aug. 1859, and died only a month after his arrival, at Lucknow, Sept. 16, 1859.

Charles Wesley Judd. B. Jan. 31, 1829, in Berkshire, Tioga Co. N. Y., U. S. A. Called to the ministry in 1849. M. in 1856. O. D. in 1857: O. E. 1859. Labored as a pastor six years before coming to I. A. in Aug. 1859. S. 1859-62, Moradabad: 1862-65, Lucknow: 1865-69, Presiding Elder of Lucknow and Bareilly Districts: (1869-71, H. to America): 1872-73, Bareilly: 1874-75, Nynee Tal: 1876, Kumaon District, Presiding Elder. H. 1879. L. Translated "Hayat-ul-Mattaqin"; M. E. Church Press, Lucknow. D. at Wilkesbarre, U. S. A. Feb. 11, 1880.

John David Brown. B. Nov. 8, 1834, in Mifflin Co. Penn., U. S. A. Entered the East Baltimore Conference in March, 1859. O. D. by Bishop Simpson. O. E. by Bishop Baker, in 1861. M. June 11, 1861. A. in Jan. 1862. S. Moradabad, 1862: Shahjehanpore, 1863-64; Seetapore, 1865-70. H. to America in 1871 : while there had pastoral charge for one year at Carlisle, Penn. Rt. in Dec. 1872. S. Shahjehanpore, 1873: Bareilly, 1874-76. L. "Talib-ul-Haqq": "Naqliyat-i-Dilchasp": several Sunday-school books (pictorial series): translated into Urdu Dr. Mitchell's "Letters to Indian Youth": and "Girdab-i-Nashabazi" (partly original): M. E. Church Press, Lucknow. Ret. to America in broken health, Jan. 1876. D. at Harrisburg, Pa., Feb. 17, 1878.

Henry Martyn Daniel. E. at the Secundra Orphanage, Agra, and dated his conversion from truth received there. O. at Lucknow by Bishop Thomson in Dec. 1864. S. Lucknow, 1865: Hurdui, 1866: D. at Lucknow, in Feb. 1867.

Melville Cox Elliot. B. in 1839, in Me, U. S. A. E. at the Wesleyan Univ. A. in 1869 as a traveller in search of health. The climate agreeing with him he engaged in educational work, in Lucknow, and in 1870 at Moradabad. In Jan. 1871, he was appointed to Bahraich, but his health failing he proceeded to the Hills, and D. at Almorah Aug. 26, 1871.

II.—THE SOUTH INDIA MISSION.

THE name of this Mission was given to distinguish it from the North India Mission of the same Church, rather than to specify its geographical situation. It originated chiefly through the evangelistic work of the Rev. William Taylor, and was formally organized in 1872. At the outset it was less a "Mission," in the usually accepted sense of that word, than a work among English-speaking people. Churches were organized, pastors appointed, and all the customary appliances of regularly established European Churches were brought into use. From the beginning, however, it was accepted as the settled aim of the organization to use these English congregations as agencies through which to reach the outlying masses of the people of India, and with a view to developing the largest possible amount of indigenous help, it was resolved to accept no aid from Missionary Societies. Each pastor was to be supported by the people among whom he lived and labored, and it was hoped that when in due time Native Churches should be organized, they would follow the same example.

The result of this policy has not, thus far, fully met the expectations of those who inaugurated it, and yet it has been sufficiently encouraging to confirm their faith in its final success. The claims of the purely English part of the Mission absorb most of the time of the missionaries, and hence some of them have done nothing in a direct way among the heathen and Mahomedans. It is hoped, however, that from year to year many lay members may be induced to undertake informal missionary work, as already a goodly number have done with very fair success. Meanwhile a Native Church is slowly growing up, and the proportion of Native to English members steadily increases from year to year. Vernacular Sunday-schools have been opened at various points, and in all the large cities vernacular preaching is regularly carried on. An orphanage for both sexes has been opened among the Telugus of the Nizam's territory and is in a prosperous condition. Thirty-eight ordained ministers are employed in this Mission and a large number of lay preachers assist them in their work. A number of young men are studying the vernaculars of various parts of India with a view to joining the Mission at a future day, and it is also expected that Native preachers will from year to year be ordained to the work. The present number of communicants is 2,012, about one-seventh of whom are Natives.

[J. M. T.]

MEMBERS OF THE MISSION.

BLACKSTOCK, JOHN. B. Ontario, Canada, Sept. 8, 1834. E. Indiana Asbury Univ. A. Dec. 18, 1875. S. Bombay, 1876; Poona, 1877-78; Nagpur, 1879-80; Madras, 1881. Ad. *Madras.*

BOWEN, GEORGE. B. April 30, 1816. A. Jan. 19, 1848, and has labored since at Bombay, engaged in preaching, and editing the *Bombay Guardian.* In 1855 resigned his connection with the American Board: since 1871 has been connected with the Methodist Episcopal Church. Ad. *Bombay.*

BOVARD, MELVILLE Y. A. 1879. Ad. *Jubbulpore, C. P.*

BOWSER, WELLINGTON. B. Echo, Penn. U. S. A. Sept. 13, 1852. O. D. A. Nov. 27, 1879. S. Cawnpore, Principal Memorial School, 1880; since, Roorkee. Ad. *Roorkee, N. W. P.*

BROWN, WILLIAM D. B. Delhi, April 17, 1850. Not O. Ad. *Hurdàh, C. P.*

BRUERE, WILLIAM W. B. Pennington, N. J. U. S. A. Jan. 10, 1857. A. March 5, 1880, S. Ahmedabad, Poona. Ad. *Poona.*

CARTER, ROBERT ELMER. B. in Ohio, U. S. A. March 10, 1854. O. D. and O. E. March 20, 1879 at New Castle Del. by Bishop Simpson. A. May 19, 1879. S. Rangoon, 1879; since, Bangalore. Ad. *Bangalore.*

CHRISTIAN, CHRISTOPHER WILLIAM. B. in Bombay, Dec. 24, 1848. Called to the ministry in Oct. 1873. O. at Allahabad by Bishop Harris, Jan. 25, 1874. S. Calcutta, from Dec. 1873 to July, 1875: since, Darjeeling, Agra, Chadarghat. Ad. *Chadarghat, Deccan.*

CURTIES, FRANCIS WILLIAM GRANT. B. Kampteo, Aug. 10, 1852. O. Bombay, Nov. 1876. S. Jubbulpore, Secunderabad, Madras, Railway Lines, Hyderabad, Bellary, Mhow, Allahabad. Ad. *Allahabad.*

DAVIS, FRANKLIN GRASSON. B. Gallipolis, Ohio, U. S. A. June 16, 1844. E. Garrett Biblical Institute, Evanston, Ill. graduating in 1874, O. D. Oct. 13, 1872, O. E. Oct. 20, 1875. Pastoral work in Ohio and Ill. before coming to I. A. June 5, 1876. S. Madras, 1876-77; Blacktown, Madras, 1878-79; since, Secunderabad, W. Engl. M. Jan. 30, 1880. Ad. *Secunderabad, Deccan.*

FOX, DANIEL ORMSBY. B. Canajoharie, New York, U. S. A. 1835. O. 1862. E. North-western Univ. (M. A.) and Garrett Biblical Institute Evanston, Ill. (B. D) A. Dec. 1, 1872. S. Poona, 1872-75; Kurrachee, 1876-78; Bombay, 1879 to present: Presiding Elder Bombay District. Ad. *Bombay.*

GILDER, GEORGE K. O. at Allahabad, Jan. 25, 1874, by Bishop Harris. Has labored since at or near Bombay. Ad. *Egutpoora, Bombay P.*

GLADWIN, WALLACE JONATHAN. B. Aug. 15, 1842, at Corning, New York, U. S. A. Labored two and a-half years in the "Christian Commission," 1864-66. Entered the ministry in 1866. Pastoral work in Missouri and Arkanas until 1871. A. Dec. 14, 1871. S. Cawnpore, 1872-74, Agra, 1875, Nagpur, 1876; since, Bombay. M. Jan. 3. 1874. Ad. *Bombay.*

GOODWIN, F. A. A. 1873. S. Kurrachee, 1873-76. since, Calcutta. H. to America 1881. Ad. 805 *Broadway, New York City, U. S. A.*

JACOBS, S. P. B. Jan. 14, 1837, near Shanesville, Tuscarawas Co., Ohio, U. S. A. Converted Jan. 30, 1857. Joined the North Ohio Conference in Sept. 1860. O. D. Sept. 7, 1862, by Bishop Scott: O. E. Sept. 4, 1864 by Bishop Ames. Pastoral work eighteen years in North Ohio and Kansas Conferences. A. March, 1880. S. Calcutta, 1880, since, Bombay. Ad. Grant Road, *Bombay.*

JANNEY, LEVAN R. B. Allowaystown, N. J, U. S. A. March 12, 1849. E. Ohio Wesleyan Univ. graduating in 1876. O. Sept. 10, 1876, by Bishop Ames. A. Nov 6, 1876. S. Allahabad, Jubbulpore, Kurrachee. Ad. *Kurrachee, Scindh.*

LEE, DAVID H. B. in Carroll Co., Ohio, U. S. A., June 29, 1850. O. Youngstown, 1875. A. Dec. 11, 1875. S. Agra, 1876, Roorkee, 1877-78, Darjeeling, 1879, Roorkee, 1880; Bangalore, 1881. Ad. *Bangalore.*

LYON, JAMES. B. Harwick. Scotland, April, 1848. O. Delaware, U. S. A. 1879. A. Nov. 1879. S. Agra and Mhow. Ad. *Mhow, C. P.*

MARTIN, CHARLES A. B. Meadville, Pa. U. S. A., 1859. Not O. A. Dec. 21, 1880. S. Calcutta, W. Educational; Principal Calcutta Boys' School. Ad. *Calcutta.*

MOORE, WILLIAM ARNOLD. B. Balarum, Hyderabad, July 26, 1857. Ad. *Bellary, Madras P.*

MORTON, THOMAS EDWARD FRANK. B. Madras, Feb. 22, 1855. S. Bellary and Railway circuit, 1879-80. Ad. *Nagpore, C. P.*

NICHOLS, MILTON HOPKINS. B. Nov. 7, 1835, in Ross Co., Ohio. U. S. A. O. D. Oct. 2, 1870. O. E. March 3. 1872. Pastoral work in Ill. before coming to I. A Dec. 18, 1875. *Now in America.*

NEWLON, WILLIAM E. A. at the close of 1875. S. Bangalore and Madras. *Now in America.*

OAKES, THOMAS HENRY. B. Madras, Sept. 28, 1853. O. Nov. 12, 1876. A. 1877. S. Calcutta, 1876; Drew Theol. Sem. Madison, N. J., U. S. A., 1877-80; Calcutta, 1881. Ad. *Calcutta.*

OSBORN, WILLIAM B. Pastoral work in U. S. A. before coming to I. A. Nov. 1876. S. Bombay and Madras. Ad. *Madras.*

OSBORNE, DENNIS. B. at Benares, Oct. 11, 1844. M. July 20, 1864. Was for sixteen years in the service of Government: resigned this to enter the ministry. O. at Lucknow by Bishop Harris Jan. 11, 1874, and appointed to Allahabad, where he has since labored. W. Engl. and Ver. Ad. *Allahabad.*

NORTHRUP, JAMES ABRAHAM. B. Cove Spring, Ky., U. S. A. Dec. 26, 1848. O. D. Bloomington, Ill. by Bishop Wiley, Sept. 28, 1873. O. E. Princeton, Ill. by Bishop Merrill, Oct. 14, 1877. A. Dec. 20, 1877. S. Calcutta, 1878; since. Poona. Ad *Poona.*

PETERS, BENJAMIN. B. Madras, July 28, 1844. O. In Bombay. Dec. 19, 1881. Ad. *Bangalore.*

RICHARDS, IRA A. B. in Indiana, U. S. A. Dec. 30, 1854. O. D. and O. E. Sept. 25, 1879, at Akron, Ohio by Bishop Foster. A. Nov. 27, 1879. S. Bellary, Madras, Bangalore. In charge of M. E. School at (Ad). *Bangalore.*

ROBBINS, WILLIAM EDWIN. B. Orange Co., Ind. U. S. A. March 8, 1845. O. Sept. 8, 1872. A. Nov. 22, 1872. S. Bombay, Nagpore, Poona. Ad. *Poona.*

ROBINSON, JOHN EDWD. B. in Ireland in Feb. 1849. Removed to America in 1865. Called to the ministry in 1873. O. in Oct. 1874: A. Dec. 18, 1874. S. Secunderabad and Rangoon. W. chiefly Engl. Ad. *Rangoon.*

ROW, ISAAC FRANCIS. B. Plymouth, Eng. Sept. 23, 1840. O. D. at Worcester, Mass. March 31, 1872 and O. E. at Boston, April 12, 1874. Graduate of Boston Theol. Sem. Pastoral work six years before coming to I. A. Nov. 9, 1876. S. Bombay, 1876-80: since, Madras. M. Ad. *Madras.*

SHAW, JAMES. B. at Dublin, Ireland, July 12, 1845. A. in 1866. Was appointed a Scripture reader and served as such during the campaign in Abyssynia. R. to Bombay and labored among the soldiers more than four years. O. at Bombay in Jan. 1874, by Bishop Harris. S. Bombay, Secunderabad, Bangalore, Chadarghat, Madras and (Ad). *Lahore.*

SHREVES, ORAMIL. B. Columbiana Co., Ohio, U. S. A. Aug. 4, 1847. O. D. and O. E. Lima, Ohio, by Bishop Simpson, in 1879. A. Dec. 27, 1879. Ad. *Bombay.*

STEVENS, WILLIAM H. Ad. *Bombay.*

STONE, GEORGE IRVIN. B. Erie, Penn. U. S. A. 1839. O. A. Dec. 31, 1879. S. Calcutta. W. among seamen. Ad. *Calcutta.*

STONE, J. SUMNER, (M. D.) B. at Wheeling, Va. U. S. A. 1856. A. 1880. Ad. *Calcutta.*

TAYLOR, WILLIAM. Entered the ministry in early life and preached two years in Georgetown, D. C. (U. S. A.) and one year in Baltimore. Was then sent, in 1849, as a missionary to California, where he labored seven years. From 1856 to 1861 was engaged in evangelistic labors in the United States and in Canada. From Canada proceeded to Australia by way of Great Britain and Palestine. After laboring here three years he went, in 1866, to South Africa where he spent several months in general evangelistic labors, returning to London at the close of the year. He afterwards returned to Australia where he spent several years. Came to India in 1870. Labored for a time in North India, and afterwards at Bombay, Calcutta, Madras and elsewhere. In 1875 R. to visit America. L. (in Engl.): "The Election of Grace": "The Model

Preacher": "California Life Illustrated": "Reconciliation, or How to be Saved": "Infancy and Manhood of Christian Life": "Seven Years' Street Preaching in San Francisco": "Christian Adventures in South Africa": "Four Years' Campaign in India": etc. London, Hodder and Stoughton: New York, Phillips and Hunt. Ad. No. 805 Broadway, *New York, U. S. A.*

THOBURN, JAMES MILLS. B. March 7, 1836, in Ohio, U. S. A. Began preaching in July, 1857. O. in April, 1859. A. Aug. 21, 1859. S. at Nynee Tal till Oct. 1863. H. to America: R. in Jan. 1866. S. Garhwal, 1866-67: Moradabad, 1868-69: Lucknow, 1870-73: since, Calcutta. To America temporarily in 1876, and in 1880. M. W. has been in both Engl. and Ver. Ad. *Calcutta.*

WARD, CHARLES BENJAMIN. B. in Kendall Co., Ill., U. S. A. March 23, 1853. O. at Pekin, Ill. Sept. 24, 1876. A. Dec. 22, 1876. S. 1877-79, Bellary, since, in charge of Telugu Mission in the North-eastern part of the Nizam's Dominions, Ad. *Chaderghat, Deccan.*

WOODALL, GEORGE W. A. 1879. Ad. *Ahmedabad, Bombay P.*

DECEASED MISSIONARIES.

Hiram Torbet. A. in Dec. 1878. Was accidentally killed at Bombay, March 12, 1879, by falling into the hold of a ship.

William Isaacson. B. in India. O. D. in 1878. S. Allahabad and Futtehpore. D. Dec. 10, 1880.

CHAPTER XXIII.

CHRISTIAN VERNACULAR EDUCATION SOCIETY.

THE Christian Vernacular Education Society for India was established in 1858 as a memorial of the Mutiny. Its objects are thus defined: "The primary objects of the Society shall be to establish in the great towns of India, Christian Vernacular Training Institutions, Male and Female, and to supply as far as possible in each of the native languages of India, school-books and other educational works prepared on Christian principles. The General Funds shall be applicable to assist in the establishment of vernacular schools in India supported by fees, local, or other resources." "Instruction in English may be given at the discretion of the Local Committees." In 1874 it was decided, in friendly concert with the Religious Tract Society to extend the Publication Department by adding to educational works, "All books of a healthy moral tone possessing a Christian tendency, which treat of subjects affecting the social or moral improvement of the people, and upon which the native mind requires enlightenment."

The Society originated with the late Rev. Henry Venn, of the Church Missionary Society. Its first regular Secretary, and till the day of his death, its warmest friend, was the late H. Carre Tucker, Esq., C. B., formerly Commissioner of Benares. Mr. John Murdoch, Secretary of the South India Christian School Book Society, was invited, in 1858, to become the Society's Agent in India, and the Publication Department soon afterwards made a beginning.

Mr. William Yorke, of the Training College, Westminster, was sent out in 1860 to train teachers in South India. Mr. James S. Haig, of the Free Church Training College, Edinburgh, was sent out in 1863 to Western India. Mr. C. J. Rodgers of the British and Foreign School Society's Training College, London, was sent out in 1864 to the Punjab.

In 1880 the number of students in the Training Institution

at Dindigul, South India, was 47; the Ahmednagar Institution had 44 students; and the Amritsar Institution had 33 students.

Efforts have been made, chiefly in Bengal, to improve indigenous schools, through the visits of Christian Inspectors; the native teachers receiving so much per pupil. The Society has also day-schools under trained Christian teachers. In 1880 the number of children under instruction was about 7,000.

During 1879 there were printed 636,440 copies of 147 separate publications. The sales realized Rs. 36,768. The total number of works published in 16 languages is 737; the total number of copies printed is 8,360,310.

During the last few years the Society has also taken up the work of Colportage. In 1879, forty-two colporteurs were employed in India, who sold 141,656 publications, including 6,615 Scriptures, the proceeds amounting to Rs. 5,891. The total income of the Society in 1879 amounted to £ 9,803.

[J. M.]

AGENTS OF THE SOCIETY.

Evans, I. E. Esq. Ad. *Dindigul, Madras P.*

Haigh, James S. Esq. A. 1863. *Now in Europe.*

Keyworth, E. Esq. Assistant Principal. Ad. *Amritsar, Punjab.*

Murdoch, John, Esq. B. at Glasgow, Scotland, in 1819. E. Glasgow Univ. In 1844 he went to Ceylon to take charge of the Government Schools at Kandy. In 1849 he resigned his connection with Government to devote himself to the publication of Christian literature, his support being kindly undertaken by the Wellington Street Congregation, Glasgow, to which he belonged. In 1854 he went to India to obtain catechists to labor among the coolies on the coffee estates in Ceylon. This led him afterward to visit Madras when the South India Christian School Book Society was established. The following year he was recognised as an agent of the United Presbyterian Church of Scotland. In 1858 he became the Indian agent of the Christian Vernacular Education Society, still retaining his connection with his own Church. In 1867, in addition to his previous duties he became Indian agent of the Religious Tract Society. The honorary degree of LL. D. was conferred on him by the Univ. of Glasgow in 1871. The following are his principal publications: a Series of School Books: the Indian Missionary Manual: the Indian Student's Manual: Catalogue of the Christian Vernacular Literature of India: Hints on the Management of Tract Societies in India: with a number of tracts and pamphlets. Ad. *Madras.*

Rodgers, Charles James Esq. B. at Wilne, Derbyshire, April 10, 1838. A. Dec. 15, 1863. H. 1874-75. Ad. *Amritsar, Punjab.*

CHAPTER XXIV.

THE RAJPOOTANA MISSION.

THE Missionary Society of the United Presbyterian Church in Scotland began its operations in India in the year 1860, selecting Rajpootana as its field of labor. This region was altogether unoccupied, and the subsequent history of the Mission thus planted shows the wisdom of the choice. The first missionary was the Rev. William Shoolbred, who arrived in October, 1859: the first station occupied was Beawr. An orphanage was formed here, and also a church now the largest in the Mission. Mr. Shoolbred was joined in 1860 by the Rev. Messrs. Martin and Robson, and other stations were soon occupied. Nusseerabad was taken up in 1861: Ajmere, in February, 1862: Todgurh, in December, 1863: Jeypore, in 1866: Deolee, 1871: Ashapura, 1872; Oodeypore, 1877: Ulwar, 1880.

Great attention has been paid by the members of this Mission to the healing of the sick: at present there are four medical missionaries in connection with the Mission. Dispensaries have been opened at Beawr, Ajmere, Nusseerabad, and Oodeypore. In the four during the year 1880, no less than 85,000 cases, new and old, were treated. Both medical and other missionaries attach much importance to itinerations, and have thus been enabled to spread throughout many towns and villages of Rajpootana a knowledge of the Redeemer's name. A lithographic press is located at Beawr and is kept constantly employed. A number of popular tracts have been published. Orphanages were established in five of the seven stations; in 1880 these were all united in one, at Beawr which contains 109 orphans. There were also in 1880, 83 schools with a total attendance (including orphans) of 3,375: and 28 Sunday-schools attended by 1,364 children.

The number of Native Christians in 1880 was 601, and of communicants 360. The Society has in India 14 missionaries (including three in Europe), an increase of 5 since 1871.

MISSIONARIES, ACTIVE, RETIRED AND DECEASED.

Name.		Arrived in India.		Address, or Remarks.
Bonnar, William, [1]	...	January,	1870	*Deoli, Rajpootana.*
Clark, W., M. D.	...	Do.,	1873	*Nusseerabad, do.*
Glardon, Auguste,	...	Do.,	1862	*Retired in* 1866.
Gray, James,	...	December,	1863	*Ajmere, Rajpootana.*
Gray, A.D.	...	Do.,	1875	*Nusseerabad, do.*
Hendrie, J.	...	January,	1870	*Retired.*
Husband, J., M. D.	...	December,	1870	*Now in Europe.*
Jameson, Alex. P. C. [2]	..	October,	1873	*Ulwar, Rajpootana.*
Macalister, George,	...	January,	1872	*Beawr, do.*
Martin, William,	...	November,	1860	*Ashapoora, do.*
Martin, Gavin,	...	December,	1873	*Died in* 1874.
McQuistan, John, Esq.	...	...		*Ajmere, Rajpootana.*
Robb, W.	...	November,	1862	*Now in Europe.*
Robson, J.	...	Do.,	1860	*Retired in* 1871.
Shepherd, James, M. D. [3]	...	January,	1873	*Oodeypore, Rajpoot.*
Shoolbred, W.	...	October,	1859	*Beawr, do.*
Sommerville, J. M. D.	...			*Ajmere, do.*
Traill, J.	...	January,	1870	*Jeypore, do.*

[1] B. in Fifeshire, Scotland, 1842. O. Oct. 1869. S. 1870, Nusseerabad, since, Deoli. H. 1874-76.

[2] B. at Manchester, Oct. 16, 1847. O. 1873. S. Todgurh, Beawr, Ulwar.

[3] B. Feb. 2, 1847. O. Oct. 28, 1880. S. Deoli, 1873, Ajmere, 1874-76, Deoli, 1877 ; since, Oodeypore.

CHAPTER XXV.

THE DANISH EVANGELICAL LUTHERAN SOCIETY.

THE old Danish Missionary Society, which sent out the first Protestant missionaries to India, having been dissolved, a new Society was founded in the year 1826. This Society had for many years no Missions in India, as its former field of operations with Tranquebar as its centre had been made over to the Leipzig Lutheran Society. In 1863 it entered into connection with the Rev. C. Ochs, who had opened a mission in the South Arcot District. Soon after, several missionaries were sent out to assist him, and he was supported by funds from Denmark till his death, when he left his station at Pattambaukam as the property of the Danish Society. Since, the Society has operated in the South Arcot District, where it now has two stations and several out-stations. Work at Madras has also been taken up.

The following statistics (December, 1880) are about the same as those for 1871 : Foreign missionaries, 3 : Native Christians, 50 : Communicants, 23.

MISSIONARIES OF THE SOCIETY.

IHLE, A. Ad. *Trikalur, Madras P.*

JENSON, HERMAN, B. Aug. 11, 1842, in Denmark. Studied in the Mission Institution at Copenhagen. A. in Sept. 1872. O. in Trikalur in Jan. 1876. S. Trikalur and Madras. Ad. *Madras.*

SCHLESCH, CHR. Ad. *Trikalur, Madras P.*

DECEASED AND RETIRED MISSIONARIES.

Carl Ernst Christopher Ochs. B. Feb. 10, 1812, at Greglineng, Wurtemberg. E. at Dresden Seminary. O. at Greiz, April 27, 1842 : A. Dec. 11, 1842. M. in Dec. 1846. H. April 3, 1855 to Dec. 28, 1856. Left the Leipzig Mission June 2, 1859, and began a mission of his own. In 1863 joined the Danish Lutheran Society ; established a new station at Pattambaukam, where he died, Nov. 16, 1873.

Peder Anderson. B. June 30, 1835, on the Island Fyen. E. in the Mission Inst., at Copenhagen. A. Dec. 18, 1865. O. in the Lutheran Church at Pattambaukam. R. to Denmark in 1876.

Niels Thomsen. A. Dec. 18, 1865. O. in Pattambaukam, Nov. 1, 1868. Left the Mission in 1869. Is now a minister in U.S.A.

Jesper A. Pedersen. B. E. and O. in Denmark. A. Feb. 17, 1871 Left the Mission Sept. 1874.

CHAPTER XXVI.

Hermannsburg Evangelical Lutheran Society.

This Society began its operations in India by sending out in 1865 the Rev. A. Mylius to establish a Mission. He proceeded to the Nellore district and in 1866 occupied Naidupett. In the same year he was joined by two other laborers: others subsequently arrived. Gudur was occupied in 1867; Venkatagiri, in 1868: Vakadu, in 1870; Rapur, in 1872; Kalastry, in 1873: Tirupati, in 1877. The Native Christian community is steadily increasing.

The following statistical items (1880) indicate the progress since 1871:—

Stations occupied,	9 : ...	increase,	8
Foreign missionaries,	8 : ...	do.	0
Native Christians,	714 : ...	do.	515
Communicants,	331 : ...	do.	302

MISSIONARIES OF THE SOCIETY.

Kiehne, A. A. 1871. H. 1878-79. Ad. *Naidupett, Madras P.*

Mylius, August. B. Nov. 20, 1819, at Baneik, Hanover. E. at Gottingen: O. at Ratzeburg, 1846. A. in connection with the Leipzig Society March 5, 1847: R. to Europe, sick in 1847. Rt. in 1866 as Senior to the Hermannsburg Society and has labored since at Naidupett. Ad. *Naidupett, Madras P.*

Petersen, Thomas Friedrich. B. Haderleben, Germany, Dec. 17, 1838. O. Hanover, 1866. A. Sept. 2, 1866. S. Gudur, 1867-72; Venkatagiri, 1872-75; Naidupett, since 1878. H. to Germany, 1875-77, L. Biblical History, Telugu. Ad. *Naidupett, Madras P.*

Petersen, Paul Otto. B. in Schleswig, Germany, Jan. 24, 1844. O. Hanover, March 12, 1875: A. Sept. 26, 1875. S. Naidupett and Tirupati. Ad. *Tirupati, Madras P.*

Rammee, Heinrich. B. Hanover, Dec. 16, 1851. A. Jan. 24, 1880. O. Naidupett, June 24, 1880. Ad. *Tirupati, Madras P.*

Schepman, G. A. 1871. Ad. *Kalastry, Madras P.*

Scriba, Carl. B. in Germany. O. July 22, 1867. A. Feb. 22, 1868. S. Gudur, 1868-69, since, Sulurpett. Ad. *Sulurpett, Madras P.*

Worrlein. Johann. B. at Windsheim, Bavaria, Oct. 22, 1837. E. at the Mission Institute, Hermannsburg; ordained by the General Superintendent, Dr. Niemann, at Hanover, July 22, 1867. A. Feb. 21, 1868. M. Oct. 24, 1873. S. Calastry, Feb. 1873 to June, 1877; Tirupati, 1877-79, since, Vakadu. Ad. *Vakadu, Madras P.*

CHAPTER XXVII.

FRIENDS' FOREIGN MISSION ASSOCIATION.

THE first missionary of this Society sent to India was Miss Rachel Metcalfe, to Benares in October, 1866. Three years later Mr. Elkanah Beard and his wife from America joined the Mission, but on account of ill health were obliged to return home in 1872. The Mission had meanwhile been transferred to Jubbulpore. Mr. Charles Gayford came out in 1873, and in 1874 the Mission was moved to Sohagpur. Here one of the first conversions took place, that of a young Brahmin. The Mission was finally fixed in 1875 at Hoshungabad, the important towns of Sohagpur, Itarsi, and Seonee being still frequently visited for bazaar preaching. The foundation stone of the mission-house at Hoshungabad was laid early in 1876. Mr. Gayford left for England in the spring of 1879. The Mission had meanwhile been strengthened by the arrival from England of Mr. Samuel Baker and Mr. John H. Williams in December, 1878. There are now 13 Native members. Boys' and Girls' day-schools and Sunday-schools are in full operation, and a handsome church-building has been erected in the city, which was opened in November, 1880.

[H. S. N.]

MEMBERS OF THE MISSION.

BAKER, SAMUEL. B. Clontarf, Dublin, April 21, 1856. Not O. A. Dec. 1878. Ad. *Hoshungabad, C. P.*

WILLIAMS, JOHN HANDAYSIDE. B at Edinburgh, Feb. 22, 1841. A Dec. 1878. Not O. Ad. *Hoshungabad, C. P.*

RETIRED MISSIONARIES.

Elkanah Beard. A. 1869. S. Benares. Ret. to America in 1872.

Charles Gayford. A. 1873, S. Jubbulpore and Hoshungabad. Ret. to Eng. in 1879.

---o---

CHAPTER XXVIII.

THE INDIAN HOME MISSION TO THE SANTALS.

THIS interesting and flourishing Mission was begun in 1867 by the Rev. Messrs. Boerresen and Skrefsrud, the one a Dane, the other a Norwegian. It is not connected with any Missionary Society. Concerning its methods of work and present status one of the missionaries gives the following account:

"We work on the principle of preaching: to concentrate our labor in a certain limited circle, hoping when the people therein are Christianized they will spread the Gospel of their own accord in all directions, the circle being our stronghold: we endeavor to get the converts (who are not taken to the station but remain in their villages and calling) to extend the Kingdom of Christ gratis: we attach ourselves in our preaching to the traditions of the people in which traces are found of the original light of God. We have almost exclusively Christian schools: we believe in the missionary living only in the very midst of the people, not in civil stations, hence we live by ourselves surrounded only by Santals: we do not direct our preaching to the individual principally, but to the individual as one of the people, *i. e.* our endeavor is to impress the people —"Ye men of Santalistan"—and get them to act and react upon one another. By a council some five or six years ago we got the heathen to agree not to put the Christians out of the community, but to eat with them and even to intermarry if any one should choose to do so, on the principle that the Christians worship the creator of heaven and earth, of which their traditions tell: our Christians do not intermarry with them (they keep the heathen partner) but by heathen decree it is open to them. We have a nominal Christian population of about 6,000: commmunicants, about 2,100. The Christians live in about 150 villages and are divided into 30 churches: the Christian Government Patshala masters look after them and hold service gratis. We have two ordained Santal helpers: 30 Elders who visit all the churches; and 10

Deaconesses to visit their own sex; the first of these get two rupees a month for a time and the latter, one rupee: these are the only ones paid for religious work, and as we are getting better off Elders and the churches stronger we will do away with even this pay.

We have one principal station, Ebenezer, and five out-stations: three missionaries and two European school-masters, two training schools, one containing 55 boys, the other, 63 girls; and 32 village schools. Grammar, Dictionary, school-books, works on Traditions and Institutions have been prepared, but not all printed, as is the case with the New Testament and a larger Hymn-book with notes. A printing-press was presented to the Mission in 1880 by friends at home."

[L. O. S.]

The statistics mentioned above indicate the following progress since 1871 :—

Native Ordained Agents,	2 :	increase,	2
Native Christians,	7,000 :	do.	6,965
Communicants,	2,756 :	do.	2,065

MISSIONARIES OF THE MISSION.

Boerresen, Hans Peter. B. in Copenhagen, Nov. 29, 1825. O. in Copenhagen. A. in connection with Gossner's Society, April 6, 1865. In 1867 helped to found the Santal Mission. Has since labored at Ebenezer. H. to Europe, 1876-77. Is Secretary and Treasurer of the Mission. Ad. *Ebenezer*, (*via* Rampore Haut, E. I. R.) *Bengal.*

Bunkholdt, W. T. A. in Dec. 1874 to labor as a school-master. Is a Norwegian. Ad. *Ebenezer, Bengal.*

Jensen, M. C. Ad. *Asanbani, Bengal.*

Muston, Harington James. B. at Midnapore, July 11, 1846. A. Dec. 11, 1866, joined the Mission Feb 26, 1878. Has labored since at Ebenezer. Ad. *Ebenezer, Bengal.*

Seeram. O. in 1875. Ad. *Aludoha, Ebenezer, Bengal.*

Skrefsrud, L. O. A. in connection with Gossner's Society in 1865. In 1867 became one of the founders of the Santal Mission. Has prepared a Grammar, Dictionary and several other books in Santali. In 1873 failing health compelled him to proceed to Europe on furlough: R. in Dec. 1874. Ad. *Ebenezer*, (*via* Rampore Haut, E. I. R.) *Bengal.*

Soorjoo. O. in 1875. Ad. *Naya Dumka, Ebenezer, Bengal.*

———o———

CHAPTER XXIX.

THE CANADIAN BAPTIST TELUGU MISSION.

THIS Mission was established about 1868 by the Rev. Thomas Gabriel, who resigned a Government situation and began traveling among the villages and preaching to the Telugus, being dependent upon his own resources. In 1870 he was ordained as an evangelist at Madras. He continued to labor, and his membership increased to 150, with several teachers and preachers. Funds failing, the Mission was offered through the Rev. J. McLaurin to the Baptists of Canada, who took it up and appointed Mr. McLaurin to Cocanada in March, 1874.

The Mission became more distinctly Canadian in 1875, by the co-operative union entered into by the Baptists of the Western and Maritime Provinces of the dominion, which resulted in sending out four families. These with the missionaries from Western Canada constitute the "Canadian Baptist Telugu Mission."

The work of the Mission is now carried on in various places from the Kistna river to Orissa and in the Jeypore country. Five stations have been occupied.

The following statistics indicate the progress since 1871 :—

Foreign Missionaries,	7 :	increase	7.
Native Christians,	1,000	do.	900.
Communicants,	473	do.	430.

MEMBERS OF THE MISSION.

ARMSTRONG, W. F. A. 1875. S. Chicacole. *Now in Europe.*

CHURCHILL, GEORGE. B. Hartford, Nova Scotia, Jan. 18, 1842. O. Aug. 12, 1873. A. July 10, 1875. S. first Siam, afterwards, Bobbili. H. to Australia, 1876. Ad. *Bobbili, Vizagapatam, Madras P.*

CRAIG, JOHN. B. Yorkville, Canada, June 4, 1852. O. Nov. 17, 1876. A. Jan. 4, 1878. S. Cocanada, 1878-80, Akidu, since Nov. 1880. Ad. *Akidu, Godavery, Madras P.*

CURRIE, GEORGE F. B. Fredericton, N. B., March 8, 1844. O. at Andover, N. B. July 29, 1874. A. Feb. 12, 1876. S. Cocanada, 1876, Tuni, 1878. Ad *Tuni, Godavery, Madras P.*

McLAURIN, JOHN. B. Aug. 9, 1839, Carleton County, Ontario, Canada. Called to the ministry in 1863. Graduated at Col. in 1868. O. July 24, 1868. M. Oct. 12, 1869. Pastoral work at home between one and two years. A. Feb. 11, 1870. Labored in connection with the A. B. M. U. at Ramapatam two years, and at Ongole two years : work, wholly ver. In March, 1874, took charge of the mission at Cocanada, where he has since labored, teaching and preaching both in Engl. and ver. Ad. *Cocanada, Madras P.*

SANFORD, RUFUS. B. Cornwallis, Nova Scotia, April 7, 1842. O. Billtown, Cornwallis, Aug. 20, 1873. A. at Rangoon Jan. 21, 1874, at Cocanada, July 24, 1875. Ad. *Bimlipatam, Madras P.*

TIMPANY, AMERICAS V. B. Dec. 21, 1840, at Vienna, Ontario, Canada. Licensed in 1860. Took literary and Theol. courses at Woodstock, Ontario. Pastoral work for two years in Western Ontario. O. at Brantford Oct. 14, and M. Oct. 15, 1867. A. in connection with A. B. M. U. April 5, 1868. S. Nellore, 1868-70 : Ramapatam, 1870-76 : In 1876 joined the Canabian Mission. W. ver. L. " Compendium of Theology" (Telugu), Madras. Ad. *Cocanada, Madras P.*

DECEASED NATIVE PREACHER.

Thomas Gabriel. Converted early in life and joined the Evangelical Lutheran Church at Rajamandry. He was at this time connected with the telegraph department. While in Madras, in 1867, he united with the Baptist Church. On returning to Cocanada he began preaching and in order to devote himself wholly to this work he resigned his position. He joined the mission of the Plymouth Brethren at Nursapur, where he labored about a year. After this he labored independently. O. as an evangelist at Madras in 1870, and continued to labor at Cocanada until his death, Jan. 1. 1875.

---o---

CHAPTER XXX.

THE GERMAN EVANGELICAL MISSIONARY SOCIETY.

THE German Evangelical Mission Society in the United States of America was organized in 1866. It is supported by German Congregations of different denominations, as Germans, Dutch Reformed, German Presbyterians and Evangelicals, etc. Its operations are confined to India, where it began its labors in 1869, sending the Rev. Oscar Lohr to open the Mission. He arrived at Raepore, Central Provinces in 1869, and bought a tract of waste land about 36 miles distant, and built mission houses: he collected a number of young Chamars who were trained as school-masters and are now, after having been converted, employed as school-masters, readers and catechists. A colony of Christian cultivators was also founded, and several schools established in surrounding villages. Since 1870 four missionarios sent out to assist Mr. Lohr, have been obliged on account of sickness to leave the country. A mission was subsequently opened at Raepore.

The following statistics (for 1880) denote the progress since 1871:

Missionaries,	2:	increase.	
Native Christians,	330:	do.	256
Communicants,	125:	do.	106

MISSIONARIES OF THE SOCIETY.

LOHR, THEODORE OSCAR. B. in Silesia, Prussia, March 24, 1824. In 1850 was sent to I. by the Rev. Mr. Gossner to join the Mission among the Kols in Chota Nagpore, where he labored until the Mutiny in 1858. Went that year to America and labored as minister of the German Reformed Church in the state of New Jersey. In 1868 was sent out again to India by the German Evangelical Society (U. S. A.) to establish a Mission in some part of India unoccupied by any Society. A. in Raepore May, 1869, where he has since labored. W. entirely ver. L. (1) *A Hindee Catechism:* (2) *A Hindee Hymn-book:* (3) *A Hindee Primer:* Mission Press, Bisrampore. Ad. *Bisrampore, (Raepore District) C. P.*

STOLL, A. Ad. *Raepore, C. P.*

RETIRED MISSIONARIES.

J. Hauser, A. in 1873. R. to America in 1876.

J. J. Weiss. A. in 1874. R. to America in 1876.

———o———

CHAPTER XXXI.

The Canadian Presbyterian Mission.

The Presbyterian Church in Canada was formed June 15, 1875 by the union of four branches of the Presbyterian denomination, representing in the Eastern and Western Provinces respectively the Church of Scotland and the non-established Presbyterian Churches of the parent countries. Before the union, missionaries from two of these had at different times laboured in India in connection with other churches, and three had Missions in the South Seas and elsewhere, but they had no Mission in India. Steps were however being taken in that direction, the largest of the four having had Indore State suggested to it as a field by other Missions in India, and the matter having so far been taken up that the Rev. J. F. Campbell, one of the present staff, had been invited to become the first missionary. Circumstances at the time prevented, and in June, 1875 he was appointed so labour in alliance with the Church of Scotland among the educated natives in Madras, on which work he entered in December, 1876.

Meanwhile the Rev. J. M. Douglass was appointed to the projected mission in Central India: he arrived in Bombay in December, 1876, and in Indore in January, 1877. Mr. Campbell, in accordance with his instructions finding that he was more needed in the new field, in July of the same year removed to Mhow. In December, 1879 the Mission was strengthened by the coming of the Rev. John Wilkie.

The field is large and populous and the people generally accessible. The work is prosecuted by the same means as in other Missions; preaching, schools, zenana visitation, itinerancy, dissemination of Scriptures and tracts, and the dispensing of medicines—the last especially by Mr. Wilkie who took a partial Medical course in Edinburgh. A Press was early started by Mr. Douglass in Indore which has been employed principally in printing small portions of scripture for gratuitons distribution. Ten adults and thirteen children have been baptized. About thirty Native Christians are connected with the Mission.

[J. F. C.]

MEMBERS OF THE MISSION.

CAMPBELL, JAMES FRASER. B. Baddeck, Nova Scotia, Canada, Oct. 16, 1845. O. Oct. 19, 1871. A. Dec. 6, 1876. S. Madras, until May, 1877, since, Mhow. Ad. *Mhow, C. P.*

DOUGLASS, J. M. A. in Dec. 1876. Began the Mission at Indore in Jan. 1877. Ad. *Indore, C. P.*

WILKIE, JOHN. B. Fifeshire, Scotland, Aug. 2, 1851. O. Guelph, Canada, Sept. 10, 1879. A. Dec. 22, 1879. Ad. *Indore, C. P.*

———o———

CHAPTER XXXII.

SWEDISH EVANGELICAL MISSIONARY SOCIETY.

THIS Society has its head quarters at Stockholm. In 1877 it sent to India four missionaries, who spent some time at Chindwara, studying the vernacular. At the close of 1878 two stations were occupied, Saugor and Narsinghpur. Another laborer arrived in 1878, and a sixth, in 1880.

A vernacular school has been opened at Saugor. At present the Native Christian community consists of 8, of whom 5 are communicants.

MISSIONARIES OF THE SOCIETY.

CARLSSON, P. A. Dec. 1880. Ad. *Narsinghpur, C. P.*

DANIELSSON, ANDERS GUSTAF. B. Westgotland, Sweden, Dec. 23, 1849. E. Mission Col. Stockholm. A. Dec. 14, 1877. Not O. Ad *Saugor, C. P.*

EDMAN, L. A. B. Dec. 1877. Ad. *Narsinghpur, C. P.*

ERIKSSON, E. M. A. Dec. 1877. Ad. *Do. Do.*

LUNDBORG, N. E. A. Dec. 1878. Ad. *Do. Do.*

UNGERTH, L. E. A. Dec. 1877. Ad. *Saugor, C. P.*

---o---

CHAPTER XXXIII.

PRIVATE AND INDEPENDENT MISSIONS.

I. THE GODAVERY DELTA MISSION.

THE idea of this Mission originated with the late Mr. A.N. Groves, who, returning to England from India about 1834, induced Messrs. William Bowdon and George Beer to come to India and labor among the Telugus. They arrived at Masulipatam in August 1836, and in 1837 began the Mission at Narsapur. They continued preaching and teaching six years before the first convert was gained. There has been a gradual increase in the number of converts since.

Mr. Beer died in 1853 and Mr. Bowden, in 1876 : they have been succeeded by their sons.

An Anglo-vernacular school has been established at Narsapur : also a Boarding-school. There are several village schools. A monthly Telugu newspaper is conducted by one of the missionaries.

The statistics are about the same as in 1871 : there are six European missionaries (unordained) : 1,000 Native Christians : 350 communicants.

MEMBERS OF THE MISSION.

BEER, CHARLES HENRY. A. 1866. Ad. *Narsapur, Madras P.*

BEER, JOHN WILLIAM. A. 1861. Ad. *Do. Do.*

BORDEN, EDWIN SKINNER. B. in Masulipatam, Oct. 26, 1845. Went to Eng. in 1851. Rt. 1870. Joined the Mission in June, 1876. Ad. *Narsapur, Madras P.*

HEELIS, THOMAS. Joined the Mission in 1855. W. preaching. Ad *Narsapur, Madras P.*

MACRAE, F. A. Dec. 1876. Ad. *Narsapur, Madras P.*

MILES, E. Joined the Mission Jan. 1881. Ad. *Do. Do.*

II. THE RAMPORE BAULEAH MISSION.

THIS Mission was founded in 1862 by the Rev. Bihari Lal Singh (*vide* p. 123), on behalf of the Presbyterian Church of England. He labored here twelve years and died in 1874. After his death the Mission was without a missionary four years.

At the close of 1877, Dr. D. Morison arrived and has since had charge. At present the Native Christian community numbers 32: communicants, 18. There are several schools with 164 pupils. In addition to evangelistic work there are two dispensaries.

MISSIONARY IN CHARGE.

MORISON, DONALD. (M. B. C. M.) B. Starnoway, (Island of Lewis) Scotland, 1846. Not O. A. Dec. 6, 1877. S. *Rampore Bauleah, Bengal.*

III. THE PUNRUTTI MISSION.

THIS Mission was commenced in May, 1871, by Mr. C. W. Reade. It was at first carried on by Native helpers: afterwards Miss C. M. Reade (accompanied by Miss Lowe) came out from England and took charge of the work. An orphanage has been established and a dispensary opened: there are two out stations. Much attention is given to open-air preaching. The Mission is conducted on the principles of the Plymouth Brethren.

At present the Native Christian community numbers 36: communicants, 28. Miss C. M. Reade has charge of the Mission. Ad. *Punrutti, Arcot, Madras P.*

IV. THE SEONI MISSION.

ANDERSON, GEORGE. O. 1871. A Dec. 13, 1871, being sent out by the Original Secession Synod of Scotland. Founded the Seoni Mission in 1871. W. has been chiefly ver. also, some Engl. preaching. An orphanage was formed in 1875. The number of Native Christians in 1880 was 34. H. to Europe Sept. 18, 1879. Ad. *Seoni, (Chhapara) C. P.*

V. THE GOPALGUNGE MISSION.

BOSE, MATHOORA NATH. B. in Jessore, 1843. O. in the Free Mission Church, Calcutta, March 2, 1874. Set apart to labor among the Chandals of Gopalgunge, Farreedpore, where he has since been stationed. During the year 1875 he baptized 11 persons, who form the nucleus of a Christian community. At present there are 60 Native Christians, of whom 30 are communicants. Ad. *Gopalgunge, Bengal.*

VI. THE ELLICHPOOR MISSION.

THIS Mission was commenced in 1875 by the Rev. A. Norton. During 1875, 20 Koorkoos were baptized. Another laborer arrived in 1878 and the work was extended. An orphanage has been established. At present there are 11 Native Christians connected with the Mission.

MEMBERS OF THE MISSION.

NORTON, ALBERT. E. at Evanston, Ill. U. S. A., graduating from the Northwestern Univ. and, in 1872, from Garrett Biblical Institute. A. in Nov. 1872, being connected with the Methodist Episcopal Church Mission. Labored several months at Bombay and afterwards in Central India. In 1874-75 he opened an independent mission at Ellichpoor, withdrawing from the Methodist Church. H. to America in Aug. 1879. Ad. *Alabama, Genesee Co., N. Y., U. S. A.*

SIBLEY, JAMES WILLIE. B. Litchfield, Ohio, U. S. A., 1847. O. Litchfield, 1877. A. March, 1878. Ad. *Ellichpoor, E. Berar.*

VII. BETHEL MISSION, JAMTARA.

HAEGERT, ALBERT RUDOLPH ERNST. Born November 2, 1844, at Auclam, Germany. Arrived in India May 21, 1868. Was engaged in business four years and left the Public Works Department in January, 1873 to join the Indian Home Mission to the Santals. In April, 1875 opened an independent mission among the Santals, at Bethel. During 1875 baptized 15 persons. The Mission is supported by private funds and subscriptions. It now has 1 training and 2 village schools, 1 church, 1 Native pastor and 15 Native Christians. Address, *Bethel*, (near Jamtara) *Bengal.*

VIII. MISSION TO LEPERS IN INDIA.

THIS Mission was commenced by Mr. W. C. Bailey, a missionary of the Church of Scotland, in March, 1878: head-quarters, Dublin. Its objects are, to relieve the sufferings of, and preach the Gospel to, lepers in India: the work is carried on by aiding existing Leper Asylums in connection with various Missions and building other Asylums where necessary. At present operations are carried on at Chumba, Almorah, Sabathu and Amballa. In all there are 105 Native Christians, connected with the various Missions laboring in these places. Mr. W. C. Bailey is Hon. Sec. for India. Ad. *Chumba, Himalayas.*

IX. FREE METHODIST CHURCH MISSION.

THIS Church (U. S. A.) has no Foreign Missionary Society. In 1880, however, it sent its first missionary to India, the Rev. E. F. Ward. At present he is at Ellichpoor, studying the language, and has not yet decided what field to occupy.

MISSIONARY IN CHARGE.

WARD, E. F. B. at Elgin, Ill., U. S. A., April 25, 1853. O. Oct. 10, 1880. A. Jan. 16, 1881. Ad. *Ellichpoor, E. Berar.*

X. THE AGRA MEDICAL MISSION.

Valentine, Colin Strachan. (L. R. C. S. Ed., L. R. C. P. Ed.) B. Brechin, Forfarshire, Scotland, June 7, 1834. A. as Medical missionary of the United Presbyterian Church of Scotland, Nov. 12, 1861. S. Beawar, 1862-66, Jeypore, 1866-78. Went to Scotland in 1879. R. to I. in 1881, as Superintendent, Agra Medical Missionary Training Inst. L. Several Hindi and Urdu Tracts. Ad. *Agra.*

XI. OTHERS.

Banerjea, Chandra Nath. B. Kalighat, 1836. E. at L. M. S. Inst. Calcutta, (B. A. 1871). O. in connection with L. M. S. at Union Chapel, Calcutta, 1860. S. Behala, 1860-69; self-supporting missionary at Allahabad, five years: for several years has served as Pastor of an Independent Bengali Congregation at Calcutta. L. Bengali, "Khrista Sangit," a hymn-book, and "Beerangona Upakhayan," a brief account of Indian Female celebrities. Edited one year "*Pakhik Sambad,*" a Bengal Periodical, and one year "*Bongo-Meheer,*" and "*Satya Pradeep,*" (Lamp of Truth) three years. Translated, for C. V. E. S. "Hints on Education," and "Third Book." Ad. *Bhowanipore, Calcutta.*

Hobbs, William Ayers. B. Margate, Kent, April 12, 1828. O. Margate, July, 1859. A. Dec. 11, 1859. S. Jessore 1859-69; H. to Eng. 1869-71; Beerbhoom, 1871-76. Resigned in 1876 on account of bad health. Rt. 1879 as a private missionary. L. (1) "Christianity God's Revelation to man" (in Engl.); (2) "The Gospel in Twenty paragraphs" (Engl. and Bengali); (3) "An aid to Light and Life," (Engl. and Bengali); Calcutta. Ad. *Calcutta.*

Scudder, Henry Martyn Esq., m. d. B. March 23, 1851, at Arcot. E. in America, receiving the degree of M. D. in July, 1874. M. 1873. A. Nov. 18, 1874. S. Ranipett, 1874-80 in charge of civil and mission dispensary. W. Engl. and ver. Left the Mission Oct. 1, 1880. Ad. *Coonoor, Madras P.*

CHAPTER XXXIV.

DISCONTINUED MISSIONS.

I. MADRAS MISSION, AMERICAN BOARD.

THIS Mission was founded in 1836, the Rev. Messrs. Winslow and Scudder being designated by the Ceylon Mission to open the work. They arrived in Madras in September, 1836, and took up their residences, the one at Chintadrepettah, the other at Royapuram. Dr. Scudder devoted himself chiefly to preaching tours, and Mr. Winslow was mainly employed on a revision of the Tamil Scriptures. In 1838 a printing establishment was purchased of the Church Missionary Society, and in 1840, Mr. Hunt arrived as a printer. Thousands of Scripture portions in various native languages were printed at the expense of Bible and Tract Societies. In 1842 a church was erected at Royapuram. About this time the Mission was reinforced from Ceylon and Madura. In 1848 a house of worship was opened at Chintadropettah. Including children the two congregations at Madras numbered 1,000. Dr. Scudder and Mr. Winslow continued the chief workers of the Mission. The former while recruiting his health at the Cape of Good Hope ended his labors in January, 1855. In the same year Mr. Winslow visited America, returning in 1858. About 1855 the English portion of the printing establishment was sold. The vernacular department was carried forward with great energy and success. In 1858 the printing of the Scriptures in Tamil amounted to 14,000,000 pages. In 1862 Mr. Winslow's Tamil and English Dictionary was completed, an elaborate and useful work. On account of failing health Mr. Winslow sailed for America in August, 1864, but died on the way, at Cape Town in October of the same year. Soon after Mr. Hunt was obliged to return to America to recruit his health, and as he was the only remaining missionary and as it was thought that the Mission had accomplished its object, the Board decided to relinquish the field. From July, 1848 to December, 1864 the printing amounted to 228,000,000 pages of Scripture;

106,000,000 pages of tracts, and 110,000,000 of other works; in all 454,000,000 pages. The English department had been sold and the vernacular was now made over to the Society for Promoting Christian Knowledge. The Chintadrepettah station was transferred to the Church Missionary Society and the church building at Royapuram to the Medical Missionary Society of Edinburgh. The schools and converts were also made over to other Societies, and the Board thus withdrew from the field.

MEMBERS OF THE MISSION.

John Scudder, M. D. B. Sept. 3, 1793, at Freehold, Monmouth Co., N. J., U. S A. Graduated at Princeton Col. in 1813, and afterwards at the New York Medical Col. United with the Reformed Dutch Church while in New York. Gave up his medical practice to come to I. Sailed (under the auspices of the American Board) from Boston June 8, 1819: arrived at Calcutta in Oct. of the same year and soon after proceeded to Ceylon. His first station was Panditeripo, where he removed in July, 1820. Aug. 8, 1820 he was licensed to preach. He labored in Ceylon until 1836; at Madras from 1836. H. to America, 1841. While in America, 1842-46, he traveled extensively making missionary addresses. Rt. in March, 1847. Soon after his return he proceeded to Madura, where he labored until 1849 when he returned to Madras. After the death of his wife in Nov. 1849, his health was very poor, and in 1854 he consented to take a sea voyage. He reached the Cape of Good Hope in November, 1854. His health improving, he had engaged his return passage, when on 13th of Jan. 1855, he passed away to his eternal reward. (*See Memoir.*)

Miron Winslow, D. D. Joined the Ceylon Mission Feb. 18, 1820. H. to America in 1834. With Dr. Scudder opened the Madras Mission in 1836. Early in 1856 he again visited America, returning in 1858: while at home the degree of Doctor of Divinity was conferred upon him by Harvard College. He continued his literary labors until 1864, when his health gave way and he was obliged to leave India. He embarked Aug. 20, 1864 and reached Cape Town on the 20th of October, but in an exhausted condition. He died two days after his arrival, at the age of seventy-five. While in I. for many years he was Secretary of the Revision and Publication Committee of the Madras Bible Society, and gave much attention to this work. He compiled a Tamil and English Dictionary, and also wrote one or more books in English.

Samuel Hutchings. A. in Ceylon Oct. 28. 1833. Joined the Madras Mission in April, 1842. R. to America broken in health in 1843.

Phinehas R. Hunt, Esq. A. at Madras, March 19, 1840, and took charge of the printing establishment of the Mission. He labored here continuously and successfully until 1866 when failing health obliged him to return to America. In June, 1868 he proceeded to China and took charge of the Mission Press at Peking. D. in 1879.

John W. Dulles. A. at Madras Feb. 20, 1849. Ret. 1852, to America.

Isaac Newton Hurd. A. at Madras July, 1852. Labored here until Aug. 27, 1858, when he Ret. to America.

II. MR. START'S MISSION.

Among the private efforts made to establish Missions in India that of the Rev. William Start deserves a prominent place. A man of means and of zealous missionary spirit, he applied to Pastor Gossner of Berlin for missionaries and promised to defray the expense out of his own purse. His idea was to form a mission on the self-supporting, Moravian plan: the candidates were to be supported only till they could earn their own living, and then their earnings were to form a common store and they were to preach to the heathen. The plan had to be abandoned: but Mr. Start's object was not altogether fruitless, several of the missionaries entering business and doing good missionary work besides, in various places, until their removal by death, though not in connection with the Mission. In other cases it was found better to leave the missionaries free from secular work and to support them. Their work was all vernacular. At first the work was only in the Plains, Hajipur being the chief station. Thence it extended to Chupra, and other stations, and in 1841, to the Darjeeling Hills. The first missionaries were the Revs. Brice and Kalberer, followed by three other companies in 1838, 1839 and 1840.

Mr. Start was himself a laborer in the Indian mission field some years, working in the Plains in the cold months and in the Hills in the hot. His health failing, he returned to England in 1852. From that time the work was carried on by the Rev. C. J. Niebel, who translated portions of the Scriptures and wrote several tracts in Lepcha and Nepalese, and was engaged in preaching and itinerating among the Hill tribes.

The Mission maintained close relations with Gossner's Mission, many of the missionaries joining this, when Mr. Start was no longer able to support them.

[A W.]

MEMBERS OF THE MISSION.

Name.		Year of Arrival.	Field of Labor.		Remarks.
Nathaniel Brice,	...		Patna,	etc.	D.——.
Louis Kalberer,	...		Do.	do.	*Vide* P. 16
A. McCumby,	...		Dinapur,	do.	Do. 25
Louis Brandin,	...	1831	Hajipur,	do.	Do. 173
G. Trentler,	...	1838	Do.	do.	
Joachim Stolke,	...	1838	Do.	do.	
Andrew Wernicke,	...	1838	Do.	do.	
Gustav Holzenberg,	...	1838	Do.	do.	
Charles Baumann,	...	1838	Do.	do.	Do. 173
——Paproth,	...	1838	Do.		Do. 173
H. Heinig,	...	1836	Do.	do.	Do. 15
W. Rebsch,	...	1838	Do.		Do. 87
——Maass,	...	1838	Do.		Do. 173
Charles Stulpnagel,	...	1838	Do.	do.	Do. 173
Charles Damenberg,	...	1838	Do.	do.	
——Kluge,	...	1839	Do.		Do. 173
——Schorisch,	...	1839	Do.	do.	Do. 173
W. Sternberg,	...	1839	Do.	do.	Do. 173
A. Rudolph,	...	1839	Do.	do.	Do. 136
J. F. Ullmann,	...	1839	Do.	do.	Do. 136
J. D. Prochnow,	...	1840	Do.	do.	Do. 92
——Schultze,	...	1840	Do.	do.	
Charles G. Niebel,	...	1840	Do.	do.	D. 1865.

APPENDICES.

I. THE MARTYRED MISSIONARIES OF 1857.

Names.	Society or Mission.	Station.
J. E. and Mrs. Freeman, ...	American Presbyterian Mission,	Futtegurh.
D. E. and Mrs. Campbell, ...	Do. do. do.	do.
A. O. and Mrs Johnson, ...	Do. do. do.	do.
R. and Mrs. McMullin, ...	Do. do. do.	do.
W. H. and Mrs. Haycock, ...	Gospel Propagation Society,	Cawnpore.
H. E. Cockey, ...	Do. do. do.	do.
A. R. Hubbard, ...	Do. do. do.	Delhi.
D. C. Sandys, ...	Do. do. do.	do.
——Cocks, ...	Do. do. do.	do.
Louis Koch, ...	Do. do. do.	do.
T. and Mrs. Hunter, ...	Church of Scotland Mission,	Sealkote.
J. Mackay, ...	Baptist Missionary Society,	Delhi.

II. MISSIONARIES OF WOMAN'S SOCIETIES.

FREE CHURCH OF SCOTLAND.

NAME.		ARRIVED.	REMARKS.
Miss Laing,	...	1843	Ret. 1857.
Miss J. Shaw,	...	1844	M. 1846.
Miss Locker,	...	1846	Now Mrs. J. Anderson.
Miss Adamson,	...	1848	M. 1850.
Miss J. McCarter,	...	1856	Ret. 1862.
Miss Goulding,	...	1858	D. 1861.
Miss A. Laird,	...	1858	M. 1863.
Miss Don,	...	1859	D. 1860.
Miss E. Macniven,	..	1863	Ret. 1867.
Miss M. Urquhart,	...	1863	Do. 1868.
Miss Taylor,	...	1864	Do. 1870.
Miss C. Ewing,	...	1867	M. 1870.
Miss Brown,	...	1870	Ret. 1875.
Miss J. Sloan,	...	1872	M. 1873.
Miss Liddell,	...	1874	D. 1875.
Miss Griffin,	...	1875	Ret. 1877.
Miss E. MacRitchie,	...	1875	M. 1877.
Miss A. Ross,	...	1875	M. 1877.
Miss Berrie,	...	1876	Ret. 1878.
Miss A. Small,	...	1876	Chindwara, C. P.
Miss Manson,	...	1876	Now Mrs. K. S. Macdonald.
Miss Hubbard,	..	1876	Calcutta.
Miss Skirving,	...	1877	Do.
Miss Mackay,	...	1877	Bombay.
Miss J. Paterson,	...	1878	Do.
Miss C. Paterson,	...	1878	Do.
Miss Duncan,	...	1878	Do.
Miss L. J. Wolff,	...	1878	Madras.
Miss Warrack,	...	1880	Calcutta.

FREE BAPTIST MISSION.

NAME.	ARRIVED.	WORK.	STATION.
Miss L. Crawford, ...	1851	Orphanage,	Jellasore.
Miss S. L. Cilley, ...	1873	Zenana,	Ret. 1876.
Miss S. R. Libbey, ...	1874	Do.	D. 1877.
Miss M. E. French, ...	1874	Do.	Ret. 1876.
Miss M. W. Bacheler,	1876	Do.	Midnapore.
Miss I. O. Phillips, ...	1877	Do.	Balasore,
Miss H. P. Phillips, ...	1878	Schools,	Midnapore.
Miss B. J. Hooper, ...	1878	Do.	Do.
SOCIETY FOR PROMOTING FEMALE EDUCATION IN THE EAST.			
Miss Packer,* ...	1854	Zenana,	Cuttack.
Miss Hart,† ...	1859	Superintendent,	Madras.
Miss Jerrom,‡ ...	1860	Zenana,	Ret. May, 1879.
Miss Davidson, ...	1869	Do.	Agra.
Miss Andrews, ...	1869	Do.	Lodiana.
Mdlle. Ponsaz, ...	1872	Do.	D ——.
Miss Needham, ...	1872	Do.	Ret.——.
Miss Leigh, ...	1872	Teaching,	Cuttack.
Miss Bland, ...	1874	Zenana,	Agra.
Miss F. Andrews, ...	1875	Teaching,	Ret.——.
Miss Greenfield, ...	1875	Zenana,	Lodiana.
Miss E. Davidson, ...	1875	Do.	M.——.
Miss Thorn, ...	1875	Do.	Delhi.
Miss Reuther, ...	1877	Do.	Lodiana.
Miss West, ...	1878	Teaching,	Do.
Miss Briggs, ...	1880	Zenana,	Mooltan.

* Calcutta, 1854-61 ; 1861-67, Berhampore ; 1867-74, Piplee ; H. to Eng. 1874-75 ; since, Cuttack.
† Landour, 1859-70.
‡ Amritsar, 1860-66.

NAME.	YEAR OF ARRIVAL.	WORK.	STATION OR REMARKS.
AMERICAN PRESBYTERIAN MISSION.			
Mrs. Scott, ..	1854	Teaching,	Landour.
Miss Beatty, ..	1864	Do.	D. 1870.
Miss J. Woodside, ..	1867	Teaching, Zenana,	Futteguth.
Miss Thiede, ..	1868	Teaching, Zenana,	Lahore.
Miss M. Wilson, ..	1869	Medical,	D. 1879.
Miss M. Craig, ..	1870	Teaching,	Dehra.
Miss J. A. Nelson, ..	1870	Teaching,	Ret. 1878.
Miss M. E. Pratt, ..	1872	Teaching,	Dehra.
Miss J. W. Bacon, ..	1872	Do.	Kasauli.
Mrs. Warren, ..	1872	Zenana,	Gwalior.
Miss S. Seward, M. D.	1873	Zenana,	Allahabad.
Miss L. M. Campbell,	1874	Teaching, Zenana	Ret. 1878.
Miss A. Campbell, ..	1874	Do. Do.	Ret. 1878.
Miss A. E. Scott, ..	1874	Teaching,	Landour.
Mrs. S. J. Millar, ..	1874	Teaching, Zenana,	Ret. 1878.
Miss C. Beltz, ..	1875	Zenana,	Etawah, N. W. P.
Miss E. Walsh, ..	1876	Zenana,	Etawah.
Miss McGinnis, ..	1876	Do.	Kolhapur.
Miss A. Fullerton, ..	1877	Teaching,	Landour.
Miss S. Hutchison, ..	1879	Zenana,	Etawah.
Miss S. M. Wherry, ..	1879	Do.	Lodiana.
Miss I. Griffith, ..	1879	Teaching,	Landour.
Miss Seeley, ...	1879	Zenana,	Fattehgurh.
Miss F. Perley, ..	1879	Do.	Etawah.
Miss E. E. Patton, ..	1880	Do.	Panhalla.
AMERICAN UNITED PRESBYTERIAN MISSION.			
Miss E. G. Gordon * ..	1855	Zenana,	Sealkote.
Miss E. Calhoun, † ..	1870	Do.	Gujranawala.
Miss C. E. Wilson, ..	1875	Do.	Do.
Miss E. McCahon, ..	1875	School,	Sealkote.
Miss R.A. McCullough,	1879	Zenana,	Jhelum.
Miss E. E. Gordon, ..	1881	Medical,	Gurdaspur.

* H. 1864; and 1871-74.
† H. March, 1880.

Name.	Year of Arrival.	Work.	Station or Remarks.
Church of England Zenana Mission Society.			
Miss Blanford, ..	1863	Superintendent,	Trevandrum.
Miss Good, ..	1871	Zenana,	Barrackpore.
Miss Henderson, ..	1872	Supt. of School,	Amritsar.
Miss Wauton, ..	1872	Zenana,	Do.
Miss Raikes, ..	1874	Do.	Chinsurah.
Miss Branch, ..	1875	Do.	Jubbulpore.
Miss Thom, ..	1875	Do.	Kurrachee.
Miss Brandon, ..	1875	Do.	Masulipatam.
Miss I. Brandon, ..	1875	Do.	Do.
Miss Tucker, ..	1875	Do.	Batala.
Mrs. Lewis, ..	1875	Do.	Palamcottah.
Miss J. Thom, ..	1876	Do.	Kurrachee.
Miss Clay, ..	1876	Do.	Jhandiala.
Miss Axley, ..	1876	Do.	Madras.
Miss L. Axley, ..	1876	Do.	Do.
Miss Macdonald, ..	1877	Do.	Palamcottah.
Miss Gebrich, ..	1877	Do.	Do.
Miss Condon, ..	1877	Supt. of School,	Calcutta.
Miss Collisole, ..	1877	Zenana,	Krishnagar.
Miss Williamson, ..	1877	Do.	Jubbulpore.
Miss Haitz, ..	1877	Do.	Meerut.
Miss M. Smith, ..	1878	Do.	Amritsar.
Miss Hewlett, ..	1879	Medical,	Do.
Miss Hoernle, ..	1879	Zenana,	Meerut.
Miss Clifford, ..	1879	Do.	Agarpara.
Miss Gregg, ..	1879	Supt. of School,	Madras.
Miss Scott, ..	1879	Zenana,	Peshawar
Miss Clay, ..	1880	Do.	Jhandiala.
Miss Gorch, ..	1880	Do.	Do.
Miss Grime, ..	1880	School,	Amritsar.
Miss Vette, ..	1880	Do.	Do.
Miss F. Butler, ..	1880	Medical,	Jubbulpore.
Mrs. Webb, ..	1881	School,	Calcutta.
Miss Chettle, ..	1881	Zenana,	Barrackpore.
Miss Baily, ..	1881	Do.	Amritsar.

NAME.	YEAR OF ARRIVAL.	WORK.	STATION OR REMARKS.
AMERICAN UNION ZENANA MISSION.			
Miss H. G. Brittan, ..	1863	Superintendent,	Retired, 1877.
Mrs. Page, ..	1867	Orphanage,	Calcutta.
Miss L. M. Hook, ..	1868	Superintendent,	Do.
Miss C. Norris, ..	1868	Zenana,	Died in 1868.
Miss M. C. Lathrop, ..	1870	Zenana,	Allahabad.
Miss G. R. Ward, ..	1870	Do.	Cawnpore.
Miss E. Chase, ..	1870	Do.	Died, 1874.
Miss F. Seelye, M. D. ..	1871		Died, 1875.
Miss Harris, ..	1872	Zenana.	Retired.
Miss Smith, ..	1872	Do.	Calcutta.
Miss J. Kimball, ..	1875	Do.	Retired.
Miss E. Marston, ..	1875	Zenana,	Calcutta.
Miss L. Woodward, ..	1875	Do.	Retired.
Miss A. H. Jones, ..	1876	Zenana,	Allahabad.
Miss Gardner, ..	1879	Zenana,	Cawnpore.
AMERICAN BAPTIST MISSIONARY UNION.			
Mrs. J. P. Binney, ..		Zenana,	Rangoon.
Mrs. M. B. Ingalls, ..			Thongzai.
Miss S. B. Barrows, ..			Moulmain.
Miss M. Sheldon, ..			Do.
Miss E. H. Payne, ..			Do.
Miss S. J. Higby, ..			Do.
Miss E. Lawrence, ..			Do.
Miss E. E. Mitchell, M. D.			Do.
Miss A. M. Barkley, ..			Do.
Miss E. T. McAllister,			Bassein.
Miss I. Watson, ..			Do.
Miss K. Evans, ..			Thongzai.
Miss J. C. Brownley, ..			Prome.
Miss L. E. Rathbun, ..			Rangoon.
Miss A. L. Buell, ..			Do.
Miss L. E. Miller, ..			Tavoy.
Mrs. C. B. Thomas, ..			Henthada.
Miss H. N. Eastman, ..			Toungoo.
Miss E. O. Ambrose, ..			Do.

NAME.	YEAR OF ARRIVAL.	WORK.	STATION OR REMARKS.
Miss Palmer,			Toungoo.
Miss Rockwood,			Do,
Miss Upham,			
Miss M. Russell,			Tura, Assam.
Miss M. M. Day,			Nellore.
Miss M. Menke,	1880		Madras.
UNITED PRESBYTERIAN MISSION (SCOTLAND).			
Mrs. Drynan,	1866	School, Zenana.	Ajmere.
Miss Guillamet,	1874	Do. Do.	Beawar.
FRIENDS' MISSION.			
Miss R. Metcalfe,	1866	Zenana,	Hoshungabad.
THE AMERICAN BOARD.			
Miss M. S. Taylor,	1867	Teaching,	Mandapasalai, M.
Miss H. S. Rendall,	1870	Do.	Madura, do.
Mrs. W. B. Capron,	1871	Zenana,	Madura, do.
Miss S. F. Norris, M. D.	1873	Medical,	Bombay.
Mrs. J. M. Minor,	1875	Zenana,	Battalagundu, M.
Miss G. A. Chandler,	1880	Do.	Palani, do.
I. F. NOR. SCHOOL AND INSTRUCTION SOCY.			
Miss Fuller, ...	1867	Zenana,	Lahore.
Miss Harding, ...	1870	Do.	Benares.
Miss Fallon, ...	1874	Do.	Bombay.
Miss Trott, ...	1874	Do.	Do.
Miss Baumann, ...	1874	Do.	Lucknow.
Mrs. Fallon, ...	1875	Superintendent,	Bombay.
Miss Malloch, ...	1875	Zenana,	Do.
Miss Hadden, ...	1875	Do.	Lucknow.
Miss Beilby, ...	1875	Medical,	Do.
Miss Kay, ...	1879	Zenana,	Lahore.
Miss Lockhart, ...	1879	Do.	Do.
Miss Falconer, ...	1880	Do.	Do.
Miss Brett, ...	1880	Do.	Benares.
Miss Brennan, ...	1880	School,	Do.
Miss Patteson, ...	1880	Zenana,	Lucknow.
Miss J. Childs, ...	1880	Do.	Do.
Miss H. Schwarz, ...	1880	Do.	Bombay.

NAME.	YEAR OF ARRIVAL.	WORK.	STATION OR REMARKS.
AMERICAN REFORMED CHURCH, ARCOT MISSION.			
Miss M. J. Mandeville,	1870	Teaching,	R. to America, 1881.
Miss J. Chapin,	1870		Retired.
Miss J. Scudder,			Vellore.
METHODIST EPISCOPAL CHURCH.			
Miss I. Thoburn, ...	1870	School,	Now in America.
Miss C. Swain, M. D.	1870	Medical,	Bareilly.
Miss F. J. Sparkes, ...	1870	Orphanage,	Do.
Miss J. M. Tinsley, ...	1871	Zenana,	Now Mrs. J. W. Waugh.
Miss C. McMillan, ...	1871	Do.	Now Mrs. P. M. Buck.
Miss L. E. Blackmar,	1872	Do.	Now in America.
Miss L. M Pultz, ...	1872	Do.	Ret. 1877.
Miss N. Monelle, M. D.	1873	Medical,	Now Mrs. H. Mansell.
Miss S. F. Leming, ...	1873	Zenana,	Ret. 1874.
Miss A. J. Lore, M. D.	1874	Medical,	Mrs. G. H. McGrew.
Miss L. H. Green, M. D.	1876	Do.	D. Sept. 30, 1878.
Miss M. F. Cary, ...	1876	Orphanage,	Now Mrs. F. G. Davis.
Miss S. A. Easton, ...	1878	School,	Cawnpore.
Miss E. Gibson, ...	1878	Do.	Lucknow.
Miss M. E. Layton,...	1878	Do.	Calcutta.
Miss Woolston, M. D.	1878	Medical,	Ret. 1880.
Miss L. Kelley, ..	1880	Zenana,	Moradabad.
Miss F. M. Nickerson,	1880	Do.	Lucknow.
Miss M. B. Spence,...	1880	School,	Allahabad.
IRISH PRESBYTERIAN MISSION.			
Miss S. Brown, ...	1878	School, Zenana,	Borsad, Gujerat.
Miss M. Patteson, ...	1876	School,	Ret. 1878.
Miss M. Forrest, ...	1876	Medical,	Surat.
Miss M. Long, ...	1878	School,	Do.
Miss Armstrong, ...	1878	Do.	Now Mrs. Shillidy.
BAPTIST MISSIONARY SOCIETY.			
Mrs. Dakin, ...	...	Zenana,	Calcutta.

Name.	Year of Arrival.	Work.	Station or Remarks.
Canadian Pres. Misn.			
Miss Rodger, ...	1874	Zenana,	Indore.
Miss Fairweather, ...	1874	Do.	Ret. 1880.
Am. Luth. Mission.			
Miss K. Boggs, ...	1881	Zenana,	Guntur.
Others.			
Miss M. E. Leslie, ...	...	Teaching,	Calcutta.
Miss L. H Anstey,..	...	Orphanage,	Colar, Mysore.
Miss C M. Reade, ...	...	Evangelistic,	Punrutti.
Miss L. R. Wheeler,...	1878	Do.	Basim.
Miss L. W. Sisson, ...	1878	Do.	Do.

III. MISSIONS IN CEYLON.

(I.) THE BAPTIST MISSION—*BEGAN WORK*, 1812.

Name.	Arrival or Ordination.	Station.
James Silva, ...	O. 1841	Colombo, W. Prov.
Peter Pereira, ..	O. 1845	Hanwella, do.
C. P. Ranesinghe, ...	O. 1846	Gampola, C. P.
C. Carter, ...	A. 1853	Kandy, do.
M. H. Pereira, ...	O. 1858	Chilaw, N.-W. P.
Inwan Silva, ...	O. 1859	Moratuwa, W. P.
I. S. Pereira, ...	O. 1862	Kandy, C. P.
Amaris Silva, ...	O. 1862	Kadugannawa, C. P.
H. R. Pigott, ...	A. 1862	Ratnapura, W, P.
F. D. Waldock, ...	A. 1863	Colombo, do.
D. Boteju, ...	O. 1863	Jayala, do.
I. M. Pereira, .	O. 1865	Do. do.
J. J. Gunasekere, ...	O. 1866	Heneratgoda, do.
H. Markus, ...	O. 1869	Awisawella, do.
Charles Pieris, ...	O. 1870	Matale, C. P.
D. B. Lewis, ...	O. 1870	Colombo, W. P.
J. G. Ratnayake, ...	O. 1871	Mahara, do.
T. R. Stevenson, ...	A. 1874	Colombo, do.
H. A. Lapham, ...	A. 1880	Kandy, C. P.

(II.) WESLEYAN MISSIONARY SOCIETY—*BEGAN WORK*, 1814.

Name.		Arrival or Ordination.	Field of Labor.
J. A. Poulier,	..	1825	South Ceylon.
D. H. Pereira,	..	1851	Do.
H. Pereira,	..	1852	Do.
J. Fernando,	..	1852	Do.
G. E. Goonewardene,	..	1852	Do.
John Scott,	..	1852	Do.
O. J. Gunesakera,	..	1860	Do.
S. Pieris,	..	1860	Do.
J. Nicholson,	..	1861	Do.
Z. Nathanielsz,	..	1864	Do.
P. B. Pereira,	..	1864	Do.
D. D. Pereira,	..	1864	Do.
J. Benjamin,	..	1865	N. Ceylon.
J. Brown,	..	1865	Do.
E. Rigg,	..	1865	Do.
J. W. Philips,	..	1865	S. Ceylon.
J. O. Rhodes,	..	1865	Do.
J. A. Sparr,	..	1865	Do.
S. Niles,	..	1866	N. Ceylon.
D. P. Ferdinando,	..	1867	S. Ceylon.
J. H. Abeyasakara,	..	1868	Do.
J. Shepstone,	..	1868	Do.
R. Tebb,	..	1868	Do.
H. Fernando,	..	1868	Do.
H. Warthenez,	..	1869	Do.
W. M. Walton,	..	1869	N. Ceylon
D. P. Niles,	..	1870	Do.
J. M. Osborn,	..	1870	Do.
D. Fonseka,	..	1870	S. Ceylon.
P. R. Willenberg,	..	1870	Do.
J. A. Well,	..	1871	Do.
C. Parinbanayagam,	..	1871	N. Ceylon.
J. G. Pearson,	..	1871	Do.
J. V. Benjamin,	..	1872	Do.
W. R. Winston,	..	1872	Do.
S. Langdon,	..	1872	S. Ceylon.
S. R. Wilkin,	..	1872	Do.
E. P. Fonseka,	..	1873	Do.
J. H. Nathanielsz,	..	1874	Do.
I. Peento,	..	1874	Do.
A. Shipham,	..	1874	Do.
C. Wickramasingha,	..	1874	Do.

NAME.		ARRIVAL OR ORDINATION.	FIELD OF LABOR.
D. Valupillai,	..	1874	N. Ceylon.
J. C. Fletcher,	..	1875	Do.
R. N. Sethakavaler,	..	1875	Do.
B. A. Wendis,	..	1875	S. Ceylon.
B. S. Wendis,	..	1875	Do.
S. Silva,	..	1875	Do.
D. P. Ferdinando,	..	1876	Do.
E. S. Adams,	..	1876	N. Ceylon.
J. Appapillai,	..	1876	Do.
E. Strutt,	..	1876	Do.
R. A. Barnes,	..	1877	D
J. G. Trummer,	..	1877	Do.
M. P. Fernando,	..	1877	S. Ceylon.
S. E. A. Gasperson,	..	1877	Do.
L. S. Lee,	..	1877	Do.
C. W. Silva,	..	1877	Do.
D. S. Silva,	..	1877	Do.
S. Hill,	..	1878	Do.
M. H. Pereira,	..	1878	Do.
Thomas Little,	..	1878	Do.
J. Parinbanayager,	..	1878	Do.
F. M. Webster,	..	1878	Do.
C. S. Casinader,	..	1879	Do.
A. Nallathamby,	..	1879	Do.
F. H. Pieris,	..	1879	S. Ceylon.

(III) THE AMERICAN BOARD.—*BEGAN WORK,* 1816.

NAME.		ARRIVAL OR ORDINATION.		STATION.	
W. W. Ho[illegible],	...	A.	1846	Oodoovillo,	Jaffna.
E. P. Hastings,	...	A.	1847	Batticotta,	do.
T. P. Hunt,	...	O.	1855	Chavagacherry,	do.
D. Stickney,	...	O.	1858	Udupitty,	do.
F. Asbury,	...	O.	1861	Navaly,	do.
B. H. Rice,	...	O.	1867	Batticotta,	do.
M. Welch,	...	O.	1870	Allavutty,	do.
T. S. Smith,	...	A.	1871	Tillipally,	do.
A. Bryant,	...	O.	1872	Chaugany,	do.
S. W. Howland,	...	A.	1873	Udupitty,	do.
H. R. Hoisington,	...	O.	1874	Oodoovillo,	do.
J. S. Christmas,	..	O.	1875	Tillipally,	do.
R. C. Hastings,	...	A.	1879	Batticotta,	do.
G. W. Leitch, Esq.,	...	A.	1880	Manippai,	do.
S. John,	...	O.	1880	Moolai,	do.

(IV.) CHURCH OF ENGLAND MISSION.—*BEGAN WORK*, 1818.

NAME.		ARRIVAL OR ORDINATION.	STATION.
William Oakley,	...	A. 1835	Nuwara Eliya, Cent. Prov.
John Ireland Jones,	...	A. 1857	Kurunegala, N.-W. P.
Stephen Coles,	...	A. 1860	Kandy, C. P.
William E. Rowlands,	...	A. 1861	Nuwara Eliya, Do.
J. Hensman,	...	O. 1863	Kapay, Jaffna.
John Allcock,	...	A 1865	Badagama, S. P.
T. P. Handy,	...	O. 1865	Nellore, Jaffna.
G. Champion,	...	O. 1865	Kokuville, do.
Elijah Hoole,	...	O. 1865	Chundically, N. P.
Henry Gunesakera,	...	O. 1867	Kandy. C. P.
Richard T. Dowbiggin,	...	A. 1867	Cotta, W. P.
David Wood,	...	A. 1867	Colombo, do.
D. Jayasingha,	...	O. 1868	Cotta, do.
H. De Silva,	...	O. 1868	Talanagama, do.
H. Kannanger,	...	O. 1869	Do. do.
B. P Weerasingha,	...	O. 1869	Kandy, C. P.
Pakkyanathan Peter,	...	O. 1872	Pellmadulla, do.
Gerard F. Unwin,	...	A. 1873	*Now in England.*
J. D Simmons,*	...	A. 1874	Nellore, Jaffna.
A. R. Cavalier,	...	A. 1874	*Now in England.*
Thomas Dunn,	...	A. 1874	Kandy, C. P.
J. I. Pickford,	...	A. 1878	Maradana, W. P.
John Gabb,	...	O. 1879	Colombo, W. P.
G. T. Fleming,	...	A. 1880	Chundically, Jaffna.
John G. Garrett,	...	A. 1880	Kandy, C. P.

* *Vide* P. 94.

(V.) SOCIETY FOR THE PROPAGATION OF THE GOSPEL, —*BEGAN WORK*, 1824.

Name.		Arrival or Ordination.	Station.
R. Edwards,	...	1852	Manaar, N.-W.P.
F. DeMel,	...	1853	Pantura, W. P.
J. DeSilva,	...	1856	Matara, S. P.
C. Sennanayake,	...	1861	Galkisse, W. P.
T. Christian,	...	1863	Kurena, Do.
T. Mortimer,	...	1864	Putlam, N.-W P.
P. Marks,	...	1866	Buona Vista, S. P.
A. Vethakan,	...	1866	Kayman's Gate, W. P.
G. H. Gomes,	...	1870	Badulla, C. P.
F. D. Ederesinghe,	...	1871	Tangalla, W. P.
C. DeMel,	...	1873	Kurena, W. P.
C. David,	...	1876	Do. Do.
H. Wikkramanayake,	...	1876	Kollupitiya, N.-W.P.
C. A. W. Jayasakera,	...		Tangalla, W. P.
J. Peter,	...		Chilaw, N.-W. P.
J. S. Lyle,	...		Matara, S. P.
E. C. Miller,	...		St. Thomas Col. Colombo.
J. F. Falkner,	..		Do. Do.

—o—

IV. STATISTICAL TABLES.

(I.) YEARS OF SERVICE OF MISSIONARIES.

No.	Mission.		Over 50.	40 to 50	30 to 40.	20 to 30.	10 to 20.	Under 10.	Total.
1	Baptist M. Soc'y,	...	1	4	1	8	5	12	31
2	London M. Soc'y,	...	...	2	2	7	14	20	45
3	Am. Board,	...	...	...	7	3	4	10	24
4	C. M. Soc'y,	...	...	2	5	19	29	48	103
5	Gospel P. Soc'y,	...	...	1	2	10	15	20	48
6	Wes. M. Soc'y,	...	...	...	1	8	8	27	44
7	Gen. Bapt. Mision,	...	...	1	2	1	...	4	8
8	Ch. of Scotland,	..	...	...	...	...	7	10	17
9	F. Ch. of Scotland,	...	...	1	...	3	10	13	27
10	Am. Pres. Mission,	...	...	4	2	5	11	7	29
11	Basel Mission,	...	...	...	2	10	21	42	75
12	A. B. M. U,	...	...	...	1	...	3	14	18
13	Free B. Mission,	...	...	1	...	...	1	4	6
14	Gossner's Mission,	...	...	...	1	2	7	11	21
15	Leipzig Mission,	...	...	...	3	5	7	6	21
16	Irish P. Mission,	...	...	...	1	...	3	5	9
17	Welsh C. Mission,	...	...	...	...	...	4	3	7
18	Am. Ev. Luth. G. Synod,	...	...	...	...	1	...	3	4
19	Am. Ref. Mission,	...	...	...	...	3	...	2	5
20	Moravian Mission,	...	...	...	...	2	...	1	3
21	Am. U. P. M.	...	...	...	...	1	3	1	5
22	M. E. Church,	...	...	...	1	5	10	49	65
23	U. P. Scotland,	...	...	...	...	2	5	7	14
24	Dan. Ev. Luth. M.	...	...	...	...	...	...	3	3
25	Hermannsburg Mission,	...	...	...	1	...	4	3	8
26	Strict B. Mission,	...	...	...	...	...	...	...	...
27	Friends' Mission,	..	...	...	...	...	...	2	2
28	Ind. Home Mission,	...	...	...	...	...	2	3	5
29	Am. Ger. Ev. Mission,	...	...	...	1	...	...	1	2
30	Assam and Cachar Do.	...	...	...	...	...	...	...	...
31	Can. Bapt. Mission,	...	...	...	...	...	2	5	7
32	Am. Ev. Luth. G. Council,	...	...	...	...	...	1	3	4
33	Can. Pres. Mission,	...	...	...	...	...	...	3	3
34	Swedish Ev. Do.	...	...	..	...	...	...	6	6
35	Private Missions, etc.,	...	...	...	...	5	3	12	20
	Total,	...	1	16	33	100	179	360	689

(II.) STATISTICAL SUMMARIES FOR 1871 AND 1880.

No.	Names of Societies and Missions.	Began work in India.	1871. Foreign Ordained Agents.	Foreign and other Lay Agents.	Native Ordained Agents.	Native Christians.	Communicants.
1	Baptist Missionary Society,...	1793	26	5	3	6,509	1,902
2	London do. do. ...	1798	44	4	27	39,879	3,900
3	American Board, ...	1813	19	1	19	8,161	2,112
4	Church Missionary Society,...	1814	102	33	67	69,114	13,106
5	Gospel Propagation do. ...	1817	41	21	37	45,083	10,604
6	Wesleyan Missy. do. ...	1817	22	6	6	1,011	494
7	General Baptist do. do. ...	1822	6	1	10	2,439	646
8	Church of Scotland Mission,	1828	4	6	4	681	326
9	Free Church of Scotland do.	1828	19	14	9	1,650	750
10	American Presbyterian do.	1834	32	1	8	1,334	563
11	Basel Missionary Society, ...	1834	42	16	6	4,612	2,272
12	Am. Bapt. Missy. Union, ...	1836	11	0	2	6,810	2,478
13	Am. Free Baptist Mission,...	1836	5	0	2	599	276
14	Gossner's Missy. Society, ...	1840	12	6	1	14,804	4,636
15	Leipzig do. do. ...	1841	19	0	4	9,265	4,837
16	Irish Presbyterian Mission,...	1841	8	1	0	532	131
17	Welsh. Cal. Meth. do. ...	1841	5	0	0	61	16
18	Am. Ev. Lu. Miss. Gen. Syn.	1842	3	1	0	2,470	731
19	American Reformed Miss. ...	1853	6	0	3	2,478	712
20	Episcopal Moravian do. ...	1854	2	0	0	17	8
21	Am. Un. Presbyterian do. ...	1855	3	1	1	120	63
22	Meth. Episcopal Ch. do. ...	1856	21	5	6	1,835	1,074
23	Unit. Pres. (Scotland) do. ...	1860	9	3	0	494	66
24	Danish Lutheran do. ...	1861	3	0	0	246	71
25	Hermannsburg Missy. Socy.	1866	8	0	0	199	29
26	Strict Baptist Mission, ...	1866	0	1	2	104	50
27	Friends' Mission, ...	1866	...	...	...	...	...
28	Indian Home do.	1867	1	3	0	35	35
29	German Ev. (U.S.A.) Socy.	1868	2	1	0	74	...
30	Assam and Cachar Mission,	1868	2	0	0	61	...
31	Canadian Baptist Mission, ...	1868	...	..	..	...	...
32	Am. Ev. Lu. Miss. Gen. Coun	1870	...	...	...	...	...
33	Canadian Pres. Mission, ...	1876	...	...	...	...	...
34	Swedish Ev. do. ...	1878	...	...	...	...	...
35	Private Missions, etc. ...		11	4	4	3,581	928
	TOTAL, ...		488	134 622	225	224,258	52,816

No.	1880. Foreign Missionaries.	1880. Native Ordained Agents.	1880. Native Christians.	1880. Communicants.	Increase; or Decrease (—) Foreign Missionaries.	Increase; or Decrease (—) Native Ordained Agents.	Increase; or Decrease (—) Native Christians.	Increase; or Decrease (—) Communicants.	Remarks.
1	31	8	10,000	3,000	0	5	3,491	1,098	Wherever a discrepancy occurs between these figures and those on preceding pages, these are to be taken as correct. In order to make a comparative statement Burmah Missions are omitted.
2	45	30	50,098	4,632	—3	3	10,219	732	
3	24	35	13,485	3,765	4	16	5,324	1,653	Including Ceylon and Burmah, the present number of Missionaries and Native Ordained Agents is 946, as compared with 838, in 1871.
4	103	107	75,998	19,401	—32	40	6,884	6,295	
5	48	56	51,391	15,305	—14	19	6,308	4,701	
6	44	8	2,000	1,000	16	2	989	506	
7	8	10	2,722	997	1	0	283	351	
8	17	4	860	326	7	0	179	0	
9	27	8	1,476	891	—6	—1	—174	141	
10	29	15	2,100	971	—4	7	766	408	
11	75	8	7,337	3,727	17	2	2,725	1,455	
12	18	51	55,633	18,653	7	49	48,823	16,175	
13	6	4	970	534	1	2	371	258	
14	21	7	29,285	11,091	3	6	14,481	6,455	
15	21	9	11,981	6,000	2	5	2,716	1,163	
16	9	0	912	198	0	0	380	67	
17	7	0	1,659	920	2	0	1,598	904	
18	4	2	5,423	2,193	0	2	2,953	1.462	
19	5	4	3,199	1,322	—1	1	721	610	
20	3	0	35	17	1	0	18	9	
21	5	2	536	335	1	1	416	272	
22	65	15	5,855	2,897	39	9	4,020	1,823	
23	14	...	601	360	2	...	107	294	
24	3	...	250	50	0	0	4	—21	
25	8	...	714	331	0	0	515	302	
26	...	...	...	...	—1	2	--104	—50	
27	2	...	13	13	2	0	13	13	
28	5	2	2,756	2,000	1	2	2,721	1,965	
29	2	...	330	125	—1	0	256	125	
30	...	...	...	..	—2	0	—61	0	
31	7	1	1,000	473	7	1	1,000	473	
32	4	2	560	216	4	2	560	216	
33	3	...	30	10	3	0	30	10	
34	6	...	8	5	6	0	8	5	
35	20	1	1,406	686	5	—7	—2,175	—142	
	689	389	340623	102444	67	164	116305	49,628	

(III.) NATIONALITY OF MISSIONARIES.

No.	MISSIONS.		Great Britain.						The Continent.								
		Sons of Miss. B. in I.	England.	Scotland.	Ireland.	Wales.	Canada.	West Indies.	Sweden.	Norway.	Denmark.	Holland.	Belgium.	Russia.	Germany.	France.	Switzerland.
1	B. M. Society,	2	21	...	1	4	1	...	...	...	...	...	...	...	1	...	...
2	L. M. do.	2	34	5	1	2	...	1	...	...	...	...	...	...	...	...	...
3	Am. Board,	6	...	...	...	1	2	...	...	...	...	...	...	...	...	...	...
4	C. M. Society,	2	89	1	...	...	2	...	...	...	...	...	1	...	8	...	...
5	S. P. Gospel,	1	39	...	...	...	...	...	...	...	...	...	...	...	6	2	...
6	Wes. Mission,	...	42	...	...	2	...	...	...	...	...	...	...	...	...	...	...
7	Gen. Baptist Mission,	...	8	...	...	...	...	...	...	...	...	...	...	...	...	...	...
8	Ch. of Scotland,	1	...	14	1	...	...	...	...	...	...	...	...	...	...	...	1
9	F. Ch. of Scotland,	...	...	27	...	...	...	...	...	...	...	...	...	...	...	...	...
10	Am. Pres. Mission,	5	...	1	3	...	...	...	...	...	...	...	...	...	2	...	...
11	Basel Mission,	...	...	...	...	...	...	...	...	...	...	1	...	1	61	...	12
12	A. B. M. Union.	2	...	...	...	...	1	...	...	...	...	...	...	...	...	...	...
13	F. Baptist Mission,	1	1	...	...	...	...	...	...	...	...	...	...	...	...	...	...
14	Gossner's do.	...	...	...	...	...	...	...	...	...	...	...	...	...	21	...	...
15	Leipzig do.	...	...	...	...	...	...	...	3	...	...	...	...	...	18	...	...
16	Irish P. do.	...	...	...	7	...	...	...	...	...	...	...	...	...	...	...	...
17	Welsh C. Mission,	...	2	...	...	5	...	...	...	...	...	...	...	...	...	...	...
18	Am. Ev. Luth. G. S.,	...	...	...	...	...	...	...	...	...	...	...	...	...	...	...	...
19	Am. Ref. C. Mission,	...	2	...	...	...	...	...	...	...	...	...	...	...	...	...	...
20	Moravian do.	...	...	...	...	...	...	...	...	...	...	...	...	...	3	...	...
21	Am. U. Pres. do.	...	...	...	1	...	...	...	...	...	...	...	...	...	...	...	...
22	M. E. Church,	...	2	1	3	1	2	...	...	...	...	...	...	...	...	...	...
23	U. P. Mission (Scot,)	...	1	13	...	...	...	...	...	...	...	...	...	...	...	...	...
24	Dan. Ev. Luth. Mission	...	...	...	...	...	...	...	...	...	3	...	...	...	...	...	...
25	Hermannsburg do.	...	...	...	...	...	...	...	...	...	...	...	...	...	8	...	...
26	Strict B. Mission,	...	...	...	...	...	...	...	...	...	...	...	...	...	...	...	...
27	Friends' Mission,	...	...	1	1	...	...	...	...	...	...	...	...	...	...	...	...
28	Ind. Home do.	...	...	...	...	...	...	...	...	2	2	...	...	...	...	...	...
29	Am. Ger. Ev. Mission,	...	...	...	...	...	...	...	...	...	...	...	...	...	2	...	...
30	Assam and Cachar do.	...	...	...	...	...	...	...	...	...	...	...	...	...	...	...	...
31	Can. Bapt. Mission,	...	...	...	...	...	7	...	...	...	...	...	...	...	...	...	...
32	Am. Ev. Lu. G. Coun.,	...	...	...	...	...	...	...	1	2	...	...	...	...	...	...	...
33	Can. Pres. Mission,	...	1	...	...	...	2	...	...	...	...	...	...	...	...	...	...
34	Swedish do.	...	...	...	...	...	...	...	6	...	...	...	...	...	...	...	...
35	Private Missions, etc.,	4	5	4	...	...	...	...	...	...	...	...	...	...	1	...	...
	TOTAL,	30	244	67	19	15	17	1	10	4	5	1	1	1	131	2	13

NATIONALITY OF MISSIONARIES.—(*Continued*).

No.	United States.																		Others.	Total.
	Maine.	Vermont.	New Hampshire.	Massachusetts.	Connecticut.	New York.	New Jersey.	Pennsylvania.	Ohio.	Virginia.	Kentucky.	Tennessee.	Indiana.	Illinois.	Iowa.	Wisconsin.	Michigan.	Other States.		
1	...	...	...	...	...	...	...	...	...	...	...	...	...	...	...	...	...	...	1	31
2	...	...	...	...	...	...	...	...	...	...	...	...	...	...	...	...	...	...	...	45
3	...	...	...	6	4	1	...	...	...	...	...	...	...	...	...	...	...	4	...	24
4	...	...	...	...	...	...	...	...	...	...	...	...	...	...	...	...	...	...	...	103
5	...	...	...	...	...	...	...	...	...	...	...	...	...	...	...	...	...	...	...	48
6	...	...	...	...	...	...	...	...	...	...	...	...	...	...	...	...	...	...	...	44
7	...	...	...	...	...	...	...	...	...	...	...	...	...	...	...	...	...	...	...	8
8	...	...	...	...	...	...	...	...	...	...	...	...	...	...	...	...	...	...	...	17
9	...	...	...	...	...	...	...	...	...	...	...	...	...	...	...	...	...	...	...	27
10	...	...	...	...	1	1	1	3	3	...	1	1	...	1	...	...	1	5	...	29
11	...	...	...	...	...	...	...	...	...	...	...	...	...	...	...	...	...	...	...	75
12	1	...	...	1	...	5	1	1	1	...	...	...	...	1	1	...	...	3	...	18
13	...	...	1	...	...	1	...	...	...	...	...	...	1	...	...	...	...	1	...	6
14	...	...	...	...	...	...	...	...	...	...	...	...	...	...	...	...	...	...	...	21
15	...	...	...	...	...	...	...	...	...	...	...	...	...	...	...	...	...	...	...	21
16	...	...	...	...	...	...	...	...	...	...	...	...	...	...	...	...	...	...	...	9
17	...	...	...	...	...	...	...	...	...	...	...	...	...	...	...	...	...	...	...	7
18	...	...	...	...	...	...	...	2	1	...	...	...	...	...	...	...	...	1	...	4
19	...	...	...	...	...	...	1	...	...	...	...	...	...	...	...	...	...	2	...	5
20	...	...	...	...	...	...	...	...	...	...	...	...	...	...	...	...	...	...	...	3
21	...	...	...	...	...	2	...	1	1	...	...	...	...	...	...	...	...	...	...	5
22	1	2	1	...	...	5	3	4	11	2	2	...	4	1	...	1	...	13	6	65
23	...	...	...	...	...	...	...	...	...	...	...	...	...	...	...	...	...	...	...	14
24	...	...	...	...	...	...	...	...	...	...	...	...	...	...	...	...	...	...	...	3
25	...	...	...	...	...	...	...	...	...	...	...	...	...	...	...	...	...	...	...	8
26	...	...	...	...	...	...	...	...	...	...	...	...	...	...	...	...	...	...	...	...
27	...	...	...	...	...	...	...	...	...	...	...	...	...	...	...	...	...	...	...	2
28	...	...	...	...	...	...	...	...	...	...	...	...	...	...	...	...	...	...	1	5
29	...	...	...	...	...	...	...	...	...	...	...	...	...	...	...	...	...	...	...	2
30	...	...	...	...	...	...	...	...	...	...	...	...	...	...	...	...	...	...	...	...
31	...	...	...	...	...	...	...	...	...	...	...	...	...	...	...	...	...	...	...	7
32	...	...	...	...	...	...	...	1	...	...	...	...	...	...	...	...	...	...	...	4
33	...	...	...	...	...	...	...	...	...	...	...	...	...	...	...	...	...	...	...	3
34	...	...	...	...	...	...	...	...	...	...	...	...	...	...	...	...	...	...	...	6
35	...	...	...	...	...	1	...	...	1	...	...	...	...	1	...	...	...	...	3	20
	2	2	2	7	5	16	6	12	18	2	3	1	5	4	1	1	1	29 117	11	689

INDEX.

THE END.

ERRATA.

P. 32, L. 46 for "A" *read* "O."
P. 35, L. 8 for "Bengal" *read* "Bangalore."
P. 83, L. 17 for "Palcutta" *read* "Calcutta."
P. 136, L. 30 for "1849" *read* "1839."
P. 228, L. 24 for "Borden" *read* "Bowden."

ADDENDA.

P. 135, L. 12 (The Rev. J. J. Hull) add:—
Died, 1881.
P. 167, bottom, add:—
Curtis, Silas. B. 1830. O. 1872. Ad. *Jellasore, Orissa.*
Naik, K. B. 1837 O. 1871. Ad. *Balasore, Do.*
P. 204, after Paul, Ambica Charn, add:—
Peters, William. O. January 9.1881. Ad. *Gonda, Oudh.*
P. 230, under VII. Bethel Mission. add:—
Patterson, Hugh. Ad. *Bethel, Bengal.*

THE END.

THE PUNJAB RELIGIOUS TRACT AND BOOK SOCIETY, LAHORE.—*CONTINUED.*

URDU BOOKS FOR CHILDREN.

Nasíhat i Tiflán, Harry's Catechism, cloth as. 4, paper cover, ...	,,	0	3	0
Talím dar Talím, Line upon Line,...	,,	0	4	0
Takmíl ut Talím, Children's Reading Book, ...	,,	0	4	0
Bible Stories, S. P. C. K. series, with coloured Illustrations, in 24 parts, each, ...	,,	0	2	0
The Second and Third Readers, (C. V. E. S) In the Press.				
Books of the A. L. O. E. Series, 18 different kinds (C V. E. S.) each 6 pie and	,,	0	0	3
Panoramic Series, R. T. S. coloured Illustrations : including the story of David, Joseph, and Samuel, River Scenes, Scenes from the Acts of the Apostles and the Journeys of Israel, each, ...	,,	0	3	0

ROMAN-URDU BOOKS.

Mushabrah Fiqrat Injil, Annotated Paragraph New Testament, R.T.S.	,,	3	0	0
Masíhí dín aur Kalísiyá ki tawáríkh, Church History, Re. 1-8 and...	,,	1	4	0
Intikháb Táríkh i Kalísiyá, Selections from Church History. In Press.				
Áína e dil, The Heart Book, translated by Rev. Mr. Deimler, Illustrated Re. 1-8. plain, ...	,,	0	4	0
Suwál o Jawáb i Rúh. The soul's enquiries, Re. 1, as. 12, 8, and ...	,,	0	6	0
Alqáb i Masíhí, The Christian Titles, coloured as. 10, stiff cover, as. 8, paper cover, ...	,,	0	6	0
Dáktar Jadsan Sahib kí Sarguzasht, Life of Dr. Judson, coloured as. 6, stiff cover, as. 4, paper cover, ...	,,	0	3	0
Masíhí Musáfir, Bunyan's Pilgrim's Progress, complete in one volume, with beautiful coloured Illustrations, ...	,,	2	8	0
Kitáb i Muqqaddas ká Ahwal, Barth's Scripture History, cloth, ...	,,	0	5	0
Kháxagí Duáen, Family Prayers,...	,,	0	2	0
Panoramic Series, R. T. S. Counterpart of the Urdu, 6 Nos. each, ...	,,	0	3	0
The Lord's Prayer, large sheet exquisitely illuminated, ...	,,	1	0	0
The Second Reading Book, In the Press, (C. V. E. S.)				
The Third Reading Book, Do. (C. V. E. S.)				

With many other books too numerous to mention. For a detailed list of Society's Publications, and other available works, see Appendix to Reports of the Society, published annually.

Applications to be forwarded to

BABU P. R. RAHA,

Assistant Secretary

Religious Tract and Book Society,

ANARKALLE, LAHORE.

MEMORIAL SCHOOL, CAWNPORE.

BOARD OF TRUSTEES

BOARD AND TUITION.

		PER MENSEM.
For single boarders, ...	Rs.	16
,, two or more boys of one family, each	,,	15
,, single day-scholars, ...	,,	5
,, two or more boys of one family, ...	,,	4
Instruction on Piano or Harmonium, ...	,,	8

INCIDENTALS.—An *annual entrance fee* of Rs. 10 is required from each pupil; and Rs. 1-8 half-yearly for repairs of shoes and clothes.

"*This School is one of the best in these Provinces.*" *EXTRACT FROM REPORT OF THE DIRECTOR OF PUBLIC INSTRUCTION, N.-W.P.*, 1880.

This old and established School combines cheapness with thoroughness. The only boy who went to the Entrance Examination last year passed in the first division.

Buildings airy. Compound large. The Memorial School is situated near the Memorial Garden.

☞ SPECIAL ATTENTION given to the HEALTH of the Pupils.
The Civil Surgeon of the station has constant oversight.
There is no charge for medical attendance.
Term begins February 1st and ends November 30th.
For further particulars *address*,

REV. F. L. NEELD, B. A.,
Principal.

THE GREAT INDIAN REMEDY

FOR ALL BILIOUS COMPLAINTS,

INDIAN FEVERS, INDIGESTION, SPLEEN, AGUE, JAUNDICE, PILES, COSTIVENESS, GENERAL WEAKNESS, and every disorder depending on FUNCTIONAL DERANGEMENT OF THE LIVER is

Dr. E. J. LAZARUS'S

ESSENCE OF CHIRETTA

Prepared only by MESSRS. E. J. LAZARUS & Co., Medical Hall, Benares, from the original receipt of E. J. LAZARUS, M. D. and sold by all Medicine Venders, at Rs. 1-8—2-8 and 4-0 per bottle.

☞None other is genuine.☜

An indubitable proof of the great value of this wonderful remedy is the various imitations which are being made.

THE GRAND INDIAN ALTERATIVE TONIC.

Dr. E. J. LAZARUS'S

ESSENCE OF HEMIDESMUS.

This preparation of the INDIAN SARSAPARILLA, UNUNTAMUL, is equal, if not superior to the more costly Jamaica or Honduras Sarsaparilla. INDIAN MEDICAL AUTHORITIES, both European and Native with one accord bear testimony to its valuable alterative, tonic, diuretic and diaphoretic properties pronouncing it a most efficacious remedy in all those diseases arising from an *impure state of the blood* and most strongly recommend it in SCROFULOUS COMPLAINTS BOILS, PIMPLES and BLOTCHES OF THE SKIN, CONSTITUTIONAL DEBILITY, CACHEXIA, especially of Children, CONSTITUTIONAL SYPHILIS, CHRONIC RHEUMATISM certain diseases of the Skin, &c., &c.

Prepared only by MESSRS. E. J. LAZARUS & Co., Medical Hall, Benares, from the original receipts of E. J. LAZARUS, M. D., and sold by Medicine Venders, at Rs. 2-8 per bottle

Dr. LAZARUS'S DOMESTIC MEDICINES.

		Per Bottle
INFANTILE FEVER POWDER (for Fevers, Teething, &c., &c.), ..	Rs.	1 4
TONIC ANTIPERIODIC PILLS (Invaluable in Intermittent Fevers, Ague and Spleen and diseases of a periodic character), ...	,,	1 4
SPLEEN PILLS (has cured thousand of cases of enlarged spleen), ...	,,	2 0
RESTRINGENT MIXTURE (for Diarrhœa, Colic, Gripes, Cramps, &c.),	,,	2 0
CHOLERA DROPS (most effectual if taken in time), ...	,,	2 0
BALSAMIC EXPECTORANT DROPS (for Coughs Colds, Hoarseness, Asthma, Pain in the Chest, Chronic Pleurisy, &c.), ...	,,	1 8
FAMILY LAXATIVE. A safe, certain and useful purgative, ...	,,	2 0
,, APERIENT PILLS (mild, prompt and safe), ...	,,	1 4
,, ANTIBILIOUS PILLS (stronger than above),...	,,	1 4
,, CARMINATIVE (Invaluable for Children), ...	,,	2 0
,, HAIR TONIC (unrivalled for producing growth of the Hair),...	,,	2 0
,, EMBROCATION (for Sprains, Chronic Rheumatism, &c.) ...	,,	1 8

The above are most strongly recommended to parents, guardians and others residing in Districts where medical aid is not available. Thousands of cases have been cured by their judicious use.

A printed pamphlet giving full instructions is wrapped round each bottle.

Prepared only by MESSRS E. J. LAZARUS & Co., at the Medical Hall, Benares, from DR. LAZARUS'S original receipts and sold by all Medicine Venders.

BASEL GERMAN EVANG. MISSION

Balmattha Weaving Establishment.

MANGALORE,

ESTABLISHED 1844.

THE undermentioned manufactures made of the best Manchester Twist, are now well known throughout India.

Damask Table Cloths

in several patterns, are made in eight different sizes, as to the breadth, viz., 5½, 6, 6½, 7, 7½, 8½, 9½, and 10 feet, and as to length, anything that may be desired,

Damask Table Napkins 20 & 24 in. square.

Damask Side Slips in any length desired.

Diamond Table Cloths

Are made in *five* different sizes, as to the breadth, viz., 5½, 6, 6½, 7, and 7½ feet, and as to length, anything that may be desired.

Diamond Table Napkins :

Diamond Side Slips :

Table Covers, in colours :

Counterpanes

For single & double Cots.

Toilet Table Covers.

Furniture Cover Cloth, 6½ feet wide, Fancy Scotch pattern.

Toilet Towels.

Washing Towels.

Bathing Towels, rough and large.

Trowserings, Coatings, Tweeds, Diagonal, Drills, Canvas, Jhoolings Bed-Ticking, Ginghams, Abyssinian Thirtings, tout Clothing, for Boarding Schools :

The favorite **Shikaree**.

☞ Price Lists and Patterns will be sent FREE on application.

TH. DIGEL,

Superintendent.

Cawnpore Girls' School,

Cawnpore.

BOARD AND TUITION.

		Per Mensem.
For Single Boarders, ...	Rs.	16
Two or more of one family, each, ...	,,	15
Single Day-scholars, ...	,,	5
Two or more of one family, each,...	,,	4
Instruction on Piano or Harmonium	,,	8

An entrance fee of Rs. 10 is required from each pupil.

The school is pleasantly located in the suburbs of Cawnpore. The compound is large, the buildings well adapted for school use. The lady Principal devotes her entire time to the school, living with the pupils.

The School passes pupils in the Entrance Examination.

Habits and manners of the pupils are strictly attended to, and their moral education is made of prime importance.

The Civil Surgeon has constant oversight.

CALENDAR.

Term begins February 1st, and ends November 30th.

For prospectus and further particulars address the Superintendent,

MISS EASTON, M. A.,

Cawnpore.

Cannington Girls' School,

ALLAHABAD.

This School, opened in 1879, is now in charge of
MISS M. B. SPENCE

A thoroughly qualified and experienced Educator,

who has just arrived from America. It receives both Boarders and Day-scholars, and teaches from the lowest rudiments to the University Entrance standard.

The Boarding Department

is replete with every comfort,—the object being to offer to those who come, a truly attractive and pleasant home.

The School Staff

includes an efficient Music Teacher and a competent Matron.

The School has just removed into one of the most commodious and pleasant buildings in Allahabad, having an excellent situation. The government of the School is mild but firm. The closest attention is paid to correct deportment, as well as to moral and religious culture.

For further particulars, apply to MISS SPENCE, Superintendent; or to the REV. D. OSBORNE, Clive Road.

PUBLICATIONS
OF THE
METHODIST EPISCOPAL CHURCH PRESS.
LUCKNOW.

Hymn-Book.

SPECIAL attention of the *Missionaries* in North India is called to the series of **Cheap-Hymn Books** published at this Press. It was the first to publish such books. They are needed. There is the same power in Christian song in India as there is in England and America and our Sunday-schools and General Services need to have a good supply of the book next to the Bible, the Hymn-Book. To supply it to all the **New Edition** is brought out in the three characters, **Hindi Persian Urdu** and **Roman-Urdu** : and the price, which does not cover the cost, is placed low.

It should be stated that this hymn-book contains a collection of 300 hymns : among them are translations of standard hymns, and of a number of the best of Sankey's hymns; also the best native compositions in the form of the *bhajan* and *gazal*. By the kindness of missionaries of different Societies the editors have had access to the collections which have to the latest date accumulated. From all the sources open to them the best have been gathered.

Price, single copies 2 as. ; 12 copies Rs. 1-8 ; 100 copies Rs. 12-8 ; 500 copies or more. at the same rate, but postage or carriage will be paid. These rates are nett. and for cash.

The Roman Urdu Edition is ready. The Hindi and Persian Urdu Editions will be ready this present year.

The Holy Scripture.

The attention of missionaries is also respectfully invited to the small portable style in which the Gospels and Acts of the Apostles and Proverbs have been produced.

PERSIAN URDU.—Gospels of Matthew, Mark, Luke and John, Acts of the Apostles and Proverbs. Each 6 pies.

ROMAN-HINDI.—The New Testament, cloth bd. (P. 2 as.) 8 As.

ROMAN-URDU.—Gospel of Mathew, Mark, Luke and John : each 6 pies. The four Gospels bound together (P. 1) 2 as.

Commentaries, Concordance.

Concordance of the Holy Scriptures Compiled by the Rev. R. Hoskins : over 100,000 references, Cloth bound, 900 pp.	2-8-0
Commentary on Matthew and Mark by the Rev. T. J. Scott, D. D. cloth bd. (Roman-Urdu)	1-8-0
,, ,, ,, (Lith. Urdu)	2-0-0
Commentary on the Book of Genesis, by the Rev. D. W. Thomas, M. A. (Roman Urdu) cloth bd.	1-8-0
Commentary on John's Gospel, Lith. Urdu	8-0

Educational Works.

Attention of Missionaries is called to the books under this head. While not obtrusively direct it is well that our Educational books should be pure, and directly favorable to the one great work to be accomplished. With this principle in view the Superintendent has thus far published the following books :—

URDU READERS. First Reader, Mufíd ul Atfál .. .. 6 pie.
Second Reader, Talím ul Atfál .. .. 9 pie.
Third Reader, Hidáyat ul Atfál .. 1 as.

ZENANA READER, ADVANCED.—The Heart's Delight with large page illustrations, beautiful and attractive ... 2 as.

This series has been carefully compiled by the Rev. T. Craven, M. A. They will be found to be correctly graded. Their popularity is great where known. The three numbers of the "*Atfal*" have gone through several editions.

HISTORY, LITH. URDU.—Translation of Mrs. Handyside's History of India. Several chapters have been added to the original English edition bringing the History down to the close of 1880. The chapter on the growth of Christianity in India has been carefully revised by the Rev. B. H. Badley, M. A. Price (P. 1) 6 as.

GEOGRAPHY LITH URDU.—Catechism of Geography, ... 1-
Roman Urdu, " " ... 1-6
GRAMMAR.—Roman Urdu, Elements of Urdu Grammar. ... 2-0
LOGIC.—English and Roman Urdu. The Elements of Logic by the Rev. T. J. Scott. D. D. 1-8-0
Lith. Urdu. do. do. 0-6

DICTIONARIES.—Compiled by the Rev. T. Craven, M. A.
English and Urdu. The People's Dictionary with idioms and their meaning and illustrations. 12,000 sold, ... 8-0
English and Rom. Urdu. The Royal Dictionary with Derivatives, Synonyms, Idioms and 400 Illustrations : 10,000 sold,—
Stiff Cover. 1-0-0
do. do. do. (cloth bd) 1-6-0
Eng. and R. Urdu and R. Urdu and English. Two Volumes in one—Popular Dictionary, 12,000 copies sold. ... 1-0-0

Others in preparation. The compilation of this series of Dictionaries has met with the most flattering success. In the short period of 12 months 40,000 copies have been ordered.

Sunday-School Books and Cards.

Though it was our happy privilege to initiate the Sunday-school Book with colored pictures we have not been able to increase or even replenish our rapidly taken stock as we desired. It has been impossible to give every department of literature the attention it deserved. We hope however that greater assistance will be obtained for this work and consequently greater activity maintained in the manufacture of suitable books for all classes but more especially for the young. Our new Catalogue will be ready, shortly.

Photographic Artist

NAINI TAL, RANI KHET AND LUCKNOW.

Mr. Sache divides the year between these Stations as follows :—

April 15 to **October 15**.—*Naini Tal and Rani Khet.*

October 20 to **April 1**.—*Lucknow.*

The finest productions as well as the latest novelties in Photography can be seen and had at Mr. Sache's studios.

Views of India for Sale.

The Catalogue of over *one thousand views* embraces the more prominent places of History as well asthe most beautiful scenes of all the promineut Stations, Hill and Plain in India. As there is no present generally so acceptable as an Album of views the attention of missionaries and others is called to the fine collection found in Mr. Sache's Catalogue.

CATALOGUES SENT ON APPLICATION

www.ingramcontent.com/pod-product-compliance
Lightning Source LLC
Chambersburg PA
CBHW031408270326
41929CB00010BA/1376
9783337060572